When Everything Changed

A Keepsake Journal

From: _____

To: _____

Date: _____

"Fascinating.... This story of how ideas that were once the norm began to seem unfair and then absurd is what Gail Collins tells in her lively new book. Until now, the second wave women's movement hasn't had its big ambitious history — the equivalent to Taylor Branch's multivolume narrative of the civil rights movement. There have been brilliant memoirs and revealing biographies and scholarly books that took slices of the movement and put them under a magnifying glass, but nothing as sweeping and accessible as this."

— Margaret Talbot, Slate.com's "DoubleX"

"It is a sign of just how intelligent and generous a writer Collins is that by the end of her book, the feminist dilemma [between motherhood and career] seems less an incurable virus than a challenge, one that has already been met with so much energy, stubborn courage, and radical hope, not to mention desperation, drama, and, sometimes, in retrospect, downright silliness, that we feel we are all on a human adventure, and all on it together.... Collins is a serious and accomplished journalist who here regards the journalistic reports of her predecessors with wit, fascination, and skepticism.... Whether she writes about fashion or the great political and social events of the day, she observes the telling details that an academic writing in greater depth or a polemicist offering stronger theoretical arguments might pass over. With deadpan comic restraint Collins provides that unexpected detail or statement or

observation that can put an entire episode into its legitimately absurd perspective."

— Cathleen Schine, *New York Review of Books*

"Social history at its best, an engaging and accessible collection of facts fleshed out with cameo appearances by and capsule biographies of people who played a role in transforming the lives of American women."

— MiChelle Jones, *Pittsburgh Post-Gazette*

"The early pages of Ms. Collins's book are peppered with accounts of incidents so outrageous they almost seem like jokes.... But she underlines the serious consequences of such risible moments by including the stories of individual women — from overworked housewives to marginalized politicians — whose lives were cramped and deformed by the culture's low opinion of their capabilities.... Ms. Collins reminds us of how many aspects of our lives were affected by the battles these women fought. And even readers who lived through this era may be surprised to discover how much they never knew, or have forgotten.... Among the impressive features of Ms. Collins's book is her genial, fair-minded sympathy, her refusal to smirk at the excesses of the most radical seventies feminists or at the stance of women, among them Phyllis Schlafly, who counseled their sisters to stay home where they belonged."

— Francine Prose, *New York Times*

"Collins's message is inspiring and timely, and all the techniques she employs to make this book fun to read—and impossible to deny—deserve critical praise as well as popular success."
—Elaine Showalter, Progressive Book Club

"*Did feminism fail?* Gail Collins's smart, thorough, often droll, and extremely readable account of women's recent history in America not only answers this question brilliantly, but also poses new ones about the past and the present.... Collins begins *When Everything Changed* with the best summary of American women's social and political history that I've read.... One of the many pleasures of the book is that Collins also reminds us of what women did in private."
—Amy Bloom, *New York Times Book Review*

"Women aren't nostalgic for the old days. If anyone is, just watch a few episodes of *Mad Men* as an antidote, with its suffocated Mad Wife Betty Draper and its slapped-down Working Woman Peggy Olson. If you prefer nonfiction, leaf through the early chapters of Gail Collins's history *When Everything Changed* to those magical yesteryears when a flight attendant was weighed, measured, and hired to be a flying geisha."
—Ellen Goodman, *Seattle Times*

"What better time to look at American women's progress since the sixties, now that the dust has settled on the 2008 presidential election when so much was won (and lost) by women?... Gail Collins's near epic history *When Everything Changed* also captures the playfulness and humor in women's advancement."
—Elizabeth Toohey, *Christian Science Monitor*

"Famous names and familiar stories appear, but what is most compelling are the vignettes of women who would have remained obscure without the work of Collins and her research team. Through their stories we experience the rat-a-tat-tat of daily indignities—big and small—that built to a crescendo we now call the women's movement."
—Connie Schultz, *Cleveland Plain Dealer*

"Exhilarating, accessible, and inspiring.... *When Everything Changed* fills a major gap on the big shelf of books about modern feminism.... That shelf has lacked, up until now, one book that captures the sweep of the whole story for the general reader.... *When Everything Changed* captures better than any other book I've read the daring, the brio, the intoxicating release of powerful creative energies that began in the 1960s and exploded in the early 1970s.... The stereotype of feminism is that it was only of interest to educated middle-class whites, but Collins shows that some of the most important battles were fought by, and benefited, working-class women.... Collins skillfully conveys how wide, and how deep, the women's movement and its ripple effects have been."
—Katha Pollitt, Slate.com

"A rich account of the past fifty years of the women's movement.... Collins's fast-moving history reminds us of the triumphs, mortifications, and hilarity of the early decades, as well as the personalities."
—Liza Mundy, *Washington Post*

"Collins's penetrating social history charts the progress of women by combining the 'public drama of the era'—from bra burnings to class-action lawsuits—'with the memories of regular women who lived through it all.' Those regular women include a three-generation Wyoming trio—grandmother, mother, daughter—whose individual stories capture the rise of female independence across the United States as vividly as any longitudinal, scientific study."
—Steve Weinberg, "Top Five Current Affairs Books of 2009," National Public Radio

"Fascinating to those of us under thirty.... We have no real concept of how different things were.... Collins's unfussy account of other women's lives is both witty and accessible, making even the most potentially dry political scenes entertaining."
— Nina Boutsikaris, *Ms. Magazine*

"'The past is a foreign country' is the kind of hallowed quotation that's resolutely opaque until you stumble on something that drives home its emotional truth. The uncanny feeling it references is one that recurs frequently as you read *When Everything Changed,* the absorbing history of feminism and American women's lives.... Ho-hum, you think — been there, done that, or Mom told me about it, and at rather tiresome length. Except that what Collins does, which so pitiably few pop-history writers do, is *bring the stories,* the anecdotes that come to life and pull you in."
— Ben Dickinson, *Elle*

"This is not only a fascinating record of how far women have come, it is also a missive to a new generation of women, reminding them to keep the faith."
— Katherine Boyle, *Booklist*

"Collins is such a delicious writer, it's easy to forget the scope of her scholarship in this remarkable look at women's progress over the past fifty years....

Next time you're sitting by yourself, happily, in a café, thank Betty Friedan, who was kicked out of a Ritz-Carlton bar for drinking alone, wrote about it — and helped spark a revolution."
— Judith Newman, *People*

"Compulsively readable.... Millions lived through the material Collins covers in her new book. To those who did not, it might read a little like science fiction." — Chris Vognar, *Dallas Morning News*

"An enormously entertaining cultural and social history.... Without preaching, Collins shows the sexism that women (and men) once accepted as the norm, and she backs up her often eye-opening stories with hard facts and solid statistics.... Collins can be deadly serious and great fun to read at the same time. A revelatory book for readers of both sexes, and sure to become required reading for any American women's-studies course."
— *Kirkus Reviews* (starred review)

"Riveting and remarkably thorough in its account of this tumultuous period.... Collins draws on an impressive variety of sources [and] employs her engaging and accessible writing style to create a very readable history book."
— Rasha Madkour, Associated Press

ALSO BY Gail Collins

America's Women: Four Hundred Years of Dolls,
Drudges, Helpmates, and Heroines

Scorpion Tongues:
Gossip, Celebrity, and American Politics

The Millennium Book (WITH DAN COLLINS)

When Everything Changed

-‹‹ ·›»-

THE AMAZING JOURNEY OF AMERICAN WOMEN FROM 1960 TO THE PRESENT

A Keepsake Journal

-‹‹ ·››-

Gail Collins

LITTLE, BROWN AND COMPANY

NEW YORK   BOSTON   LONDON

For Danny

———

Little, Brown and Company
Hachette Book Group
237 Park Avenue, New York, NY 10017
littlebrown.com

Originally published in hardcover by Little, Brown and Company, October 2009
First Back Bay paperback edition, October 2010
First Keepsake Journal edition, April 2014

Little, Brown and Company is a division of Hachette Book Group, Inc.
The Little, Brown name and logo are trademarks of Hachette Book Group, Inc.

The publisher is not responsible for websites (or their content) that are not owned by the publisher.

Library of Congress Cataloging-in-Publication Data
Collins, Gail.
    When everything changed : a keepsake journal : the amazing journey of American women from 1960 to the present / Gail Collins. — 1st ed.
      p. cm.
    Includes bibliographical references and index.
    ISBN 978-0-316-05954-1 (hc) / 978-0-316-01404-5 (pb) / 978-0-316-36982-4 (Keepsake Journal)
    1. Women—United States—History. 2. Women—United States—Social conditions.
3. Women—United States—Social life and customs.   I. Title.
    HQ1421.C64 2009
    305.40973'09045—dc22   2008054933

10 9 8 7 6 5 4 3 2 1

Q-KY

Printed in the United States of America

CONTENTS

✣ ✣

Author's Note   XI

Introduction   3

PART I
1960

1. Repudiating Rosie   11
   Keepsake Pages   *19*

2. The Way We Lived   25
   Keepsake Pages   *35*

3. Housework   39
   Keepsake Pages   *48*

PART II
WHEN EVERYTHING CHANGED

4. The Ice Cracks   57
   Keepsake Pages   *73*

5. What Happened?   77
   Keepsake Pages   *83*

6. Civil Rights   87
   Keepsake Pages   *110*

7. The Decline of the Double Standard   115

    Keepsake Pages   *130*

8. Women's Liberation   135

    Keepsake Pages   *151*

PART III

FOLLOWING THROUGH

9. Backlash   159

    Keepsake Pages   *173*

10. "You're Gonna Make It After All"   177

    Keepsake Pages   *194*

11. Work and Children   199

    Keepsake Pages   *210*

12. The 1980s — Having It All   215

    Keepsake Pages   *235*

13. The 1990s — Settling for Less?   241

    Keepsake Pages   *253*

14. The New Millennium   257

    Keepsake Pages   *270*

15. Hillary and Sarah . . . and Tahita   273

    Keepsake Pages   *283*

Epilogue   287

Acknowledgments   295

Notes   297

Bibliography   309

Index   313

Author's Note

➤ ◀

A while back I was in a bookstore in Austin, meeting readers, when a woman came up and showed me a copy of *When Everything Changed* that she had footnoted to illustrate where she was and what she was doing when all the above-mentioned changes occurred. "I'm giving it to my grandchildren, so they'll know the story in a personal way," she said.

I cannot tell you how much I loved that idea. Everybody who was around for the 1960s has stories about how different life was for women back then. (Very frequently, at least one of those stories involves not being allowed to wear slacks.) Every woman who was around for the 1970s has memories of the transformation that happened—being part of it or watching from afar and thinking about what it all meant. And it's my strong impression that virtually every woman who was around for the 1980s has a tale about having a work "uniform" that involved a blouse with a big floppy bow around the neck under a suit jacket.

If the women who talk with me are any indica-tion, many of them wish they could find a way to tell the younger generations how different things are now, how much it cost to make those changes happen, and what it felt like to live through them. And younger women are surprised by how much they enjoy hearing about it. I sent a small army of twentysomething researchers out to interview their mothers and grandmothers and aunts for this book, and many of them were thrilled by the terrific conversations that resulted.

Ever since my Austin encounter, I've been try-ing to think of a way to make it easy for that kind of conversation to happen. A Web site would be the obvious solution, but there's something so cool about the idea of an actual document that could be handed over, saved, passed on.

So here it is. At the end of every chapter, you'll find some extra pages, waiting for personal memo-ries. And just to get you started, I've included some possible questions. For heaven's sake, don't feel obliged to ask/answer them all. Just let them prod your memory, and have some fun.

When Everything Changed

A Keepsake Journal

⤙ ⤚

INTRODUCTION

→→ ←←

"Do you appreciate you're in a courtroom in slacks?"

On a steamy morning in the summer of 1960, Lois Rabinowitz, a 28-year-old secretary for an oil-company executive, unwittingly became the feature story of the day in New York City when she went down to traffic court to pay her boss's speeding ticket. Wearing neatly pressed slacks and a blouse, Lois hitched a ride to the courthouse with her husband of two weeks, Irving. In traffic court, Magistrate Edward D. Caiazzo was presiding.

When Lois approached the bench, the magistrate exploded in outrage. "Do you appreciate you're in a courtroom in slacks?" he demanded, and sent her home to put on more appropriate clothes. Instead, the secretary gave the ticket to her husband, who managed to finish the transaction and pay the $10 fine—but not before the magistrate warned the newlywed Irving to "start now and clamp down a little or it'll be too late." When it was all over, Lois diplomatically told the courthouse reporters that "the way the judge thinks about women is very flattering" and promised to "go home and burn all my slacks."

Since Caiazzo had no known record of tossing out male petitioners who showed up in overalls or sweatshirts, it was pretty clear that the showdown was really about women's place in the world, not the dignity of traffic court. "I get excited about this because I hold womanhood on a high plane and it hurts my sensibilities to see women tearing themselves down from this pedestal," the magistrate told reporters. It was a convoluted expression of the classic view of sexual differences: women did not wear the pants in the family—or anywhere else, for that matter. In return, they were allowed to stand on a pedestal.

"She has a head almost too small for intellect."

The idea that women were the weaker sex, meant to stay at home and tend to the children while the men took care of the outside world, was as old as Western civilization. The colonists who came over on the *Mayflower* believed that women were morally as well as intellectually and physically inferior, and that they should be married off as early as possible so their husbands could keep them on the straight and narrow. Their ministers enjoyed quoting St. Paul, who had urged the Corinthians to "Let your women keep silence in the churches...And if they will learn any thing, let them ask their husbands at home." But it was occasionally difficult to wring the proper degree of deference out of women who had crossed the ocean in small boats, helped carve settlements out of the wilderness, and spent their days alone in isolated farmhouses surrounded by increasingly ticked-off Indians. One early settler wrote with some irritation that his sister was "not so humble and heavenly as is desired."

The colonial farmwife actually enjoyed considerable status within her family, because she manufactured many of the things her husband and children needed to survive and contributed greatly to the family fortunes. (One New England Quaker remembered her colonial grandmother being busy with "candle making, soap making, butter and cheese making, spinning, weaving, dyeing, and of course all the knitting and sewing and dressmaking and tailoring and probably the shoemaking and the millinery" for her husband and fourteen children.) But in the nineteenth century, the industrial revolution kicked in, and families began moving to cities. The middle-class housewife stopped spinning thread and making candles, and instead focused her considerable energies on household duties that had been given short shrift in the countryside: nurturing her children like tender little sprouts, cleaning, and cooking effortful dinners. It was all very important, everyone agreed. (And very difficult, considering that making a simple cake before the invention of the eggbeater required three-quarters of an hour of hand beating.) But it did not create wealth, and America was a society that had trouble taking anyone without an economic role seriously.

To raise their stature, women were given the morality franchise. Middle-class society, with women's eager cooperation, placed them on that pedestal. (It was a good metaphor—they got higher status but precious little room to maneuver.) If colonial women were thought to be rather lax and lascivious by nature, in need of correction by their fathers and husbands, Victorian women were elevated as the moral guardians of their families. Men, who used to have that job, could hardly afford to focus on virtue when they had to wring out a living in the dog-eat-dog marketplace. Their wives were going to have to be good enough for both of them. Women were supposed to protect that goodness by staying far away from the outside world of business and politics. "Our men are sufficiently money-making. Let us keep our women and children from the contagion as long as possible," wrote Sarah Josepha Hale, the editor of the hugely popular *Godey's Lady's Book*.

This new feminine portfolio was both empowering and humiliating. A woman's impulse toward goodness was seen as instinctual, a God-given gift in a being who was still regarded as none too bright and weak in the face of the terrors of the outside world.

"She reigns in the heart...The household altar is her place of worship and service," said Dr. Charles Meigs in a famous lecture to nineteenth-century male gynecology students. "She has a head almost too small for intellect and just big enough for love."

The central point in the Western vision of sexual differences was that a woman's place was in the home, leaving men to run everything that went on outside the front door. Men provided and protected; women served and deferred. It was an ancient and extremely durable theory but riddled with holes. For one thing, it ignored the problem of what happened to these dependent creatures if their husbands failed to live up to their end of the bargain by dying, taking to drink, or abandoning the family. (*Ladies' Magazine*, a popular periodical in the early nineteenth century, helpfully recommended that if a wife felt her husband was in danger of decamping, she should win him back with "increased anxiety to please.") And, of course, the idea that women were meant to work only within their own homes was never applied to large chunks of the population. After the Civil War, ex-slaves who wanted to take care of their families full-time were hounded into domestic service or fieldwork amid white denunciation of black female "loaferism." Most rural farmwives had to labor in the fields with their husbands rather than presiding over the hearth, and many urban women, black and white, had to earn wages to help feed their families.

But for the middle class, the rule about women's place endured. Remarkable women might, on occasion, merge marriage, motherhood, and work, or carve out a career for themselves in traditionally male occupations. But women who worked as doctors, architects, and politicians were always the rare exceptions, never the precursors of change. They were depicted in the media as strange mutations—"female physician" or "lawyer and grandmother"—whose achievements could never be mentioned except in the context of their femaleness. A 1960 story in the *New York Times* about Peggy Keenan, a mine operator in South Dakota, was headlined "Feminine Fashion Has a Place in the Mine." When Betty Lou Raskin, a member of the Society of Plastics Engineers, wrote an article for the *New York Times Magazine* on the shortage of young scientists, the editors' subhead announced: "A Lady Chemist Argues That the Answer Is to Tap Female Brainpower."

"Talk of an American spacewoman makes me sick to my stomach."

In 1960, when our story begins, although computers were still pretty much the stuff of science fiction, almost all the other things that make modern life feel modern—jet travel, television, nuclear terror—had arrived. But when it came to women, the age-old convictions were still intact. Everything from America's legal system to its television programs reinforced the perception that women were, in almost every way, the weaker sex. They were not meant to compete with men, to act independently of men, to earn their own bread, or to have adventures on their own. While circumstances varied by state, many American women lived under laws that gave their husbands control of not only their property but also their earnings. They could not go into business without their husbands' permission or get credit without male cosigners. Women were barred from serving on juries in some states. The rest made it either very difficult for women to serve or very easy for them to avoid serving. (No one questioned why a movie about a troubled jury was called *Twelve Angry Men*.) Supreme Court Chief Justice Earl Warren was advised, in a memo from his clerk, that permitting women to serve "may encourage lax performance of their domestic duties."

At work, employers routinely paid women less than men for doing the same jobs. The National Office Managers Association found that a third of the companies it surveyed had dual salaries as a matter of policy. Many employers cited the extremely convenient assumption that working women were either single and living with their parents or married and bringing in extra "pin money" to supplement their husbands' earnings. Maria K., a single mother working in upstate New York, remembered objecting to the fact that men doing the same things she did "made twice as much," and being told in response that "they had families to support."

Given the assumption of male superiority in everything related to the world of work, the different pay scales made sense. So did simply refusing to hire women at all. (In 1961 there were 454 federal civil-service-job categories for college graduates, and more than 200 of them were restricted to male candidates.) To facilitate employers' ability to discriminate, newspapers invariably divided their classified ads into HELP WANTED—MEN and HELP WANTED—WOMEN. Medical and law schools banned female students or limited their numbers to a handful per class. There was, for all practical purposes, a national consensus that women could not be airplane pilots, firefighters, television news anchors, carpenters, movie directors, or CEOs.

Then, suddenly, everything changed. The cherished convictions about women and what they could do were smashed in the lifetime of many of the women living today. It happened so fast that the revolution seemed to be over before either side could really find its way to the barricades. And although the transformation was imperfect and incomplete, it was still astonishing. A generation that was born into a world where women were decreed to have too many household chores to permit them to serve on juries, and where a spokesman for NASA would say that any "talk of an American spacewoman makes me sick to my stomach," would come of age in a society where female astronauts and judges were routine. Parents who hoped for a child to carry on the family business, or for another doctor in the family, or for a kid to play ball with in the backyard at night, no longer drooped with disappointment when the new baby turned out to be a girl. It was the liberation that countless generations of American women had been waiting for, whether they knew it or not. And it happened in our time.

PART I

❯❯ ❮❮

1960

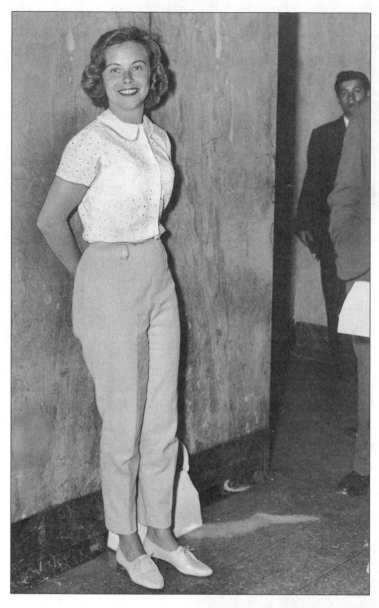

Lois Rabinowitz, after being ejected from traffic court for wearing slacks, August 9, 1960. *(AP Images)*

One of the duties of flight attendants on the all-male Executive Flight between New York and Chicago was to light their passengers' cigars. *(United Airlines)*

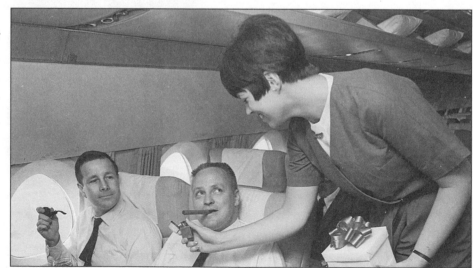

The seventeen women who served in Congress in the late 1950s, including Margaret Chase Smith, eighth from left, stand on the Capitol steps for a group portrait. *(AP Images)*

Nothing represented the evolution of beauty standards for black women in the 1960s better than the change in hair styles. Willie Mae Johnson kept to the traditional straightened style when she was crowned Miss Tan America in 1965. *(AP Images)*

Angela Davis (right) wore her trademark Afro when she showed up for a court appearance in 1972. "The hair thing made a huge difference," said Mary Helen Washington, then a Detroit graduate student. *(AP Images)*

1. Repudiating Rosie

"Some of you *do* wear a cautious face."

In January 1960, *Mademoiselle* welcomed in a new decade for America's young women by urging them to be...less boring. "Some of you *do* wear a cautious face," the editors admitted. "But are you really—cautious, unimaginative, determined to play it safe at any price?" *Mademoiselle* certainly hoped not. But its readers had good reason to set their sights low. The world around them had been drumming one message into their heads since they were babies: women are meant to marry and let their husbands take care of all the matters relating to the outside world. They were not supposed to have adventures or compete with men for serious rewards. ("I think that when women are encouraged to be competitive too many of them become disagreeable," said Dr. Benjamin Spock, whose baby book had served as the bible for the postwar generation of mothers.) *Newsweek,* decrying a newly noticed phenomenon of dissatisfied housewives in 1960, identified the core of the issue: menstruation. "From the beginning of time, the female cycle has defined and confined woman's role," the newsmagazine wrote. "As Freud was credited with saying: 'Anatomy is destiny.' Though no group of women has ever pushed aside these natural restrictions as far as the American wife, it seems that she still cannot accept them in good grace."

Most girls grew up without ever seeing a woman doctor, lawyer, police officer, or bus driver. Jo Freeman, who went to Berkeley in the early '60s, realized only later that while she had spent four years "in one of the largest institutions of higher education in the world—and one with a progressive reputation," she had never once had a female professor. "I never even saw one. Worse yet, I didn't notice." If a young woman expressed interest in a career outside the traditional teacher/nurse/secretary, her mentors carefully shepherded her back to the proper path. As a teenager in Pittsburgh, Angela Nolfi told her guidance counselor that she wanted to be an interior decorator, but even that very feminine pursuit apparently struck her adviser as too high-risk or out of the ordinary. "He said, 'Why don't you be a home-economics teacher?'" she recalled. And once *Mademoiselle* had finished urging its readers to shoot for the sky, it celebrated the end of the school year with an article on careers that seemed to suggest most new college graduates would be assuming secretarial duties, and ended with tips on "pre-job hand-beautifying" for a new generation of typists.

Whenever things got interesting, women seemed to vanish from the scene. Outside of golfing, there was no such thing as a professional female athlete—even in schools, it was a given that sports were for boys. An official for the men-only Boston Marathon opined that it was "unhealthy for women to run long distances." When *Mademoiselle* selected seven "headstrong people who have made names for themselves lately" to comment on what the 1960s would bring, that magazine for young women managed to find only one headstrong woman to include in the mix—playwright Lorraine Hansberry, who did double duty as the panel's only minority.

"Women used to be the big stars, but these days it's men."

Nothing sent the message about women's limited options more forcefully than television, which had just finished conquering the nation with a speed that made Alexander the Great look like an underachiever. In 1950 only about 9 percent of American homes boasted a set, but by 1960 nearly 90 percent of families had a TV, and those who didn't were feeling very deprived indeed. Beverly Burton, a Wyoming farmwife, had been estranged throughout the 1950s from a mother who had once told her she was sorry Beverly had ever been born. When her mother decided to mend fences, she sent Burton a note saying, "I hope this will cover the past"—attached to a television set. And it did indeed become a turning point in the relationship.

The postwar generation that was entering adolescence in the 1960s had grown up watching *Howdy Doody*, the must-see TV for the first wave of baby boomers. *Howdy* was a raucous puppet show in which the human performers interspersed broad physical comedy with endless pitches for the sponsors' products. "But all the slapstick stopped when they brought out Princess Summerfall Winterspring," remembered Stephen Davis, a childhood fan whose father worked on the show. The princess, played by a teenage singer named Judy Tyler, was the only long-running female character in *Howdy Doody*'s crowded cast. The role had been created when a producer realized "we could sell a lot of dresses if only we had a girl on the show," and the princess spent most of her time expressing concern about plot developments taking place while she was offstage. Adults approved. "The harshness and crudeness which so many parents objected to in *Howdy Doody* now appears to have largely been a case of too much masculinity," said *Variety*. But the stuff that made kids love the show—the broad comedy and bizarre plots—was all on the male side of the equation. Princess Summerfall Winterspring sang an occasional song—and watched.

The more popular and influential television became, the more efficiently women were swept off the screen. In the 1950s, when the medium was still feeling its way, there were a number of shows built around women—mainly low-budget comedies such as *Our Miss Brooks*, *Private Secretary*, and *My Little Margie*. None of the main characters were exactly role models—Miss Brooks was a teacher who spent most of her time mooning over a hunky biology instructor, and Margie lived off her rich father. Still, the shows were unquestionably about *them*. And the most popular program of all was *"I Love Lucy,"* in which Lucille Ball was the focus of every plotline, ever striving to get out of her three-room apartment and into her husband Ricky's nightclub show.

But by 1960 television was big business, and if women were around at all, they were in the kitchen, where they decorously stirred a single pot on the stove while their husbands and children dominated the action. (In 1960 the nominees for the Emmy for best comedy series were *The Bob Cummings Show*, *The Danny Thomas Show*, *The Jack Benny Show*, *The Red Skelton Show*, *The Phil Silvers Show*, and *Father Knows Best*.) When a script did turn its attention to the wife, daughter, or mother, it was frequently to remind her of her place and the importance of letting boys win. On *Father Knows Best*, younger daughter Kathy was counseled by her dad on how to deliberately lose a ball game. Teenage daughter Betty found happiness when she agreed to stop competing with a male student for a junior executive job at the local department store and settled for the more gender-appropriate task of modeling bridal dresses.

In dramatic series, women stood on the sidelines, looking worried. When Betty Friedan asked why there couldn't be a female lead in *Mr. Novak*—which was, after all, a series about a high school teacher—she said the producer explained, "For drama, there has to be action, conflict...For a woman to make decisions, to triumph over anything, would be unpleasant, dominant, masculine." Later in the decade, the original *Star Trek* series would feature a story about a woman so desperate to become a starship captain—a post apparently restricted to men—that she arranged to have her brain transferred into Captain Kirk's body. The crew quickly noticed that the captain was manicuring his nails at the helm and having hysterics over the least little thing.

Cowboy action series were the best-loved TV

entertainment in 1960. Eleven of the top twenty-five shows were Westerns, and they underlined the rule that women did not have adventures, except the ones that involved getting kidnapped or caught in a natural disaster. "Women used to be the big stars, but these days it's men," said Michael Landon, one of the leads in *Bonanza,* the long-running story of an all-male family living on a huge Nevada ranch after the Civil War. Perhaps to emphasize their heterosexuality, the Cartwright men had plenty of romances. But the scriptwriters killed their girl-friends off at an extraordinarily speedy clip. The family patriarch, Ben, had been widowed three times, and his three sons all repeatedly got married or engaged, only to quickly lose their mates to the grim reaper. A rather typical episode began with Joe (Landon) happily dancing with a new fiancée. Before the first commercial, the poor girl was murdered on her way home from the hoedown.

"ALL THE MEN BECOME LAWYERS AND ALL THE WOMEN WORK ON COMMITTEES."

TV created the impression that once married, a woman literally never left her house. Even if the viewers knew that this really wasn't true, many did accept the message that when matrimony began, working outside the home ended. In reality, how-ever, by 1960 there were as many women working as there had been at the peak of World War II, and the vast majority of them were married. (Young single adult women were, as we'll see, as rare as female action heroes at this point in history.) More than 30 percent of American wives were holding down jobs, including almost 40 percent of wives with school-age children.

Yet to look at the way Americans portrayed themselves on television, in newspapers, and in magazines, you'd have thought that married women who worked were limited to a handful of elemen-tary school teachers and the unlucky wives of sharecroppers and drunkards. Marlene Sanders, one of the very few women who managed to do on-

the-air reporting for network television, left in 1960 to give birth to a son. "After about six weeks, I thought, 'I will go crazy,'" she recalled. She hired a housekeeper and offered a male college student free room and board in return for filling in when she, her husband, and the housekeeper were all unavail-able. It seemed to work, but Sanders had no idea whether the arrangement was normal or bizarre. She knew no other working mothers, and there was, she said, "no public discussion of the child-care problems of working couples." One of the first articles she ever saw on the subject, she added, was one "about how I had this male babysitter."

If all the working women were invisible, it was in part because of the jobs most of them were doing. They weren't sitting next to Sanders in the network news bureaus. They were office workers — receptionists or bookkeepers, often part-time. They stood behind cash registers in stores, cleaned offices or homes. If they were professionals, they held — with relatively few exceptions — low-paying posi-tions that had long been defined as particularly suited to women, such as teacher, nurse, or librarian. The nation's ability to direct most of its college-trained women into the single career of teaching was the foundation upon which the national public school system was built and a major reason Ameri-can tax rates were kept low. The average salary of a female teacher was $4,689 at a time when the gov-ernment was reporting the average starting salary for a male liberal-arts graduate fresh out of college as $5,400. (Women graduates' salaries were signifi-cantly lower, probably in part because so many of them were going into teaching.)

Another reason the nation ignored the fact that so many housewives had outside jobs was that working women tended not to be well-represented among upper-income families. The male politicians, busi-ness executives, editors, and scriptwriters who set the tone for public discussion usually felt that wives not working was simply *better.* After the war, Ameri-cans had a powerful and understandable desire to settle down and return to normal. Since they were doing so in an era of incredible economic growth, it was easy to decide that stay-at-home housewives were part of the package. Women could devote all their energies to taking care of their children and husbands (politicians, businessmen, and editors included). If some of them wanted a break from domestic routine, they could volunteer to work on the PTA or, if they were wealthy enough, the charity fashion show. ("It is a tradition in the Guggenheimer family that all the men become lawyers and all the women work on committees," said a story in the *Times* about some well-to-do New Yorkers.) Men were supposed to be the breadwinners. A woman who worked to help support her struggling—or striving—family might want to downplay the fact rather than make her husband look inadequate. As late as 1970, a survey of women under 45 who had been or were currently married found that 80 percent believed "it is much better for everyone involved if the man is the achiever outside the home and the woman takes care of the home and family."

The limited options for women who did work, and the postwar propaganda about the glories of homemaking, convinced the young women who were graduating from high school and college in the early 1960s that once you married, the good life was the stay-at-home life. Prestige lay in having a husband who was successful enough to keep his wife out of the workplace. Esther Peterson, the top-ranking woman in the Kennedy administration, asked an auditorium full of working-class high school girls in Los Angeles how many expected to have a "home and kids and a family," and the room was full of waving hands. But when Peterson wanted to know how many expected to work, only one or two girls signified interest. She then asked how many of their mothers worked, and, she recalled later, "all those hands went up again." The girls were disturbed by the implicit message. "In those days nine out of ten girls would work outside the home at some point in their lives," Peterson said. "But each of the girls thought that she would be that tenth girl."

"I'D KNOW WE WERE GETTING THE WRONG KIND OF GIRL. SHE'S NOT GETTING MARRIED."

Employers happily took advantage of the assumption that female college graduates would work for only a few years before retiring to domesticity. They offered up a raft of theoretically glamorous short-term jobs that were intended to end long before the young women would begin to care about things like health care or pensions or even salaries. The sociologist David Riesman noted that instead of contemplating careers in fields such as business or architecture, "even very gifted and creative young women are satisfied to assume that on graduation they will get underpaid ancillary positions, whether as a *Time-Life* researcher or United Nations guide or publisher's assistant or reader, where they are seldom likely to advance to real opportunity."

First and foremost among these mini–career paths was being a stewardess. Girls in the postwar era had grown up reading books such as *Julie with Wings,* in which beautiful and spunky young women beat out the massive competition to become flight attendants. Along with teenage fiction about Cherry Ames, the inexhaustible nurse, the stewardess novels were virtually the only girls' career books around—unless you counted the girl detectives, who didn't seem to get paid for their efforts. Winning your "wings," readers learned, might require leaving behind an unimaginative boyfriend. ("Tug, there's a whole world for me to discover before I marry and all its people for me to know. I must follow the silver path for a while. Alone.") There would be difficult passengers and—according to the novels—an extraordinary number of airborne criminals. But the rewards were great. Within a few chapters, the heroine of *Silver Wings for Vicki* had attracted two new boyfriends, met a movie star, and helped the police arrest a smuggler. In the real world, the job was a lot more mundane, but it was still virtually the only one a young woman could choose that offered the chance to travel. As a result, the airlines got more than a hundred applicants for every opening. Schools sprang up, offering special courses that would improve the odds of getting into a flight-attendant training program. (The Grace Downs Air Career School breathlessly asked potential clients to envision themselves being able to "greet oncoming passengers at lunchtime in New York and say farewell before dinner in Minneapolis!")

Despite the fact that the American experience was built around women who ventured off to create homes in an unexplored continent, there had always been a presumption that a proper woman didn't move around too much, and there was certainly a conviction that sending a woman on a business trip raised far too many risks of impropriety. Georgia Panter, a stewardess for United Airlines in 1960, noticed that except for the occasional family, her flights were populated only by men. One regular run, the "Executive Flight" from New York to Chicago, actually barred female passengers. The men got extralarge steaks, drinks, and cigars—which the stewardesses were supposed to bend over and light.

Women had been eager participants in the early years of flying, when things were disorganized and open to all comers. But any hopes they had for gaining a foothold in commercial aviation were dashed when the Commerce Department, under pressure from underemployed male pilots, exiled women from the field by prohibiting them from flying planes carrying passengers in bad weather. Instead, they got the role of hostess. The airlines originally hired nurses to serve as flight attendants, but by the postwar era, trained health-care workers were long gone and the airlines were looking for attractive, unmarried young women whose main duty would be to serve drinks and meals.

Georgia Panter and her sister—who also became a United stewardess—grew up in Smith Center, Kansas, a Plains town so remote "we used to run outside if a car went by to see who was in it." When the Panter sisters joined United, they became celeb-

rities back home, and the local paper ran a picture of them in their uniforms. They quickly learned the downsides of the job, from the very low salary to the indignity of constantly being weighed and measured by "counselors" watching to make sure they kept their slender figures. "We had inspections often," Georgia said wryly. "Everybody seemed to think they should inspect us. Every department." (Besides limits on weight and height, stewardesses were required, according to one promotion, to have hands that were "soft and white"—a hint as to how welcome African-American applicants were at the time.) But despite the "appearance police" and pay that was lower than she had received working as a clerk for the University of Denver, Panter loved having the chance to travel. She and her sister gradually accumulated enough seniority to allow them to fly around the world on their airline passes, and they found that single-women tourists were about as rare as female businesswomen on airplanes. "People were fascinated. They'd come up to us, talk to us, invite us to their homes. They thought it was so unusual."

The airlines tried to make sure their stewardesses didn't stay around long enough to become dissatisfied with their benefits or acquainted with their union. The average tenure when the Panter sisters arrived was about eighteen months, thanks to a rule requiring the women to quit if they got married. In an era that was breaking all records for early weddings, that was all it took to ensure very rapid turnover. If a stewardess was still on the job after three years, one United executive said in 1963, "I'd know we were getting the wrong kind of girl. She's not getting married." Supervisors combed through wedding announcements looking for evidence of rule breaking. They discovered one stewardess was secretly married while the young woman was working with Georgia Panter on a cross-country flight. When the plane was making its stop in Denver, a supervisor met the flight. "He pulled that poor woman off," Panter said, "and we never saw her again."

"HELL YES, WE HAVE A QUOTA."

Women were vigorously discouraged from seeking jobs that men might have wanted. "Hell yes, we have a quota," said a medical school dean in 1961. "Yes, it's a small one. We do keep women out, when we can. We don't want them here—and they don't want them elsewhere, either, whether or not they'll admit it." Another spokesman for a medical school, putting a more benign spin on things, said, "Yes indeed, we do take women, and we do not want the one woman we take to be lonesome, so we take two per class." In 1960 women accounted for 6 percent of American doctors, 3 percent of lawyers, and less than 1 percent of engineers. Although more than half a million women worked for the federal government, they made up 1.4 percent of the civil-service workers in the top four pay grades. Those who did break into the male-dominated professions were channeled into low-profile specialties related to their sex. Journalists were shuttled off to the women's page, doctors to pediatric medicine, and lawyers to behind-the-scenes work such as real estate and insurance law.

Since it was perfectly legal to discriminate on the basis of sex, there was no real comeback when employers simply said that no women need apply. A would-be journalist named Madeleine May, looking for her first reporting job, applied to the *Providence Journal* and was rebuffed by an editor, who said, "The last woman we hired got raped in the parking lot." She applied to the *Washington Post* and was told she was a finalist, then later was notified that "we decided to give the job to a man." After going to Columbia Journalism School for further training, she applied to the *New York Times*, hoping to become a copyeditor. "We don't have anything in the newsroom for you, but I could see if we could get you a waitressing job in the *Times* cafeteria," said the personnel director.

Sylvia Roberts graduated in the late 1950s from Tulane Law School, intent on having a legal career in her beloved home state of Louisiana. But the placement officer was opposed to women lawyers, Roberts recalled. Furthermore, "there weren't any firms in New Orleans that would allow a woman to apply." She eventually did find a job that the Louisiana legal community considered particularly suited to a woman—the clerk to the chief justice of the state supreme court. These days, we think of a law clerkship as a high-prestige post, but back then in Louisiana, people took the word "clerk" literally. "My judge felt all women lawyers should take shorthand and should type," Roberts recalled. She lasted a year and then embarked on another job search, which landed her a starting position with a small law firm—as a secretary.

The belief that marriage meant an end to women's work life provided an all-purpose justification for giving the good opportunities to young men. Joanne Rife, a college graduate in California who was interested in industrial psychology, had a job interview in which she was pitted against a man with an inferior college record. "They asked me very pointedly if I was going to get married...and you know I probably waffled around a little," she recalled. In the end, the male student got the opening and Rife was offered a secretarial job. When Ruth Bader Ginsburg, the future Supreme Court justice, went to Harvard Law School, the dean held a dinner for the handful of women in the class. He jovially opened up the conversation by asking them "to explain what we were doing in law school taking a place that could be held by a man."

Once hired, women had virtually no hope of moving up. A report on women in management by *Harvard Business Review* in the 1960s said there were so few such women that "there is scarcely anything to study." The idea that men were supposed to be in charge went beyond conventional wisdom; it was regarded by many as scientific fact. A federally funded study of college students' career objectives concluded that the typical coed "most easily finds her satisfaction in fields where she supports and often underwrites the male, such as secretarial work or nursing, or in volunteer work which is not paid and is clearly valued by the sentimental side of community attitudes."

"My name wasn't even on it."

Not long ago Linda McDaniel, a Kansas housewife, came across the deed to the house she and her husband had purchased when they were married in the 1960s. "It was made out to 'John McDaniel and spouse.' My name wasn't even on it," she said.

Men, in their capacity as breadwinners, were presumed to be the money managers on the home front as well as in business, and women were cut out of almost everything having to do with finances. Credit cards were issued in the husband's name. Loans were granted based on the husband's wage-earning ability, even if the wife had a job, under the theory that no matter what the woman said she planned to do, she would soon become pregnant and quit working. A rule of thumb that banks used when analyzing a couple's ability to handle a mortgage or car loan was that the salary of the wife was irrelevant if she was 28 or under. Half of her income was taken into consideration if she was in her 30s. Her entire salary entered the calculations only if she had reached 40 or could prove she had been sterilized. Marjorie Wintjen, a 25-year-old Delaware woman, was told her husband's vasectomy had no effect on the matter "because *you* can still get pregnant."

Even when a woman was living on her own and supporting herself, she had trouble convincing the financial establishment that she could be relied upon to pay her bills. The *New York Times* was still reporting horror stories in 1972, such as that of a suburban mother who was unable to rent an apartment until she got the lease cosigned by her husband—a patient in a mental hospital. A divorced woman, well-to-do and over forty, had to get her father to cosign her application for a new co-op. Divorced women had a particular problem getting credit, in part because of a widely held belief that a woman who could not keep her marriage together

might not keep her money under control, either. (Insurance companies held to the same line of reasoning when it came to writing policies for car owners, theorizing that a woman who broke the marital bonds would also break the speed limit.) Joyce Westrich, a program analyst, wanted to buy a house in New Jersey for herself and her two children after she and her husband legally separated. All the banks she approached turned her down, to Westrich's befuddlement, until her real estate broker "whispered...in the manner of a character in a deodorant commercial, 'Maybe it's your marital situation.'" Although her about-to-be ex-husband's income was much lower than hers, once he agreed to cosign, Westrich had no further troubles.

"Men needed faster service than women."

The presumption that women needed men's protection in every aspect of life led to a kind of near-infantilization. Looking back on her life as a housewife in the 1960s, the writer Jane O'Reilly recalled that she had "never earned my own living, never taken a trip alone, never taken total responsibility for a single decision. The only time I tried to give a speech, I fainted. I had been divorced once, and lasted only four months before I remarried in a fit of terror. I had never gone to a party by myself, never gone to the movies by myself. I wanted to run away from home but I felt I had to ask permission."

When women ventured into the outside world, they often felt tentative, unsure of their welcome. And it was no wonder. The Executive Flight to Chicago was not the only service that barred them at the gate. The world was full of men's clubs, men's gyms, and men's lounges, where the business of business was conducted. Even places that were theoretically open to the public reserved the right to discriminate. The public golf course in Westport, Connecticut, would not allow women to play during prime weekend hours, claiming that men deserved the best spots because they had to work during the week. Heinemann's Restaurant in Milwaukee banned women from the lunch counter because "men needed faster service than women because they have important business to do." Many upscale bars refused to serve women, particularly if they were alone, under the theory that they must be prostitutes.

Early in the 1960s, a freelance writer from New York, traveling to Boston to interview a psychologist for a book she was working on, stopped by the Ritz-Carlton Hotel and ordered a drink at the bar. "We do not serve women," the bartender said, and whisked her off to a little lounge off the women's restroom, where he brought her the whiskey sour. It was a moment Betty Friedan recalled with humiliation decades later, long after she helped spark a movement that made sure nobody ever got consigned to that lounge again.

Keepsake Pages

You're now beginning your self-interview—or questioning a friend or relative.

Perhaps you'd like to start with something easy. (Did you read *Mademoiselle* back in the 1960s? What were your favorite TV programs when you were in high school?)

Or take the middle road. (Did you feel obliged to lose when you played games with boys?)

Or dive in deep. (Who were your female role models when you were growing up?)

Begin any way you want. You can always go back and expand.

And on the following pages, you'll find a few more memory stimulators.

_____

_____

_____

_____

_____

_____

_____

_____

_____

_____

_____

_____

_____

_____

Did you know any women who worked when you were growing up? What did they do?

_____

_____

_____

_____

_____

_____

_____

_____

_____

_____

In high school, did you talk about careers or husbands, or both?

_____

_____

_____

_____

_____

_____

_____

_____

_____

_____

Did you read any of those old books-for-girls series, such as those starring Sue Barton or Cherry Ames, or the stories about Julie and Vicki the flight attendants?

_____

_____

_____

_____

_____

_____

_____

_____

When did you first take a plane alone? Do you remember thinking the stewardesses had a really glamorous job?

_____

_____

_____

_____

_____

_____

_____

_____

_____

Do you remember being told, "Girls don't [do whatever]"?

_____

_____

_____

_____

_____

_____

_____

_____

_____

If you went to college in the '60s, did you have any female professors?

_____

_____

_____

_____

_____

_____

_____

_____

_____

_____

More Thoughts and Memories

More Thoughts and Memories

2. The Way We Lived

"WE WERE THE GUILTY ONES."

The previous chapter made American women circa 1960 sound very badly treated. But at the time, most of them would not have seen things that way. The economy was booming; their standard of living was, in general, at an unprecedented high. They expected to do much better than their parents and to have children who progressed even further. If their options were limited by their sex, it was due to social traditions that had existed for so long that few questioned or even noticed them. Most tended to compare their opportunities and achievements to those of other women, not men. And for those who did venture into the public world, the mere fact of being allowed to take part was so exciting that the details scarcely mattered.

When Anne Tolstoi Wallach graduated from Radcliffe, she talked to Time-Life Publishing about a job in magazines, which for a woman always involved a typing test. "I was a terrific typist, and they offered me a typing-pool job that might lead to research," she recalled. In all the big newsmagazines, men were reporters and writers, and women were researchers, collecting information for reporters and fact-checking their final product without receiving any credit. When Nora Ephron graduated from college, she applied for a job at *Newsweek* and was told, "Women don't become writers here." At the time, Ephron recalled, "It would have never crossed my mind to say, 'How dare you.'"

Wallach didn't find this division of labor shocking, either. Just being offered a job, she thought, was "wonderful." Her attitude was typical. In a survey for the *Saturday Evening Post*—at a time when it was both legal and common to declare some jobs off-limits for women, and to automatically pay them less in others—George Gallup found that only 19 percent of married women and 29 percent

of single women said there was sex discrimination in the professions.

Wallach ultimately chose a career in advertising, which was, for all its discrimination, far more open to women than were most business fields. She began as a writer with the powerful J. Walter Thompson agency, which employed a Women's Copy Group that handled products such as dish soap and fashions. The women's group was segregated in a special part of the building that was staffed with maids who served the female writers their lunches on trays. (The men, Wallach recalled, had a fabulous dining room that had been brought over, brick by brick, from an English castle. The women were permitted to use it one day a week.) The management was apparently convinced that women were frail things, because their restroom was equipped like a hospital, with cots and a nurse. "You could go in and say, 'I need to be up at two,' and they would tuck you in and the nurse would wake you at two and you'd go back to work," Wallach said.

Unlike the vast majority of upper-middle-class women, she kept working when her son and daughter were born. In one sense, juggling a job and children was less difficult for her than it is for professional working mothers today because the employers were less demanding. In the postwar era, when the United States had very little international competition, profits were high and pressure for productivity was low. "The whole time I worked, it was pretty much nine to five," Wallach said. "And in Thompson's women's group, nearly everybody had a secretary. And when you were promoted you had two secretaries, and if you were really important you had three secretaries. There was a lot of make-work." But on the downside, when Anne got home there was absolutely no expectation that her husband should help with housework or child care just because his wife had spent the day in an office. She and most of her female colleagues were working to support their families—many were married to artists or writers whose careers were more creative than profitable. Nevertheless, she said, "We were the guilty ones." The women saw the fact that they went out to work as a kind of privilege, and Anne and her best friend used to swear to each other that their husbands would "never have to give up anything that a stay-at-home wife would give them."

Most women who worked did so because their families needed the money, and very few made enough to hire people to help with child care and cooking as Wallach did. But rich or poor, they had a shared sense that all domestic responsibilities were on their shoulders. When Gloria Vaz, an African-American mother of four in Brooklyn, got a nine-to-five job, her husband, a cab driver, agreed to be home when the children arrived from school. But that was the extent of his help, she said. "In fact sometimes as soon as I would get home, he would go out...to hang out with his friends and, I found out later, he had other women."

June LaValleur had always intended to work—her father committed suicide when she was 16, and her mother told June that she "really needed to have an occupation in case my husband died." So even though she was engaged to be married when she graduated from high school, she trained as a lab technician. She and her husband, a gas-station owner, lived in a mobile home in rural Minnesota. While they both worked full-time, "it was just assumed I did all the cooking, all the cleaning, all the baking, all the clothes shopping. He didn't even buy his own underwear...Over the years there was a lot of resentment." But LaValleur, the product of a stoic farm culture, said there were few fights. "The heritage was, you didn't talk much."

"...COULDN'T WEAR PANTS AT ALL."

When we look at how women lived day-to-day in 1960, it seems appropriate to go back to that matter of pants, so comfortable and so freighted with symbolism. Through most of American history, women's clothing seemed to have been designed to make it difficult to move, let alone get any work done. In the nineteenth century, when middle-class women were weighed down with floor-length skirts and corseted within an inch of their lives, reformers had tried to popularize the bloomer dress—a short skirt over billowing Turkish-style trousers. But the women who dared to wear them were denounced by preachers and tormented by small boys, who threw pebbles at them when they ventured out in public. (Susan B. Anthony had to be rescued by police in New York City after she was surrounded by a "wall of men and boys" who jeered at her costume and refused to let her pass.) As time went on, pants became acceptable for golf or for some kinds of factory work. But even during World War II, four female pilots who had been ferrying new military fighter planes to an airport in Georgia were arrested as they walked to their hotel for violating a rule against women wearing slacks on the street at night.

In 1960 the old dress code was still holding firm. In advertisements, women were always shown wearing dresses—whether they were lab workers at the General Foods Kitchens, an older housewife bent over with arthritis, or a younger one pulling sheets out of the washer. Outside of factories, there was little room for slacks in the public world. Virginia Williams, who was a file clerk at a Social Security office in New York, recalled that women "couldn't wear pants at all. If you wore pants in the dead of winter, you wore them to the office, but then when you got ready to start working, you had to have on a skirt." Louise Meyer, a Wyoming farmwife whose list of daily chores would have made a stevedore quail, still wore a housedress and apron while she worked. Beverly Burton, one of Meyer's neighbors, said she wore pants at home but nowhere else. "We didn't even go to the post office in them."

Women who held white-collar jobs wrestled

with a demanding wardrobe that included nylon stockings, heels, gloves, and hats. For the women who worked on ad accounts at J. Walter Thompson, Anne Wallach recalled, the hats were particularly important. "They distinguished you from the secretaries," she said. "The minute you stopped being a secretary and became a junior writer, you put a hat on. I wore glasses and had trouble juggling the hat and the glasses, but I never would have taken the hat off. Even in the bathroom." Shirley Hammond, a Washington, DC, schoolteacher in the 1960s, remembers wearing high heels when she stood in front of her class every day. "I guess that's why so many of us have problems with our legs and hips and knees now...It all could very well have been from teaching in high-heeled shoes on those hard floors." The students were required to dress up for school as well, and that was okay with many young women who liked pretty, very feminine outfits—matching skirt-and-sweater sets, worn over a girdle and nylon stockings. "Picture me in salmon-pink A-line skirts, little black collars with little floral patterns all over, and a little sweater that matched with a little pin with my initials," said Margaret Siegel, a doctor's daughter who grew up in New Jersey. "I had the salmon outfit and I had a powder-blue one."

Hems had begun wandering above the knee, but parents and teachers waged a never-ending war to keep anything resembling a thigh out of sight. "My mother was the home-ec teacher, and the dress code was that your skirts could be no higher than one inch above your knee, and since she was in charge of enforcing the rule...my skirts were never higher," said Barbara Arnold. In parochial schools, the nuns often employed the time-honored method of making the girls kneel, and sending home anyone whose skirt didn't touch the floor.

Women generally wore sanitary napkins when they menstruated, and it took a remarkably long time for manufacturers to figure out that these could be attached to underpants with a strip of adhesive. In the '60s they were still being secured by a small belt with tabs in the front and back, to which the pad could be attached. Female athletes were bedeviled by the bulkiness of the napkins—Wilma Rudolph, the Olympic track star, vividly remembered "how uncomfortable it was running with sanitary pads." But while tampons existed—and were beginning to be promoted in advertisements filled with extremely clinical copy—many girls were dubious about their effects. The closest thing Margaret Siegel ever had to a discussion about sex was debating with her friends "whether you were going to lose your virginity if you used tampons."

"I dreamed I sang a duet at the Met in my Maidenform bra."

The first Barbie dolls appeared in American toy stores in 1959, and they were a revelation. Dolls had always been shaped more or less like little girls, with a firm, stocky, and undefined body. But Barbie was *built*. Sylvia Peterson vividly remembered the family trauma when her little sister received her first Barbie. "My father saw that doll...and when he saw that she had boobs, he got really mad. It was at her birthday party, and he really exploded." Anne Wallach's daughter, Alison, was a Barbie fiend. "I was Career Barbie. I was Stewardess Barbie. And I had the Ken doll and the Dream House. Every time I could save up five dollars, I bought a new outfit. So I had a lot of outfits, and I mixed and matched clothes." It took a while—and the civil rights movement—to prod Mattel to create African-American Barbies. But Yana Shani Fleming remembers that her grandmother created them herself. "She had painted lots of black Barbies. So I had these interesting Barbies whose skin would peel like a suntan."

Even for grown-ups, the beauty ideal in 1960 was a Barbie-like woman with a small waist and large, firm breasts—the kind of figure that was difficult to achieve without a great deal of reinforcement. The bras of the era were serious pieces of underwear. "I dreamed I sang a duet at the Met in my Maidenform bra," ran an ad in a long and successful campaign that showed well-endowed young women directing traffic, fighting bulls, or playing the cello with nothing on above the waist except a bra with cups so pointy they resembled lethal weapons. Women wore "panty-style" girdles that sometimes reached midthigh, with hooks to hold up their nylon stockings. (One book on dressing tips for wives proposed that they wear girdles even while scrubbing the floor.) *Mademoiselle* advised that when it came to Bermuda shorts, the best underwear was "a svelte panty girdle, long and leggy, in giddy pink and white or blue and white checked nylon power net." Even the individual least in need of foundation garments—Barbie—had a girdle. Tawana Hinton remembers starting junior high school in the early '60s "and I probably weighed all of eightysomething pounds, but you wore a girdle and hose that hooked to the girdle or garter belt... It was just crazy." Susan and Lorna Jo Meyer, living in rural Wyoming, wrestled with the local fashion dictate for pure white sneakers—which required the constant application of white shoe polish—at a time when the dress code required skirts and nylon stockings. "Oh, that was awful," recalled Susan. "If you crossed your legs at your ankles, then that stuff would get on your nylons."

The movies were full of voluptuous stars such as Marilyn Monroe and Elizabeth Taylor, and the nation still generally embraced the 1950s standard of beauty that held that it was definitely possible for a woman to be too thin. But a second model had already entered the consciousness of younger women. Debbie Reynolds and Sandra Dee were both among the top ten box-office stars of 1960, playing tomboys named Tammy/Gidget who were transformed into women by true love but hung on to their childlike figures. The new first lady, Jackie Kennedy, would cement the trend away from curves—a campaign she and her upper-class friends had been fighting since childhood. (When her 12-year-old sister, Lee, asked for advice on how to lose weight, the teenage Jackie suggested she take up smoking to curb her appetite.)

"HAIR WAS HUGE."

The obsession with hair in the early 1960s was something that spanned all class distinctions. "Hair was huge," said Laura Sessions Stepp, who went to high school in West Virginia. "We talked about hair. We didn't talk about clothes because in West Virginia they didn't have a lot of money. But hair was something you could do a lot with, and the boys loved hair." The postwar approach to hair curling had been a fearsome rite of beauty-parlor "permanents" that often left their victims looking very much like the Bride of Frankenstein. "It looked bad!" recalled Verna Bode, a former teacher from Kansas. "Your hair would be so fuzzy. But it would last maybe half a year." The 1960s required a different, smoother look that girls acquired by going to bed with a head bristling with instruments of torture. Stepp, who was striving for "the perfect flip," rolled her hair around orange-juice cans. "And I slept on them every night. I don't know how in the world."

Many women wanted a classic bouffant, which in its most effortful incarnation was an architectural wonder built around copious applications of hair spray. A serious bouffant was not something that could be created without considerable assistance from a girlfriend or hairdresser, and once constructed, the hairdo tended to be left in place for some time. Legends grew among '60s high school girls about a teenager who left her bouffant untouched for so long that a nest of spiders set up residence, nibbling away at the girl's scalp until she contracted a fatal case of blood poisoning.

For black girls, the hair issue was complicated by standards of beauty that valued white features such as light skin and straight hair. The battle to keep naturally frizzy hair looking straight and smooth went on forever. "You could wear it any way you wanted, as long as it was straightened within an inch of its life," said Mary Helen Washington, who grew up in Cleveland. "When relaxers came in, we were in heaven! We could get it relaxed, and it stayed straight for months!" Until the advent of those chemical treatments, girls did their straightening with hot combs or irons, but their hair would betray them whenever it came in contact with moisture—a fact that made swimming classes extremely unpopular with many black teenagers of the era. "In Detroit you'd have those basement parties, right?" reminisced Valerie Chisholm. "It'd get really sweaty down there, so if you were dancing with somebody, your hair would be messed up on one side—it had gone back—and the other side would be looking good!"

"HE SQUEALED HIS TIRES!"

The typical teenage girl of 1960 was far less sexually sophisticated than girls of the same age are today, but she in no way resembled the demure Victorian young woman who spent every New Year's Eve making resolutions about how to be a better person. Many girls embarked on the pursuit of a steady boyfriend when they were still in elementary school. That was a new phenomenon for a nation that had spent the previous decades extending childhood for as long as possible. But the race to premature adolescence seemed unstoppable. In the fall of 1960, an ad in the *New York Times* for little girls' dresses was headlined: "She Too Can Join the Man-Trap Set."

One of the least-appealing characteristics of early '60s adolescence was that there was little room for the idea that girls and boys could be friends. Laura Sessions Stepp recalled, "I had no male friends. Except boyfriends. You were a boyfriend or no friend." Mary Helen Washington credited the rigid racial rules of the early '60s with allowing her, in a backhanded way, to get to know men as people. As an African-American graduate student at the University of Detroit, she was in classes where all of the male students were white, and since "interracial dating was just something that wasn't done," she said, it provided an opportunity to relate to the opposite sex in a nonromantic context.

Girls' real friends were other girls, but even those relationships were drowned in the obsession with dates. "We had a gang of girls, about six of us, that kind of hung out together," said Gayle Lawhorn. "But most of the time we hung out together, we just talked about boys. Or we'd walk up and down the street, hoping our boyfriends would drive by. One guy I was really crazy about… he had a souped-up car and he'd drive by and make it squeal—the tires. And we'd go, 'Oh, he likes me. He squealed his tires!' We'd have pajama parties, and all we did was talk about, swoon about, whoever the boy was at the time that we cared about."

While girls were obsessed with boys, they weren't able to take much initiative beyond walking down the street and looking available. As the essayist Jane O'Reilly recalled years later, "The one absolutely unbreakable rule, guiding and controlling all contacts with the opposite sex, was *never call a man.*" Phoning a boy, any boy, was regarded as shockingly forward. If a girl called a boy in her math class to ask about an assignment, she left herself open to a misinterpretation of her motives. Only 26 percent of high school students surveyed in 1961 agreed that it would be good if girls "could be as free as boys in asking for dates." The rules were so powerful that they lasted into adulthood. A woman who had reached the position of assistant vice president for personnel at a San Francisco bank told the author Caroline Bird, "I suppose I could be a branch manager if I really wanted the job. But then I would have to call up perfectly strange men and invite them to lunch." Writing in the late 1970s, O'Reilly admitted that she still couldn't shake the feeling "that if I pick up the phone and dial a man, my hand will grow warts and I may even go blind or insane."

Teenage culture was distinctly separate from the world of adults. Once the transistor radio went on the market in the mid '50s, young people could summon music anytime they wanted. And for the first time, no matter where they lived or how popular they were, they could learn the latest dances on *American Bandstand,* an after-school program broadcast from Philadelphia that featured local teenagers dancing to popular songs. "It was almost like a soap opera because the same kids were on, dancing every week, so we'd get to know them," said Judy Riff, who was raised in New Hampshire. In public, girls danced with boys, but in private they could practice with each other, since unlike the dances of their parents' generation, the new ones did not require them to follow a boy's lead. In fact, the dance sensation of the early '60s, the Twist, did not really require a partner at all — dancers just rotated their hips and swung their arms to the music. It was a great liberation for women, who had typically been the better dancers. Literally dancing by yourself was unthinkable — a girl always twisted with a boy. But she was no longer dependent on his skill to enjoy herself.

One of the great postwar social developments was the concept of going steady. Before, a popular girl had been the one with a long string of suitors — whether they were the gentlemen callers lined up at the front porch for Scarlett O'Hara or "stags" breaking in, one after another, to dance with the prettiest jitterbug during the war. "We dated three or four people at a time," recalled Lillian Andrews, who was dating two other men while being courted by her future husband, John. (When she announced her engagement, she added, "I naturally told the other two fellows.") But in the 1950s and early 1960s, playing the field was regarded as somewhat fast, or at least reckless. *Harper's* bemoaned the fact that "young people often play with the idea of marriage as early as the second or third date, and they certainly think about it by the fifth or sixth. By the time they have been going steady for a while, they are apt to be discussing the numbers and names of their future children."

"IT WAS NOT A MATTER OF CHOICE."

Teenage girls in the early 1960s were as obsessed with matrimony as the young ladies in a Jane Austen novel. That was natural. While the twentieth-century girls might have understood that they were capable of getting a job that would bring in enough money to keep body and soul together, the vast majority had no more confidence in their ability to earn a good living than did Jane's heroines. "The most important thing back then was finding a husband with a good job... We never thought about having to provide for ourselves," said Gayle Lawhorn. Lillian Andrews's daughter, Pam, always planned to go to college, "but I was going to college to find a husband."

In 1962 a former ad copywriter named Helen Gurley Brown created a sensation with a little book called *Sex and the Single Girl,* which argued that a single woman could not only support herself but have fun, independence, and a full sex life. That was a startling proposition at the time. Not getting married — as soon as possible — was regarded as almost unthinkable. In one much-quoted postwar survey, fewer than 10 percent of those interviewed believed an unmarried woman could be happy. "If fun in life is based on marriage, single women recognize the fact," said George Gallup, whose 1962 *Saturday Evening Post* poll was an effort to draw a portrait of the typical American woman. When the participants were asked whether married or single women were happier, 96 percent of married women opted for marriage — and 77 percent of single women agreed.

Gurley Brown would turn out to be a prophet of a new era, but you'd never have seen it coming in 1960. Marriage fever was in the air. "Almost all young women between 16 and 21 want to be married by 22," said the indefatigable Gallup when he was commissioned by *Ladies' Home Journal* to study "the young American woman's mind." (In fact, the median age of marriage was 20.) Gallup found that most of his respondents wanted four children. They intended to work until their first pregnancy. "Afterward, a resounding no!"

Even women who intended to have lifelong careers could not escape the sense of urgency to marry. Joan Bernstein graduated from Yale Law School in the 1950s and managed to land a job at a Wall Street firm by the time she was 25. Nevertheless, she was "nervous" about the fact that she had yet to find a husband. "Society dictated that a woman unmarried had no place and was a failure," she said later. "It was not a matter of choice. If a woman, lawyer or not, was unmarried, it was assumed no one had asked her." As much as Bernstein was interested in her career, she did not want "to be forever considered a slightly eccentric maiden lady lawyer who was never quite socially acceptable."

"I can't think of one, to be honest."

Once married, people were expected to stay that way. Divorce, though hardly unknown, was regarded dimly. "I just think back to when I was in high school and how unusual it was for anybody I went to school with to have divorced parents. I can't think of one, to be honest. It was very unusual. I remember hearing stories of abuse, of fathers who drank, but divorce was almost never an option," said Maria K., the single mother from upstate New York. Her own father was a devoted family man who provided his wife and child with a big house and servants. But he died when Maria was 6, and within a few years, her mother, who had never worked, was struggling. "My father didn't think she needed to know how to drive a car, write a check, take care of money, and of course she had gone right from her father's home to my father's. She didn't know how to do anything; she had an eighth-grade education... So the first thing she did was put all her money into a dress shop, which went belly-up and left her with nothing. She didn't have

anyone to advise her, so she was just muddling around as best she could." Facing penury, Maria's mother got a job as a cook in a nursing home, and she and her daughter wound up "living in one room together, at the home for aging women in Homer, New York."

The government could not keep husbands from dying, but it did try to make it as difficult as possible for a couple to divorce. Most states worked under the theory that divorce was not a right but a punishment that could be requested only by the innocent, aggrieved spouse when his or her partner had done something truly awful. In New York, adultery was the only grounds for divorce under a 1787 law that had resisted all attempts at amendment. Couples who wanted to end their marriage had to convince friends to testify that one of them — usually the husband — had been found in a "compromising" situation. (In the cynical can-do spirit that always marked New York City, some women set up small businesses playing "home wrecker" in scenes staged so that the witnesses would actually have something to witness.) In Chicago, which had very specific rules for what constituted cruelty, one study noted the "remarkable" number of spouses who "strike their marriage partner in the face exactly twice, without provocation, leaving visible marks" — the precise criteria for divorce. The idea that someone had to be "at fault" was so pervasive that in Oregon, a husband and wife who accused each other of "nearly every variety of cruelty for which descriptive words could be found" were not allowed to end their marriage because the state supreme court ruled neither one was innocent of blame.

"Sometimes you wonder what you're teaching them for."

In colleges around the country, Christmas break was engagement time. When everyone returned to school, coeds would wait for their friends to reenter the dorm and would quickly scan their hands for the diamond. "It was understood that you'd be engaged for a year and then you'd get married as soon as you graduated," said Judy Riff, who jumped the gun and got married in January of her senior year at Rivier College in New Hampshire. *Harper's* claimed, "A girl who gets as far as her junior year in college without having acquired a man is thought to be in grave danger of becoming an old maid." That wasn't much of an exaggeration. Muriel Fox remembered a pregraduation class party at Barnard when "they handed corsages to the girls who were engaged and lemons to those of us who weren't." (In the class of 1960, two-thirds of the seniors were corsage-material.)

Professors watched in frustration as their prize pupils raced from final exams to wedding showers. A science teacher told the *New York Times* that his pet student, a woman "who gave every indication of deep and original thinking in genetics," had married six months after graduation and passed up a career to raise a family. "I hope she's happy, but sometimes you wonder what you're teaching them for," he said. Many didn't even wait for commencement. *Newsweek* reported in 1960 that 60 percent of the young women who entered college dropped out before graduation, "most to get married."

There had always been a division on American campuses between the goal-oriented women who went to college to prepare for a career and those who regarded it as a sort of glorified finishing school where they could find a husband among the ranks of future high-earners. The young women who were intent on making careers for themselves were still on campus, but the flush economic times had allowed more and more families to feel they could afford to subsidize college for their daughters even if they never used their degrees, and many bright young women embarked on a college career with no more sense of mission than the sorority girls in movie musicals. Pam Andrews, who went to Wellesley, said the only students who put their energies into planning for a career were "people

who had no social life." At a soon-to-become-famous class reunion at Smith College, Betty Friedan asked a graduating senior what courses students were excited about these days and said she was told, "Girls don't get excited about things like that anymore. We don't want careers. Our parents expect us to go to college. Everybody goes. You're a social outcast at home if you don't. But a girl who got serious about anything she studied—like wanting to go on and do research—would be peculiar, unfeminine. I guess everybody wants to graduate with a diamond ring on her finger. That's the important thing."

"SUCCESS AND A WELL-DRESSED WIFE GO TOGETHER."

If the popular culture was giving young women very few role models outside of marriage, there was a great deal of attention being paid to the duties of the wife of the striving young executive. "Success and a Well-Dressed Wife Go Together for Young Executives," announced a headline in a *New York Times* story about a meeting in Miami of the Young Presidents Organization, a group of under-40 CEOs. "Five hundred young men of distinction met here this week and most brought positive proof of their business success—a presidential title and an attractively dressed wife." The women, the reporter noted approvingly, had "outstanding personalities, meet strangers easily, and above all, are carefully gowned and groomed...Almost every wife has an impressive diamond ring and a mink coat or stole."

The postwar era produced a raft of novels and movies about the corporate wife who helped her husband with his climb to the top or—even more often—showed him the true joy that comes with staying in middle management and spending more time with his family. At her most sympathetic, the wife always seemed to be played by June Allyson. In the end, however, she had little to do but look supportive: the husband was always the star of the show. "It will make you very lonely at times when he shuts you out of his life," Barbara Stanwyck, playing the mistress of a recently deceased CEO, says when June's husband (William Holden) is named the successor in *Executive Suite*. "But he'll always come back to you. And you'll know how fortunate you are to be [short pause, as the mistress recognizes the superior attachment of the marriage license] his wife."

In 1960 a new and far more thrilling model of wifely success arrived on the scene. During the year's presidential campaign, John F. Kennedy's handlers had tried to keep Jackie Kennedy in the background because they didn't believe she fit the image of a proper first lady. Presidents generally had wives like Mamie Eisenhower, the middle-aged Army spouse who painted the White House interiors "Mamie pink," banned alcohol at social functions, and spent quiet evenings with her husband eating dinner off trays and watching TV. And at times it did seem as if Mrs. Kennedy might be a political liability. Her biggest campaign splash came when *Women's Wear Daily* wrote that she spent $30,000 a year on Paris fashions—a sum far above the average income of middle-class Americans. She indignantly compared the story to attacks on her husband's Catholicism.

But then Jackie arrived in the White House, leading a train of interior decorators and landscapers, and many young women saw a whole new vision of how glamorous the life of a wife could be. For the first time, young women wanted to resemble the first lady in ways that were not related to domestic or political virtue. Only 31, Mrs. Kennedy could enchant her husband's business associates with witty repartee (in several languages), fill the house with silver bowls of flowers that looked both informal and spectacular, and throw parties that everybody would rave about for months afterward. "The food is marvelous, the wines are delicious…people are laughing out loud, telling stories, jokes, enjoying themselves, glad to be there…You know, I've never seen so many happy artists in my life. It was a joy to watch," said Leon-ard Bernstein after a famous dinner at which the great cellist Pablo Casals entertained. (Jackie was the sort of person who knew that Pablo Casals had been boycotting the United States since the Spanish Civil War and that getting him to the White House was a coup.) "What I learned from her is that life is not just politics or hard work; you needed something beautiful in your life," said Sylvia Peterson, who was a working-class teenager in New Hampshire. In Connecticut, 18-year-old Carol Rumsey spent an idyllic afternoon at an amusement park with an about-to-be-married friend who was "an exact replica of Jackie Kennedy." It was the day Rumsey realized, for the first time, that she was gay.

Jacqueline Kennedy took the role of corporate wife far beyond the ability to wear a mink coat well and make small talk at parties. To the outside world, her marriage looked like a partnership of talented equals—an impression reinforced when she accompanied her husband to France, the country that made even the most self-confident American feel socially insecure. With her elegant look, her charm, and her perfect French accent, she created a sensation. When the president described himself as "the man who accompanied Jacqueline Kennedy to Paris," her triumph was complete.

It soon seemed as though almost every woman had a Jackie-type pillbox hat or a daring set of capri pants that resembled the ones Mrs. Kennedy wore. One day Georgia Panter, the flight attendant, was walking to work in Manhattan when a limousine pulled up at a light as she waited to cross the street. Inside the car was Jacqueline Kennedy. As the two women exchanged glances, Panter was very much aware that the uniform she was wearing was an obvious copy of one of Mrs. Kennedy's suits. "I saw her and she saw me and I was thinking, 'Does Jackie see how much we're looking like her?'"

Jacqueline Kennedy was a transitional figure, like her era. When she wrote in her high school yearbook that her ambition was "never to be a housewife," she didn't mean that she wanted a career but rather that she wanted to be a woman wealthy enough never to have to think about the mundane aspects of housekeeping. She had been reared to know how to behave when one's husband was having multiple affairs, but it would be much later that she would discover the capacity to live as something other than a wife. In the White House years, her aura of independence and marital partnership was part of the same calculated effect as her parties and clothes.

There was no policy-making "pillow talk" in the Kennedy White House. During the Cuban Missile Crisis, one of the junior assistants to the president's staff told friends that he would come upon the first lady "wandering sadly around the halls and she would say to me, 'Mike, what's the news?' ... Nobody took the trouble to tell her." A family friend concluded, "I suppose the president didn't want to talk about it ... He probably wanted a stiff martini and a little food and gossip. News about what the children's day had been, that sort of thing."

Keepsake Pages

If you worked in the 1960s, you've probably got stories to tell. How were the men and women treated differently on the job? And what about pants? When did you first wear slacks to school or work? Do you remember wearing a girdle and nylons? How did they feel?

_____

_____

_____

_____

_____

_____

_____

How did you wear your hair in high school? How much trouble did you have to go through to get it right? Did you sleep in rollers? African-American chroniclers: Do you remember the days when everybody straightened their hair? When did you go natural?

_____

_____

_____

_____

_____

_____

_____

_____

Did you go steady in high school? Did you have boyfriends who were only friends? Did you ever call a boy up when you were a teenager, or was that forbidden?

_____

_____

_____

_____

_____

_____

_____

_____

_____

_____

Do you have any memories of Jackie Kennedy in the White House?

_____

_____

_____

_____

_____

_____

_____

_____

_____

More Thoughts and Memories

More Thoughts and Memories

3. Housework

"I MIGHT GET UP ABOUT FOUR THIRTY
AND THEN I'D GO WEED UNTIL
SIX O'CLOCK."

When Louise Meyer and her husband were newly-weds in the 1950s, they lived in a two-room farmhouse in Eden Valley, Wyoming, that had no electricity or running water. There were no screens in the windows, and at night the moths swarmed over everything that moved, including the baby. (It has been only recently, historically speaking, that Americans have been able to obtain window screens as easily as handguns.) Instead of a refrigerator, the house had an icebox that was cooled with blocks of ice cut from the local reservoir. "It was kind of rough...but I loved it," Meyer said.

In 1960 she was 27 and pregnant with her third child. Her house had two more rooms by then, and electricity. But she still baked her own bread, churned her own butter, and waited for the glorious day when an indoor bathroom would replace the family outhouse. Her chores were very similar to the ones that had exhausted women pioneers or even the early colonists. She was a farmwife, just as the vast majority of women have been for most of recorded history. If, like Louise, they had husbands who appreciated them and establishments that prospered, it could be a full and rewarding life. As to whether it was happy or unhappy, there was seldom much time to reflect on it.

On the farm, Bob Meyer would rise at four in the morning to begin his farm chores, and Louise would follow close behind: "If I had to weed in the garden, I might get up about four thirty and then I'd go weed until six o'clock." They grew all the produce for the family table, including carrots, beets, turnips, parsnips, beans, tomatoes, peppers, and rutabagas. "We used to raise a ton of potatoes," she said. "In fact, that's what we used to put our

kids through school, was money from potatoes." After the children woke up, Louise cooked breakfast—typically sourdough pancakes, eggs, and ham or bacon. At busy times on the farm, when workers came to assist with jobs such as branding the new calves, she cooked for everyone. Her husband, she recalled, laughing, "always branded on Mother's Day." After the family and hired help were fed breakfast, she began her household chores, helped her husband with the milking, and sewed clothes for her daughters. In the winter, she canned "anywhere from three hundred to five hundred quarts of food a year." (In canning season, her workday continued until midnight.) Virtually everything the family ate came from their farm. "Basically the only thing we bought for years was spices and flour and sugar, coffee and rice," she said. They raised their own pigs, cured their own ham and bacon, made their own sausage. When her children were grown and the Meyers sold the farm, "I said there's five things I'm not going to do anymore. Raise a garden, render lard, butcher chickens, can—and I don't remember the fifth."

In early America, washing clothes was a chore so exhausting that most housewives simply didn't do it. As a newlywed, Louise did laundry in much the same way colonial women did but with more determination to follow through. She heated water on a wood-burning stove and washed the clothes in a tub, scrubbing the soiled pieces against a washboard to loosen the dirt. The clothes were then wrung by hand and hung outside on a line. (In Wyoming, winter meant collecting stacks of stiff, frozen diapers and bringing them into the kitchen to thaw.) To eliminate wrinkles, she used a flatiron—basically a heavy piece of cast iron with a handle—that was left on the stove until it got hot. "Well, I'll tell you, with flatirons it wasn't a lot of fun," she said. "Because you'd get them hot, and when they were really hot, they'd be too hot, and about the time they were just right, they'd get too cold." She progressed from a tub and washboard to a washing machine with a gas motor, which used water that still had to be heated on the stove. The sopping-wet clothes were then wrung through a hand-turned wringer. That wringer could be a frightening presence. Remembering her childhood in rural Minnesota, June LaValleur recalled the day she did the laundry for her ailing mother: "My sister Sharon, who was about 8, wanted to help…and her hand got caught in the wringer. Instead of pushing the release button, all I could think of was to turn the reverse button, so it ran her hand back out again."

"I THRIVED ON HIS COLORFULNESS."

Wyoming calls itself the "Equality State" and takes pride in the fact that it was the first to give women the right to vote in 1869. (At the time, with only one woman for every six men in the state, legislators were hoping that suffrage would serve as a kind of advertisement. "We now expect quite an immigration of ladies," editorialized the *Cheyenne Leader* hopefully.) There was a genuine sense of equal partnership embedded in traditional Wyoming farm life. To prosper, both husband and wife had to be good at their work. No matter how industrious the man, he needed his wife to sew the clothes and grow the vegetables, make the butter and sausage, and perform hundreds of other tasks on which the family's comfort or even survival depended. And no matter how energetic the woman, she was dependent on her husband's ability and initiative. Virginia McWilliams, who wed a Wyoming cowboy, said, "Back in those days, when they hired a man to work on the ranch, for the most part they hired the whole family. But if the man screwed up, then the whole family had no place to go."

McWilliams's husband, Ike, followed the rodeo as a bronc rider. "He was colorful and I was quiet. I thrived on his colorfulness," she said. In 1961, when their fifth child was born, Ike and Virginia returned to Wyoming and began working on a large ranch. She says they shared the domestic duties. "When they were little, he got up at nights with the children and things like that. And he cooked a lot when there weren't any men around to catch him." And although Bob Meyer never helped with the indoor chores, Louise said he "always made me feel like what I did was just as important as what he did." Life, she reflected, "was never easy…and it took both adults to keep a family going."

It took all the children as well. Wilma Mankiller was born in Oklahoma, on land her family had owned since the Cherokee were driven out of their original homes in the southeast. (The family name had originally been a Cherokee military title, the equivalent of a major or a captain.) Her mother, who married at 15 and had eleven sons and daughters, relied on the children for endless assistance, including toting water from a spring a quarter mile away for the washing. "Everybody did it," Wilma said. "Whoever was there did that job." While she would later run into plenty of set ideas about women's roles when she became involved in tribal politics, she recalls her childhood as gender-neutral: "I can't remember anyone saying you can't do this or that because you're a woman. Maybe my parents had too many kids and were too busy."

"IT WAS SORT OF A FABULOUS TIME."

Farm life could be harsh and bleak; many young people fled as fast as they could to the more varied and colorful world of the cities. But for families that were both loving and reasonably successful, farming seemed—at least in retrospect—idyllic. "We would gather in the evening and sing hymns and that sort of thing," recalled Mary Bell Darcus, who raised a large family on a modest farm in Virginia. "When I look back, it was sort of a fabulous time compared to now."

But it was a life that was beginning to fade into history. Children who had gathered for singing hymns and playing Monopoly with their parents lost their attachment to simple pleasures when television moved into the neighborhood. "To me, television is one of the worst things that ever happened to the world," said Louise Meyer, who believes her oldest children, who grew up pre-TV, "had a lot happier childhood, were a lot more contented." Her older daughters seem to agree: they have clear memories of how much they enjoyed diversions that kids of the TV age would have found unfathomable. "Do you remember when Grandpa used to come down to the house and he and Mom would share the *National Geographic*?" Jo Meyer Maasberg asked her older sister, Susan. "He would ask her, 'Now, have you read this story about...?' and they would discuss it, and it was almost like we got to go around the world through their eyes."

By 1960 the United States was no longer a farming country — only 30 percent of families lived in rural areas. The nation was booming, and its prosperity reached farther down into the working class than ever before. Sixty percent of families lived in a home they owned, and 75 percent had a car. A quarter of all families were living in the suburbs, the much-exalted fulfillment of the American dream — to own a nice house on a plot of land, with healthy children going to good schools and destined for even higher levels of prosperity.

In the beginning, the newly constructed dream houses were, by our current standards, very small. (In the famous Levittown development on Long Island, the basic house was a 750-square-foot, four-room Cape Cod with one bath and two bedrooms.) Their owners had, for the most part, only one car, which was taken to work by the husband. The wives were left behind in neighborhoods that were filled with other women of the same age and circumstances, whose lives revolved around their household chores and children. "I had a friend who had a date calendar with all the things she had to do. I thought that was the biggest show-off thing I ever saw," said Edna Kleimeyer, who was living in a suburb outside Cincinnati with her husband and three small children. Some of the women who found themselves in a sea of similar-looking houses full of stranded housewives were appalled by the sameness, and never adjusted. But many were delighted to have a ready-made community. "The neighborhood was so new that immediately you became best of friends with the people who were buying the houses," said Lillian Andrews, who moved to the suburbs of Washington, DC, with her husband in 1958. "So the neighborhood became a social thing. Everybody had parties all the time. That was wonderful."

The early suburbs were singularly unfriendly to the concept of a two-income family. Day care was virtually nonexistent, and relatives who might have been available for babysitting had been left behind in the cities or on the farms. The new housing developments were still remote from stores, offices, or almost anything that might have provided employment. Besides, many of the young couples setting up housekeeping were escaping hard times, and a stay-at-home wife was a kind of trophy — a sign that the family had made it to middle-class success and stability.

Josephine Elsberg was a secretary in Washington, DC, who had grown up in a family struggling to survive after the father deserted them. After she got married, she recalls, she sat her new husband down and told him, "Harold, you're going to take care of me from now on. I'm not going to support myself any longer. That's why I married you."

"I was wondering how long you'd want to work," said Harold.

"I never did want to work," his new wife told him. "I always wanted to be stay-at-home."

She was hardly alone, and thanks to the postwar prosperity and the easy mortgage credit of the GI bill, many couples found they could purchase a home and do very well on just the husband's income. Black women, who had always worked in much larger proportions than white women, were eager for the opportunity to take care of their children full-time — particularly if they had been employed to look after someone else's house and family. When the economic boom allowed many to do just that, *Ebony* celebrated with an article titled "Good-bye Mammy, Hello Mom." Joyce Ladner, growing up in a small black community in Mississippi, still recalls the day her father told her mother, "You'll never clean another woman's house."

It's a mistake to see the race to housewifery as a lack of enterprise on the part of the women who were so eager to marry and stay home. They knew that if they had a job, it would involve working under a boss — be it a housewife in need of cleaning help, a store owner, or a school principal. Ever since colonial days, the part of full-time homemaking that women treasured most was the ability to be in charge. "I guess I just liked the freedom of being at home and not having someone tell me what to do," said Marylyn Weller, who gave up a job as a bookkeeper in Oklahoma to raise her three children.

"I COULD NOT DO A SHIRT IN LESS THAN TWELVE MINUTES."

In the suburbs of 1960, nobody had to churn butter or boil water for the laundry on a woodstove, but homemaking was still more than a full-time job. Typically, the postwar wives had several youngsters to take care of — the birthrate for third children doubled in the postwar years, and that for fourth children tripled. And although the country was on a tear of appliance buying, the new suburbanites were still awaiting the arrival of conveniences such as disposable diapers. Betty Riley Williams, the wife of a Marine, lived in a trailer in Camp Lejeune, North Carolina, with her baby daughter, Anita, in 1960, and she diligently followed her mother's instructions on how to wash the baby's clothes. "There was a diaper pail. It was white, enamel...I put the diapers in that and the baby clothes," she said. Williams then boiled water, and added the water and soap to the pail. "I had to stir it with a wooden spoon for fifteen minutes. Then I'd drain them and rinse them three times and

then I'd hang them on the line until they were done." Mae Ann Semnack, who was married to a steelworker in Boston, still remembers her struggle to wash the sheets in a big tub as a weekly wrestling match. "One time, I got in there with them."

There were no permanent-press clothes yet, and even spray-on starch was still beyond the horizon. Edna Kleimeyer used packets of starch that had to be dissolved in water. "You dipped in the collars and cuffs and hung them up to dry. Then you would take them off the line and sprinkle them, roll them up, and put them in the wash basket and cover it with a towel. And you'd start ironing. I could not do a shirt in less than twelve minutes. If you didn't finish, you'd put what was left in the refrigerator so the clothes didn't dry out." Automatic washing machines had begun to drive away the dreaded wringers, but most women still hung the clothes up on a line to dry. The Kleimeyers once went to a party at the home of a man who had connections in the appliance industry and was eager to show them a brand-new acquisition — an automatic dryer. "His wife brought out the towels, and we all had to feel them."

The idea of being a good cook was intertwined with being a good wife. "Nothin' says lovin' like something from the oven," said an omnipresent Pillsbury ad. There was virtually no such thing as fast food, and while frozen meals had arrived, they were regarded dimly. (In *The Apartment*, which won the Academy Award for best picture of 1960, director Billy Wilder emphasized the pathetic loneliness of Jack Lemmon's bachelor life by having him dine on a frozen dinner.) Women also tended to look down on desserts that weren't made from scratch. A doctoral student who conducted a study on cake mixes in 1958 found that two-thirds of the housewives shunned them when baking for their families.

But the food industry, which knew that convenience foods would form its next generation of profit centers, was doing everything it could to eliminate the prejudice against shortcuts. With the help of cooperative women's magazines, the industry stressed the idea that housewives were too busy to cook from scratch and that they could personalize a dish by taking a package of frozen vegetables or a cake mix and "glamorizing" the final product with a special touch such as a can of fried onions or a maraschino-cherry garnish. Pragmatic mothers began giving their newly wed daughters copies of *A Campbell Cookbook: Cooking with Soup*—perhaps with a bookmark on the recipe for the classic casserole, composed of cream of mushroom soup and frozen green beans. "In those days you did a lot of things with cream of mushroom soup," recalled Angela Nolfi of Pittsburgh, who had given up her interior decorator ambitions to become a secretary and then a full-time housewife. "You would open up things like tuna fish and put them together." And almost every social occasion, she added, involved Jell-O salad. "We were always looking for a new, interesting way to use Jell-O."

"I THOUGHT EVERYTHING SHOULD BE CLEANED EVERY DAY."

In the 1960s new time-saving appliances kept marching off the assembly lines and into American homes. Almost all the women who were using them could remember a time, barely twenty years in the past, when a great many people did not have running water and a third of the nation's housewives cooked on wood- or coal-burning stoves. Many still referred to their purring refrigerators as the "icebox" because they had grown up in houses where food was chilled in boxes filled with ice, and the "iceman" was as regular a visitor as the milkman and the coal man. Now, the suburban kitchen refrigerators not only ran on their own but were beginning to defrost themselves and produce ice at the touch of a button. The dreaded laundry chores were tamed by the arrival of permanent-press clothing, better steam irons, and those automatic dryers. "Wash-and-wear clothing and the steam iron were the real liberation for women," said Edna

Kleimeyer. Once they were all in place, it was possible to get the basic household chores done relatively quickly.

Yet the housewives did not seem to be working any less. The amount of time spent on housework was very difficult to quantify. A methodical study by the sociologist Joann Vanek that used pretty much all the data available concluded that in the 1960s, the full-time homemaker spent fifty-five hours a week on her domestic chores. That was actually a little more than in the 1920s, when women were washing by hand and keeping their food cold in iceboxes. On the other hand, Vanek found that women who had outside jobs spent less than half as much time on housekeeping. That held true even when Vanek considered factors such as children and outside help. (Husbands' contributions were so minimal at the time that they didn't really figure into the equation.)

Clearly, women were responding to their time-saving appliances by raising the bar for housekeeping. They bought their family more clothes and washed them more often. (In the 1950s the average household laundry soared from thirty-nine pounds to sixty-five pounds a week.) Once they had acquired a second car, they became chauffeurs, driving their children around to lessons and sports. Vanek found that between shopping and ferrying children, "contemporary women spend about one full working day per week on the road and in stores." They took up gourmet cooking or interior decorating. Myrna Ten Bensel, who had four children in St. Paul, decided to up the ante by making her own diapers: "You could buy diaper fabric in the dry-goods store, and I would cut them and hem them."

Josephine Elsberg, who made it clear to her husband that she didn't want to work outside the home, was a dynamo inside. "I thought everything should be cleaned every day," she recalled. "Have to vacuum every day. Have to clean the bathroom every day. I was a fanatic." When the family became prosperous enough to acquire a maid, Elsberg never allowed her to do the cooking or the laundry. She ironed everything herself, including the bedsheets, which she washed twice a week. She spent every winter personally repainting the entire house and every summer planting in the garden. The local beautification program gave her multiple commendations, and when her daughter went off to college, she wrote back about how much she missed the feel of freshly ironed sheets. "And I said, 'That made it all worthwhile,'" Elsberg recalled.

"NO ONE EVER DIED FROM SLEEPING IN AN UNMADE BED."

The very fact that there were so many women ready, willing, and able to purchase a new washer/dryer or self-cleaning oven made the nation's advertising industry deeply interested in the suburban housewife. She was the consumer in chief who had to be flattered and assured that there was no human gratification greater than the sight of a perfect white load of laundry or a shiny kitchen floor. The women's magazines—all edited by men—could not say enough about the glories of housekeeping or how enthusiastic husbands and children would be over a well-washed shirt or the cherries on that newly baked cake.

"Togetherness" was the *McCall's* magazine watchword for the new American family partnership, in which the stay-at-home wife took an interest in her husband's job while the husband took a *deep* interest in issues such as interior decor and family fun. One *New York Times* columnist, commenting on the "extraordinary" new emphasis on shared family lives, quoted a male friend as saying, "If my wife had her way, I think we'd all breathe in unison." The housewives often were equally skeptical of the magazines' romanticism, having spent years experiencing just how much reaction a load of clean clothes really got. They fell in love with a generation of female humorists who wrote about families and homemaking with wry realism, like the columnist Erma Bombeck ("No one ever died from sleep-

ing in an unmade bed"). Jean Kerr's chronicles of her move to the suburbs with a husband and three sons, *Please Don't Eat the Daisies,* was so popular it was made into both a movie and a TV series. "I know that small children have a certain animal magnetism. People kiss them a lot," wrote Kerr in an essay that questioned why etiquette books were written for grown-ups rather than 3-year-olds. "But are they really in demand? . . . No. For one thing they bite, and then they keep trying to make forts with mashed potatoes. It holds them back, socially."

"THE OTHER HALF ARE FREE IN SPIRIT ONLY."

While the women's magazines went into ecstasy over the accomplishments of the new suburban housewife, the rest of the mass media were somewhat less enthusiastic. *Playboy,* which would open its first, much-touted Playboy Club in 1960, was a center of rebellion against the new postwar order of domesticity. It celebrated the freedom of the cool bachelor, who had jazz on the stereo, martinis at the bar, and a long line of playmates who were willing to provide sex without commitment. "Approximately half of *Playboy*'s readers are free men," the magazine noted in 1958, "and the other half are free in spirit only." Popular magazines began theorizing that the pressure on men to provide well for their families might be sending them into premature heart attacks. Women's life expectancy, it was noted repeatedly, was outstripping men's. "You can hardly pick up a paper, a magazine, a book, go to a play, movie, or watch TV without discovering what the American wife is doing to the ego, the maleness, the very essence of her man," complained Margaret Taylor Klose in *McCall's.*

The national move to the suburbs had changed things for men, too. They lost the old urban patterns of nights out with male friends or visits to neighborhood bars. Social life revolved around couples at cocktail parties or families watching movies at drive-in theaters, with the children bouncing around in their pajamas in the backseat. Most of the husbands seemed to like their new lives, but the American decision makers and commentators who were based in big cities found it hard to believe they were really happy. The prototypical suburban husband, as many editors and writers saw it, was going off to work at a white-collar job that often entailed a great deal of psychological stress. And where did his salary go? To pay for more work-saving appliances for his nonworking wife! There was a great deal of talk about the emasculation of men who had to labor at stultifying jobs in the city and then come home to a demanding wife who had spent the whole day doing—whatever it was women did. And in the black press, the rising number of female-headed households was being blamed on black women who, the editors charged, failed to respect their husbands properly and made too many material demands. "The life of many a 'wealthy' Negro doctor is shortened by the struggle to provide diamonds, minks, and an expensive home for his wife," claimed the sociologist E. Franklin Frazier.

"IT DOES NOT LAST VERY LONG."

Whether they were being overpraised or underestimated, most of the women who had raced to marry after World War II were plenty busy in the 1950s and early '60s, inundated with the responsibilities of rearing offspring they had borne quickly and close together. A typical woman married at 20 and had three children, completing her family before she was 30. Anyone with two or three preschoolers in the house generally does not have much leisure time to wonder about the meaning of life, let alone the long-term sociological impact of washer/dryers and microwave ovens. But by 1960 the first wave of the baby-boom generation was already in high school. Many housewives would still be in their prime when the nest emptied out entirely, and without children, mothers would likely find that house-

keeping was not all that challenging. What would happen then?

It was a question remarkably few women seemed to ask themselves, even though almost everyone who paid attention saw what was coming. "Whether one finds it richly rewarding or frustrating, there is one trouble with motherhood as a way of life. It does not last very long," wrote the editors of *Harper's* in a special issue on American women in 1962. George Gallup, conjuring up his average American woman for the *Saturday Evening Post* in the same year, had much the same thought: "One real problem shows clear in the silhouette we have cut: the empty years to be faced by the typical American woman—perhaps half her lifetime—after the children are grown and gone. She has not prepared for them, and is not preparing now...In fact, throughout the whole study, few women seemed aware of the lonely years ahead." Even *Newsweek*, in its cranky feature about dissatisfied housewives who failed to understand that biology is destiny, mentioned that the average housewife had "forty-five years of leftover life to live" when her last child entered school.

It was not a problem previous generations had faced. The average woman born in 1900 could expect to live to be only around 50. She would have continued to have children until menopause—leaving the nest stuffed until she died. If she did survive to old age, she would probably finish her life in the home of a son or daughter, as a live-in babysitter. That pattern was as old as memory, and although it had been changing gradually over the century, a country distracted by two world wars and a massive depression had failed to notice.

"I WAS HANGING CLOTHES ON THE LINE WITH TEARS JUST STREAMING DOWN MY FACE."

Even those short-lived days of full-time motherhood in the nation's suburban homes didn't satisfy every woman who found herself living the new

American dream. Some young housewives discovered, to their shock, that they didn't really like the existence they had been groomed from childhood to believe would make them fulfilled. In 1960 *Redbook* magazine ran an article called "Why Young Mothers Feel Trapped" and invited readers to write in, with a $500 prize for the best description of the feeling. The editors were stunned with the avalanche of mail: 24,000 replies.

Housewives who felt trapped were not a new phenomenon, even if nobody had done a poll or requested reader responses on the topic in earlier eras. But personal happiness had not been regarded as an entitlement then. And it surprised the nation—or at least the media—that the women who had acquired better homes and more conveniences than any previous generation should seem to be particularly miserable. "She is dissatisfied with a lot that women of other lands can only dream of," said *Newsweek*.

Many of the most unhappy—and vocal—housewives were college graduates who had gone to school under the peculiar conditions of the postwar era. For most, it was a given that they would marry in their early 20s, start families almost immediately, and dedicate their lives to homemaking. Yet as students they had taken the same courses the career-bound men had, passed the same tests, and researched the same papers to prepare for a future they never actually intended to have. Inevitably, many of them wound up feeling disoriented. "It was odd when you think about it. You didn't think about it, though," said Joanne Rife, who graduated from Occidental College, married the same year, and moved to Santa Barbara County in California with her husband, a rancher. By 1960 Rife was pregnant with her third child. She felt exhausted all the time, even though the housework wasn't physically challenging and she enjoyed her children. "I think it was mental fatigue more than physical... It was not a fulfilling kind of thing," she recalled. "The kids were fulfilling but not the house." Within another few years, "I was really at the end of my rope. I felt trapped by my situation...

I was hanging clothes on the line with tears just streaming down my face."

"... HUNCHED OVER THIS PAPERBACK, FROWNING."

Since the phenomenon of the unhappy homemaker seemed to center around the college-educated women, then perhaps it was the fault of... college. Rather than questioning why so many of their graduates were being cut off from any chance of using their education in the outside world, college presidents had spent the 1950s striving to prove that their curriculum was designed to create competent and *happy* housewives. The (male) president of all-female Radcliffe celebrated the beginning of every school year by telling the freshmen that their college education would "prepare them to be splendid wives and mothers and their reward might be to marry Harvard men." The (male) head of Mills College in California proposed that female students be schooled in the "theory and preparation of a Basque paella, of a well-marinated shish kebab, and lamb kidneys sautéed in sherry."

Betty Friedan, a freelance writer in suburban New York, got a commission from *McCall's* magazine to write a defense of the kind of well-rounded education she had gotten at Smith fifteen years earlier—a piece that was supposed to depict college as the perfect preparation for life as a "togetherness" wife and mother. A psychology degree from Smith had not actually kept Friedan from becoming a pretty unhappy housewife herself. The mother of three, she lived with her family in a restored Victorian house on the Hudson River. While she passed as a stay-at-home housewife in the neighborhood, she was in fact an accomplished writer whose work had been published in a number of national magazines. But she was restless and dissatisfied, and it was not—at least not entirely—because her marriage had plummeted to the stage where Friedan's fights with her husband left her trying to conceal the bruises.

Before her fifteenth Smith reunion, Friedan spent an entire year preparing an alumnae questionnaire "of inappropriate and unnecessary depth" that was going to form the basis of her *McCall's* article. Her former classmates were stunned by the length and specificity of Friedan's questions, but many of them plunged ahead gamely and provided information that sparked one of the most influential books in American history. Rather than revealing that college-educated women had been given the ideal preparation for their careers as full-time housewives, the survey responses showed Friedan that a number of her peers were slowly going crazy in their well-appointed homes, just as she felt she had been doing. The material formed the basis of *The Feminine Mystique,* in which Friedan wrote about a kind of vague despair that left women asking themselves, "Is this all?" One young mother of four told Friedan, "There's no problem you can even put a name to. But I'm desperate. I begin to feel I have no personality. I'm a server of food and a putter-on of pants and a bedmaker, somebody who can be called on when you want something. But who am I?"

The Feminine Mystique was like an earthquake compared to the tremors about unhappy housewives that had registered before. Friedan described the problem in scorching prose that made it seem much worse than anyone had previously suggested. "You'd be surprised at the number of these happy suburban wives who simply go berserk one night, and run shrieking through the street without any clothes on," she quoted an unnamed doctor as saying. And unlike most of the other panels and probing essayists, Friedan told the American housewife (specifically the well-educated, middle-class suburban one) that she was absolutely right to feel dissatisfied. There were, according to Friedan, no "happy housewives"—or scant few. Women were being forced to waste their lives on meaningless household chores in order to create profits for the manufacturers of household goods. They were being duped into believing homemaking was their natural destiny by gushy, unrealistic articles in women's magazines—all edited by men. It was natural to want marriage and children, she wrote, but housekeeping was no full-time job for a smart, well-educated woman. "The feminine mystique has succeeded in burying millions of American women alive. There is no way for these women to break out of their comfortable concentration camps except by finally putting forth an effort—that human effort which reaches beyond biology, beyond the narrow walls of home, to help shape the future," she concluded in a call to arms—or at least to outside employment.

The power of Friedan's writing, the wealth of statistics and anecdotes (after years of freelancing, she was especially devastating on the subject of women's magazines), and the fact that she was writing from the same place as her audience made *The Feminine Mystique* a sensation when it was published in 1963. Madeleine May Kunin, the would-be journalist who was offered a waitressing job in the *New York Times* cafeteria, argued about it with her book club in Cambridge, Massachusetts, where her husband was at Harvard Medical School. "Some of the women were outraged that *The Feminine Mystique* had placed their choices into question," she remembered. "And others, like myself, felt at last they had been understood." Joanne Rife, who had been hanging the family laundry with tears running down her cheeks, picked up a paperback copy, and "it really got me fired up...I mean, like, ninety-five percent was true to my experience." She gave the book to a good friend, she recalls, "and she read it and got a divorce. She should've. He was a jerk." Anna Quindlen, the novelist and columnist, says she remembers few specific details from her childhood, but one of the most vivid is seeing her mother "hunched over this paperback, frowning, twin divots between her dark brows."

Keepsake Pages

Where did you grow up? How did you get to school and to the stores? Did your mother have a car?

_____

_____

_____

_____

_____

_____

_____

_____

How was housework different then? Do you remember when there was a *lot* of ironing? Old-fashioned refrigerators? What kinds of things did your mom cook? Did you have brothers, and if so did they help with housework the same way the girls did?

_____

_____

_____

_____

_____

_____

_____

_____

Did your mother prepare for the time when she'd have an empty nest?

_____

_____

_____

_____

_____

_____

_____

_____

Do you remember reading _The Feminine Mystique_? If so, what was your reaction?

_____

_____

_____

_____

_____

_____

_____

_____

_____

More Thoughts and Memories

More Thoughts and Memories

More Thoughts and Memories

PART II

→ ⤙

When Everything Changed

Betty Friedan, shown here in her apartment in 1981, founded the National Organization for Women by passing notes around a government luncheon in Washington. (*Neal Boenzi* / New York Times)

Pauli Murray, lawyer, educator, minister, and civil rights leader, said her work for the Commission on the Status of Women was a "memorial" to her friend and mentor, Eleanor Roosevelt. (*Frank C. Curtin / AP Images*)

Ella Baker, who the student civil rights activists called "our Gandhi." (*Photographs and Prints Division, Schomburg Center for Research in Black Culture, The New York Public Library, Astor, Lenox and Tilden Foundations*)

Marian Anderson during her concert at the Lincoln Memorial in 1939. (*Thomas D. McAvoy / Time & Life Pictures / Getty Images*)

Fannie Lou Hamer speaks to supporters of the Mississippi Freedom Democratic Party in 1965. (*AP Images*)

Muddy tracks show the path made through the grass by the car in which Viola Liuzzo and Leroy Moton were traveling when Liuzzo was shot to death by members of the Ku Klux Klan in Alabama.

(*Liuzzo and car photographs: © Bettmann / Corbis; Moton photograph: AP Images*)

Members of Women Strike for Peace picket the White House in 1967. "We'd get dressed in mink coats and hats and gloves to look like the woman next door," said an organizer. *(© Bettmann / Corbis)*

Women protesting the Miss America pageant at the breakthrough demonstration in 1968. *(AP Images)*

Gloria Steinem. *(AP Images)*

4. The Ice Cracks

On Election Day in 1960, women around the country celebrated the fortieth anniversary of their constitutional right to vote, and newspapers noted that for the first time in the nation's history, there were likely to be more women than men casting their ballots for president. "Women now hold the balance of power," said the assistant chair of the Republican Party, Clare B. Williams Shank. It was hard to say exactly what that meant in practical terms. The suffragists of the early twentieth century had presumed that when women got the vote, they would press for a specific pro-family agenda—things like better care for infants and pregnant women, and better schools. But it turned out that women voters made their choices much like their husbands and fathers and brothers did—on the basis of class, ethnicity, or regional loyalties. In the first national election after passage of the Nineteenth Amendment, women helped choose the utterly inept Warren Harding, who would distinguish himself for his perennial appearance on the ten-worst-presidents-of-all-time lists.

The women who were cutting the anniversary cake might also have contemplated the fact that the highest-ranking female judge in the nation served on the Customs Court and that in forty years, only two women had ever been appointed to cabinet-level posts in the federal government: Frances Perkins, during the Roosevelt administration, and Oveta Culp Hobby, who was the first secretary of the Department of Health, Education, and Welfare under Dwight Eisenhower. The record was not going to be improved under the about-to-be-elected President John Kennedy or by his immediate successors. At the end of the decade, when Richard Nixon brought the White House back under Republican control, some of his women supporters expressed hope he might follow Eisenhower's example and appoint the first female cabinet member since the 1950s. Unenthusiastically, a spokesperson pointed out that "the departments had grown" since then.

Women took part in the presidential-nominating conventions that summer, but newspaper accounts of their gatherings did not suggest deal-making in smoke-filled rooms. "The meal begins with 'Swan Canterbury,' which consists of fresh pineapple on a bed of laurel leaves surrounded by swans' heads in meringue," the *New York Times* reported in a story headlined "GOP Women Facing a Calorie-Packed Week." Meanwhile, nearly two-thirds of women ages 18 to 60 who were surveyed by George Gallup said that they didn't approve of the idea of a female president.

The Eighty-seventh Congress that was elected in 1960 included two women in the Senate and seventeen in the 435-member House, and that would turn out to be the high-water mark for the next decade. Both of the female senators and half the women in the House had gotten to their exalted positions through the same time-honored career path: marry a congressman, and succeed him when he passes away. Edna Simpson of Illinois, the ultimate congressional widow, was just finishing her first and last term in office. Simpson's congressman-husband had died just nine days before the election of 1958, and she bowed to pleas from Republican leaders and let her name go on the ballot in his place. She did not campaign, and after she was elected she never spoke on the floor of the House or—it seemed—to any of her fellow members. Her only legislative initiative was to protest when her name appeared in the *Congressional Biographical Directory* as Edna Oakes Simpson rather than as her preference: Edna (Mrs. Sid) Simpson.

Even the congresswomen who didn't succeed their husbands tended to be widows—voters were wary of female candidates with family obligations.

The disasters that could befall them were vividly displayed in the case of Coya Knutson, who had managed to topple an incumbent House member in Minnesota in 1954 and win a seat in her own right. Her alcoholic husband, Andy, who was left behind to run the family hotel, torpedoed her career in 1958 by issuing a "Coya, Come Home" letter claiming his marriage was being destroyed by her political success. She became the only Democratic incumbent to lose the 1958 election. Her marriage did not last much longer than her congressional career.

"TELL HER YOU'VE JUST STARTED RUNNING."

Throughout American history, the best way to get to the top in politics was to begin by practicing law. In 1960 the only woman in the House with a law degree was Martha Griffiths. A Democrat from Michigan, she had a family tree that included Daniel Boone and the first woman lawyer in the state of Missouri. She and her husband, Hicks, were a political couple—something the United States had seen a lot of since Abigail Adams spent the Revolution writing letters to John, urging him to keep up the fight and to remember that the ladies had rights, too. But the Griffithses were different from their predecessors in that their joint efforts were directed at *her* political career. In her unpublished autobiography, Martha said that when Hicks was accepted at Harvard Law, which did not take female students, he told her, "We will find another law school. You are going, also." They graduated together from the University of Michigan, then started a law practice in Detroit, where Hicks became active in Democratic politics. But in 1946 it was Martha who got a phone call urging her to run for the state legislature—from a longtime local women's-rights advocate with the memorable name of Phoebe Moneybean. Martha demurred, but when her husband heard about the conversation, he told his wife, "Call her back right now and tell her you've just started running."

After a stint in the state legislature, Martha set her sights on Congress. Hicks managed the campaign while she drove around the district in a house trailer—a rarity at the time—and lured curious voters in to examine the interior and meet the candidate. Griffiths estimated that she talked to 40,000 prospective voters in her first unsuccessful race in 1952. It paid off two years later when she won. She went on to become the leading advocate of women's rights in the House of Representatives during the critical years of the 1960s. "She was wonderful. She was gutsy—very outspoken and friendly," said Muriel Fox, the public-relations executive who became one of the founders of the National Organization for Women. Griffiths and her husband, who did not have children, were "totally dedicated to each other," a friend said, and her political success was the crowning achievement of both of their lives. Nevertheless, she felt obliged to assure an interviewer that "if there was any question that my career was interfering with my husband's happiness, and I had to make a choice, I would definitely give up my career."

"I'M NOT SURE I CAN GO TO THOSE LENGTHS."

The greatest irony of the celebration of forty years of suffrage was that it seemed that once women had gotten the right to vote, they never got anything else. There was an endless list of ways they were discriminated against or treated unfairly, from lower salaries to inferior facilities for girls' sports in public schools to the different—and less generous—way that Social Security benefits were computed on women's wages. Few people seemed to think all this posed much of a problem. Many of the women who had experienced the most discrimination took it for granted; those who didn't saw little possibility for major change.

The new president, John Kennedy, had called on the nation to throw off the restraints of decades of depression and war, and move forward into the exciting and challenging future he called the New Frontier. He didn't necessarily envision a major role for women in it. In her memoirs, the publisher Katharine Graham recounted how the president had once demanded to know why Adlai Stevenson, the balding, chubby United Nations ambassador, was regarded as so attractive by his many female friends. Told that it was because Stevenson actually listened with interest to what women had to say, the president responded, according to Graham, "Well, I don't say you're wrong, but I'm not sure I can go to those lengths."

During his run for the White House, Kennedy had kept the female volunteers at arm's length when it came to decision-making. Margaret Price, an official on the Democratic National Committee with the inevitable title of vice chair for women's activities, called the campaign staff an "all-male cast." After the election, 2.4 percent of the executive positions in the forward-looking New Frontier went to women—exactly the same as under the placid administration of Dwight Eisenhower. Yet the ice was starting to crack, and things began to move.

"ESTHER, THE LADIES ARE HERE."

Early in 1960, just as in every other year when Congress went into session, a group of mostly elderly women emerged from a brick house on Constitution Avenue and walked up Capitol Hill to request the introduction of the Equal Rights Amendment (ERA). They were members of the National Woman's Party, led by the redoubtable Alice Paul, the heroine of the battle for suffrage who had stoically endured hunger strikes and prison terms to win the right to vote. She was consumed by the fight for women's rights. "There is no Alice Paul. There is suffrage," wrote a magazine writer who had tried, and failed, to find the person behind the cause. Paul seemed to have no private life and to be indifferent to anything that did not relate directly to her obsession. Since 1920 she and her followers had devoted all their attention to getting a constitutional amendment barring discrimination on the basis of sex.

"Esther, the ladies are here," the president pro tem of the Senate told Esther Peterson, the head of the Department of Labor—Women's Bureau and the highest-ranking woman in the Kennedy administration. As always, the bill would be introduced. Then, as always, a poison pill would be added, declaring that the amendment would not apply to any laws aimed at protecting women—such as common state regulations limiting the number of hours they could work. The Woman's Party members would then declare that the amendment was unacceptable, ask that the ERA be withdrawn, and trot sadly back down the hill to their headquarters.

Most people in the Kennedy administration regarded the Woman's Party as an anachronism at best—the original "little old ladies in tennis shoes"—and at worst a bunch of wealthy conservatives who cared only about other well-to-do white women like themselves. (Esther Peterson called them the "Old Frontier.") But complaints had already been raised about the way Kennedy and his aides were ignoring women's issues, and Peterson had worked out a plan for both avoiding the ERA and mollifying the critics. Like Peterson herself, it was practical and aimed at incremental change. It would turn out to be the catalyst for much more.

"GOD SAW HIM AS A BIGGER COG THAN ME."

As a good Mormon girl growing up in Utah, Esther Eggertsen was troubled by religious doubts, which she confided to her boyfriend. Religion, he told her, was much like a pocket watch: "God is the mainspring, and we are the cogs turning round him. Each of us has an ability to lead or follow, each doing our part." Esther listened intently. "From his description," she recalled years later, "I got the clear idea that God saw him as a bigger cog than me." Much to her mother's distress, she broke off the relationship and went east to study at Columbia University. Realizing her family's worst fears, she was attracted to a doctoral student, Oliver Peterson, who "was a socialist who drank coffee and smoked a pipe." When the two of them wound up getting kicked out of a park "because we argued about the business practices of Henry Ford into the early-morning hours," she knew it was love.

After their marriage, the Petersons moved to Boston, where Esther taught gym at an upscale school by day and volunteered to teach a night course at the YWCA for young factory workers. When a favorite student failed to show up one night, she sought the girl out at her family's slum tenement and entered a room where a mother and five children sat around a table under a bare lightbulb, doing take-home work for which they were paid by the piece: "Even the youngest child, no more than three years old, worked. He sat in a high chair, counting out bobby pins into piles of ten." The student had skipped school to take part in a strike against a factory that had reduced the payment for piecework, putting the already-impoverished workers in danger of starvation. The next morning, Peterson was out on the picket line with her. It was the beginning of a forty-year career in the labor movement.

Calm and steady—she relieved anxiety with bouts of manic bread-making—Peterson wore her hair in an old-fashioned braid around her head. (Later, when she became Lyndon Johnson's assistant for consumer affairs, the outraged advertising industry would refer to her as "the woman with the tight hairdo.") After her family moved to Washington, she became the only woman lobbyist for the Amalgamated Clothing Workers. The union leadership, wary of giving her any serious responsibility, assigned Peterson to follow the most insignificant freshman representative on the Labor Committee. "Give her to Kennedy—he won't amount to much," someone said. The two bonded, and when John Kennedy ran for president, she became one of the first labor-union officials to support him.

"What do you want?" Kennedy asked when he won the election.

"The Women's Bureau," she replied. It was an uninspired choice, but Peterson's husband was ill with cancer and she wanted a job in which she knew she would feel comfortable. The Department of Labor—Women's Bureau was the traditional spot where presidents stashed a female appointee deserving of a policy-making position. It was supposed to fight for better working conditions for women, but it also frequently and defensively acknowledged that no job should take second place to domestic duties. ("It is not the policy of the Women's Bureau to encourage married women and mothers of young children to seek employment outside the home," said a 1964 publication.) The highest salary anyone in the bureau could be paid was $2,000 a year, since Congress had decided that, in the words of one lawmaker, "no woman on earth is worth more than that."

But Peterson had made her choice, and she was reminded quickly of where it left her in the political hierarchy. When the incoming Kennedy administration organized a lunch for all its new labor officials and the Eisenhower appointees they were to replace, the secretary of labor, Arthur Goldberg, asked Peterson to take the outgoing Women's Bureau head to lunch so the men could get together on their own. "Like a fool, I did it," she said.

"MEN HAVE TO BE REMINDED THAT WOMEN EXIST."

Republican women tended to favor the Equal Rights Amendment, but it raised hackles among many Democrats because it would eliminate the protective laws they had struggled to pass during the last generation. Esther Peterson had spent much of her life working with desperate women who were crippled by the physical demands of their jobs, sexually harassed by their supervisors, and deprived of enough time to be proper mothers to their undernourished children. She resented the "elite, privileged old ladies" who cared about only their own emancipation. "Are women better off being singled out for protection, or are they better served by erasing all legal distinctions between women and men? As the lettuce pickers and cafeteria workers know, it depends on your status," she said.

But even some Democrats felt the protective laws did more harm than good, giving employers an excuse to discriminate against women and deprive them of the chance for promotion and overtime. During the 1960 presidential campaign, a prominent Democratic clubwoman wrote to Kennedy, asking him to support the ERA. Kennedy had replied carefully and vaguely—in a note that was probably written by Peterson. The disappointed petitioner then took the extraordinary step of having a friend on the campaign committee type a different letter on Kennedy's stationery, announcing his support for the amendment and signing it with the automatic pen that the campaign used to duplicate the candidate's signature. Rather than raise a controversy, Kennedy tried to ignore it, but the letter got some attention.

While the ERA was hardly a major problem hanging over the new administration, it worried Peterson. She decided to bury the issue by proposing a special Presidential Commission on the Status of Women that could be stacked with ERA opponents and then eventually issue a report on how to improve the lives of American women without the help of a constitutional amendment. Every politician seeking to avoid a sticky issue loves a study, and for the president, the commission was a win-win that got even better when Eleanor Roosevelt agreed to serve as the symbolic head.

Roosevelt had always been a one-person network for smart, talented women who had been cut out of all the male power circles in the New Deal and beyond. She had introduced them to one another, put in calls when they needed political pull, and lobbied for them when they were seeking jobs and promotions. ("When I wanted help on some definite point, Mrs. Roosevelt gave me the opportunity to sit by the president at dinner and the matter was settled before we finished our soup," said one of her protégés.) Kennedy's relationship with the great former first lady had always been chilly, and when the new administration failed to include any high-ranking female appointees, she told reporters, "Men have to be reminded that women exist."

"She would train the men."

The Commission on the Status of Women was made up of people you would expect to find on a panel that was meant to be modestly useful but not controversial. The male members were mainly educators and cabinet officials whose interest in the subject was in some cases nonexistent. (Hyman Bookbinder, who served on the commission as the representative of the secretary of commerce, cautioned that the commission "should not pretend that women as a group are equal to men as a group in qualifying for participation in the world of work and public affairs.") Among the women, Kennedy had included the presidents of the National Council of Negro Women, the National Council of Jewish Women, and the National Council of Catholic Women, along with an editor from *Ladies' Home Journal*. The commission would eventually issue a very responsible report that would be quickly forgotten in the anguish over the president's assassination a few days after its release.

Nevertheless, it is important to our story. The commission—and the state commissions on the status of women it spawned—brought together smart, achieving women who might otherwise have never met. And it required them to talk about women's rights, a subject that seldom came up in their normal work in government or academia. It created a special chemistry, a kind of synergy that made things happen.

Most of the people on the commission and its staff tended to treat discrimination as a simple fact of life. (Mary Eastwood, the brilliant Justice Department attorney, said she had thought nothing of it when she was interviewed for one of her first government jobs and told that she would of course "have to be a lot more qualified for a job than a man in order to get it.") While many of them had wanted different careers than the ones they got, the women were almost universally successful by 1960 standards. They were polite, well-behaved, and committed to working within the system. But they were about to enter into what Pauli Murray, a commission lawyer, called "the first high-level consciousness group." By the time they were through, many would realize that inwardly, they had been seething all along.

Marguerite Rawalt, a government tax attorney, was appointed to the commission as a token ERA supporter. She was a tall, middle-aged Texan who never lost her Southern charm, universally described as "a lady" or "a very, very nice woman." Rawalt had always quietly dreamed of one day becoming a judge. After law school, she had taken a job with the Internal Revenue Service that provided her with security and enough income to help support her family back home during the Depression. Her bosses must have been equally pleased by her impressive work habits and her hesitation about ever asking for a promotion. When she did ask, late in her career, her supervisor expressed amazement that she had never been elevated before—and raised her one grade. When Lyndon Johnson, an old Texas associate, became vice president, Rawalt finally dared to lobby for a judgeship, but she was told she was too old. "She was a lovely woman," said Mary Eastwood, who worked for Rawalt's group on the commission. "She had been passed over for the head of her section year after year. She would train the men."

Disappointed in her work life, Rawalt directed her considerable energies to professional women's clubs. (She was once simultaneously elected president and vice president of the National Association of Women Lawyers due to an overenergetic write-in campaign.) She used her various posts whenever possible to push for women's issues, but it was a crusade that often concerned her fellow club members less than it did her. When she was elected head of the DC chapter of the Federation of Business and Professional Women, a Washington columnist enthused that Rawalt, "magnetic and winning instant attention and admiration for her legal acumen, knows the art of correct dressing as well."

She also knew how to write letters—hundreds and hundreds of letters. It's hard to imagine how important a talent that was in the era before e-mail. In the early 1960s, long-distance telephone calls were pricey, generally reserved for emergencies or at least special occasions. People did not have access to even the most basic office copying equipment. The only method of duplicating a letter or an announcement, short of shipping it off to the printer, was a mimeograph machine, which could reproduce text that was painfully—and often messily—typed on waxed sheets of paper.

Whenever anything happened in the inchoate struggle for women's rights, Rawalt reached for her stamps. If a critical congressman needed to be pressured, she urged her fellow letter writers to start sending in petitions. If some minor triumph occurred—a successful meeting or a new volunteer to the cause—she sat down at her desk and dashed out notes to anyone she felt might be interested. Correspondence, for her, was a matter of bulk. Mary Eastwood remembered being in awe of Rawalt's extraordinary efficiency at sealing envelopes. "She'd lay them all out with the sticky part showing and get a damp sponge and run it down them." At a time when women who did succeed made every effort to avoid anything that resembled secretarial work, Rawalt was the one who was never afraid to get her hands inky.

One of Rawalt's chief allies on the commission staff was Pauli Murray, the extraordinary African-American lawyer who had been hired from Yale, where she was pursuing a PhD. Murray, like some other talented black Americans forced to prove themselves over and over, was an almost compulsive academic overachiever. She had worked her way through Hunter College in New York despite financial troubles that left her suffering from malnutrition. She graduated in 1933, one of four blacks in a class of 247. After an unsuccessful attempt to integrate the University of North Carolina graduate school, she went to law school at Howard University, the only woman in her class. Scrimping as always, she lived in an unused powder room in a girls' dormitory.

While she was at the all-black Howard (which discriminated against her because of her sex nearly as much as other schools did because of her race), Murray wrote to Franklin Roosevelt, criticizing his failure to do more for African-Americans. The president failed to respond. But Eleanor Roosevelt wrote back, defending her husband and calling Murray's letter "thoughtless." When Murray stood up for her position, the first lady invited her to come to her New York apartment "to talk these things over." Their meetings continued, and when Murray graduated from law school, a huge bouquet of flowers appeared at the commencement exercises. The black newspaper the *Pittsburgh Courier* proudly reported that the flowers were sent to the "brilliant, active, strong-willed Pauli Murray" from "Mrs. Roosevelt, wife of the president of the United States."

Murray went to New York, struggling to find a job and living on such cheap food that she got a tapeworm. Eventually she landed a spot with a major law firm, but because she was the only woman, the only minority, and twenty years older than her peers, she was never comfortable. She accepted a post teaching in Ghana and then a fellowship at Yale, where she was doing graduate study in law. Later in life, after receiving her Yale doctorate and teaching at Brandeis University, she would attend divinity school and end her career as an Episcopalian minister. "Pauli was like a pixie—petite and energetic, even when she was in her 60s," said Mary Eastwood, who worked with her on the commission staff. "She was afraid of nothing in terms of action. She even submitted her résumé when there was a vacancy on the Supreme Court—applied for the job!"

One constant in her life had been Eleanor Roosevelt, who continued to exchange letters with Murray and invite her for afternoon teas and weekend visits. But Mrs. Roosevelt died in 1962, before the Commission on the Status of Women could finish its work. "It became my memorial to her last public service," Murray said.

"I AM ALWAYS STRONG FOR WOMEN, YOU KNOW."

In 1964 Representative Howard Smith of Virginia appeared on *Meet the Press* to answer questions about the Civil Rights Act, which was moving through Congress. Its most controversial section was Title VII, prohibiting racial discrimination in employment. For once, there was a woman among the reporters doing the questioning. May Craig of Gannett News Service asked Smith if he would add women to the minority groups to be protected from discrimination in Title VII.

"Well, maybe I would. I am always strong for women, you know," he said.

Smith, 80, was the chairman of the Rules Committee, a post that gave him enormous power to stop or at least delay any legislation of which he disapproved. And there was a lot Smith disapproved of—including aid to education, welfare, and minimum-wage laws. He kept Alaskan statehood bottled up in his committee for nearly a year, and he once delayed civil rights legislation by simply disappearing for several days and making it impossible for his committee to schedule a time for the measure to be considered in the House. When he returned, he claimed he had been called home to his dairy farm when a barn burned down. "I always knew Howard Smith would do anything to block a civil rights bill, but I never supposed he would resort to arson," said Sam Rayburn, the Speaker of the House.

Of all the forces of progress Smith wanted to stop, civil rights was at the top of the list. "Congressman Smith would joyfully disembowel the civil rights bill if he could. Lacking the votes to do so, he will obstruct it as long as the situation allows," said a writer in the *New York Times Magazine*.

When the Civil Rights Act came up for a vote in the House, Smith got up and offered an amendment that would add women to the groups who would be protected from job discrimination. In case anyone might have imagined he was actually concerned about a serious social issue (Smith was, after all, a friend of Alice Paul's), he began by jocularly reading a letter from a woman complaining about the lack of marriageable men: "Just why the Creator would set up such an imbalance of spinsters, shutting off the 'right' of every female to have a husband of her own is, of course, known only to nature. But I am sure you will agree this is a grave injustice to womankind and something Congress and President Johnson should take immediate steps to correct, especially in an election year."

The proposal that women should have equal opportunity to be considered for any job was an idea that struck a great many otherwise open-minded people as absolutely ridiculous. The debate over Smith's amendment reflected that. Emanuel Celler of New York, who was managing the Civil Rights Act and attempting to deflect any amendment that might endanger it, stood up. "I can say as a result of forty-nine years of experience—and I celebrate my fiftieth wedding anniversary next year—that women, indeed, are not the minority in my house...," he said. "I usually have the last two words and those words are 'yes, dear.'"

Amid the hoots from the other male legislators, Representative Leonor Sullivan of Missouri turned to Martha Griffiths. "If you can't stop that laughter, you're lost," she said.

Griffiths, unlike much of the House, was dead serious about adding women to Title VII, but she knew that between the lawmakers who flat-out opposed the idea and the ones who simply feared doing anything to endanger the Civil Rights Act, there would not be enough votes to support her if she offered such an amendment. When she heard Smith's comments on *Meet the Press*, she saw a new opening. Smith had the consistent support of dozens of Southern conservatives in the House. Add those to the numbers she could round up on her own power, and there might be a majority. Griffiths had some chips in the favor bank herself. (She was the first woman to serve on the Ways and Means Committee, which approved all those obscure little tax exemptions so dear to the hearts of campaign contributors.) She had been working to collect votes, and she had thought carefully about what she would say when she rose to her feet. "I presume that if there had been any necessity to point out that women were a second-class sex, the laughter would have proved it," she said.

That got their attention.

"In my judgment, the men who had written the Equal Employment Opportunity Act had never even thought about women," Griffiths said later. She was convinced the authors wanted to "give black men some rights, and that black women would be treated about like white women." But whatever their motives, Griffiths said, "I made up my mind that if such a bill were going to pass, it was going to carry a prohibition against discrimination on the basis of sex, and that both black and white women were going to take a modest step forward together."

Eleven of the twelve women serving in the 435-member House rose to support the act. The holdout was Edith Green of Oregon. A member of the Commission on the Status of Women, Green had just finished a long and depressing struggle to pass a bill prohibiting employers from paying men and women different wages for the same job. Her Equal Pay Act had been amended until it was riddled with holes, including an exemption for professional, executive, and administrative positions. (Green remembered a male colleague asking her incredulously if she would actually "pay a woman administrative assistant in your office as much as you would pay a male administrative assistant.") For the minimal reform that was left, Green had still had to fight every step of the way. At one point, when she went looking to make sure the bill hadn't disappeared in committee, she found that a male colleague had filed it under "B"— for "broads." It was no wonder, really, that Green had a reputation for crankiness.

Green herself had thought of proposing an amendment to add women to the Civil Rights Act. But the Johnson White House had convinced her that it could endanger the legislation's chance of passage. In this matter, she decided, black Americans had to come first. "For every discrimination that has been made against a woman in this country, there has been ten times as much discrimination against the Negro," she said.

It was a very old and very painful debate. The fight for women's rights and the struggle for racial justice had almost always been linked in America. Abolition of slavery had been the first political issue that brought large numbers of women into the public world, and many of them pointed out the similarities they saw in the treatment of women and African-Americans. Black leaders were grateful for the support but tended to feel that however bad and repressive Victorian marriages were, they were not quite as grim as slavery and lynching. From the beginning, each cause was keenly aware that when they presented a joint front, critical support tended to dwindle away. Many male politicians who supported abolition felt very strongly that a woman's place was in the home, and many Southern politicians who were willing to consider legislation of benefit to women drew back fast when civil rights were added to the equation. During the Civil War, abolition leaders felt that it would be much harder to amend the Constitution to give African-Americans the full rights of citizenship if women had to get the vote as well, and they decided that the black cause was by far more urgent. Women such as Elizabeth Cady Stanton and Susan B. Anthony were furious, and Stanton shocked her old friend and ally Frederick Douglass by denouncing the idea of immigrants and freed slaves—"Patrick and Sambo and Yung Tung"—making laws for the disenfranchised "daughters of Adams and Jefferson...women of wealth and education."

When women once again rose up and demanded the right to vote during World War I, Alice Paul and her lieutenants had no intention of alienating Southern supporters with a show of sympathy for African-Americans. When Paul staged the famous women's rights parade of 1913 in Washington, she ordered black suffragists to march at the back of the line in order to spare the feelings of Southern sympathizers. (Ida Wells-Barnett, who had been leading a group of black women from Chicago, vanished into the crowd along the sidewalk, then stepped back into the street as the Illinois delegation marched by, joining her white friends and integrating the demonstration.) A half century later, Paul

ignored pleas that she decline to accept support for the ERA from the segregationist presidential candidate George Wallace.

In 1964 black Americans were still in a far more perilous position than white women. But women, especially poor and working-class women, desperately needed better protection. And there was no reason that a fabulously prosperous nation founded on equal rights for all shouldn't be able to attack both injustices at the same time. While all the black legislators were worried about the amendment's effect on the Civil Rights Act, they were not unanimously convinced that Griffiths was wrong. Griffiths recalled that, several days after the vote, as she was walking into the House, William Dawson, a black representative from Chicago, came up and shook her hand. "Mrs. Griffiths, during the weekend I thought about that speech you made on behalf of women and I would like to tell you that if all of your training and all of your experience had been for that one moment, it has all been worthwhile," he said.

The amendment passed the House, as Griffiths had calculated. ("We made it! We're human!" cried a woman from the gallery.) The Civil Rights Act then moved through the Senate, where Everett Dirksen, the powerful minority leader from Illinois, wanted to remove it. While Marguerite Rawalt organized one of her letter-writing campaigns, Senator Margaret Chase Smith picked up the fight on the Senate floor.

"THIS LITTLE LADY HAS SIMPLY STEPPED OUT OF HER CLASS."

Smith was another widow—at 33, after years as a single working woman, she married Clyde Smith, a 54-year-old soon-to-be congressman from Maine. She stepped into his seat when he died, and then, after four terms in the House, she shocked everyone by running for the Senate in 1948. "This little lady has simply stepped out of her class," said a state politician. Smith campaigned for the seat during the congressional session, returning home on weekends in an era when flying—especially flying to Maine— was an airborne version of taking a wagon train west. Smith headed for Portland, which required one or two changes of planes along the way. When she arrived, there was another hundred-mile trip to her home, where she picked up her car and started driving. As she traveled from stop to stop, she sometimes wound up having to ask for shelter for the night in a local farmhouse. When she slipped on the ice and broke her arm, it simply made her two hours late for her next speaking engagement. She had no paid staff, no campaign manager. And in the end she got more votes than all three of her opponents.

In 1950, when Washington was quivering under Senator Joseph McCarthy's crazed anti-Communist campaign, Smith took to the floor and became the first lawmaker to dare to stand up to McCarthyism. "I don't like the way the Senate has been made a rendezvous for vilification…I am not proud of the way we smear outsiders from the floor of the Senate and hide behind the cloak of congressional immunity…As an American I want to see our nation recapture the strength and unity it once had when we fought the enemy instead of ourselves," she said. Bernard Baruch, one of the most influential political advisers of the era, said that if the speech had been made by a man, that man would have been the next president. In retaliation, McCarthy had her tossed off the Permanent Investigating Committee and tried to run a candidate against her in Maine in 1954. She simply ignored the challenger. "My record is so outstanding and so effective that there isn't any use running around the state defending it," she said. And she was right.

The only woman in the Senate for most of her career, Smith had to stand in line at the public bathroom because she was barred from the senators' lounge. When she served on the Naval Affairs Committee, one of the staff members took her for a walk during long sessions so the men would have a break from the burden of a female presence. Once, on a flight home from Europe with other lawmakers, the plane developed trouble serious enough that everyone was given a life jacket and told to pre-

pare for a possible crash. In response, Smith pulled out some harmonicas she had purchased as presents for her nieces and nephews and persuaded everyone to start singing. Later, she told reporters she was as terrified as everyone else, "only as a woman I couldn't have the luxury of showing my fear."

On the issue of women's rights, Minority Leader Dirksen was no match for the senator from Maine. The Civil Rights Act passed with the amendment intact and was signed into law. Years later, the very elderly Howard Smith—retired and no longer the terror of liberal legislation in the House of Representatives—visited the Capitol and ran into Martha Griffiths. "You know, our amendment is doing more than all the rest of the Civil Rights Act," she told him. Smith, Griffiths said, responded, "Martha, I'll tell you the truth. I offered it as a joke."

"AN AIRLINE OR A WHOREHOUSE?"

Howard Smith was not the only person who thought the idea of giving women workers equal protection under the law was hilarious. Once the Civil Rights Act was on the books, it looked as if the section protecting women from job discrimination was going to do nothing but spawn endless jokes about the "bunny law" that, wags predicted, would require the Playboy Club to give men equal opportunity to don puff tails and silk ears, and work as one of its scantily clad waitresses. The *Wall Street Journal* invited its readers to imagine "a shapeless, knobby-kneed male 'bunny' serving drinks to a group of stunned businessmen" while on the other side of town "a matronly vice president" was chasing her male secretary. "Bunny problems indeed!" giggled a *New York Times* editorial, which also raised the specter of male chorus-line dancers. *The New Republic*, a bastion of liberal commentary, said the sex provision should simply be ignored. "Why should a mischievous joke perpetrated on the floor of the House of Representatives be treated by a responsible administrative body with this kind of seriousness?" the magazine asked.

Very few people involved with enforcing the act seemed to believe women should be a serious concern. The Equal Employment Opportunity Commission was set up to arbitrate complaints under the new law, and Aileen Hernández, the only woman among the five commissioners, said other members responded to sex-discrimination complaints with "boredom" or "virulent hostility." The EEOC ruled that help-wanted ads could not mention a preferred race for applicants, but it did nothing to stop the newspapers' practice of dividing the ads into HELP WANTED—MALE and HELP WANTED—FEMALE.

Yet when the EEOC opened for business, its first complainants were neither oppressed black workers nor men hoping to break into the ranks of the Playboy Bunnies. They were stewardesses. The commission's clerical staff, which had been told that their job was to help fight racial discrimination, was still unpacking when Barbara Roads, a union leader for the flight attendants, and another stewardess arrived. "We walked in and looked around at a sea of black faces. Their typewriters were still in boxes. This woman came up to us, two blondes in stewardess uniforms, and she said, 'What are you doing here?'" Roads recalled. The two women helped the brand-new workers set up their typewriters and told them about the airline ban on marriage, the age discrimination, and the endless measurements to check for weight gain. "They couldn't believe it," she said.

The black women behind the typewriters may have been sympathetic, but the flight attendants' complaints brought out the same somber deliberation on the part of male officials that the Playboy Bunny theories did. When a House labor subcommittee held a hearing on the issue, Representative James Scheuer of New York jovially asked the flight attendants to "stand up, so we can see the dimensions of the problem." The airline industry continued to argue with a straight face that businessmen would be discouraged from flying if the women handing them their coffee and checking their seat belts were not young and attractive. "What are you running, an airline or a whorehouse?" Martha Griffiths demanded. The

remark got into public circulation just as Griffiths was concluding a reelection campaign, and even her ever-supportive husband, Hicks, worried she had made a potentially fatal error. But the next morning he called from Michigan to report, "I am wrong. Everybody I have seen in Detroit is in hysterics. They are shouting at me from across the street, saying, 'Tell Martha it was the greatest question ever asked.'"

"AN NAACP FOR WOMEN."

Howard Smith's decision to play games with the Civil Rights Act was an extraordinary example of unintended consequences. At the time he introduced his amendment, the idea of ending job discrimination against women was on almost no one's radar. Only two states — Hawaii and Wisconsin — included women in their fair-employment laws. At the Commission on the Status of Women, Mary Eastwood and Pauli Murray had intended to sneak in a proposal that states should *study* whether women ought to be protected against job discrimination. It had seemed like a rather radical recommendation. But, of course, once the Civil Rights Act was amended, expectations rose. Nobody was going to settle for a study when the law of the land said that female employees could not be treated differently than men. And when it became clear that the EEOC had no intention of protecting women workers as the law required, it created instant militancy.

Betty Friedan was among the frustrated. She was going to Washington for a few days every week in the mid-'60s, allegedly to research a book. Perhaps, given her fractious marriage, she was merely trying to get away from home. Perhaps, as she said later, she was networking with the small group of senior women government officials she had unearthed with the help of Pauli Murray—people who Friedan called the "underground network of women in Washington." (The practical government women found the term wildly overdramatic, even though they secretly liked it.) They "maneuvered me into place all right," Friedan wrote later, "recognizing that I, famous for writing a controversial book about women, could do publicly what they could only do underground: organize a women's movement."

In the summer of 1966, at a conference of state commissions on the status of women, delegates, guests, and lookers-on arrived in Washington steaming about the way the new law against job discrimination was—or rather was not—being enforced. Friedan ran into Pauli Murray, and they agreed to invite "whomever we met who seemed interested in organizing women for action" to a strategy session that night. The meeting, in Friedan's hotel room, is now famous as a turning point in the history of the women's movement, but certainly no one at the time would have imagined she was taking part in a legendary event. It was crowded, the conversation disjointed and testy, and the women, who had spent a long day in nylons and girdles, must have been tired and a little uncomfortable. The radical forces called for "an NAACP for women" that would identify discrimination and fight it in the courts and in the legislatures. The moderates suggested proposing a resolution calling for the enforcement of the Civil Rights Act ban on sex discrimination in employment. Others just wanted to send a telegram to whoever was chairing the meeting the next day. At one point in the long, heated discussion, Friedan irately demanded that everyone leave and, when no one did, locked herself in the bathroom. The meeting went on anyway; Friedan eventually emerged, and a resolution was drafted. The next day it was introduced, then promptly ruled out of order.

During the conference lunch, while various members of the Johnson administration gave utterly forgettable speeches, Friedan and a dozen or so other women seated at the front tables were buzzing among themselves, making a mini-spectacle as they talked, dashed notes on napkins, and passed them back and forth. They were creating, on the spot, a version of that long-awaited "NAACP for women." They called it NOW, the National Organization for Women, and agreed to ante up $5 each to get the ball rolling. As word of what was going on spread around the room—it would have been hard for the conferees to miss the fact that something was up—Friedan remembered that "those five-dollar bills kept coming at us, one from Eleanor Roosevelt's granddaughter, Anna."

"THE MYTHICAL MARCHING MILLIONS."

Given the fruit it bore, NOW seems to have been a plant that required only a seed and a thimble of water before it sprouted into something terrific. Members joked about "the mythical marching millions" when in reality there were only about three hundred members. In the months right after its founding, NOW existed in one of those golden moments when the winds of change seemed to be virtually impelling it to success. "We were totally confident we were making history," said Muriel Fox.

During NOW's first protest, a picketing of EEOC offices in cities around the country, Friedan was so carried away with the excitement and the news cameras that she decided to announce a legal action. Mid-demonstration, she dashed into a secretary's cubicle in the New York EEOC and called Mary Eastwood, who was providing surreptitious support from her government perch in the Justice Department. "What do you call it when you sue the government for not enforcing a law?" Friedan asked.

"A writ of mandamus," said Eastwood.

Friedan put down the phone, marched back out, and announced that NOW was "going into court for a writ of mandamus against the U.S. government" for not enforcing the Civil Rights Act when it came to sex discrimination. At the time, she recalled later, NOW had "only two members in Atlanta, six in Pittsburgh, a dozen in Chicago and California, and not much more in between."

It was not that people didn't want to join. As soon as Jo Freeman, a young Chicago community organizer, read about NOW, she wrote asking to become a member but got no answer. "Over the next year I wrote a few more letters to NOW names in the news, including Betty Friedan, but again got no reply," she remembered. Just finding NOW was a "little like trying to find the early Christians," said one early liberationist. Martha Griffiths, who had naturally been enlisted as a charter member as well as a member of the advisory committee, said later she was never called to a meeting. "They weren't organized well enough, you know."

The women on top of the very small pyramid that was the early NOW membership understood about the law and the media, but they were not necessarily prepared to grow a mass movement. "With no money, no office, no staff, it was impossible to answer all the letters and calls from women who wanted to join NOW," Friedan wrote later. "When someone would get so impatient that she'd call long distance...I'd make her the local NOW organizer—if she didn't sound too crazy." Fox recruited a woman to serve as Friedan's secretary, and for want of a better workplace, the new employee sat perched behind a typewriter table in Fox's office at the public relations firm Carl Byoir. Much of the printing and phone calling was done in Michigan by NOW supporters in the United Auto Workers union. The mail drop for the infant organization was in Washington, and Friedan, the leader, was in New York. It was little more than a small cadre of far-flung acquaintances who suddenly discovered they had a tiger by the tail.

"... AND MAKE UP FOR THE LACK OF HARRY AT HOME TO CARE."

Word started going around that there was, indeed, an "NAACP for women" that would champion the victims of sex discrimination and take their legal cases. NOW's legal committee was exactly like that of the NAACP—except that the NAACP had a history of fighting racism through the courts, a veritable army of experienced attorneys at its disposal, and a long, although painfully acquired, list of financial backers. NOW had a handful of volunteer lawyers, most of whom worked for the government and were unable to take a public role. At the beginning only Marguerite Rawalt, who had retired, was able to treat NOW as a full-time—albeit unpaid—job. In 1966 she was newly widowed and eager to throw herself into the cause. "You have not heard from me because I have been so overwhelmed with work and travel and making talks that I can hardly keep myself going," she wrote a friend. "I seem to lose myself that way, and make up for the lack of Harry at home to care."

But Rawalt was no match for the flood of letters NOW received from women looking for legal help. "I must have relief...I can't do it all," she wrote Friedan. Many of the women who wrote were the victims of all the protective laws the labor unions and well-intentioned politicians had gotten passed in state legislatures, prohibiting businesses from asking women to lift heavy objects or work long hours. In the real world, companies used the weight rules to disqualify women from high-paying jobs, and the regulations restricting them to forty-hour workweeks cut them out of lucrative overtime. Companies also took it upon themselves to create rules for women's alleged benefit. Some refused to employ women with preschool children under the theory that mothers with young sons and daughters should not have jobs that were too demanding. In Orlando, Ida Phillips applied for an assembly-trainee job at Martin Marietta and was rejected because she had preschool children. When she sued, the lower court rejected her claim, saying that employers had a right to consider job applicants' outside responsibilities. But it was an illusion to imagine that the women who sought to be assembly workers had other options that would make it easier to take care of their families. While she fought her case in court, Phillips was forced to take a job as a waitress—for less money and longer hours.

"WOMEN WORKED AND NEEDED A PLACE IN THE WORLD."

Lorena Weeks was 9 years old when her father was killed in a sawmill accident. Her mother was 29, with four children. "She had never worked and she did have a hard time," Weeks recalled in her Georgia drawl. "That's one thing I knew. All men weren't breadwinners and women did have to work for what they got. So I always assumed I would work, and I did work. I went to work at a five-and-ten-cent store when I was 9 years old. I could hardly see over the counter because I was small in stature. I worked for one dollar a day."

Her mother died of a cerebral hemorrhage nine years later, leaving 18-year-old Lorena with a 9-year-old brother and 15-year-old sister to raise and support. She worked four hours a night as a waitress in her hometown of Louisville, then caught a bus to her overnight job as a telephone operator in Wadley, ten miles away. "I worked from eleven at night until seven in the morning and caught the mail carrier back to Louisville. I got home in time to fix breakfast. We had one room and a tiny kitchen. My brother and sister went to school during the day and I slept," she recounted. "I was determined and I had the Lord on my side."

She also had a suitor—William Weeks, a part-time electrician and rural letter carrier who shared her last name. "All my life I knew I would marry a black-haired, blue-eyed man and I did," said Weeks, who is now a widow. "When I was a little girl my daddy used to rock me on the porch and I'd say I wanted to marry him and he'd say, 'Sissy, you can't marry Daddy.' And I'd say, 'I want to keep my name, Daddy. I want to always be a Weeks.' And he said, 'You'll just have to find a man who has the same name.' So it just happened like that." Billy Weeks courted Lorena by phone for three months before they ever met. "He called me every night. He said, 'I saw you eating a piece of pie in the restaurant and I just wanted to talk with you.'

"I loved him before I even knew him, really."

They married and set up housekeeping, and she continued to work for the telephone company, Southern Bell, with a five-year break when she had her three children in rapid succession. "When my little girl was old enough to call me on the phone to talk, I went back to work," she said. "We needed the money."

The Weeks were determined that their son and two daughters would be able to go to college, and all their efforts were aimed at saving up for their schooling. Everything else—including the long-dreamed-of house Billy intended to build on some land they owned—was put on indefinite hold. At Southern Bell, Lorena was always on the lookout for a chance to make overtime or to move up to a better-paying job. She was a phone-company clerk when a notice came out that a switchman's job had opened up. The work involved making sure routing equipment in the central office was functioning properly, and Weeks felt confident she could do the job as well as anyone else. But when she applied, the phone company sent back her application. "They said they appreciated that I wanted to advance within the company, but it's a job not awarded to women." The head of her union told her she did not get the promotion because "the man is the breadwinner in the family and women just don't need this type of job."

There was a large sign in the office informing employees that if they felt discriminated against, they could contact the EEOC, signed by the commission's head, Franklin D. Roosevelt Jr. Weeks wrote to the late president's son and eventually got a notification that a representative of the Atlanta office was coming to investigate. The company refused to bend, citing a Georgia rule that prohibited women from lifting anything heavier than thirty pounds. The switchmen used a piece of testing equipment that just qualified. But it was pushed around on a dolly, while the thirty-four-pound manual typewriter Weeks used as a clerk had to be lifted by hand onto her desk every morning and stored away every night.

Weeks filed a legal appeal, to the dismay of her husband. "He called me Butch, and he said, 'Butch, you're not going to accomplish anything and we're going to lose friends.' Billy just loved people...So I just kept quiet. I didn't come home and talk about it at all. My children knew very little about it. I just didn't want to upset them. This was a thing unheard-of."

Weeks understood that no one she knew had ever considered the prospect of a woman going to court to demand a job that had always been held by men. "I even heard about a preacher preaching about women trying to take men's jobs and things like that. And I was a devout Christian, and I went to church and Sunday school every Sunday and taught," she said. "Well, I just stopped going to church and Sunday school. I was a loner, really. I felt like I was so alone, and yet I knew I was doing what God wanted me to do. Going way back to the fact that my mama had died working so hard. And I knew women worked and needed a place in the world."

Weeks lost her case in district court. (The judge, Frank Scarlett, was an infamous segregationist who had attempted to dismiss a school-integration case on the basis of "expert" testimony from witnesses who said blacks were less intelligent than whites.) Her attorney — who was paid for by the same union that had tried to tell her the job should go only to a man — assured her that the situation was hopeless. When she got the news, Weeks could hear her supervisor and some other men "standing outside my office door, laughing and having the biggest time over it you had ever heard in your life." The next morning, when she came into work, instead of lifting her typewriter onto her desk, she began writing out her reports by hand. When her supervisor protested, Weeks pointed out that she had just lost a lucrative job because of a machine that weighed thirty and three-quarters pounds. "I said, 'This typewriter right here weighs thirty-four and three-quarters pounds.' I said, 'Now if you will reach under the desk and lift it out for me and put it up here where I can type, I'll type all day long. But I don't intend to break a Georgia rule.'" The supervisor told her she was suspended and sent her home.

"It hurt me so much I didn't know what to do. I loved the telephone company. So I went home and I cried all weekend," she said.

It was about then that Weeks found Marguerite Rawalt, who told her NOW would take the case and represent her without charge if she would promise to stick it out.

"I was meant to do this," Weeks told Rawalt.

"You will be on the job tomorrow."

The closest lawyer to Georgia on Rawalt's tiny list of volunteers was Sylvia Roberts, the young Louisiana woman who had to work as a secretary in order to get a starting job in a law firm.

"Sylvia Roberts was the one who kept me from drowning, almost," Weeks said. "She's never gotten credit and she was the most wonderful thing. And Marguerite Rawalt. She was just wonderful to me."

Roberts and her client were kindred spirits who had both grown up with an instinctive understanding that women needed to be able to take care of themselves. "I knew at a very early age that if you didn't have your own money and your own life...that just seemed like a very precarious position," said Roberts. She wanted a profession of her own, and given her lack of interest in science and math, she gradually determined that she was going into law, "although I had never seen a woman lawyer. So this was all on faith."

At that point, none of NOW's efforts to use the new civil rights law to fight discrimination in the courts had been successful. Everyone understood the potential importance of Lorena Weeks's case. Southern Bell was pointing to a section in the Civil Rights Act that allowed an employer to declare a job was open to men only or women only if there was some reasonable qualification that only one sex could fulfill. Corporations regarded it as "a huge loophole," Roberts said, while NOW felt it should appropriately be applied only to jobs for "sperm donors and wet nurses." But there was a distinct danger that the courts might lean more toward the employers' interpretation. Lorena Weeks's appeal seemed like the perfect vehicle for putting things straight. The idea that no woman could lift thirty pounds was ridiculous, Roberts said, given the number of Georgia women who routinely carried around thirty-pound children.

"Our argument was that you can't prejudge," she said. "Women come in all shapes and sizes. I'm an undersized person. I'm not of average height or weight. So I had things brought into the courtroom and I lifted them." Perhaps moved by the sight of Roberts hoisting a workbench, the Fifth Circuit Court of Appeals overturned the lower court ruling and decided in favor of Lorena Weeks, in language that thrilled her young lawyer. Southern Bell's argument was just "romantic paternalism," the opinion said. The new Civil Rights Act had left it up to the women, not the employers, to decide if they wanted to take on untraditional jobs such as telephone-company switchman. "It's been quoted in case after case," said Roberts.

Weeks v. Southern Bell was one of the first big victories on the road to ending job discrimination against women, a huge cause for celebration at NOW. But for Lorena Weeks herself, it was just another marker in a long and tortuous road. She was still in limbo at work and still shuttling to Savannah and Atlanta for hearings, endless hearings. Roberts, who would go on to become an expert in sex-discrimination cases, marveled at the "heroism of the plaintiffs. Their life is such agony while they're going through this and they don't know if they'll get any relief. And all their neighbors think they're doing the wrong thing."

For two more years, the telephone company dragged its heels about letting Lorena Weeks take the test for the switchman's job, let alone finding her a position. Griffin Bell, the distinguished Fifth Circuit judge who would later become Jimmy Carter's attorney general, had been assigned to mediate. Bell seemed dubious that a woman could handle telephone-routing equipment, Roberts remembered. "We were in his office. It was real hot. He had this rickety air conditioner on. Judge Bell kinda turned to look at the air conditioner and said, 'I don't really know how you could do this, Miss Weeks. If I had to fix this air conditioner, I don't believe I could do it.'"

Roberts thought for a moment and said in desperation, "Well, Judge, Lorena's husband is an electrician."

It was, she said, as if a lightbulb went on. "He said, 'Oh well, I guess that's all right.'" Roberts thought Bell might have been instinctively returning to the hoary legal principle that held that husband and wife were one person. Or—she laughed—he might have simply concluded that "if she ever got into a dilemma, she could call Billy."

Still, the fight kept dragging on. Lorena was using Valium to quiet her nerves, trying to keep a low profile at work, worrying that she might accidentally come in late and face the wrath of supervisors who had warned her that any signs of tardiness would lead to dismissal. Meanwhile, her husband had been severely injured in a car wreck. "She was so worried," said Roberts. "She had to make sure her child was at school, plus whatever Billy needed."

At yet another hearing in Judge Bell's chambers, Lorena bitterly said, "I hope everybody here had a very merry Christmas," and noted that in her own family, the girls got only miniature sewing machines to make up for the fact that their parents could not afford to buy them clothes.

"Miss Weeks, you aren't on the job yet?" said the judge in surprise. And then, as Lorena remembers it, he told her, "You will be on the job tomorrow. I'm going to write an order."

"And that," she concluded triumphantly, "is exactly what saved everything."

On the train home, Lorena showed all the other passengers her court order, and during a brief stop at Macon, she jumped off the train to call her husband while the conductor yelled at her to get back on board.

"She believed so much," said Roberts. "She just had this wonderful faith: we have a law, then it's got to apply. The system will work." Lorena received the hard-won check for $31,000 in back pay and the switchman's job. Southern Bell stopped being a company where the lowest-paid man made more than the highest-paid woman. Once they were sure all the children's education would be paid for, Lorena and Billy built their long-deferred house.

Later, when Lorena retired and applied for Social Security, the clerk who was processing her claim at the local office said she had never before seen a woman with such a high income.

Keepsake Pages

When you were growing up, did your parents ever discuss politics? Were you involved in politics when you were young, and if so how did you get drawn in?

_____

_____

_____

_____

_____

_____

_____

_____

_____

What did we do without cell phones and e-mail? Do you remember when calling long distance was a big deal?

_____

_____

_____

_____

_____

_____

_____

_____

When you left school, what was your first job? What did you envision it leading to?

_____

_____

_____

_____

_____

_____

_____

_____

_____

_____

Do you think, back in the day, that there was more discrimination against women in blue-collar or professional jobs?

_____

_____

_____

_____

_____

_____

_____

_____

_____

_____

More Thoughts and Memories

More Thoughts and Memories

5. What Happened?

Not to give the plot away, but the rebellion that began amid all that hilarity over male Bunnies and husband-hungry spinsters is going to go much farther, much faster, than anyone who was there at the beginning might have imagined. Soon, the NOW founders will be joined by more radical women, mostly younger and schooled in the ways of confrontation by the civil rights protests, whose demands will go way beyond antidiscrimination laws. In almost no time, a new women's movement will be attacking the very core of the social roles assigned to the sexes. It will be known as women's liberation — although after a few years of jabs about "libbers," many people will grow tired of the term.

It seemed that overnight everything that America had taken for granted about a woman's role was being called into question. Her place was in the home, and then — zap — she was applying to medical school or going for an MBA. She was supposed to defer to her husband as head of the house — except suddenly there she was, holding consciousness-raising meetings in the living room to discuss his failure to give her help with the baby or the right kind of orgasm. "I always felt bad for the guys who had gotten married under the old rules," said Nora Ephron wryly. "It was like — *What?*" One day coeds were in school just to earn an MRS degree, and then — whoops — there were so many qualified, competitive young women winning the best places in the best colleges that the media worried about what would become of the boys. One year little girls were learning the importance of losing gracefully, and the next they were suing for admission to the Little League. It left many people shaking their heads, wondering what propelled such extraordinary changes so rapidly.

The apparent suddenness of it all was not due to the arrival of a great leader, although some of the leaders were amazing. If the only thing women needed was a powerful voice to articulate their grievances, everything would have been worked out in the nineteenth century when Susan B. Anthony and Elizabeth Cady Stanton were around. The female colonists and pioneers, the early-twentieth-century settlement-house workers, and the World War II nurses who lived with the old gender biases were not less resourceful or insightful than the women of 1968. There was something else — or a collection of something elses — buried deep in the social fabric.

"EXPERIENCE IN BUSINESS BROADENS A WOMAN'S MIND."

Now that we've marveled at the rapidity of the change, we have to acknowledge that it didn't really happen overnight. Women's lives had been evolving throughout the century. They had been having fewer children, marrying later, and taking jobs outside the home more often. In a placid world, the changes might have looked like a gentle slope on a chart. But the Americans had to struggle through two world wars, with the Great Depression sandwiched in between. All of this left the charts looking less like a gentle slope and more like the peaks and valleys of an EKG for a heart-attack patient.

There was no "normal" in the twentieth century, but there was one near constant: a changing economy put a higher value on women's skills. Telephone companies started by hiring men as operators, but they found that women were better at handling customers and less likely to argue with the people on the other end of the line. American businesses found they needed fewer laborers and more customer-service representatives. At the same time, work conditions became more pleasant. Once glamorous department stores took the place of small, dingy shops, and the growing office bureaucracies needed typists, clerks, and receptionists, not-so-poor young women who would have shunned a job in a factory were tempted to think about working. And as the economy's demand for women to take these positions grew, society regarded their participation in the workforce with increasing benevolence.

This was an old pattern. Whenever the nation suddenly required a large supply of new workers—particularly literate workers for relatively low-paying jobs—the answer was women, and the nation's position on women's place adapted quickly. When the public-school system began growing after the Revolutionary War, society decided teaching was a maternal function that respectable women could perform. (And, as one nineteenth-century school superintendent in Ohio happily reported, perform at half the male teachers' wages.) When the industrial age produced far more clerical, sales, and other low-paying white-collar jobs than the male population could fill, the nation readily agreed that a few years of typing or manning department-store counters was an excellent preparation for marriage. "Experience in business broadens a woman's mind and makes her views more practical," concluded *Harper's Weekly* in 1903.

During World War II, women were asked—actually the better word would be nagged—to go to work. There were more than three million jobs going begging as men left civilian work for the military, and the government propaganda machine warned housewives that if they refused to join the factory assembly line, defective weapons might go uninspected and airplanes might be improperly welded. *A soldier might die*, the stay-at-home women were told, and it would be their fault. Those who responded were celebrated for breaking out of their sexual roles and becoming streetcar conductors or welders. *("She's making history, working for victory, Rosie the Riveter...")* The Office of War Information urged newspapers and magazines to run "sto-

ries showing the advent of women in logging camps, on the railroads, riding the ranges, and showing them not as weak sisters but as coming through in manly style."

Some of the women who responded—particularly married women who had always worked but who loved the higher pay in the war-industry jobs—were dismayed to find themselves elbowed out of the way when peace broke out and the soldiers came home. But most of the single women readily complied with society's demand that they go back home and leave the jobs for the returning veterans. They made up for lost nesting time by marrying early and having several children in rapid succession. The government generously underwrote the impulse to domesticity with cheap mortgages, college scholarships, and a huge program of public works that sent incomes shooting up.

"SO THEY HIRE WOMEN."

After the war, the economy didn't just improve. It exploded. Americans were producing half the world's goods in the mid-'50s, even though they made up only 6 percent of the world's population. Business was expanding by leaps and bounds, but the available workforce was relatively small. The "baby-bust" generation of men born during the Depression could not supply enough labor to fill the need. In the 1960s, as the economy was constantly creating employment, two-thirds of those new jobs went to women.

"A Good Man Is Hard to Find—So They Hire Women," announced *Time* in November 1966. That year, President Johnson urged employers to consider hiring women (along with teenagers, the handicapped, and immigrants) to fill their openings. Large firms such as IBM and Texas Instruments targeted stay-at-home moms in recruiting campaigns. So did temporary-employment agencies. "First, we must overcome the married woman's prejudice against returning to work, and this prejudice, in most cases, boils down to her conviction that a mother's place is in the home so long as there are children there," said Manpower's public-relations counsel.

The idea of married women working was indeed hard for middle-class Americans to swallow. Their benevolent attitude toward women employed in department stores or business offices was limited, in the main, to young singles. Even during World War II, very few stay-at-home wives took off their aprons and signed up to become welders or street-car conductors. But the ones who answered the call were proud. "Darling—you are now the husband of a career woman. Just call me your Ship Yard Babe!" wrote one new defense worker to her husband in the service. And after the fighting was over, as single women left the workforce in droves to start families, many of the older married women continued on the job. They were joined by other housewives who were attracted by the pleas of employers and the rising salaries they could earn—especially for part-time white-collar jobs. These working wives and mothers still tended to be below the top of the social scale, so it was easy to under-rate the trend. That was particularly true since, as we've seen, the nation preferred to ignore the fact that they were working at all.

The fact that the percentage of married women in the workforce kept quietly going up was really the key to women's liberation. The nation had to accept the idea that most women would work through their adult lives. That didn't mean, of course, that every woman had to hold down a job all the time. But as a sex, they were not going to have standing in the public world unless men saw them as having an important economic role. If young women did not expect to work after marriage, most of them would not plan for serious careers. Most schools would not want to train them. The nation might honor them for their roles as wives and mothers, but they would not be taken seriously in business, academia, the arts, or politics.

Even within the family, women who made a substantial contribution to the household's finances tended to have more power and respect. And, of course, the ability to support themselves gave them far more independence when it came to handling an unsatisfactory spouse, or filling in for one who vanished.

"A DESIRE FOR ALL THE ADVANTAGES OF THE 'TWO-INCOME' FAMILY."

The consultant for Manpower who was trying to figure out how to lure married women into the postwar workforce had another suggestion beyond eliminating the prejudice against working wives. "Second, we must develop a desire for all the advantages of the 'Two-Income' family," he proposed.

Business was not only offering women incentives to work; it was in overdrive when it came to wooing them to spend. American families were willing consumers, but before World War II their vision of what they should—and could—acquire was limited. A significant minority of households had no electricity to power modern conveniences. Louise Meyer of Wyoming was hardly the only housewife laundering clothes with boiled water and eliminating wrinkles with a piece of iron heated on a wood-burning stove. During the war, the nation's premier washboard manufacturer churned out more than a million boards a year for housewives who were still doing their clothes by hand. Half of American homes had no central heating, and a quarter lacked flush toilets. Even in the best times most people could remember—the boom years before the Depression—less than a third of the country had a middle-class standard of living. But after the war, thanks to the stunning economic boom and generous federal spending in the 1950s, 60 percent of American families reached the middle class. Family income, adjusted for inflation, rose 42 percent in the 1950s and 38 percent in the 1960s.

For the economy to keep growing, consumers had to keep buying. Helped along by the new, mighty voice of television, advertisers were constantly expanding family visions of what the good life entailed. The number of families living in their own homes soared, and most of those new homes were in the suburbs. Family cars, then second cars, became necessities. So did—as far as most people were concerned—second televisions and summer camp for the kids. An entire middle-class generation grew up in the postwar era taking for granted a lifestyle of three-bedroom homes, washer/dryer combos, annual family vacations, and college education for their children.

Then the economy began to slow. Fewer and fewer families could afford to buy the things they had gotten used to having on one person's salary. Over the '70s and '80s, the weekly earning of non-management workers fell 19 percent. While women continued to drop in and out of the workforce, often taking time off when their children were young and working more when the kids went to school full-time, they no longer regarded their work as optional or as a matter of bringing home pin money. In the 1970s wives who worked provided, on average, a third of the family's income.

"THAT DEFINED THE TWENTIETH CENTURY."

Until the postwar baby boom, American women had been having fewer children for as long as the nation had been keeping population statistics. That was a rational response to the change from an agricultural to an industrial economy. An extra child on a farm was usually an unalloyed benefit—another little helper who, in relatively few years, would be available to work the fields or spin the thread or tend the chickens. But as people moved into cities and developed higher expectations for the next generation, children moved from being an economic plus to an economic drain. They had to be fed, clothed, educated, and—in a middle-class family—supported for eighteen or more years without any return on investment. Obviously, parents got their reward in other ways. But it was much easier to

appreciate the pluses if there were only two or three little minuses to take care of.

The baby boom was an exception—an extraordinarily large exception—to the pattern of smaller families. The men and women who produced it had grown up in the Depression, fought World War II, and then returned home to a booming economy to have more children than any Americans since the beginning of the twentieth century, their reproductive enthusiasm rivaling countries like India. It was no wonder we called them the Greatest Generation, but their offspring had no intention of repeating the performance.

American women had always been fairly adept at limiting the size of their families when they wanted to, through means ranging from diaphragms to abstinence. However, all their strategies worked best when the goal was to reduce the odds of pregnancy rather than to prevent it entirely. A woman who wanted a family of two or three children rather than six or seven had good odds for success, but not a woman who wanted to be sexually active without reproducing.

The birth control pill was simpler and far more reliable than anything that came before. It had only a fourth the failure rate of condom use and a seventh of diaphragms. The Pill, which went on the market in 1960, not only gave women more confidence about their ability to plan a career; it gave employers more confidence that when a woman said she wasn't planning to get pregnant, she meant it. "There is, perhaps, one invention that historians a thousand years in the future will look back on and say, 'That defined the twentieth century,'" wrote *The Economist* at the end of 1999. "It is also one that a time-traveler from 1000 would find breathtaking—particularly if she were a woman. That invention is the contraceptive pill."

Young unmarried women did not have widespread access to the Pill until the early 1970s—which not coincidentally was the same time they began to apply to medical, law, dental, and business schools in large numbers. This was an enormous shift. American girls had always done better than boys in most subjects in high school, but those who went to college had been funneled into relatively low-paying careers such as nursing and teaching—professions that you could pursue for a few years before marriage, and return to when your children were grown.

Once young women had confidence that they could make it through training and the early years in their profession without getting pregnant, their attitude toward careers that required a long-term commitment changed. And the sexual revolution, which arrived at the same time as widespread Pill use, reassured them that even if they delayed marriage, they would have the same opportunities as unmarried young men for a satisfying sexual life.

"JUST A HOUSEWIFE."

There were other social forces at work that, while perhaps not as sweeping, were combining to make the old patterns of women's lives look less attractive. The first wave of the baby-boom generation grew up hearing their mothers describe themselves, self-deprecatingly, as "just a housewife," and in truth, the status of homemakers was dwindling. Perhaps it was due in part to complaints from magazines such as *Playboy* about men being trapped in marriage, forced to support unproductive wives. Perhaps it had to do with changes in the homemakers' jobs. Before the automated kitchen and laundry, running a house was a daunting responsibility. You needed to be a good manager and to have, particularly when it came to cooking, a lot of skill. But the postwar housewife's duties were more about driving children to multitudinous activities, microwaving quick dinners for family members on different schedules, and constantly running washing machines and dryers. Once children were out of the nest, some mothers found new challenges in volunteer work or caring for the offspring of their working daughters. But many women, still in the prime of their lives, were left with no real role at all. The

attractions of marriage and motherhood didn't fade, but women felt an increasing need for a second string—a place in the working world that would provide them with a sense of identity and usefulness once the children had grown.

At the same time, the rising divorce rate was driving home the peril of trusting your future entirely to a spouse's ability and willingness to support his family. Divorce, like the tendency toward smaller families, had been on an upward trend for a long time, until the postwar period disrupted the graph. But that dip was followed by a huge surge of divorce in the 1970s, along with an increase in unmarried couples living together and never-married mothers. The message to younger women was clear: marriage was an unreliable basket in which to put all of your eggs.

"THE WHOLE LAND SEEMS AROUSED."

The civil rights battles of the 1960s went to the core of the nation's identity, forcing the country to grapple with the fact that it had never lived up to the standards it set for itself in the Declaration of Independence. White Americans who accepted the message of what had happened went through a moral shock, made all the worse for the realization that they and their leaders had not been all that eager to rectify the injustice when it was driven home to them. As a result, young people became more skeptical about the wisdom of traditional cultural rules. Americans grew extremely sensitive to questions of fairness, and that opened the way for other discriminated-against groups, including women, to demand their rights.

The effect of the civil rights movement was crucial for women, because their fight was unique. It was, as the sociologist Alice Rossi said, the only instance in which people being discriminated against lived in much more intimate association with the "enemy" than with other members of their own group. Women's interests were bound up with those of their fathers, husbands, brothers, and sons in every aspect of their lives. It was difficult for them to mount the kind of clear-cut fight that racial or ethnic minorities were able to make against an establishment that had discriminated against them. That was probably why the women's movement always tended to ride on the wake of other fights for justice.

Fighting slavery had been the first moral issue so grave that housebound middle-class Victorian matrons felt compelled to go into the outside world and engage in politics. "We have given great offense on account of our womanhood, which seems to be as objectionable as our abolitionism. The whole land seems aroused to discussion on the province of women, and I am glad of it," said Angelina Grimké, the abolitionist lecturer who was one of the first to consider the plight of African-Americans and find similarities to the condition of white American women. The earliest women's rights movement grew up out of antislavery actions, and in the twentieth century, the suffrage cause finally succeeded during the Progressive era, when the nation was focused on the evils of poverty and unbridled capitalism. In the 1960s women's greatest legislative victory was an amendment tacked onto the Civil Rights Act.

Many of the young women who took the lead on the radical side of women's liberation had been trained in confrontation by their involvement in the civil rights movement. All of them had learned from that struggle how injustice can run deep in a nation's laws, traditions, and customs. They did not believe that the fact that things had always been done one way made them right. To the contrary, that made them suspect. And they could see, even by the late 1960s, that history was going to celebrate the people who had the strength to stand up against popular conventions and demand justice for black Americans. They had confidence from the beginning that women, too, would win.

So there it was: the postwar economy created a demand for women workers, and the postindustrial economy created jobs that they were particularly suited to fill. The soaring expectations of the postwar boom, followed by the decline in men's paychecks in the 1970s, made wives' participation in the workforce almost a requisite for middle-class life. The birth control pill gave young women confidence that they could pursue a career without interruption by pregnancy. The civil rights movement made women conscious of the ways they had been treated like second-class citizens and made them determined that their own status was one of the things they were going to change. It was, all in all, a benevolent version of the perfect storm.

Keepsake Pages

Did any of your female relatives work during World War II? Did they talk about it in later years?

_____

_____

_____

_____

_____

_____

_____

_____

_____

Did you grow up in the suburbs? Did you think it was boring or a paradise? How did your mother feel?

_____

_____

_____

_____

_____

_____

_____

_____

Do you remember the era of women's consciousness-raising groups? Did you ever belong to one?

_____

_____

_____

_____

_____

_____

_____

_____

Do you think men had a hard time adjusting to all the changes women went through in the '60s and '70s? How about the men you knew?

_____

_____

_____

_____

_____

_____

_____

_____

More Thoughts and Memories

More Thoughts and Memories

6. Civil Rights

In the late 1950s, Virginia Williams was traveling to South Carolina for a family funeral. When the bus passed near Camp Lejeune in North Carolina, a black soldier got on and tried to take a seat near the front. Williams can still remember her astonishment as the driver insisted that a man serving his country in the military go to the rear of the bus. "This was fifty years ago, and it's still right there," she said, pointing to her heart.

In the postwar era, if you had asked average black Americans such as Williams about injustice, they probably would have talked about the soldiers who risked their lives in World War II and came back to be told they did not deserve either fairness or respect. But if you had asked an average white American for an example of "injustice to Negroes," chances are the answer would have been Marian Anderson, the singer who was denied the right to perform in the nation's capital because of her race.

Anderson had been blessed with an astonishing voice that was the pride of her poor Philadelphia neighborhood. Her first direct contact with racism came when she applied to a local school of music and was told coldly, "We don't take colored." Members of her church scraped together money to pay for private lessons instead. She eventually went to study in Europe and became a world-renowned contralto with a voice that the conductor Arturo Toscanini said "is heard only once in a hundred years." Yet in 1939 she was prohibited from singing in Washington's Constitution Hall. The Daughters of the American Revolution, which owned the building, cited shadowy rules and regulations, but it was clear that the problem was Anderson was black. Eleanor Roosevelt resigned from the DAR in protest and

lobbied her husband. "I don't care if she sings from the top of the Washington Monument as long as she sings," Franklin Roosevelt told his aides, and Anderson was invited to give a concert in front of the Lincoln Memorial on Easter Sunday.

At least 75,000 people came to hear the concert, while millions more listened over the radio. With the great statue of Abraham Lincoln behind her and a crowd stretching beyond her vision in front, Anderson was almost paralyzed when she approached the microphone. "I sang, I don't know how," she wrote later. When it was over, she was nearly overrun by the adoring crowd. She had gone from being a little-known concert singer to an icon who reminded Americans not just of the evils of segregation but of their capacity to do better. She had created what her agent, Sol Hurok, called "as nearly spontaneous an arising of men and women of goodwill . . . as there can be in our times."

Marian Anderson's story had two very different lessons. One was that if the nation's attention was fixed on the evils of segregation, Americans would probably draw back in disgust and do the right thing. The other was that when it came to getting that attention, the bar was very, very, very high. Preventing an internationally acclaimed American singer from performing in the nation's capital struck even many die-hard conservatives as outlandish. And Anderson was both the most sympathetic and least threatening victim imaginable. A woman of extraordinary dignity and impeccable reputation, she was always the best-behaved person in any room. She was also reluctant to make a scene or to remind her white supporters that when it came to injustice against black people, singing venues were the least of the problem.

Her sex was also very important. White Americans had always found it easier to relate to the black struggle for equal rights when it was framed around the saga of a good, abused woman. *Uncle Tom's Cabin,* the book that drew so many Northern whites to the cause of abolition, was about mothers separated from their children and innocent young girls left at the mercy of lascivious slave owners. (Along, of course, with the extremely deferential Tom.) In the twentieth century, the stories about racial injustice that whites found most compelling were not generally about black men being lynched or black soldiers being welcomed home with discrimination and abuse. Rather, whites were moved by images of black women—mainly very young or middle-aged black women—who were both powerless and noble in the face of vicious racism.

Civil rights organizations were well aware of white America's feelings, and as the NAACP went looking for test cases to challenge segregation, the targets were new versions of Marian Anderson. That was never more true than in Montgomery, Alabama, where black working people were being tormented by a bus system that consigned them to the back, required them to relinquish their seats to whites, and left the enforcement of the rules to the drivers—who often carried guns and seemed to get particular pleasure in tormenting their black passengers. "I felt like a dog," said Jo Ann Robinson, a newcomer to Montgomery who inadvertently sat in the wrong place and was shrieked at by the driver, who leaped up and advanced on her with a raised fist. During the 1950s a number of black riders had rebelled, refused a driver's order to relinquish their seats, and suffered arrest. But to the NAACP, none of them seemed perfect test cases. Some were men. One of the women, a teenager, had a slightly disreputable family. Another seemed too confrontational. Another, a minister's wife, lacked the requisite coolness needed to face the city's angry white power structure without being flustered. Like Goldilocks wandering through the bears' bedrooms, the civil rights leaders rejected one possibility after another—until they found Rosa Parks just right.

Parks, an old schoolmate remembered, was "self-sufficient, competent, and dignified" even as a child, a student who always wore a clean uniform, planned ahead, and never sneaked over to the boys' side of the school like some of the other girls did. Even in defiance, she was a perfect lady. When the Montgomery bus driver told her to give up her seat to a white man or be arrested, the petite, middle-aged seamstress calmly replied, "You may do that." Later, when her husband begged her not to allow herself to be turned into a test case, she coolly went ahead. ("He had a perfect terror of white people," recalled a friend. "The night we went to get Mrs. Parks from the jail, we went back to her apartment and he was drunk and he kept saying, 'Oh, Rosa, Rosa, don't do it, don't do it... The white folks will kill you.'") When she appeared for her court date, she wore a long-sleeved black dress with white cuffs and a small velvet hat with pearls across the top. "They've messed with the wrong one now," cried out a black teenager, who turned out to be absolutely correct. "My God, look what segregation has put in my hands," extolled the local NAACP leader, E. D. Nixon.

"YOU ALL ARE TOO SCARED TO STAND ON YOUR FEET."

Rosa Parks's simple act of defiance in 1955 marked the beginning of the modern civil rights movement. Black Americans had always staged personal acts of rebellion and challenged segregation in court—a year earlier, the NAACP had won the landmark Supreme Court ruling on public schools, *Brown v. Board of Education.* But it was in Montgomery, after Parks's arrest, that an entire black community rose up to express solidarity, boycotting the city bus system for more than a year. The sight of elderly women walking in foul weather, of clerks and maids struggling with makeshift car pools, broadcast to the world that Southern blacks were not, as the white community had always insisted, perfectly happy with things the way they were.

The boycott was not spontaneous. It operated

on two levels: a public leadership of male ministers, headed by the charismatic young pastor Martin Luther King Jr., and an organization of women volunteers, who did the behind-the-scenes work. The women, although unsung, were not simply following the directions from above. They had long ago thought up the idea for the boycott, and they had been preparing for it for almost nine years.

The Women's Political Council, a quiet organization of Montgomery's middle-class black teachers and social workers, had struggled with hostile poll workers and arcane literacy tests to register to vote themselves and then to help others register. But the bus service had been their particular target. The council head, Jo Ann Robinson, never forgot the day her long-anticipated vacation was ruined by the driver who shrieked at her until she ran, weeping, into the street. The council leaders had met with city officials over and over to complain about the service. "True, we succeeded only in annoying [them], but this was better than nothing," said one of the members. When word of Parks's action spread around Montgomery, the women were ready. The next day they wrote a leaflet calling for a bus boycott, and that midnight they were at Alabama State University, where Robinson taught, cutting a mimeograph stencil and running off 35,000 copies. The following morning, Rosa Parks recalled, Robinson "and some of her students loaded the handbills into her car, and she drove to all the local black elementary and junior high and high schools to drop them off so the students could take them home to their parents."

The women were not only far better organized than the male ministers who were the public face of the black community but more radical. While the ministers pressed the bus company for a more orderly system of dividing the seats between the races and more courteous drivers, the women wanted total integration. The women were also more fearless. The ministers were wary of being too far out in front in so controversial an enterprise. That was why they had tapped Dr. King, a new-

comer, to take the lead, and why they originally wanted to call a mass meeting without letting the white community know that they were the ones doing the calling. (E. D. Nixon of the NAACP said he warned the ministers that if they didn't assume public leadership, he would let the black community know it was because "you all are too scared to stand on your feet and be counted.") Later, when Parks's lawyer was looking for a handful of volunteer plaintiffs to file a suit against the bus segregation in federal court, not a single minister volunteered to step forward. In the end, the plaintiffs were four women: Aurelia Browder, a seamstress, a widow, and mother of six; Susie McDonald, who was in her seventies; and two teenagers who had refused to give up their seats on the bus before Parks but who had been passed over by the NAACP as not quite right to carry their cause.

Parks herself was far from the simple, weary seamstress her backers tried to depict. She was one of the most active NAACP members in Montgomery. Like the women who organized the boycott, she had actually been preparing for this moment for years. But at the community meeting when the black citizens of Montgomery came together, inspired by her defiance to challenge segregation, the newly energized ministers monopolized the podium and told her she wouldn't be required to speak. "You have said enough," they assured her.

"OTHER NEGROES WILL HAVE THE CAREER I DREAMED OF."

When Marian Anderson was interviewed by *Ladies' Home Journal* in 1960, she was asked how it felt to have "accomplished everything you set out to do." Anderson — who had just endured a cab ride with a driver who had thought she was a maid and urged her to do well by the "boss lady" — mildly pointed out that she had actually wanted to be an opera singer. Although she did become the first black performer ever invited to sing at the Metropolitan Opera in New York, the invitation came when she was 58 and well past her prime. "Other Negroes will have the career I dreamed of," she told the interviewer.

By 1960 the Supreme Court had ruled that segregated public schools were unconstitutional and had struck down segregation in interstate transportation. (Looking for their perfect plaintiff in that case, the Virginia NAACP lawyers had found Irene Morgan, a married 27-year-old defense worker who was ill and on her way to see a doctor when she was arrested for refusing to relinquish her seat.) But on the ground in the South, very little had changed. The buses and trains were still segregated, and black students still went to separate, inferior schools. Joyce Ladner, who grew up in Mississippi, attended an all-black high school with no lab equipment in its science classes and was barred from using the city library her family paid taxes to support. "I felt the Hattiesburg public library held all the knowledge I wanted," she recalled. "But my school library consisted of one bookshelf." Blacks were still relegated to the balconies in theaters. Swimming pools and amusement parks were off-limits to black children. (Lucy Murray of Washington, DC, never forgot going on an expedition with a white friend's family to Glen Echo Park in Maryland, where the children piled onto the merry-go-round. "All of a sudden, this state trooper came over and told me to get off.") Restaurants, restrooms, and all other public accommodations were strictly segregated. When Marian Anderson arrived in a Southern town to sing, she was often escorted quickly and surreptitiously to a hotel room that had been reserved by special arrangement for the black guest who was too famous to reject.

If Anderson believed young black people would have a different life from hers, the young people intended that as well. Students from Southern black colleges had been holding classes in nonviolence and civil disobedience, and they began to claim what was being withheld from them. That meant sitting in at white-only lunch counters, picketing white-only restaurants, and allowing themselves to be dragged off to jail in defiance of unjust laws. The demonstrations spread quickly from Greensboro, North Carolina, to Nashville, Atlanta, and other cities, drawing in the best of the postwar generation of black youth. Many of them were children from poor families whose parents had placed all their hopes on their smart, striving sons and daughters. To join the protest movement was to risk the one clear path to a better future. Gwendolyn Robinson, a scholarship student at Spelman College in Atlanta, vowed to stay clear of the demonstrations: "I certainly had no intention of getting involved. I had my priorities straight. This was an opportunity of a lifetime for me; I certainly wasn't going to blow it." Despite her resolve, she was soon on the picket lines and then in jail. Worst of all, Robinson was forced to call her grandmother, who had raised her. "She said I had disgraced the family, reminding me that I was the first person in our family to ever be arrested. She sounded so sad, so pained. Her voice was all low and husky."

Spelman was the most prestigious college for black women in the country. A young Marian Wright arrived in 1956, wary of "its reputation as a tea-pouring very strict school designed to turn black girls into refined ladies and teachers." Its rigor was based, at least in part, on the widely held conviction that if black men had to be at least twice as good as whites to succeed, then black women had to be twice as respectable. Students had a nine o'clock curfew. The dress code required them to wear nylon stockings at all times—pants, of course, were banned. After Spelman dances ended, the students had fifteen minutes to get back to their dorms. Alice Walker lasted two years before transferring to Sarah Lawrence to get away from "a school that I considered opposed to change, to freedom, and to understanding that by the time most girls enter college they are already women and should be treated as women." (Spelman was hardly alone in keeping its black coeds under a tight rein. Joyce Ladner, who started at Mississippi's Jackson State in 1960, lived in a dorm where the housemother "was more strict than our parents had been…We had to be in by six o'clock in the evening or at dark…We had to go to vespers every Sunday, and she stood at the door and checked to see if we had hats and gloves on.")

The women who joined the civil rights protests of the early '60s were almost all the product of parents and teachers who believed that respectable black girls needed to be constrained, disciplined, perfect ladies. They had been raised to regard jail as the ultimate disgrace, something that happened to the other kind of black women—the ones who were living out all the worst white stereotypes. And they had not been encouraged to take the lead any more than white middle-class girls of the era were. When Diane Nash was nominated to chair the committee coordinating protests by students at the various black colleges in Nashville, she was so unnerved that she said she could not take the job because she had her period. She got the post anyway, and not long after, Nash led the students in a critical confrontation with Mayor Ben West that would become the high point of the Nashville movement. She skillfully drew West into declaring his general opposition to discrimination and bias, and then quickly asked whether that included the symbolic lunch counters. Cornered, the mayor had to agree it did, and by the end of the meeting on the city's courthouse steps, West and the students were embracing one another, and the local paper was preparing its headline: "Integrate Counters—Mayor."

"If you were going to jail, you dressed up."

Making the transition from ladylike student to jailbird was made easier by the fact that the early civil rights protests had all the decorum of a Spelman tea party. "If you were going to jail, you dressed up," recalled Lenora Taitt-Magubane. "Nobody could ever see there were some ragamuffins who don't deserve a hamburger at Woolworth's." Later, when the first Freedom Riders were preparing to challenge segregation on interstate transit with a trip that would leave them beaten, jailed, and nearly incinerated in a blazing bus, the organizers dictated that the men would wear coats and ties, and the women, dresses and high heels. "When I went to jail, I had on a skirt and a blouse, and probably a jacket," said Taitt-Magubane. "When you went on a march, you were fittingly dressed." As television cameras began to follow the students' progress, the American public couldn't help but see the contrast between the rowdy mob of white racists shrieking epithets and the well-clad black students, reading their textbooks while they sat silent and erect on the lunch-counter stools—seats that were fine for the time it took to eat a sandwich but that felt extremely uncomfortable after three or four hours. The *Richmond News Leader,* an outspoken opponent of integration, admitted to "a tinge of wry regret" at the scene. "Here were the colored students, in coats, white shirts, ties, and one of them was reading Goethe and one was taking notes from a biology text. And here, on the sidewalk outside, was a gang of white boys come to heckle, a ragtail rabble, slack-jawed, black-jacketed, grinning fit to kill…Eheu! It gives one pause."

Taitt-Magubane, who was then Lenora Taitt, got into the protests in 1960 via a musical. "I was in the drama club. My professor Howard Zinn said, 'Lenora, would you like to see *My Fair Lady*?' I said I would love to." Zinn, who was white, was arranging to take a mixed-race group of students into Atlanta's segregated downtown theater. When they sat down in the white section, the theater manager first threatened to cancel the production. "We said that would be very sad," said Taitt-Magubane. "And we didn't move." He then called the mayor, who pragmatically suggested the lights be dimmed as quickly as possible. ("We *enjoyed* that play," Taitt-Magubane recalled.) When the lights went back on, her group discovered all the nearby seats had been vacated. "So we wouldn't contaminate them, I guess," she added, laughing. Outside the theater, the press and photographers were waiting. "And the next day it was a front page story."

There was, throughout the movement, always a question about the role of black women: were they comrades in the struggle or helpless dependents to be protected? ("If anyone gets whupped out here today, it ain't gonna be our women," a student demonstrator assured reporters later in Alabama.) When the Freedom Rides began, organizers were reluctant to allow black women to be put in what was going to be obvious peril and in the end limited the female contingent to three—two of them white. But the black women had no intention of staying out of the action. "A guy might be protective of you on the march—say, 'You okay?' or whatever. But I could get beaten just like he could," said Joyce Ladner. When the Nashville students went off to the first big sit-in that was likely to result in mass arrests, James Bevel, one of the leaders, urged Diane Nash to avoid going to jail so she could coordinate from the outside. Nash thought the other students might wonder if she was a coward. If someone was not going to be arrested, she responded sensibly, it should be Bevel, who already had a reputation for fearlessness. And off to jail she went.

Angry whites didn't much differentiate between the sexes once a protest began. In February 1961 Lana Taylor, a college sophomore, was sitting in at an Atlanta restaurant when an employee walked up behind her, grabbed her by the shoulders, and said, "Get the hell out of here, nigger." But Taylor stayed put. "Lana was not going," said Jane Stembridge, a white civil rights worker. "She put her hands under the counter and held...I looked down at that moment at her hands...brown, strained...every muscle holding...All of a sudden he let go and left...He knew he could not move that girl—ever." At another demonstration, a waitress threw a Coke bottle that just missed hitting 18-year-old Ruby Doris Smith.

Smith was another Spelman student, although a young man who knew her at the time described her as "not the quintessential Spelman woman...She was not the ladylike kind." Her relatively poor family had scrimped to give their daughters extras, and Ruby had piano lessons and a debut at a ball in Atlanta sponsored by Sigma Gamma Rho Sorority. She was in many ways a typical teenager, worried about her figure, interested in clothes. Once, when a group of students were nervously preparing to leave for a protest that would inevitably lead to jail, Ruby Doris suddenly announced a delay: "My hair is not right," she declared. "And I'm rolling it and I'm not leaving until it's curled." But her determination soon set her apart. In the summer of 1960, when most of the Atlanta college students had gone home, she helped organize picketing of a local grocery, often simply marching in front of the store alone, carrying her sign. She also took part in a series of "kneel-ins" at white churches. Stunned when she was barred admission to pray at one congregation, she "pulled up a chair in the lobby and joined in the singing and the worship services, which I enjoyed immensely."

"SOMEONE WILL RISE. SOMEONE WILL EMERGE."

Ella Baker was well into middle age when the students started raising hell. She had gone to Shaw University, a proper Baptist school in Raleigh, at a time when the regulations made Spelman of 1960 look like a Woodstock reunion. Her most daring rebellion involved a petition that girls be permitted to wear silk stockings on campus. (Part of the uniform of the proper young African-American lady a generation later, silk stockings were regarded as a sign of vanity, and perhaps exhibitionism, in Baker's college days.) The petition was denied, and the girls were required to spend extra time in chapel until they repented of their folly. It was typical of Baker that she did not actually care what she wore herself. She just wanted the students to stand up for themselves, and if stockings were their priority, that was fine.

One thing that marked young Ella as different was that she absolutely refused to consider a career in teaching. Every black woman was expected to give back to the community, and if you were middle class with an intellectual bent, you did it by teaching school until you married and turned your attention to good works in the church and proper women's clubs. It broke her mother's heart, but after college Ella left home and embarked on a career as a community organizer—a job that involved traveling by herself in an era when women were still expected to have a male protector when they were away from home. Baker joined a long and distinguished line of peripatetic American heroines. Like Eleanor Roosevelt, she seemed most at home on a train, with an overnight bag and a stack of work. Even when she married, she never nested, and even when she took on the responsibility of raising her young niece, she never stayed home. "I had to move fast to keep up with her," her niece Jackie recalled. "I would sit in the back of meetings and do my homework many a night."

In 1941 Baker was hired as an organizer for the NAACP, and two things quickly became clear. The first was that she was brilliant at the job. The chairman of the Virginia NAACP had protested when he heard a woman would be sent to organize the annual membership drive. But afterward, he described Baker's visit as "one of the most important and wonderful things that has ever happened in Richmond." Unlike the many male organizers who behaved like visiting superstars, Baker had what the Richmond leaders called a "wonderful and outstanding quality of mixing with any group of people."

Her second defining characteristic was a dislike of top-down leadership. "She had an interest in the power of people," said Lenora Taitt-Magubane. "She never gave answers. Miss Ella would ask questions: What about this? Have you thought about so and so? And then let you fight it out…She felt leaders were not appointed but they rose up. Someone will rise. Someone will emerge." It was an attitude Baker shared with some of the other older women in the movement, such as Septima Clark, a venerable educator and mentor to Rosa Parks who once sent Martin Luther King a letter urging him "not to lead all the marches himself but instead to develop leaders who could lead their own marches." (It was not a successful intervention. "Dr. King read that letter before the staff. It just tickled them; they just laughed," Clark said.)

Baker became one of the founders and acting director of the Southern Christian Leadership Conference, which was meant to keep alive the spirit of the Montgomery bus boycott. But the SCLC was defined by Martin Luther King's charismatic leadership, and since Baker did not believe in charismatic leaders, she and King never hit it off. She was not offered the permanent directorship. Wyatt Tee Walker, the minister who got the job, said Baker was not even really considered: "It just went against the grain of the kind of person she was." Ella had a similar, although blunter, take. "After all, who was I?" she said. "I was female. I was old. I didn't have a PhD." On another occasion, she attributed the lack of connection between her and the male leaders to the fact that she "wasn't a fashion plate" at a time when black men—like white men—tended to judge all women by their aesthetic value. (Septima Clark once referred to the wives of early civil rights leaders as "just like chandeliers: shining lights, sitting up, saying nothing.") While Baker was a handsome woman, her appearance was the last thing people talked about when they met her. "Miss Ella was, I guess, she was about five feet tall, but she seemed to me like she was twenty feet," said Lenora Taitt-Magubane. "With her pillbox hat—always looking very crisp."

It was the old story. Women worked behind the scenes; they were not expected to head organizations or give important speeches. Lucy Murray, whose father was a black labor activist in Washington during the 1960s, remembered hearing him say that the only woman in the "inner sanctum" of the movement was Dorothy Height, the head of the

National Council of Negro Women. Septima Clark felt the established black leaders "didn't have any faith in women, none whatsoever." For the younger generation, the resistance to women leaders was perhaps more complicated. Andrew Young, who was one of Martin Luther King's top aides, said that Ella Baker and other strong women in the movement made him feel defensive. "They were too much like my mother. Strong women were the backbone of the movement, but to young black men seeking their own freedom, dignity, and leadership perspective, they were quite a challenge."

Baker's response was to found a charismatic leader–free organization that would reflect her ideas of what the civil rights movement should be all about. She threw her lot in with the students, helped them organize the Student Nonviolent Coordinating Committee, and kept them out from under the arm of Dr. King and the ministers. Unsurprisingly, SNCC (which was always referred to as "Snick") was more open to women's leadership than any of the groups that had gone before. Its heyday lasted only a few years, but while it did, SNCC was not only fighting for civil rights but also struggling to create, within itself, a "Beloved Community" in which blacks and whites, men and women, poor and middle class, lived and worked together as equals. "Remember, we are not fighting for the freedom of the Negro alone, but for the freedom of the human spirit, a larger freedom that encompasses all mankind," Baker told the students.

The idea of a leader-free, star-free organization was natural for many of the students. The Nashville contingent had picked Diane Nash as their coordinator in part because she was so ego-free, so good at letting everybody have a say. But Baker's vision was far more demanding than a simple sharing of power. She was suspicious of quick fixes such as the lunch-counter sit-ins, or any strategy that involved appealing to the federal government to save black Americans from white racists. "People have to be made to understand that they cannot look for salvation anywhere but to themselves," she said. Her

first speech to the students was called "More Than a Hamburger," and it puzzled her audience of young people, who were sure their restaurant sit-ins would bring the world's attention to the rightness of their cause and solve the problem of black oppression rather quickly. "To our mind lunch-counter segregation was the greatest evil facing black people in the country," said Julian Bond dryly.

Baker wanted the students to challenge more than the white segregationist power structure; she also wanted them to take on the class lines within the black community itself, to bypass the black leaders who had risen by mimicking the values they saw in white society, such as snobbishness and self-promotion. She had loved the black neighborhood she lived in as a child, where everyone knew and took care of one another. "Where we lived there was no sense of hierarchy, in terms of those who have, having a right to look down upon, or to evaluate as a lesser breed, those who didn't have," she said. Both she and the students wanted to live that way forever.

While it worked, SNCC was an experience so powerful that many of the people who were there for the early years seemed to live out the rest of their lives in quiet mourning for the thing they lost—the "adrenaline high" of working at fever pitch on something so charged with risk and excitement and so much greater than themselves. "There was terror in the work—but such joy and passion as well," remembered Penny Patch, a young white woman who was one of the early volunteers. "I remember dancing to the Twist one night in Maryland, high as could be. No alcohol, at least not for me. But I was just flying. We all were." Unita Blackwell, a former plantation worker from rural Mississippi, tried to explain what the SNCC experience in 1964 felt like to her:

Nobody had to say that all of us were equal; we could feel it. These were the first moments of my life when I knew that people outside my family respected me for what I knew and what

I had to offer. They wanted to know *my* ideas, to get *my* advice about what *they* should do. I was telling them what to do. Even in my own community, as a woman my opinion didn't mean much unless it was in agreement with a man's. I had been beat way down, and the realization that I had something of value to give someone else was a powerful sensation. At the time, I didn't even know how to describe it but it gave me strength.

Ella Baker, who SNCC leaders called "our Gandhi," set the example of how to proceed. There were endless stories about her willingness to do whatever was needed, no matter how mundane. She never accepted an official position with SNCC or a salary, stitching together an income from side jobs here and there. "How did I make a living? I haven't. I have eked out existence," she said later. She stayed up with the young members until late at night and sat uncomplaining through endless meetings in smoke-filled rooms. (Baker was asthmatic in an era when it was not yet regarded as acceptable to ask people to refrain from smoking. One former SNCC member said his most vivid memory of her was "sitting in on these SNCC meetings that ran for days—you didn't measure them in hours, they ran days—with a smoke mask over her nose, listening patiently to words and discussions she must have heard a thousand times.") She traveled with the students, sharing their casual and substandard living conditions even though she was nearly 60. She dressed in unmemorable gray suits or brown dresses that masked the radicalism of her vision. For the young SNCC organizers, she was the answer to all the parents and teachers who had ever told them that they would settle down and get over their wild ideas when they got a little older. "To me she was just a very special person in my life," said Lenora Taitt-Magubane. "We bonded and we never unbonded till the day she died."

Baker was an inspiration to the students who worked with her—independent, intelligent, comfortable in her own skin, and totally self-confident. That was especially true for the young black women who had come from middle-class families where girls were expected to be demure and submissive. The fact that Baker refused to ever talk about her marriage (a ten-year commitment she kept extremely private until her death) was a revelation to young women who had been raised to believe the central question of their lives would be the identity of their husbands. To fight for equal rights in SNCC did not require the perfection of a Marian Anderson or a Rosa Parks. They could be themselves and make a difference.

"If I don't come back, here's a number to call."

There was something about segregated buses and trains that had driven black women particularly crazy for more than a century. Even before the Civil War, there had been spontaneous eruptions of resistance against the system that confined them to bad accommodations and poor service. Elizabeth Jennings, a Manhattan schoolteacher, had gone into a meltdown in 1854 when a white streetcar conductor had told her to wait for a car that took colored people. She resisted furiously, was arrested, and hired the attorney Chester Alan Arthur, the future president, to press a suit that led to the integration of all mass-transit systems in New York City. Sojourner Truth and Harriet Tubman were each arrested when they insisted on riding in the same accommodations as middle-class white women. The resistance never really stopped. Pauli Murray was once barred from using the women's room at a rest stop on a long bus ride and was told "to relieve myself in an open field in full sight of the highway. My alternative was to ride in sheer agony for the remaining two hours of the journey." On a subsequent trip, she simply fell into the mind-set of Elizabeth Jennings, staging a resistance that left her spending Easter weekend in a Virginia jail.

While the Supreme Court had declared segregation unconstitutional in buses and trains that traveled across state lines, the practice was still enforced throughout the South in the early 1960s. The first group to challenge it through civil disobedience (or civil obedience, if you were paying attention to the Supreme Court) was organized by the Congress of Racial Equality. In the spring of 1961, an integrated group of ten male and three female Freedom Riders boarded two different buses in Washington, DC. They ignored seating rules and used the whites-only waiting rooms between stops. Their trip, which was supposed to end in New Orleans, got only as far as Alabama. There, one bus had its tires slashed, and when it broke down, a mob set it on fire, attempting to pen the demonstrators inside. "Oh my God, they're going to burn us up!" screamed Genevieve Hughes, a 28-year-old white civil rights worker who was separated from the other volunteers by impenetrable smoke. When they escaped through a side door, some were attacked with bats and bricks. A 12-year-old white girl from the neighborhood ran back and forth through the crowd, bringing water to the choking Freedom Riders. (As a result, her family was targeted by threats and eventually had to leave town.) The second bus made it as far as Birmingham, where another mob dragged the Riders off and beat them so badly that one man was left permanently paralyzed. The rest of the ride was canceled.

The Nashville students, led by Diane Nash, picked up the crusade. Warned that any new Riders could well be killed, Nash said, "We fully realize that, but we can't let them stop us with violence. If we do, the movement is dead." Another group of Freedom Riders took off for Alabama, where they were met in Montgomery by hundreds of men, women, and children, screaming and waving bats and tire irons. Susan Wilbur, 18, and Susan Hermann, 20, two white students, were surrounded by a mob. White women bashed them with their pocketbooks while a teenage boy, "dancing like a boxer," kept hitting Wilbur in the head. John Seigenthaler, a Justice Department official, saw the mayhem and drove onto the sidewalk, yelling for the women to get in the car. "Mister, this is not your fight! Get away from here! You're gonna get killed!" yelled Wilbur, who thought Seigenthaler was simply a well-meaning passerby. One of the rioters hit Seigenthaler on the head with a pipe, fracturing his skull. Meanwhile Lucretia Collins, a volunteer who was fleeing the scene in a commandeered cab, saw Jim Zwerg, a 21-year-old divinity student, being held against the wall and repeatedly punched. "Some men held him while white women clawed his face with their nails," she said later. "And they held up their little children—children who couldn't have been more than a couple years old—to claw his face."

The Riders spent the night with their supporters at Montgomery's First Baptist Church, surrounded by a howling mob that set the author Jessica Mitford's car on fire, threw rocks through the windows, and threatened to incinerate the church, while federal officials begged black leaders for a cooling-off period. The negotiations between the Justice Department and Martin Luther King and his lieutenants did not include Nash. (Years later, she would tell the author David Halberstam that if everything had happened fifteen years down the road, after the women's movement, she would never have stood for being excluded.) Whether the older men liked it or not, however, Nash announced that the volunteers were going forward. "We can't stop now, right after we've been clobbered," she said. A new group of Riders got back on the bus and headed for Jackson, Mississippi.

All the Riders were arrested in Jackson, and as word of the arrests spread and the media coverage of the Freedom Rides increased, new volunteers rode Greyhounds into Jackson from different parts of the country, strode right over to the whites-only waiting room in mixed-race groups, and joined the growing population of prisoners inside jammed cells. Outside, there was...Diane Nash. With no office and decades before the age of cell phones, she walked around a hostile city with change for the pay phones in her pocket. Many of the newly arrested volunteers were strangers, and Nash was terrified that she would lose track of someone, leaving him or her adrift in the Mississippi prison system. Outside of Medgar Evers, the head of the local NAACP (who would be assassinated in front of his family in 1963), she found virtually no one willing to help. Most of the city's black establishment gave a wide berth to the Freedom Riders, who they regarded as a sure source of trouble. When a local resident did step forward, it was Claire Collins Harvey, the owner of a local funeral home who saw some of the female Riders shivering in court and began collecting warm clothing for the prisoners.

The possibility of imminent death was always present on the Freedom Rides, and many of the students made out wills before leaving. "I remember saying to someone, 'If I don't come back, here's a number to call,'" said Lenora Taitt-Magubane, who was in graduate school when she volunteered to participate in a ride from Atlanta to Albany, Georgia. Her "train group" of four blacks and four whites made it to Albany and through the whites-only waiting room before being greeted by cheering black supporters and white hecklers in the parking lot. They were all arrested and taken to a jail. She was released on bond until her court appearance and spent the time attending mass meetings with supporters. Seeing Lenora enter a church for one of the gatherings, Bernice Johnson, an Albany student who had known her previously, was stunned by Taitt's transformation. "I had never seen anybody's face that was glowing like that. She was just beaming. I had never seen anybody smiling like that."

That was the joyous side of the movement, the almost physical sense of connection among kindred souls risking everything for what they firmly believed would be a historic and successful crusade. The other side came crashing down on Taitt days later, when she and the other Freedom Riders appeared in court and were taken back to a prison that was crammed with people who had been arrested during the demonstrations of the preceding week. "We had sixty people in three cells which were only meant to hold six people. The clothes we wore going in were the same clothes we wore when we came out. The jail was the worst I'd ever been in. It was filthy, decrepit. You could see the rodents. I said, 'Oh boy, a hunger strike would be easy here.'" In less than two weeks, she lost ten pounds. After her release, she discovered she had developed a throat condition that left her unable to speak above a whisper for months. In jail, the Freedom Riders would sit on the floor, reading, wearing coats in the unheated winter air, until the jailers confiscated their books. They took one woman's glasses away, and the woman, who suffered from migraines, lay moaning as Taitt rocked her between her legs.

By the end, over four hundred Freedom Riders would wind up in jail—more than a quarter of them women. The images of brutal mob violence disgusted most of the nation and eventually helped push the federal government into enforcing court rulings against segregated buses and trains. The Riders themselves did not win national sympathy overnight. At the time the demonstrations were under way, 63 percent of respondents told George Gallup's surveyors that the Riders were going too far, pushing too fast and starting trouble. But in Washington, a dying Eleanor Roosevelt begged to disagree. "Never has a tinier minority done more for the liberation of a whole people than these few youngsters," she said.

"...A 'TRIBUTE TO WOMEN.'"

The SNCC students eventually did elect a chairman, and to the surprise of some the choice was Marion Barry (the future deeply controversial mayor of Washington) rather than Diane Nash. "Diane was a devoted, beautiful leader, but she was the wrong sex," said Congressman John Lewis, who later served as SNCC chair. "There was a desire to emphasize and showcase black manhood." Whether it was among the students or the old-guard ministry, men continued to get the vast majority of leadership posts in the civil rights movement. And that was fine by many black women. "If the Negro woman has a major underlying concern, it is the status of the Negro man and his position in the community and his need for feeling himself an important person, free and able to make his contribution in the whole society in order that he may strengthen his home," said Dorothy Height, the president of the National Council of Negro Women. African-American women, particularly those in the South, were aware of how long black men had been demeaned and kept in their place by the threat of physical violence against themselves and their families. "My father could not protect my mother, unless he risked his life," said Joyce Ladner. "He could be killed for saying something to a white man who said something terrible to my mother."

If black men wanted to be in the spotlight, many women concluded, maybe they were due. Others felt that kind of thinking was a trap. Ella Baker was particularly irritated by the idea "that black women had to bolster the ego of the male" by playing "a subordinate role." In Mississippi, one male civil rights leader who was concerned about the shortage of men in the state's Freedom Democratic Party made the error of suggesting the women "step back a little and let the men move in now." Baker quickly warned him not to "make the mistake of substituting men in quantity for women of quality."

It was an argument that would go on for more than a decade. But on occasion, things would happen that would make women on both sides of the debate wonder if black men were simply trying to appropriate all the advantages of the patriarchal rule that white men had been enjoying. A dramatic example occurred during the preparations for the great March on Washington in the summer of 1963. Called by Martin Luther King Jr. to focus attention on Southern intransigence and brutality against civil rights workers, the march is remembered as the moment in which the nation finally came to grips with the breadth and sweep and moral urgency of the civil rights movement. Washington, DC, which had feared a mob of thousands of unruly black protesters, saw instead a joyous, disciplined, multiracial mass movement of a quarter million people, where everyone from sharecroppers to movie stars came together to hear King deliver his immortal "I Have a Dream" speech.

It was a glorious day, and very few people noticed that black women had been almost completely cut out of the event. Anna Arnold Hedgeman—the only woman on the nineteen-member planning committee—had been complaining that there was no role for female civil rights leaders. Rosa Parks, Daisy Bates, and the others who had stepped up when men had quailed were assigned to march with the wives of the male leaders. ("Nowadays, women wouldn't stand for being kept so much in the background," Parks said years later.) No woman was on the speaking list, although the entertainer Josephine Baker was eventually asked to say a few words. No woman was invited to the meeting President Kennedy held with civil rights leaders at the conclusion of the march. A. Philip Randolph, one of the chief organizers, gave his major address at the National Press Club, which not only did not allow women to be members but barred from the audience women reporters who were trying to cover the speech.

"Nothing that women said or did broke the impasse blocking their participation," said Dorothy Height. While Height wanted to make black men feel they were important, she did not believe that required making black women feel they were invisible. "I've never seen a more immovable force... The march organizers proffered many excuses. They said, 'We have too many speakers as it is. The program is too long. You are already represented.'" Bayard Rustin, the chief organizer, told Height that women were already included since "every group has women in it—labor, church." In the end, the only concession to protests from Hedgeman, Height, Pauli Murray, and others was a "Tribute to Women" in which Rosa Parks, Daisy Bates, Diane Nash, and a few other leaders were introduced by

Randolph while sitting silently on the podium. Hedgeman proposed that at least a woman should do the introducing—she nominated Nash or the widow of the slain Medgar Evers—but nothing happened. The men kept pointing out that they had, after all, asked Marian Anderson to sing.

"That's them!"

Of all the heroines of the civil rights movement, some of the bravest were undoubtedly black women who lived in small, rural Southern towns. Time after time, when young organizers arrived, it was local women who stepped up and volunteered to shelter them and to help them recruit others, and who agreed to register to vote. Unita Blackwell, a sharecropper who lived in little Mayersville in a remote part of the Mississippi Delta, worried that the organizers would never come to her town, and when she saw two strangers walking past her house one day, she nudged her neighbor and announced excitedly, "That's them!" When SNCC called a meeting to look for volunteers to register to vote, Blackwell's hand was the first in the air.

In the world of the Mississippi Delta, the burden of being African-American was so brutal that it would have been hard to notice that women were being restrained by their gender as well as their race. But when Blackwell, a lively young woman from Memphis, moved to Mayersville with her husband and small baby, she discovered she was "about the only black woman drinking and going places that the town had ever seen who wasn't a slut." She had been used to a great deal of independence while her husband was gone on long trips with the Army Corps of Engineers, where he worked as a cook. But women in Mayersville only went out with their husbands. They did not drive cars, and their sole social outlet was the Home Demonstration Club, where they heard lectures on housekeeping and made crafts. Blackwell tried to fit in, and she was struggling to glue cloth and macaroni on a cigar box—an effort that was supposed to create a jew-

elry case—when she succumbed to boredom. "I got up my macaroni and went home and cooked it. That was my last time at the Home Demonstration Club," she wrote later.

Her sense of emptiness, the fear of a future limited to chopping cotton and going to church, was beginning to endanger her marriage. That was what made her so eager when the two very young SNCC organizers walked past her shabby little house. Blackwell's friend Coreen advised her not to get mixed up with them: "You liable to be dead."

"I don't know what difference it would make. I'm dying anyway," Blackwell said.

Blackwell's story is more spectacular than that of most women who held up their hands and volunteered to register to vote—she was eventually elected mayor of Mayersville, served twenty years, and got a MacArthur "genius" grant for her work as a community organizer. But she was also part of a second story—that of the postwar American women of all races who loved their families but still felt a desperate need to belong to something larger. "To have wonderful new friends—black and white, educated, people of means, some of them, who'd been places and done things I'd never even dreamed of—sitting on the floor or in the old broke-down furniture in my front room, talking about our lives and times, gave me a feeling I'd never had before," she wrote.

The organizers offered poor, rural blacks the opportunity to become an important part of a great national drama of liberation, but at a cost. Their homes were often destroyed. They and their relatives could be fired from their jobs. Rifle shots smashed into their children's bedrooms; crosses were burned on their front yards. They were beaten and arrested. (Unita Blackwell estimated she was jailed about seventy-five times in her attempts to register voters.) Yet they kept going. "Violence is a fearful thing. People don't realize how frightened you get," said Avon Rollins, a male SNCC organizer who recalled moments "when the words wouldn't come out of my mouth, where my teeth were just crushing together, chattering because the fear was so strong in me, not knowing what was going to happen. Then I'd see these black females out there, and I knew I couldn't let them take the beating, and the words would come out and I would make my stand."

Black women were much more likely to step forward than men in rural communities such as Mayersville. Some estimates put them at three or four times more active in the civil rights movement of the early '6os. No one has ever been sure why that was so, although there are plenty of theories. The most common one is that black women could simply get away with more, since the white racists found them less threatening. Almost all the people who were killed during the protests and voter-registration drives were men. But Charles Payne, a Duke University professor who studied the SNCC organizing projects extensively, noted that black women were often beaten as badly as the men, and their homes and businesses were shot at and burned down. And in all his interviews with people who had been involved in the SNCC movements in Mississippi, Payne said, "No woman to whom I spoke ever suggested, even indirectly, that *her own* involvement could be explained in such terms." Payne himself suspected that black women's close ties to the community and their strong network of family and friends had the effect of pulling in others once one woman stepped forward. And he felt their religious faith gave them the courage to simply do what they thought was right and trust in the Lord to protect them.

The fearlessness of some of the women was astonishing. Laura McGhee, a widow who had a farm in Greenwood, Mississippi, invited any plantation workers who were left homeless after they tried to register to vote to move onto her land—which she also put up as security for bail so many times that the authorities finally stopped accepting it. When the white night riders shot into her home, she slept during the day and sat up on the porch all night, cradling her shotgun. Once, when she tried to visit one of her sons who had been arrested in a demonstration, a policeman tried to bar her way. McGhee, who had another son in the hospital with a bullet in his jaw, lost her interest in nonviolence and simply slugged him in the eye. "And he's losing consciousness, sliding down the door," recalled Bob Zellner, the SNCC organizer who had accompanied her. "Meanwhile, Mrs. McGhee is following him on the way down. She's not missing a lick—boom, boom, boom! And every time she hits him, his head hits the door." Although she was arrested, she was never tried for the assault, and Zellner decided that "a new day is coming when a black woman can just whip the yard-dog shit out of a white cop and not have to account for it."

Fannie Lou Hamer, who was working as a sharecropper in Ruleville, Mississippi, was the most legendary of the local women who stepped forward. The youngest in an impoverished family of twenty children, she was childless herself, having been sterilized without permission by a white doctor who was operating on her for a benign tumor. When the SNCC workers arrived and asked for volunteers to register to vote, Hamer, too, had her hand up right away. As a result, she and her husband were thrown off the plantation where they lived. The home of the friend who took them in was riddled with bullets. When Hamer finally passed the test to register—a daunting process in a state where the test for black citizens was not only complicated but also arbitrary in the scoring—her tumbledown house received a $9,000 water bill although it had no running water. But Hamer—a natural orator who soon became SNCC's star speaker—was unstoppable. She was arrested in a bus station, taken to the jail, and beaten savagely, leaving her with injuries that would torment her for the rest of her life. "She told me they had one black prisoner sit on her feet, and one with a blackjack beat her and the white guard fondled her and there was nothing she could do," said Lenora Taitt-Magubane. "But she never gave up, even after she got sick. She kept speaking, with her sixth-grade education and her powerful voice. She never lost her faith and her will to fight."

In 1964 Hamer and Blackwell became delegates from the Mississippi Freedom Democratic Party to the presidential convention—a SNCC plan to challenge the seating of the regular Mississippi delegates on the grounds that black Mississippians had been denied the right to vote. Hamer's testimony before the Credentials Committee, in which she described white harassment and her beating in jail, became the most riveting moment of the convention. "All of this is on account we want to register, to become first-class citizens, and if the Freedom Democratic Party is not seated now, I question America," she concluded. It was so compelling that President Johnson, who was planning on being nominated without totally alienating the white voters of the Deep South, suddenly called a press conference at the White House to divert the TV networks from broadcasting her appearance.

The negotiations over who would get the Mississippi seats at the convention were carried on between Senator Hubert Humphrey—the civil rights champion who wanted desperately to be Lyndon Johnson's running mate—and male black leaders. They zeroed in on a compromise that would leave the white delegates in place and give the Freedom Democrats two symbolic seats, but Fannie Lou Hamer wanted no part of it. "At first Mrs. Hamer, as vice chair of our delegation, was invited to the meetings," Blackwell wrote later. "But she was excluded after she told Humphrey to his face that he wanted to be vice president more than he wanted to do what was right and that she was going to pray for him." The only politician who "stood with us all the way," Lenora Taitt-Magubane remembered, was Representative Edith Green of Oregon.

The true import of the Freedom Democratic Party was not in what they did or did not accomplish when it came to seating delegates. It was the impact on viewers, who watched while Hamer's testimony was replayed over and over on TV.

Emma Jordan, a black college student in California, was thrilled. "I remember looking at her and thinking, you know, she spoke so powerfully. I mean, it just made me choke to listen to her... She was confronted by some of the most powerful politicians in the world. And she stood up. Hubert Humphrey, Lyndon Johnson, they were all putting enormous pressure on her to take a deal and cave." The commentary on TV, Jordan noticed, seemed to assume that in the end the powerful men would win out. "The news reporters were reporting behind the scenes, 'This is the deal. We think it's going to be resolved this way.' And she stood up and... she was not going to take a deal."

Hamer's will was strongest, and negotiations collapsed. The convention seated the regular Mississippi Democrats, who then promptly walked out anyway. The Freedom Democrats, who had been given floor passes by delegates from other states, stole onto the floor and gradually occupied those empty places, successfully resisting any attempts to dislodge them. They had the seats physically if not legally. "The spotlight was on us that night in the hall," Blackwell said. "And I had a feeling I had never had before: It was a sense of history. I felt a part of history. I felt free and significant and very much a part of the United States of America."

"THAT WAS OUR UNIFORM."

Blackwell looked on what happened to her at the convention as a triumph, while the young civil rights organizers saw it as a terrible defeat, and proof that no matter how noble their cause and how much pain they endured, the white liberal Northerners they had counted on were not really going to respond. Perhaps it was the difference in expectations that allowed Blackwell to keep growing stronger throughout the tumultuous '60s, while SNCC began to slide into an angry cynicism. "I don't think that anybody envisioned the long years of struggle and violence and... anguish," said Connie Curry, a white SNCC official. In 1960, when SNCC was formed, the students declared their commitment to the creed of nonviolence, vowing to remain "loving and forgiving even in the midst of hostility." But by 1964 the students—many by then ex-students—were growing dubious about nonviolence and less willing to put their bodies on the line just in the hope that someone in power would notice and intervene. Being beaten and thrown into jail "and trying to love everybody while they did it to you...," Curry said, "was bound to mess you up."

Dressing up for demonstrations was definitely over. The students who had worn their best clothes to sit-ins and jail were now in denim pants and work shirts. "That was our uniform," said Joyce Ladner. "I had an overall skirt I wore. That was fashionable among the movement women. The guys wore overalls, and we wore the overall skirt." The transition from dress-up to workers' clothes did not come without controversy. While some argued that wearing jeans was a sign of solidarity with the working class, others thought it was a sign of disrespect. Marian Wright Edelman said she would never forget "the disappointed looks" of rural black Mississippians "who heard there was a Black lady lawyer in town...and who came to look for and at me. When they saw me in blue jeans and an old sweatshirt, they were crestfallen. I never wore jeans in public again in Mississippi." Back in Atlanta, Ruby Doris Smith, who had taken over the day-to-day operations of SNCC, offered a compromise: "It isn't so much what you wear but the condition of the clothes worn." (Smith herself generally stuck to skirts and blouses.)

Carefully straightened hair gave way to natural Afros, some of them just a small halo around the head, others great explosions of hair. The new style created enormous generational conflicts, from Northern college towns to rural Mississippi. Unita Blackwell was disturbed when Muriel Tillinghast, the young SNCC organizer assigned to work with her on voter registration, arrived in town wearing a short Afro. "Me, I called it nappy-headed," she recalled. "I had been straightening my hair for

years, and all the other black women I knew had been, too. By the time I was 7 or 8 years old, my mother and grandmother were 'warm-combing' my hair to get the kinks out. As far as I knew, there was no such thing as a black woman not straightening her hair." She found Muriel's hair embarrassing—particularly since "all the women in church kind of sniggled about it"—and kept dropping hints about going down to the local hairdresser.

The idea of letting your hair "go natural" had begun with black artists and actresses in the 1950s, and in 1963, Cicely Tyson wore her hair in an Afro or in cornrows when she appeared in the TV series *East Side/West Side*. But the civil rights workers were the ones who brought the style into the college campuses and black neighborhoods around the country, much to the horror of their parents and teachers. When Emma Jordan got married in California, her mother made it clear that the ceremony would not go on unless the bride had her hair properly straightened. Jordan dutifully began her wedding day in compliance. Then at the last minute she went into the bathroom and put water in it, allowing it to revert to "the cutest little Afro." Her mother burst into tears, Jordan said, "but there was nothing she could do." Valerie Bradley, a black journalist, said that when she returned home to visit her family in Indianapolis, her mother refused to meet her Afro-wearing daughter at the airport. At Spelman, Gwen Robinson was already letting her hair grow natural in the early '60s. She was called into the dean's office and told she was a "disgrace" and had no hopes of finding a husband.

"The hair thing made a huge difference...," said Mary Helen Washington, who was a graduate student in Detroit when she let her hair go natural. "First of all it was a real power statement: I have all that hair walking around. But it was very freeing to have a style that white people couldn't wear that made you look gorgeous."

The Afro was an early sign of a coming explosion of anger over the standards of beauty in the black community, which had long valued features, color, and hair that looked as "white" as possible. Those standards were particularly important at the elite black colleges. It was hard to avoid noticing that Spelman girls were not only extremely well-behaved; they were also, in general, extremely light-skinned. "The best of all possible worlds is that you are light as you can be, you have green eyes, or light brown, and you have long straight hair," said Gwen Robinson, who was dark-skinned and who found that the male students from neighboring colleges were cruelly dismissive. "Some of the Morehouse guys were so nasty to a person who looked like myself. Overt, I mean, straight up." Diane Nash was universally admired for her organizing skills, but virtually every description of her by colleagues in Nashville included a reference to the fact that she was very beautiful in that traditional way—so light-skinned that if the movement needed information on what was going on inside segregated waiting rooms or restaurants, she could walk in and pass for white. "The first thing you have to say about Diane—the first thing anyone who ever encountered her noticed, and there is no way *not* to notice—is that she was one of God's beautiful creatures, just about the most gorgeous woman any of us had ever seen...," wrote John Lewis in his memoirs. "But none of this turned Diane's head. She was dead serious about what we were doing each week, very calm, very deliberate, always straightforward and sincere. As time passed, she came to be seen more as our sister than as an object of lust."

"There's no answer, really."

The small, tightly knit Beloved Community of SNCC was evolving into a large, nationally famous organization that could no longer be run by endless meetings in search of consensus. Ruby Doris Smith had taken over the central office in Atlanta—less because she was interested in the job than because she realized how desperately SNCC needed someone to impose order. "She absolutely did not tolerate any nonsense," said Stanley Wise, who worked with her.

Ruby Doris, who was still just 22, had gotten married in the summer of 1963 to Clifford Robinson, whose brother had married her sister. Robinson, who had not been involved in the movement, wound up working as a mechanic for SNCC, and the people who knew them both would debate whether they made a good couple. Many believed Clifford was no match for Ruby Doris, but Smith herself always claimed that she had finally found a man who was stronger than she was. What seemed clear, as Joyce Ladner said, was that her new husband "absolutely adored Ruby. He would just sit and look at her." Soon, she was pregnant, but she stayed on the job until she went into labor. In the hospital where her son was born, friends found her on the floor doing exercises a few hours after the delivery, intent on getting back to work. Two weeks later, Ruby Doris appeared on her sister Catherine's doorstep with her infant. When Catherine protested that she had no experience taking care of children, Ruby Doris said, "You'll find out," put the baby in Catherine's arms, and went to work.

Since twenty-first-century America has not yet figured out exactly how a woman can handle the duties of both career and family, it's not surprising that the women in the civil rights movement of the 1960s had trouble balancing husband, children, and an all-consuming cause that burned out many single, unattached people. "Well, I've found out there's no answer, really, for a woman who works in a career and has children," Ruby Doris told Josephine Carson, a writer who was collecting stories of black women in the South. "Like: my baby knows who his mother is, I think, but it's his grandmother who's giving him the food and that means something very special. He's getting more of her... uh...nature than he is of mine. He's learning to live with *her*, not me."

In 1961 Diane Nash had married James Bevel, a divinity student and SNCC leader who was, depending on who you were talking to, either one of the most charismatic or one of the most eccentric members of the organization. "He's crazy but he's a genius," said Ivanhoe Donaldson, a SNCC organizer who accepted both theories. "He's overwhelming, and I think he just overwhelmed Diane. And so she faded into his background while his star was out there shining." Nash in fact kept working, particularly on a voting-rights campaign in Alabama. When she was pregnant with her first child, she was sentenced to two years in jail for "contributing to the delinquency of minors." (She had taught techniques for nonviolent civil disobedience to high schoolers.) Nash tried, unsuccessfully, to have the judge order her to serve the whole sentence. "Since my child will be a black child born in Mississippi, whether I am in jail or not he will be born in prison," she said. Released, she simply went back to working for the cause. But soon, she had a second child and a foundering marriage. Bevel's compulsive infidelity doomed the relationship; he ultimately failed even to provide support for his children. By the end of the decade, Nash would be a single mother living in Chicago. She had once told a reporter that the civil rights movement was what she intended to be "doing for the rest of my life." But earning a living and raising her son and daughter left her limited time for anything else.

"I ASKED FOR VOLUNTEERS AND THEY SENT ME WHITE WOMEN."

In 1964 SNCC invited about a thousand students, most of them Northern whites, to come to Mississippi to work on voter-registration projects during their summer vacations. It was a controversial idea—while the exhausted organizers needed fresh manpower, many doubted that inexperienced outsiders were the answer. But the architects of the plan also hoped that white Northern America would pay more attention to the vicious resistance to black voter registration in the South if some of the people being brutalized were white. The summer had barely begun when three male civil rights workers—one of them a new white recruit from the North—were murdered. By September, there had been eighty beatings, thirty-five shootings, thirty-five church burnings, and thirty bombings. Many of the volunteers were targets, but SNCC's local black supporters suffered the most. "It was a beautiful experience until the summer of '64, when there were just too many funerals," said Taitt-Magubane.

SNCC would wind up marginalized within a few years and out of business by the end of the decade. There were endless reasons for its decline and fall. But the enormous influx of volunteers—mostly white and about 40 percent female—strained the already-existing fault lines until they cracked. The tensions between black and white women were particularly acute.

The story line was easy for everybody to discern: young black men, who had always been taught to regard white women as a forbidden—and extraordinarily dangerous—fruit, suddenly found themselves fussed over by white coeds while the black women watched from the sidelines. When Penny Patch, a longtime white organizer who was romantically involved with a black man, began to notice that the black female veterans were treating her coldly, she decided that the real cause was neither jealousy on their part nor indiscretion on hers, but history. "As the nearest and safest white women, some of us became vessels into which black women, if they chose to, could pour their accumulated anger—anger they had borne for hundreds of years...It is slavery and oppression that created the distance between black women and white women, not the fact that white women slept with black men during the civil rights movement."

Patch was right about the history. While white and black women had worked together and forged friendships in America since the seventeenth century, the more common relationship was the uneasy one of employer-employee. Some of the black women in the movement had mothers who worked as domestics and had bitter memories of the way white women had treated them. But the sex part most definitely did matter. Black women who had already suffered because their features didn't look sufficiently "white" could not possibly be thrilled when hundreds of white women arrived on the scene and started pairing off with black men. They had been putting their lives on the line, but many of their male comrades seemed to prefer the attention of the newcomers. "Our skills and abilities were recognized and respected, but that seemed to place us in some category other than female," said Cynthia Washington, who was working as a project director in one of the most dangerous areas of the South. Things weren't helped by the fact that SNCC's executive secretary, James Forman, who was married to a black woman, was having an affair with a white staff member. "There is the movement. And everybody is, like, we are a family, we are together as brothers and sisters," said Josie Bass, thinking about her days fighting for civil rights in Chicago. "But it was a fight in the back room every day about the brothers not being with the sisters while we were together in this movement. And that is the part that I don't hear people talking about anymore, but it was *so real and raw.*"

The volunteers were all well-intentioned, and most bent over backward not to offend the black people they were working with. Nevertheless, some of the recruits had a Lady Bountiful attitude toward the people they were there to help. Dr. Alvin Poussaint, who studied the way white women adjusted to the demands of Freedom Summer, said one of them told him she felt like "the master's child come to free the slaves." Others failed to understand how easily they could put black men in danger. Chuck McDew, a black organizer, was being kept incommunicado in a Mississippi jail when one of the white female volunteers had the bright idea of getting in to see him by passing herself off as his wife. The guards, who had not been particularly antagonistic toward their prisoner, changed overnight and began beating him brutally, saying, "Son of a bitch, that's what you get for marrying a white woman." The badly injured McDew, when he got out, threatened to kill the volunteer himself.

Freedom Summer was a huge success in the way SNCC had intended, drawing far more national attention to the brutality of Southern resistance to civil rights. But that very fact was as irritating as it was welcome. How could the veteran organizers not be offended to see the TV crews grow excited over the news that two bodies had been found in the Mississippi River and then quickly lose interest when they discovered the victims were black men, not white students? The white volunteers themselves were embarrassed that stories such as "They Walk in Fear but They Won't Give Up" talked all about them and failed to mention the heroic local blacks or the indomitable SNCC workers.

The white women were assigned to jobs where they would have the least contact with the white population, such as teaching in the Freedom Schools, where local youngsters were prepared to register to vote. Going out to actually register people in the community—the highest-prestige job, and the most exciting—was almost always delegated to men. Although most of the women did not complain, they certainly did notice that the male volunteers were, as one Freedom School teacher remembered, "running out…being macho men…you know, 'we're going to go out and get our heads busted and we'll come back to here where you nurse us…and otherwise service us and send us back out again.'" One of the few young white women who was able to get a field-organizing job was Jo Freeman, thanks to the hand-cranked mimeograph machine that was sent to her by friends. "Until you've written out three hundred mass-meeting leaflets by hand, you don't know how valuable this was to any project director," she said. "And I went with the machine."

Many of the new arrivals felt the coolness from the start. The summer volunteers were "often viewed as a kind of disposable labor and public relations source," said Elaine DeLott Baker, an experienced organizer from Ohio who had gone to Mississippi to stay but still felt she had "arrived too late to be incorporated into the culture of trust that was the hallmark of…the Beloved Community."

Susan Brownmiller, a white New Yorker who went with a friend to work in Mississippi, reported to a black organizer, who said with annoyance, "I asked for volunteers and they sent me white women."

"IT HAD THE APPEARANCES OF A NECKING PARTY."

The Civil Rights Memorial at the Southern Poverty Law Center in Montgomery, Alabama, honors "40 Lives for Freedom"—the men and women "who lost their lives in the struggle for freedom during the modern civil rights movement" from 1954 to 1968. Among them are Addie Mae Collins, Denise McNair, Carole Robertson, and Cynthia Wesley, remembered as the "four little girls" who were getting ready for a service at the Sixteenth Street Baptist Church in Birmingham when a bomb exploded. Johnnie Mae Chappell, who was walking down a road in Jacksonville when she was killed by white men who simply wanted to shoot a black person, was later added to the list in honor of the victims of "random racist violence" during the era.

The only other woman on the list—and the only woman to be killed during a civil rights protest—was white. Viola Liuzzo, a 39-year-old Detroit housewife and college student, was shot by members of the Ku Klux Klan while she and a black volunteer were driving between Selma and Montgomery after the Selma march of 1965. Liuzzo was a solitary figure, and the civil rights movement seemed unsure exactly what to do with her when she was suddenly thrust upon them as a martyr. Her participation had mainly involved marching in a few demonstrations in Michigan, and she had driven down to Selma alone. She seemed less like a classic civil rights worker than one of Betty Friedan's *Feminine Mystique* heroines, looking for a commitment to something larger than her home and family.

Early in life Viola Liuzzo had made bad choices that haunted her—quitting school at 14, marrying and divorcing by the time she was 16. Then she turned things around, and by the early 1960s she was living a proper middle-class life in Detroit with her husband, Jim, a teamsters official, and five children. By all accounts she was a devoted mother. But she had no interest in either housekeeping or neighborhood social life. Trying to explain Liuzzo's decision to go South, her only close friend, a black woman named Sarah Evans, said she was "searching, looking for something." Her husband and children simply said that she had a huge heart.

The march from Selma to Montgomery was a follow-up to Bloody Sunday, in which Alabama law officers had attacked six hundred people marching for voting rights. Americans saw television reports of the attack, and thousands drove to Selma to be part of the great protest being held in response. Liuzzo apparently intended to drive down with other students from Wayne State University, where she was attending classes. But in the way of college students everywhere, her companions fell by the wayside when it was time to get organized and go. Viola left by herself, driving a thousand miles in three days. When she arrived, she was assigned the unmemorable job of working at a hospitality desk and then later at a first-aid station. She stayed with a local volunteer, Mrs. Willie Lee Jackson, and befriended her daughter, an unmarried high school dropout with a new baby. Perhaps thinking of her own much-regretted decision to leave school, Liuzzo invited the girl to come to Detroit to live with her family, so she could go back to high school and get a new start.

While she was working at the hospitality desk, she loaned her car to the Transportation Committee, which was headed by Leroy Moton, a black volunteer who stood well over six feet tall but weighed less than 140 pounds, and whose slight build and big glasses made him look younger than his 19 years. Moton, who dreamed of being a barber someday, carried an American flag in the march, and people noticed him beaming with pride, occasionally bursting into a few verses of "The Star-Spangled Banner." After it was all over, Liuzzo met up with Moton and got behind the wheel herself to ferry him and five other passengers back to Selma. The two of them were returning to Montgomery down Highway 80 when they were spotted by a carful of Ku Klux Klan members, who gave chase. "We got pretty much even with the car, and the lady just turned her head solid all the way around and looked at us," said an FBI informant who was with the assailants. "I will never forget it in my lifetime, and her mouth flew open like she—in my heart I've always said she was saying 'Oh God' or something like that." Liuzzo was shot to death. Moton miraculously survived as the car plunged, uncontrolled, into a field.

For Liuzzo and Moton to be in the same car was a terrible error, one many members of the black community could not conceive of making. Unita Blackwell was also on her way home from Montgomery that day, just ahead of Liuzzo and Moton. Her passengers included one white woman who the others kept covered with a bedsheet. "Merely seeing blacks and whites together in any kind of equal situation was enough to send white law-enforcement officials and some in the general public into a frenzy, and anything might happen," Blackwell said.

Virginia Durr—whose white Southern roots did not keep her from playing a leading role in the Montgomery civil rights movement—said that in the end the violent paranoia about integration in the South "always got down to sexual relations between a black man and a white woman." The obsession with "race-mixing" comes up endlessly in antiblack rhetoric, and for Southern racists, that mixing occurred in only one direction. White men could prey on black women at their pleasure, but let a black man touch a white woman, and civilization fell. The Alabama state legislature, in a resolution denouncing the Selma march, claimed, "There is evidence of much fornication, and young women are returning to their respective states apparently as unwed expectant mothers." In Washington, the congressman who represented Montgomery said that the marchers were "rabble hired to march for ten dollars a day... and all the sex they wanted."

The theme was not confined to Southerners. FBI chief J. Edgar Hoover, briefing the attorney general on Liuzzo's death, told him "that she was sitting very, very close to the Negro in the car; that it had the appearances of a necking party."

At the first trial of Collie Wilkins, the Klansman who shot Liuzzo, defense attorney Matt Murphy launched into a tirade about the mixing of the races: "Integration breaks every moral law God wrote... No white woman can marry a descendant of Ham. That's God's law... I don't care what Lyndon Johnson or anybody else says." Questioning Leroy Moton, he demanded to know if the young man "had relations" with Viola Liuzzo. When Moton denied it vehemently, the lawyer wanted to know what other reason there could be for a white woman from Detroit to "desert her husband and children to ride around with a black man." Finally, after suggesting that Moton was a drug addict, Murphy claimed that Liuzzo "was in the car with three black niggers. One white woman and three black niggers. Black nigger Communists who want to take us over!" Wilkins was freed after the jury deadlocked, repeatedly voting 10 to 2 to convict on a lesser charge of manslaughter. Murphy assured a reporter that there would undoubtedly be an acquittal on retrial: "All I need to use is the fact that Mrs. Liuzzo was in the car with a nigger man" and, he added bizarrely, that "she wore no underpants." Murphy and the other men accused of Liuzzo's murder then embarked on a fund-raising tour for the Klan, during which Wilkins was repeatedly introduced as "the triggerman" and honored with a parade in Atlanta. (Wilkins was indeed acquitted at his second trial. Later, all three of the Klansmen implicated in Liuzzo's death were convicted in a federal trial of violating her civil rights and were sentenced to ten years in prison.)

Liuzzo was far from the only white housewife in the North who felt the call to go to Selma and bear witness. Watching the news coverage of "soldiers shooting down those black children" from her home in Boston, Betty Riley Williams, the former Marine's wife, felt she should be in Selma with the marchers.

"I was a coward because I kept thinking, 'What if I get there and I get shot? Who will bring up my children?' I've always felt a little ashamed about that, but that's how it was. I know other women have gone and they're proud they did it, but I couldn't do it." Yet Liuzzo has somehow always remained an orphaned martyr, the dead civil rights protester who no one wants to claim. Civil rights activists, black and white, almost all felt that she had behaved recklessly in driving with a black man on an open highway. And while the general public did not indulge in paranoid fantasies about drugs and necking parties, many did believe she had neglected her responsibilities to her family to go on a quixotic quest to get justice for strangers. A poll by *Ladies' Home Journal* found that 55 percent of the women questioned felt she had no right "to leave her five children to risk her life for a social cause." A little more than a quarter thought she did have a right to go. In a follow-up focus group, the magazine brought together eighteen Northern suburban women, and none of them seemed to have much sympathy for the idea that a married woman should put herself at risk for anything other than her immediate family. And the definition of what was risky appeared to be expansive. One of the women admitted that, as president of a club, she had gone out of town for three days. When she added that she had gone by plane, there was a long, and apparently disapproving, silence.

"THE DAY MIGHT COME WHEN WOMEN AREN'T NEEDED."

In the fall of 1964, after the summer volunteers had finally gone away, SNCC's regular members held a gathering at Waveland, Mississippi, to regroup. Sandra "Casey" Hayden, a longtime white organizer from Texas, wrote a memo with several other white women that proposed addressing the question of sexism in the organization. They argued that men's sense of superiority in the civil rights movement was "as widespread and deep-rooted and every bit as crippling to the women as assump-

tions of white supremacy are to the Negro." The memo would go down in women's history as one of the first attempts to expand the modern civil rights movement's concerns to include gender as well as race. But at the time, very few people paid much attention, and Stokely Carmichael—who would soon become chairman of SNCC—joked that the proper place for women in the organization was "prone." (Carmichael would both repudiate and repeat the line in later years. In an interview in 1995, he said he "would not have been taken seriously as a leader of an organization like SNCC if I had not taken seriously the leadership of women. A woman like Ella Baker would not have tolerated it.") The black women were generally dismissive of Casey Hayden's memo. "White women in the movement . . . said they were forced to type instead of being able to go out and organize. Well, I wanted them to stay in the office and type as much as the black guys," said Joyce Ladner. "If they went out in the community, they were a lightning rod for all of us to get hurt." Black women had plenty of complaints about black men, but they had no intention of sharing their dissatisfaction with the general public. "There was always this united front in front of white America that we were supporting the brothers," said Josie Bass. "But part of my anger of racism was the anger of how black men treated black women and blamed it on racism."

Meanwhile, SNCC was moving into its black-power phase. After several years of being jailed and beaten by whites, of seeing their friends killed by whites, and of witnessing the murderers shielded by whites, many of the black organizers were tired of fighting for integration, and overwhelmed by an understandable—if not necessarily practical—desire to have all white people go away and leave black people to themselves. Joyce Ladner found she went through a period "when I started to really dislike white people." The feeling was so strong that when her former roommate, who was white, called to say she was coming to visit for the weekend, Ladner could not bear to deal with her. "This thing had taken hold of me," she recalled. "I think maybe I took it out on her because she was the closest white person to me. But it was very—it was bad, so uncomfortable. I felt so awful that white people had treated us this way." (Eventually, Ladner apologized to her ex-roommate, and they resumed their friendship.)

SNCC finally voted to expel all its white members, much to the dismay of some of the veterans, such as Fannie Lou Hamer. ("I am not fighting for an all-black world, just like I am not going to tolerate an all-white world," she told one writer.) Ella Baker, who would never turn her back on the young people she had nurtured, nevertheless began to drift away. She spoke to the SNCC leaders less and less, and they seldom reached out to her for advice.

The task that Baker had imposed on the early SNCC members required humility and a willingness to continually compromise. By working with local men and women on the ground and following their lead, the young organizers were forced to bow to the ideas and needs of people with very different histories and interests. When SNCC gave up on grassroots organizing and gave up on working with whites, compromise went out the window. The leaders began to splinter into factions based on ideology or history or personality. And they began arguing that black women's chief duty in life was to follow and support black men. Having dropped the discipline required to live and work in close harmony with whites, some of the leaders had stopped bothering to try to work with women as well.

Ruby Doris Smith had been elected executive secretary of SNCC in 1966—the only woman who ever had held, or ever would hold, such an important office. But she came to power just as the organization was slipping toward irrelevance and her own health was beginning to fail. Tragically, in 1967 she fell ill and died at the age of 25 from cancer. Shortly before her death, she told *Ebony* magazine that while in the past black women had to "assert themselves so the family could survive," now that more men were joining the movement, "the day might come when women aren't needed for this type of work." It was a surprising statement from someone as independent as Smith, although it might have been understandable for an ailing woman juggling the demands of a husband, a small child, and an all-consuming job to dream about not being needed quite as much. However, if Smith was simply responding to the changing tenor of her organization, she wasn't giving too much away. The day that men would actually be ready to totally take over that desired role of all-purpose leader, she added cannily, "can't even be foreseen—maybe in the next century or so."

Keepsake Pages

When did you first hear about the civil rights movement? Were you involved? If you were, you have a story to tell—go to it.

_____

_____

_____

_____

_____

_____

_____

_____

_____

If you weren't involved in the civil rights movement, what do you remember hearing? How did it impact you?

_____

_____

_____

_____

_____

_____

_____

_____

African-American interviewees: Did you ever feel black women in the civil rights movement were getting second-class treatment from their male colleagues?

_____

_____

_____

_____

_____

_____

_____

_____

_____

There were so many unforgettable moments in civil rights history. Which ones do you remember having a particular impact on you? The death of the four little girls in the Birmingham church bombing? The Selma march? The March on Washington? Something else?

_____

_____

_____

_____

_____

_____

_____

_____

_____

More Thoughts and Memories

More Thoughts and Memories

More Thoughts and Memories

7. The Decline of the Double Standard

"They think I'm a good girl."

In 1968 the *New York Times* took note of a startling new trend: "cohabiting." A feature story introduced readers to several couples, mainly New York City college students, who were living together without the benefit of a marriage license. Everyone's identity was disguised in deference to the controversial nature of the subject. "Joan," whose parents believed she was rooming with a girlfriend, said even the mailman was conspiring with her to hide the truth from her family. "It's funny…my parents have a lot of confidence in me. They think I'm a good girl," said Joan, who clearly believed that if her parents got a load of her real roommate, "Charles," they might change their minds.

The lead anecdote, however, belonged to "Peter" and "Susan," who were part of a youthful counterculture that the *Times* was still slowly introducing to its readers. The couple was sharing a four-room apartment with "no bed in the bedroom — just six mattresses for their use and that of fellow students who need a place to sleep." And the paper reported that although Peter and Susan had been together for two years, they "had no plans for a wedding because they regard marriage as 'too serious a step.'" Susan was a student at Barnard College, which generally prohibited off-campus living arrangements. But she had gotten around the rule by having a friend tell the college employment bureau she wanted to hire Susan as a live-in nanny.

That was a little too much detail, as it turned out. It didn't take the Barnard administration long to figure out that "Susan" was actually Linda LeClair, a 20-year-old sophomore. When confronted, LeClair admitted she had deceived the housing administrator and broken school regulations. Rather than apologizing, she and her boyfriend, Peter Behr, a junior at Columbia, began

leafleting the campus, asking students to demand changes in the rules. Endless debate and newspaper headlines ensued. A student-faculty committee was called to consider the case. After five hours of deliberation, the committee announced that as punishment for deceiving the administration about where she lived, LeClair would be "denied the privilege of using the following college facilities: the snack bar, the cafeteria, and the James Room," a student lounge.

A snack-bar ban was clearly not the kind of penalty likely to deter future cohabitation, and the alumnae wrote to complain. Barnard's president, Martha Peterson, seemed torn between respecting the committee's decision and showing the college's donors that she was not going to let the matter drop. So she sent an open letter to LeClair, asking her opinion on "the importance of integrity among individuals in the college" and "the importance of respect for regularized procedures." She also wanted a letter from LeClair's parents stating whether they approved of their daughter's behavior. The result of all this was another *Times* story, titled "Father Despairs of Barnard Daughter," and an editorial noting that Barnard could have saved itself a lot of grief "by letting sleeping coeds lie."

By May, Peterson was hinting very strongly that Linda LeClair ought to go away ("…no useful purpose can be served by your continued enrollment in Barnard College"). Yet she insisted that the final judgment would be based neither on sex nor on failure to follow procedures, but on the final grades of a student who, it appeared, had been spending more time passing out leaflets than attending classes. The *Times*, which had been covering the story as if it involved the threat of nuclear war, tracked down LeClair among "a student group flying paper airplanes on the Columbia campus" and found her rather indifferent to her future as an undergraduate. The next time she made an appearance in the paper would be as one of hundreds of students arrested during sit-ins and protests over Columbia's plan to build a gym in Harlem. Ultimately, LeClair dropped out at the end of the semester, went off with Peter Behr to live in a commune in Vermont, hitchhiked to the West Coast, and returned to New York so her boyfriend could refuse induction into the Army. On her arrival, LeClair told a *Times* reporter that she had a certain sympathy for President Peterson. "She is aware... that recognizing sexual intercourse would cause embarrassment to the ladies that give money to the college."

"... WHILE I WASN'T ALLOWED OUT AFTER NINE THIRTY."

Of all the social uprisings of the late 1960s and early 1970s, none was more popular than the sexual revolution. And while men took an enthusiastic part, it was basically a story about women. Most of the world had always operated under a double standard in which girls were supposed to remain chaste until marriage while boys were allowed—sometimes encouraged—to press for whatever sex they could get. But Linda LeClair's generation had learned from the civil rights movement that just because something had always been the rule did not mean it was right—particularly if that rule gave some people more privileges than others. Even the authority figures had lost some of their confidence in the old morality. The Barnard administration, while trying to get a handle on the LeClair situation, skirted any suggestion that it was wrong for a young woman to shack up with a man she did not intend to marry. Instead, President Peterson focused on the fact that LeClair had lied about where she was living. Even in 1968, everyone on campus tended to agree that lying was bad.

Colleges had always given their unspoken endorsement to the double standard by setting far stricter regulations in girls' dormitories. In her pre-

cohabitation days, LeClair would get back to her room in time for curfew, then look out the window to watch her boyfriend walking away. "I can still see the image," she said recently, "of him going across Broadway to do whatever the heck he wanted to do while I wasn't allowed out after nine thirty at night." It was a tradition as old as women's higher education. But by the late 1960s, Barnard was hardly the only college on the defensive. Within a few years, many schools were in full-scale retreat. When Nora Ephron returned to Wellesley for the tenth reunion of the Class of 1962, she heard that one of her old classmates had gone into a dormitory bathroom and seen "a boy and a girl taking a shower together." No one, Ephron said, could believe it. "Ten years ago we were allowed to have men in the rooms on Sunday afternoons only, on the condition the door be left fourteen inches ajar." And Anne Wallach, visiting her daughter at Antioch, prided herself on not reacting when she passed a naked man on her way to Alison's room.

"... THE TECHNICAL VIRGINS ASSOCIATION."

The female warriors of the sexual revolution had been born into a world where the importance of remaining a virgin until marriage was seldom questioned. Nothing was worse than being suspected of casual sleeping around. Ellen Miller, who grew up in Kentucky, remembers that adults were extremely tolerant of their children smoking and that parents routinely chaperoned parties in which underage boys and girls drank alcohol. But permissiveness went only so far. Nobody wanted to hang out with a girl who had "a reputation," Miller said. "I guess the social mores accepted smoking, accepted drinking, but did not accept early sex."

There were, of course, many women who had clear-cut religious reasons for avoiding sex outside wedlock. But for a great many others, virginity had become a social convention without any real ethical roots. Rather, they saw it as a commodity that made women more valuable in the marriage market, and they tried to divert their boyfriends into sexual activity that would leave them satisfied without risking penetration. "We called it the TVA — the Technical Virgins Association," said one coed of the mid-'60s. The task was made all the more challenging because many women of the era found oral sex disgusting. "Now don't turn up your nose and make that ugly face," warned the author of *The Sensuous Woman* in 1969 before embarking on a discussion of oral sex.

The country had been wedded to the old Victorian belief that women had a much lower sex drive than men and that women were the ones responsible for drawing the line. For a boy, manliness meant pressing his dates to go farther, ever farther. It was the girl's duty to call a halt. "A man will go as far as a woman will let him. The girl has to set the standard," a college student told George Gallup. It was the girl who had to decide whether French-kissing on the second date was too fast, how much touching could take place and where. Advice columnists doled out leaflets with titles such as "Necking and Petting and How Far to Go," and boys reported to their friends whether they had gotten to second base or third.

If a home run had been hit, a gentleman never told — unless, of course, the girl in question had a reputation and was therefore fair game. Girls with reputations got asked out on dates for only "one thing," and most people believed they forfeited their chance of a good marriage. In the movies, unmarried women who were sexually active were punished with a life of lonely solitude or sudden death. (Elizabeth Taylor won the 1960 best actress award for *BUtterfield 8,* in which she played a "party girl" whose decision to reform wasn't enough to save her from a fatal car crash.) The most popular actress of the early 1960s was Doris Day, who specialized in playing a working woman protecting her virtue against handsome men who schemed to deflower her. Since Day was well into her 30s at the time, the films drove home the point that a woman was never too old to resist extramarital sex.

The virginity rule was a reason for early marriage — any delay would increase the chances of straying from the path of virtue. And it was an excellent argument against training women for serious careers. If unmarried women — even those as old as Doris Day — were expected to avoid sex, and if married women were not supposed to work, pursuing a career became something very close to taking the veil.

"... A LOT MORE FUN BY THE DOZEN."

In 1961 *Ladies' Home Journal* offered its readers an essay that asked, "Is the Double Standard Out of Date?" In it, writer Betsy Marvin McKinney answered her own question with a definite no. Sex for the sake of sex, without the chance of procreation, could be satisfying for a man, she conceded. His only job, after all, was to release some sperm. But a woman was built to have babies, and for her, sex for pleasure alone was far more frustrating than simply remaining chaste. Doris Day knew what she was doing, and once women started behaving like men in the bedroom, life tilted out of balance. "The end of the world would come as surely as atomic warfare could bring it," McKinney warned grimly.

One reader who came away less than convinced was Helen Gurley Brown, an ad-agency executive in her late 30s who had worked her way up from typist to secretary to a high-salaried copywriter in Los Angeles, all the while sleeping with whatever men took her fancy. She paid her own way in the world, supporting her widowed mother and disabled sister back in Little Rock and plunking down cash for an expensive, if used, Mercedes-Benz. That car impressed David Brown, a film producer who had been burned in the past by extravagant women who expected him to pay the bills. They married, and Brown urged his new wife to write an advice book for young women on how to live a modern single life. McKinney's article got Gurley Brown focused, and her response, *Sex and the Single Girl,* was published in 1962. It became a bestseller "that torpedoed the myth that a girl must be married to enjoy a satisfying life," as the cover bragged in bright yellow letters.

It also became one of those books that define an era. Whether Gurley Brown converted large numbers of people to a new way of thinking or simply announced a change that was already well under way, she captured the mood of the moment. Many American women were beginning to realize that they might be fated to be single for a long time, whether they liked it or not. Those who left school without a mate found the demographics stacked against them. Tradition dictated that they marry a man somewhat older than they were, which meant searching among the scanty population born during the war or competing with younger girls for the first wave of male baby boomers. Georgia Panter, who began a career as a stewardess at 23, said that even a job that put her in constant contact with planes full of businessmen didn't produce many prospects: "It was rare that I met single men." Gurley Brown suggested that her readers should just enjoy affairs with other people's husbands: "The statistics merely state that there are not enough *marriageable* men to go around. Nobody said a word about a shortage of *men*."

Sex and the Single Girl announced that the single woman, "far from being a creature to be pitied and patronized, is emerging as the newest glamour girl of our times." Unlike her married sisters, Gurley Brown declared breezily, the single woman got to spend her life in the interesting public world of men. She could have almost all the fruits of marriage—financial security, a nice home in which to entertain, an active social life. Children could be put off till later or borrowed for the occasional day from a harried friend or relative. "Her world is a far more colorful world than the one of PTA, Dr. Spock, and a jammed clothes dryer," Gurley Brown declared. It was the polar opposite of the conviction that George Gallup brought back from his surveys—that married women were much happier than their single sisters.

The section of the book that really caused a stir was the one in which Brown gave her single girl the right to extramarital sex—lots of extramarital sex. ("You do need a man of course every step of the way, and they are often cheaper emotionally and a lot more fun by the dozen.") For the new breed of single girl, sex was simply another part of her full, exciting life, just like dinner parties and a well-decorated apartment. It was pretty much the same game plan that *Playboy* had been urging on its male readers with so much success and profitability—except that *Sex and the Single Girl*, with a keen eye to its audience, also promised that at the end of all this glamorous independence, there would still probably be a husband. A *better* husband, in fact. Gurley Brown warned the young women of the 1960s that the men who were real catches were not looking for innocence and submission anymore; they wanted a wife who was both interesting and capable of pulling in a good paycheck. She caught her "brainy, charming, and sexy" movie producer because she had spent seventeen years becoming the kind of woman a rich, fascinating man would want to live with. "And when he finally walked into my life I was just worldly enough, relaxed enough, financially secure enough...and adorned with enough glitter to attract him."

"WE WEREN'T OF THE MIND-SET OF SAVING IT FOR THE HUSBANDS ANYMORE."

The sexual revolution hit hardest and fastest in big cities and in campus communities. But no one who read a newspaper or went to the movies could miss that something new was going on. A series of court decisions had made it far more difficult to ban pornography of any stripe, and the nation's ever-vigilant marketing community responded by churning out sexually explicit movies, books, magazines, and plays. On Broadway, audiences poured in to see the musical *Hair*, which featured onstage nudity and a cast that cheerfully sang, "Masturbation can be fun." A well-known designer introduced a topless women's swimsuit, and although only a few thousand customers actually bought one, the publicity and jokes made it seem as if everybody was going to the beach clad in just a bikini bottom. A fad for topless dancers in bars started in San Francisco, and everyone knew that at the fashionable Playboy Clubs, drinks were served by those glamorous "Bunnies" in their scanty costumes. (Before her incarnation as a feminist leader, Gloria Steinem was famous for her article "I Was a Playboy Bunny," in which she went under cover to discover that the costumes were extremely uncomfortable, the pay low, and the turnover rapid.)

There was certainly a lot more talk about sex, but it's hard to tell how much of it translated into real-world activity. Women had never shared all that much information about their sexual behavior, even with friends. Marie Monsky, who was living on her own in Manhattan and working her way through night school in the early 1960s, hung out with a fairly sophisticated crowd. But she still doesn't remember having a frank discussion about sexual experience. "There was a line you never crossed," she said. "It was a privacy issue." So it's possible that what looked like a great deal of sexual freedom was actually just a great deal more sexual frankness.

Alfred Kinsey had stunned the nation in 1953 with his famous study that found half of American women had had sex before they were married. (The study was limited to white women — Kinsey, like most of the nation, seemed indifferent to what African-Americans, Hispanics, Asians, or other minorities were doing with their private lives.) His findings were denounced as absurd, unbelievable, and morally suspect — the American Medical Association accused him of setting off a "wave of sex hysteria," and given the fact that Kinsey interviewed only people who had volunteered to talk about the most private aspects of their lives, there was reason to question whether the results were representative of the population as a whole. But his conclusions about women and premarital sex were

probably close to the mark. Most of the sexually active single women he found had slept with the men they believed would be their future husbands, something that had always been common, if not readily admitted. (As far back as 1695, a minister visiting New York wrote home that young people there seldom married until "a great belly puts it so forward that they must either submit to that, or to shame and disgrace.")

But as the '60s rolled along, it seemed clear that quite a few respectable middle-class young women had ditched the double standard completely. And the respectable middle-class young men responded enthusiastically. "There was a tremendous amount of sex," said Barbara Arnold, who was a nursing student at the University of Bridgeport. "There was a tremendous amount of, literally, free love. There were just orgies all over the place...It was a very crazy time, it really was." Pam Andrews — whose mother, Lillian, was one of the postwar housewives who enjoyed the new suburbs so much — arrived at Wellesley in 1968 and quickly went to a Planned Parenthood clinic and got a diaphragm. "I think I was one of the early ones," she said. But her classmates soon caught up with her, and when she transferred to the University of Wisconsin in 1970, Andrews found that the spirit of free love was completely in bloom. "You could sleep with everybody. Everybody was very open. It was such an unreal world." Sex in those days, she remembered, "was nothing special — just another way to get to know somebody."

In 1972 a survey of eight colleges found that less than a quarter of the women were still virgins in their junior year — the same proportion as men. "We weren't of the mind-set of saving it for the husbands anymore," said Tawana Hinton, who started college in 1970. "You know, it's like, if it feels good, do it. That was the rule. I don't have to be madly in love. It's not all about love; it's really just...no big deal. Pretty much everybody was on the Pill...and STDs and HIV wasn't of concern. Your only concern back then was, don't get pregnant."

"I PROBABLY WOULDN'T HAVE DONE THIS IF IT WEREN'T FOR THE PILL."

The young Americans who took part in the sexual revolution were living at a very particular moment in time, a brief window in which having sex with multiple partners posed very little physical peril. For most of human history, syphilis had been a scourge, and a good deal of the Victorian hysteria about sex—and prostitution in particular—had to do with women's fear that their husbands would stray and infect them with an incurable disease that could put them in peril of sterility, insanity, and death. Parents who feared their children would not be impressed by the moral arguments against premarital sex had an excellent follow-up: the Victorian version of sex education involved lantern shows of pictures of the grisly effects of syphilis. Then penicillin, which became widely available during World War II, provided a cure. By the 1960s sexually transmitted diseases were being treated like a joke by middle-class people who, as the decade went on, began experimenting with group sex, wife-swapping, and other kinds of behavior that would have been regarded as near suicidal by earlier generations.

And then there was the birth control pill, or—as the media called it in deference to its awesome powers—the Pill. The *Times,* in its survey of college cohabitation, noted that all the female roommates described in the story were taking it. "I probably wouldn't have done this if it weren't for the Pill," said Joan, the student who wistfully noted that her parents still thought she was a good girl. The older generation tended to agree with Joan— they blamed the birth control pill for what they saw as a frightening upsurge in premarital sex. "I think that's when morals started to deteriorate, because women weren't afraid they were going to get pregnant anymore, so why not?" said Louise Meyer in Wyoming. Her youngest daughter, who was born in 1968, wound up living with her future husband before they were married, she noted. It was some-thing she felt her older girls, who had been born in the early '50s, "would never have done."

The fact that the birth control pill had been invented did not necessarily mean a woman could get it. In 1960, the year the Pill went on sale, thirty states had laws restricting the sale or advertising of virtually anything related to birth control. The most draconian was in Connecticut, where anyone convicted of using, buying, or helping someone to acquire a birth control device could be fined or sentenced to up to a year in prison. The law was not one of those moldy pieces of antique legislation that the lawmakers had simply forgotten to repeal. Margaret Sanger, the birth control pioneer, had launched an attempt to eliminate it in 1923, and a bill to modify or repeal it had come up continually ever since. "It is a ridiculous and unenforceable law," complained a state senator from Greenwich in 1953, one of the few years in which advocates for change ever managed to get as far as a full debate. (The repeal bill was defeated on a voice vote by what the *Times* reported as an "overwhelming" majority.)

The law did not have much effect on middle-class married women, who could quietly get a prescription from the family doctor. But anyone who needed to go to a clinic—poor women or unmarried women seeking anonymity—was out of luck. Connecticut's Planned Parenthood League ran a van service transporting women in need of birth control pills across the state line to clinics in Rhode Island or New York. (Driving to Massachusetts would have been no help for unmarried women, since the law there barred anyone—even doctors— from helping them obtain contraceptives.) In 1958 the head of Connecticut Planned Parenthood, Estelle Griswold, designed a plan of attack. Griswold, a gray-haired, middle-aged woman of eminent respectability and an equal amount of feistiness, invited Dr. Charles Lee Buxton, the chairman of Yale Medical School's Department of Obstetrics, and Fowler Harper, a Yale law professor, to her home for cocktails. "Her martinis were always notorious," said Catherine Roraback, a

New Haven attorney. Soon after, Harper called Roraback and asked her to join the team that was going to challenge the law.

"Are you calling me as an attorney or a single woman?" asked Roraback.

Harper laughed and acknowledged that having a counsel who represented the people who suffered most under the Connecticut law would be a fine thing.

"Well, I'm not taking it," rejoined Roraback, who did not want to be a token. But she added quickly, "I'll do it as an attorney."

Harper was both a Yale professor and a famous free-speech advocate who had been an outspoken critic of the anti-Communist witch hunts of Senator Joseph McCarthy and his followers. Roraback had defended some of the victims of McCarthyism for little or no fee, and it was for that reason that Harper wanted to invite her into what everyone believed might be a history-making, career-building case.

"I think you deserve something like this," he said.

They brought their first case on behalf of a group of clients that included Dr. Buxton, who argued that he was being denied his right to practice medicine; a woman who had been warned that she would die from another pregnancy; and a couple who had had three disabled children. The case went up to the Supreme Court, which rejected it on the grounds that the laws were not actually being enforced.

That was true only if you were a middle-class woman with a private physician. "All of us knew—and Lee Buxton especially knew—that poor women couldn't get contraceptive advice," said Roraback. The last family-planning clinic had closed long ago, and hospitals did not deal in birth control because they knew they would be prosecuted. But because there were no clinics to prosecute, there were no plaintiffs who had standing to bring a case. A Catch-22.

So Griswold and Buxton opened a clinic. The Connecticut Planned Parenthood Center of New Haven immediately attracted customers, even though the women were warned that the police might arrive at any moment. "If they do that, we'll just sit down here until we get the information we came for," replied one patient. But Roraback was worried that the women's privacy might be compromised during a raid. She went to see the local prosecutor and arranged for three volunteer clinic patients to testify that they had indeed received contraceptives. Griswold and Buxton were given the choice of appearing at the police station on their own or being dramatically arrested, handcuffed, and hauled off before the TV cameras. Representatives of an older, more discreet generation, they opted for the police station. They were fined $100—and given the legal grounding they needed to go to court to challenge the law.

In 1965 the Supreme Court ruled 7 to 2 that Connecticut's law violated married couples' constitutional rights, and in 1972 the Court closed the circle by tossing out the Massachusetts law as well, making it clear that the right to use birth control belonged to everyone, not just to married couples. (In 1973, in the ultimate American benediction, the Internal Revenue Service declared that the Pill was a tax-deductible medicine.) All around the nation, women lined up to get prescriptions. "We had an option, so you took it," said June LaValleur, who had always felt using a diaphragm "kind of broke up the spontaneity of things."

Unmarried women who did not have a personal physician—or whose family doctor might disapprove—continued to have a harder time, especially if they were not living in big cities with liberal attitudes toward sex. In the 1960s, in most states, the age of adulthood was 21, and it was illegal for a doctor to prescribe birth control to an unmarried woman under that age without a parent's consent. It was not until the 1970s that Congress, embarrassed by the fact that young men of 18 were being sent off to the war in Vietnam while they were still legally children, passed the Twenty-sixth Amendment, which reduced the age of majority to 18. Until then, even unmarried 20-year-olds generally had to claim they were engaged and on the verge of marriage to cadge a birth control prescription from a physician.

College health services slowly began prescribing birth control pills for students who wanted them, and some parents made sure their children arrived on campus with a supply already in hand. When Tawana Hinton started college in 1970, her mother marched her off to the gynecologist. "It was like, 'You will go to college on the Pill,'" Hinton recalled. "And I did."

Planned Parenthood clinics were another crucial source—Alison Foster remembered that her boarding school ferried interested students to the nearest clinic. "And when I was in college, it was like candy," she said. "You just went to the health center and they gave them to you." But only 4 percent of the women who were taking the Pill in 1969 got it through Planned Parenthood, and even those who had the name of a sympathetic doctor were sometimes too embarrassed to follow through. Wendy Woythaler got the Pill while she was at Mount Holyoke in the late '60s, and when she looks back, she remembers searching for an office down a dark alley: "It was probably a fine, upstanding gynecologist somewhere in town. But when you're thinking, 'I'm not supposed to be doing this,' it feels like you're going down a dark alley."

"There was a stigma attached to it if you weren't married," said Maria K. "I didn't want to go to the drugstore and buy birth control pills because everybody would know I was having sex. Oh, heavens!"

"WHORES DON'T GET PREGNANT."

For every Linda LeClair, who seemed to have her finger right on the '60s zeitgeist, there were many more young women like Maria K. Maria—whose mother had wound up cooking in a home for elderly women when her father died—walked into the new morality without the sophistication to protect herself from its consequences. She got the news she was pregnant while she was working as a secretary at a local college in a small town in upstate New York. "At that time, if you got pregnant, you either got married or you went away and came back unpregnant," she said.

In 1967, when Maria had her child, the idea that an unmarried woman would simply raise a baby herself was almost unheard-of, particularly in small towns. Most girls just married the father. Others got abortions or went off to homes for unwed mothers, where they gave the baby up for adoption and returned from what was generally described as a long stay with an out-of-town relative. Judy Riff remembered that one of her friends at their all-girls Catholic college got pregnant her sophomore year, "and one minute she was there and the next minute she was gone. It was like she was never there...I don't know what happened to her." The very idea of having a baby out of wedlock "was just so awful...," Riff said, "that probably would have to be the worst thing that could have happened to any of us."

Most women had no idea how to obtain an abortion, which was illegal everywhere until the late 1960s. Maria, who was Catholic, never considered the option. Consulting her parish priest, she went to a home for unwed mothers in a nearby city. She was interviewed on arrival by a "kind, compassionate, and practical" woman who told her that the baby's chances of being adopted would be low. The man who fathered Maria's baby was blind, and at a time when adoptive parents had a large supply of illegitimate babies to choose from, any hint of a possible imperfection could be disqualifying. "She said even though it couldn't be genetically passed on to my son, that he would be very difficult to adopt if it was known that one of his parents was not sighted. And she told me that I seemed like a nice girl and she believed...that I would make a good mother."

When Maria decided to keep her son, her mother told her that a baby is always a wonderful thing and behaved "like an angel," her daughter recalled. But otherwise, "I became an outcast." She had trouble finding a landlord who would rent to an unmarried mother, and she lost her job. "I think they probably thought I was a bad example in the college atmosphere and so forth." And far worse trouble was around the corner. "About a year and a half later, I was pregnant again. And I was really up a creek."

When she got the news, Maria broke down in the doctor's office. "Everybody's going to think that I'm a whore," she cried.

"Whores don't get pregnant," the doctor said. "They're smarter than that."

"REMEMBER, ALL OF US HAD TAKEN THE PILL."

The Pill had been developed by Dr. Gregory Pincus, a biologist recruited by Margaret Sanger, who was more successful in revolutionizing medical contraception than she was in lobbying the Connecticut state legislature. It posed unique questions when it came to safety. Unlike most medication, it was intended to be taken over long periods of time by healthy women. Risks that might seem acceptable if you were, say, controlling diabetes loomed a lot larger if there was no disease to cure. Cases of blood clotting were reported, and women began to worry that they were being put at risk of heart attacks or strokes. The Food and Drug Administration began research, and in 1970 a Senate committee headed by Gaylord Nelson of Wisconsin held hearings on the Pill's safety. Some women immediately noticed that all the senators doing the investigating were male—no small surprise, since 99 percent of the Senate was of one gender and Margaret Chase Smith couldn't be everywhere. But all the people invited to speak were men as well. Barbara Seaman, the author of the powerful book *The Doctors' Case Against the Pill,* had not been invited. There were no women scientists or consumers who had experienced bad effects. "Remember, all of us had taken the Pill, so we were there as activists, but also as concerned women," said Alice Wolfson, who led a protest that disrupted the proceedings.

The FDA eventually ordered that birth control pills come with an insert describing possible health risks, and a Gallup survey found that 18 percent of those who had been taking the Pill stopped. Many turned to intrauterine devices (IUDs)—until the most popular model, known as the Dalkon Shield, had to be pulled from the market due to questions about its own safety. Meanwhile, researchers were discovering that the Pill was far stronger than necessary. Gradually, the amount of estrogen dropped to less than a third of what was in the earliest versions, and progesterone to less than a tenth. The controversy over the Pill died away, but it turned out to be only the first shot in what would become a long-running feud between American women and the traditional medical community.

For generations, women had been American doctors' best clients and abused guinea pigs. When physicians learned how to use a hypodermic syringe in the mid-nineteenth century, one of the first things they did was to inject opium or morphine into their patients, sometimes on a daily basis, creating legions of addicted housewives. Surgeons removed reproductive organs in women who showed signs of promiscuity or masturbation, and castrated more than 100,000 around the turn of the century. And although those abuses were long over by the 1960s, there was still a widespread presumption that a woman's uterus became useless once she passed childbearing age and should be removed—often along with her ovaries—for minor problems or as a precaution against disease developing in the future. When a doctor discovered a lump in a patient's breast, it was standard procedure to have the woman sign a form consenting to have the entire breast removed even before the biopsy was performed. (Susan Ford, whose mother, Betty, saved many American women's lives by being open about her mastectomy when she was first lady, noted that in those days, the patient woke up to discover she "either had a Band-Aid or no breast.")

Doctors, who were overwhelmingly male, had an authoritarian attitude toward all patients in the postwar era, but they saw more women, and they were particularly inclined to treat female patients as children who panicked easily and were better off knowing as little as possible. When 23-year-old Barbara Winslow of Seattle found a lump in her breast, she and her husband went to a doctor. He told them that he would do a biopsy and that if it proved malignant, he would immediately perform a complete mastectomy. He then handed a consent form to her husband to sign. When Winslow asked why she was not the one asked to give permission, the doctor said, "Because women are too emotionally and irrationally tied to their breasts." Nora Ephron wrote that it seemed every week brought "a new gynecological atrocity tale. A friend who specifically asks not to be sedated during childbirth is sedated. Another friend who has a simple infection is treated instead for gonorrhea, and develops a serious infection as a side effect of penicillin. Another woman tells of going to see her doctor one month after he has delivered her first child, a deformed baby, born dead. His first question: 'Why haven't you been to see me in two years?'"

In 1969 a small group of women in Boston decided to get together and share their "feelings of frustration and anger toward…doctors who were condescending, paternalistic, judgmental, and noninformative." As time went on, the group felt it was on to something worth sharing. The members created a course on women and their bodies that in turn became the basis for *Our Bodies, Ourselves,* a book that talked simply and explicitly about sex, birth control, venereal disease, lesbianism, childbirth, and menopause. Lessons on anatomy and basic biology were interspersed with personal testimony, offering the reader the comforting sense that whatever she was feeling or was worried about had happened to somebody else before. "I will tell you that a book we all had was *Our Bodies, Ourselves,*" said Kathy Hinderhofer, who went to college in the early '70s. "You had to have that." Other women started medical self-help projects, some focusing on informal classes that trained students in basics such as breast examinations, and others evolving into full-blown medical

clinics. (A few went over the deep end and began urging women to extract their monthly menstrual flow and perform do-it-yourself abortions with a syringe.) By 1975 nearly two thousand projects were scattered across the United States.

"IT IS AS EASY AS BEING THE LOG ITSELF."

The sexual revolution was about more than whether women should be able to feel as free as men to have sex before marriage. It was also about whether women—single or married—had as much right to *enjoy* sex. Most postwar manuals on how couples could improve their physical relationship centered on the man. The woman's role pretty much involved lying there. The experts did not generally go as far as the authors of *Modern Woman: The Lost Sex,* an influential postwar diatribe against the nontraditional female that decreed that for a woman, having sex was "not as easy as rolling off a log…It is easier. It is as easy as being the log itself." But they almost all seemed to disapprove of too much aggressive activity on her part. And there was a virtual consensus that women should attain satisfaction from conventional penetration.

Many women had little information about what went on in other people's bedrooms. The popular magazines were vague, and what specifics they did impart were about how to make husbands happy, not how to give wives sexual satisfaction. In a 1957 article called "How to Love Your Husband" in *Coronet,* for instance, author Hannah Lees approvingly described an interview with an "unselfish" wife who admitted, in the language of the era, to faking orgasms:

"I have never had that feeling," she said, "that wild emotion that many other women have. But my husband, he expects it. I love him. So I try to make him happy." She spread her hands and shrugged, and her face was soft and tender...Maybe her husband was missing something by not having a wife who could match his strong physical need with hers. But I had an idea it made no difference.

Even Helen Gurley Brown, so eager to encourage her readers to have affairs, was silent about what a single girl should do if she didn't enjoy the sex—except to suggest seeing a psychiatrist. And less than half of married women and 38 percent of single women said they talked frankly about sex with their friends or female relatives, according to that famous Gallup survey. Even if they did share confidences, what they learned could often be misleading. Jane Alpert, a high school student in the early '60s, was part of a cool bohemian crowd in Queens. Her role model, Beatrice, "the first girl I knew who claimed not to be a virgin," bragged to Alpert that she had had vaginal orgasms, "which were the best kind."

While their mothers had not necessarily been reared to expect real physical pleasure from lovemaking, the postwar generation wanted intimacy and partnership in every aspect of marriage. Many women who failed to get much pleasure themselves found solace in creating the illusion of success by writhing, moaning, and simulating orgasm. (Robin Morgan said that when she confessed to her husband that she often faked orgasm with him, she was convinced "I was the only woman in the world sick enough to have done this.") It was no wonder that experts suspected more than half of American women were "frigid."

Many women got reeducated by *Human Sexual Response*. The book, which was published in 1966 by William Masters and Virginia Johnson, was the product of eleven years of direct laboratory observation of nearly seven hundred people who had volunteered to have sex while the authors ran cameras and measured their heart and brain activity. Masters and Johnson found, among many, many other things, that women were capable of more intense and enduring sexual response than men, and that, contrary to what Jane Alpert's best friend told her, vaginal orgasms were not the best kind. While the book itself was written in hard-to-read scientific terminology, it was interpreted, summarized, explained, and debated all over the mainstream media for the rest of the decade.

Women began to argue—out loud—that the right to satisfying sexual experience was important, perhaps right up there with equal pay. In 1970 "Myth of the Vaginal Orgasm," an essay by Anne Koedt, explained that the reason "the so-called frigidity rate among women is phenomenally high" was because men were looking for their mates' orgasms in the wrong place. In a call to action that was copied, reprinted, and shared all around the country, Koedt urged, "We must begin to demand that if certain sexual positions now defined as 'standard' are not mutually conducive to orgasm, they no longer be defined as standard."

American society had always given women only one big responsibility when it came to sex—stopping boyfriends from going too far. Now they seemed to be in charge of everything, from providing the birth control to making sure they had orgasms. A great deal of research was obviously required. Workshops sprouted up on college campuses, offering women tips on all sorts of hitherto-undiscussed matters. Arriving at Antioch as a freshman, Alison Foster showed up for a meeting of the campus women's group. About half an hour into the proceedings, she recalled, "everybody was supposed to look at their cervix. We all got little mirrors." Nora Ephron, reporting on similar gatherings in New York, commented, "It is hard not to long for the days when an evening with the girls meant bridge."

"...THIS VELVET BATHROBE."

The sexual revolution was only one part of an extraordinary era, when a large number of relatively privileged young people felt free to plan the reinvention of the world, confident that the world would pay attention. They had an unprecedented amount of time to devote to the task because the still-booming economy made it easy to drop in and out of the job market at will. The cost of living was very low, particularly for those who were willing to share space in a rural farmhouse or urban tenement. Travel was cheap, and airlines gave students special passes that allowed them to fly standby for cut-rate prices. When you got to wherever you were going, there was almost always a bed where you could crash for the night in the apartments of fellow members of the youth culture.

Political activists shut down their universities over the war in Vietnam, free speech, or the administration's failure to accept their advice on matters ranging from how to invest the endowment to where to locate the new gym. And even the most apolitical took part in the cultural revolution—a '60s watchword for everything from hippie communes to the Beatles. Standards for fashion and physical appearance underwent a drastic makeover. Clothes became comfortable, colorful, and dramatic. Girls tie-dyed everything, dipping knotted fabric into bright colors to produce psychedelic patterns. ("I ruined many a sink in the dorm," recalled Barbara Arnold.) They bought long, loose-fitting peasant dresses and blouses and vintage clothes. "I was really part of that hippie, thrift-store, make-your-own-blouses-out-of-your-mother's-linen-tablecloth scene," said Alison Foster. She still has a very clear memory of the moment she stopped liking anything the department stores sold and gave her patronage to the secondhand shops downtown. "I'd go to the East Village and buy funky furs and velvet coats . . . I loved that stuff." When it was time to dress up for Sunday dinner at her boarding school, Foster donned "this velvet bathrobe—which I thought was the height of sophistication. It wasn't even mine. It was my roommate's, but I wore it as many times as I could get away with it." The whole point, she concluded, was being creative

"and not looking like our parents. That was very important to me. I look at kids now and I'm wearing very similar clothes to what a lot of the girls wear. But those days I didn't want to look like my parents."

It was nothing personal. Alison Foster got along very well with her mother, Anne Wallach. She had not minded being the only girl in her circle whose mother worked, "and I liked it that she didn't hover." Still, whether a young woman adored her mother or loathed her, if she grew up in the '60s, she probably vowed that her life would be far different—more exciting, less concerned about what the neighbors would think, more in touch with her feelings, more *real*. (Or, as Wellesley College's 1969 student commencement speaker, Hillary Rodham, put it: "A more immediate, ecstatic, and penetrating mode of living.") And no matter what else she did to align herself with the revolutions at hand, clothing marked her as part of the brave new world of change and adventure.

Everything was supposed to be natural. Some women stopped shaving their legs, which quickly turned into a political issue. There was, recalled Anselma Dell'Olio, "a tendency to gauge one's feminist credentials by look, address, and degree of hairiness." (A letter writer to the *Times* denounced "arm-pit Feminists, women whose involvement with the ethic of body hair has overpowered other considerations.") It was easy to wear shorter skirts because panty hose had arrived on the scene. Basically the same leotards that dancers had always worn, panty hose quickly displaced stockings as the undergarment of choice. (Wendy Woythaler's mother was shocked at the idea of throwing out two legs' worth of panty hose when only one had a run in it, so she cut off the offending legs and told her daughter to wear a pair with a good right leg over a pair with a good left. "Oh God, it was awful." Woythaler sighed.) And it was easy not to bother with skirts at all, because by the end of the decade women had given themselves permission to spend their entire lives in jeans if they felt like it. "I used to have to go to an Army/Navy store to buy blue jeans," recalled Alison Foster. "There was a point where nobody sold blue jeans. And then everybody sold blue jeans."

Black women let their hair blossom out into Afros, and white college students let theirs fall straight down their backs, banishing the nighttime roller routine. Neither style, unfortunately, was always as easy to achieve in reality as in theory. Most white women did not actually have perfectly straight hair, and many resorted to ironing it. Some black women discovered that their hair, when left to its own volition, just hung there. "I decided I was going to show some of my blackness and have this Afro," said Tawana Hinton. "My hair was long, and I did it by trying to roll it and wet it…It didn't work. It didn't last but a minute, you know." Josie Bass, who had given up trying to get her hair to cooperate, was invited to a dance at the University of Maryland by a student she fancied, who himself sported an impressive Afro, so she went downtown and invested in an Afro wig. She was so intent on her errand she didn't really notice that one of the many urban riots of the era was beginning to break out. "The dance was canceled and I never wore that wig." She laughed.

"I THOUGHT I WAS THE ONLY PERSON LIKE THAT IN THE WORLD."

It looked for a while as though the sexual revolution applied to only heterosexuals. "The whole idea of homosexuality made me profoundly uneasy," said Betty Friedan. The leader of the National Organization for Women had a tactical concern about the fact that opponents had tried to undermine the movement by depicting it as a lesbian cabal. But beyond that, it was pretty clear Friedan, like many Americans, was just uncomfortable with "the whole idea."

For most of history, lesbianism was so little understood that it was actually pretty easy for gay women to live out their lives in peace and quiet. (When Martha Peterson, the Barnard president

who fought the Linda LeClair wars, died in 2006 at the age of 90, the *Times* obituary surprised many alumnae when it reported that she was "survived by her companion, Dr. Maxine Bennett.") Women had always slept together—the draftiness of most homes made cuddling up in bed extremely popular. And they had traditionally expressed their friendship for one another in intense terms that involved kissing and hugging and declarations of love. The shortage of men after major wars created a large population of unmarried women who often lived together. No one ever thought they were sharing their lives for any reason beyond companionship and convenience.

A woman who was attracted to members of her own sex thus had an easy time hiding it, if she chose to do so. But she probably had a hard time putting her feelings in any positive context. "I thought I was the only person like that in the world," said Carol Rumsey, who was 18 in 1960 when she felt stirrings for her girlfriend, the Jackie Kennedy look-alike. They were spending a last day together before the friend's impending marriage, "and we went to the movies and it was cold in Connecticut—and we got in the backseat and we snuggled up and we were just talking and all of a sudden we kissed and that was, you know, the first time that ever happened to me." And like many other women in her circumstances, Rumsey responded to her discovery by pretending nothing had changed and getting unhappily married.

At the time, while conservatives saw homosexuality as a sin, liberals saw it as an illness. (When *Ms.* began publication in 1971, an early issue assured readers that letting their sons play with dolls would not lead them into homosexuality, since "boys become homosexual because of disturbed family relationships, not because their parents allow them to do so-called feminine things.") No one had much of anything positive to say about it. *Time*, which had put the author Kate Millett on the cover when it wrote a glowing article about the women's liberation movement in 1970, rethought the whole issue when Millett acknowledged she was gay. The revelation about Millett's sexuality, *Time* said, was "bound to discredit her as a spokesman for her cause, cast further doubt on her theories, and reinforce the views of those skeptics who routinely dismiss all liberationists as lesbians."

Homosexuality was almost never referred to in the mainstream media, and when it was, the references were generally oblique—jokes that could go over the heads of more innocent readers and viewers. In the movies, gay characters were the cause of problems, if not disaster. In 1961 *The Children's Hour,* starring Audrey Hepburn and Shirley MacLaine, tackled the subject of lesbianism with sensitivity and an ending depressing enough to make the *BUtterfield 8* finale look like a situation comedy. Hepburn's and MacLaine's characters, the owners of a boarding school for young girls, are falsely accused of having an "unnatural" affair by an extraordinarily unpleasant student. They sue unsuccessfully for libel, and the school is destroyed. Curiosity-seekers come to gawk outside the house, and MacLaine—who turns out to have been nursing a secret passion for her friend all along—hangs herself in the bedroom.

The first attempt by lesbians to organize publicly may have been the Daughters of Bilitis, founded in 1953 in San Francisco. (By 1970 the editors of their magazine, *The Ladder,* felt they had made enormous progress when they proudly estimated that each issue was read or at least seen by "approximately 1,200 people.") Gene Damon, a writer for the magazine, said that to be a lesbian was to be regarded as "automatically out of the human race" and that she was constantly being asked questions such as "But what do you Lesbians do in the daytime?" Damon contributed an essay to the feminist book *Sisterhood Is Powerful* in 1970 that captured the feelings of persecution: "Run, reader, run right past this article, because most of you reading this will be women...and you are going to be frightened when you hear what this is all about. I am social anathema, even to you brave ones, for I am a Lesbian."

"SOCIETY HAS BEGUN TO MAKE IT AS ROUGH FOR VIRGINS..."

The prophets of the sexual revolution had more in mind than simply eliminating the double standard. The big thought of the 1960s was that sex should become a perfectly natural part of everyday life, not much more dramatic and profound than a handshake. If people would just give up the idea of sex as a sacred act between a man and a woman eternally bonded together, the argument went, they could throw off their repressions and inhibitions. Sharing and good feeling would triumph over jealousy and negativism. The world could make love, not war. The other famous slogan of the '60s—"If it feels good, do it"—might mean more than just an excuse for self-indulgence. It might mean a happier society or even world peace. The hippie movement in particular gave great credence to the idea that if people were busy taking off their clothes and coupling, they were not likely to be in the mood for more negative activity.

Alison Foster experienced that side of the sexual revolution very suddenly, after spending her first two years of high school at a private all-girls school in Manhattan with a very strong sense of decorum. "We had dances where they literally had a ruler— if you were dancing too close, the ladies would come and separate you." She transferred in 1970 to a progressive boarding school, where she discovered a very different world. "Everybody was sleeping with everybody. Professors were sleeping with students. I had a poetry teacher sleeping with a tenth grader. We had professors modeling in the nude in our art classes. We had a lake that we would all skinny-dip in. So I went from what I thought was this very sophisticated New York girl to—oh my God, I am so over my head." She loved the school. ("Everybody was talking about feelings. It was just the kind of thing I liked.") But she saw the damage that the new theories about free love could do. "I had friends—they acted like it didn't bother them, but they felt very bad the next morning when he didn't call. I figured out pretty early on that I wasn't going to do that. That I could figure out."

The pressure to give in to the code of free love was a lot more difficult to resist when it was ideological as well as personal. A 1966 novel called *The Harrad Experiment* was an enormous hit on college campuses (to the tune of 2.5 million copies sold in a year and a half), and it was one of those bestsellers that attracts readers with its ideas, not riveting prose or well-drawn characters. *Harrad* was the tale of a group of wholesome college students brought together to learn how to experience sex in a completely honest, open atmosphere. By graduation, the heroes and heroines have, as promised, taken "the long step away from primitive emotions of hate and jealousy" and formed a six-person group marriage. "Every Sunday when my new husband for the week joins me in my room, I feel like a new bride all over again," reported one of the women. "Sometimes I wake up in the night and for a sleepy moment I may forget whether I am with Stanley, Jack, or Harry, and then I feel warm and bubbly." As the curtain fell, they were on their way to settle in an underpopulated state out west, where they planned to take over the legislature and create a utopia where every young citizen would have the right to a free college education, along with cohabitation, nude beaches, and humanistic group sex.

The ideology of the sexual revolution meshed into another '60s phenomenon, the political upheaval known as the New Left. Although young leftists came in all sorts of packages, many saw monogamy as just another form of private property, and free love as a kind of socialism of the flesh. "Certainly it was a time of fairly extensive sleeping around, a time when couples who remained monogamous were not proclaiming the fact from the rooftops," said Priscilla Long, a writer and political activist. Jane Alpert, who had traveled a long road from her high school in Queens to a Lower East Side household of two men and two women in intertwining relationships, became suspicious of a new couple her lover wanted to bring into the circle. "I considered their intention to marry reason enough to exclude them," she said.

Of course, if sex was all about *sharing,* anyone who refused to share was seen, in some quarters, as selfish or repressed or both. "I think there was subtle pressure," said Pam Andrews. "You were a truly liberated person that was going to build a new world, a new idealistic world." Women were still in charge of drawing the lines but were left with fewer arguments against going all the way. Rejected men told them they were sexually repressed or accused them of failing to sympathize with the fact that the men might be drafted for the war in Vietnam. At the time, one woman compared the men she knew to "rabbits," adding, "It was so boring you could die." While most women would not have wanted to go back to a time when they were expected to save themselves for the man they would marry, some did feel that things had gone overboard. "The invention of the Pill made millions for the drug companies, made guinea pigs of us, and made us all the more 'available' as sex objects," raged Robin Morgan. "If a woman didn't want to go to bed with a man *now* she must be hung up." Gloria Steinem wrote that "in the fine old American tradition of conformity, society has begun to make it as rough for virgins...as it once did for those who had affairs before marrying."

Keepsake Pages

When you were in high school and college, how far did a good girl let her boyfriend go?

_____

_____

_____

_____

_____

_____

_____

_____

Where did you get your information on sex?

_____

_____

_____

_____

_____

_____

_____

_____

If you went to college and lived in a dorm, what were the rules about entertaining boys in your room?

_____

_____

_____

_____

_____

_____

Did you assume you would have to be a virgin when you got engaged—or married?

_____

_____

_____

_____

_____

_____

Did you expect to be married soon after you got out of school? Did girls worry if they hadn't found a mate by the time they graduated?

_____

_____

_____

_____

_____

_____

When did you first hear about the Pill? When did you first use it? How hard was it to get?

_____

_____

_____

_____

_____

_____

_____

_____

_____

_____

When did you first understand about homosexuality? Who was the first person you knew who came out?

_____

_____

_____

_____

_____

_____

_____

_____

_____

_____

More Thoughts and Memories

More Thoughts and Memories

8. Women's Liberation

"A CLASSIC EXAMPLE OF LIBERAL MOTHER-DAUGHTER CONFLICT."

Jeannette Rankin, the first woman ever elected to Congress, was a Montana pacifist with extraordinary grit and unbelievably bad timing. She had been in office only four days in 1917 when she was called upon to vote on American entry into World War I. Her "nay" cost her the seat, and it took more than two decades before she was able to stage a comeback. Her constituents finally sent her to Washington again in 1941—just before Pearl Harbor was attacked. As the only member of the House to vote against going to war, she effectively ended her political career.

So what better name for a massive women's protest against the war in Vietnam than the Jeannette Rankin Brigade? Rankin herself, still going strong at 87, volunteered to lead the march. It took place on the opening day of Congress in 1968 and drew five thousand demonstrators. Many of them were dressed in black, in memory of sons, brothers, and fathers lost in combat. It was the largest gathering of women for a political event since the suffrage days, and bringing all those people together had not been easy. The organizers had cast their nets wide, hauling in church groups, civil rights groups, labor groups, and community groups, as well as the usual antiwar coalitions. Their success made two things inevitable: First, although many marchers had been hoping to do something dramatic, such as civil disobedience with mass arrests, there was no way that an event involving so many respectable organizations was going to be anything but well-behaved. Second, when it came time for speeches, there were going to be a lot of them.

Washington police had turned out in force to make sure the marchers did not get anywhere near the Capitol grounds, and the protesters obediently stood across the street, shivering in the snow, while a few representatives delivered their antiwar petition to House and Senate leaders, who promised to refer it "to the appropriate committee." Grumbling about lawmakers who didn't have the courage to take on a bunch of "old ladies," Rankin then led the demonstrators to their fallback destination—the Shoreham Hotel. There, they held a Congress of Women, in which that long list of speakers addressed the somewhat deflated protesters.

The speakers, like the audience, were mostly middle-aged veterans of earlier political struggles, from civil rights to labor organizing to protests against the testing of nuclear bombs. They had grown up in an era when any show of opposition to authority was widely viewed as subversive. Like the carefully dressed black students who sat in at the lunch counters in the South, they went out of their way to make a good impression, to convince people they were typical Americans, not Communist saboteurs. "You know, we'd get dressed in mink coats and hats and gloves to look like the woman next door," said Amy Swerdlow of Women Strike for Peace, who was one of the organizers.

Suddenly, a group of younger, rowdier, scruffier women took the stage, carrying a papier-mâché coffin decorated with curlers, garters, and hair-spray cans. Beating on drums and tooting on kazoos, they sang a dirge to the corpse—a blank-faced, blond-haired dummy representing Traditional Womanhood "who passed with a sigh to her Great Reward...after 3,000 years of bolstering the egos of the Warmakers."

This was not the way the women in the audience were used to conducting their events. Many of them had spent their lives trying to look as much as possible *like* Traditional Womanhood while they picketed the White House.

The performers were from New York Radical Women, a group that had been in existence for less than a year. While most of them had been involved in student protests and civil rights, they were making an initial foray into this particular world of older activist women. They passed out leaflets that denounced the march as too passive—all about "weakness, political impotence, and tears." They called out to all "radical women" to join them at a countercongress—a protest against the protest—and marched off to another part of the hotel.

Swerdlow had a feeling that the women onstage were looking at the audience and resentfully seeing their own mothers, who went to college and then retired to conventional domesticity. New York Radical Women had representatives on the planning committee for the march, she recalled, "and they were giving us a hard time from the beginning." Despite their status as the new group on the block, the younger women had bullied the organizers into paying for an extra hotel room to accommodate the countercongress that was going to be attacking them. It was, Swerdlow thought wryly, "a classic example of liberal mother-daughter conflict."

Swerdlow walked over to the countersession, expecting to hear "more radical and militant strategies for ending the war." Instead, she found young women "rushing to the mike to speak passionately, but often incoherently, about the way in which the traditional women's peace movement condoned and even enforced the gender hierarchy in which men made war and women wept." The gathering was so "chaotic," Swerdlow wrote later, that most of the older women "came away more confused than enlightened, but definitely shaken."

It was, in a way, the passing of a torch. Jeannette Rankin was a member of the first wave of twentieth-century American feminism, the rapidly dwindling band of suffragists who had won women the right to vote. Now the performers toting that papier-mâché coffin were heralding a second wave, which would become known as the women's liberation movement.

The first wave won the ballot but failed to eliminate the wall between women and the male-controlled public world. The second wave wanted an equal role in everything—business, the arts, sports, politics, science, and academia. It had begun a couple of years earlier, in Betty Friedan's hotel room in Washington. Now it was about to explode into a movement that included reformers such as Friedan and revolutionaries such as New York Radical Women, with countless students, factory workers, teachers, and housewives in between. It was a moment when history opened up to every woman who was ready to join a march, start a consciousness-raising group, or give her daughter a baseball and bat for Christmas.

The movement's various factions had little in common. The reformers did not want to overthrow the existing system—they wanted to open the gates so that women could become part of it. And they had little interest in changing the rules for private relationships between men and women. "This is not a bedroom war. This is a political movement," Friedan said. They envisioned themselves—and their daughters—marrying and having children while also sitting in corporate boardrooms or running for Congress. The leaders of the radical wing of the women's movement wanted to go much farther than simply leveling the playing field when it came to things like job opportunities. They were going to examine everything about American womanhood—in fact, about womanhood back to the time of the pharaohs. They intended to figure out what had kept their sex in such a secondary role. And then they were going to free women to be all they could be, even if that meant getting rid of capitalism or the nuclear family or the Judeo-Christian tradition, or anything else that got in the way. They were convinced that the things that were tormenting them in their private lives were really political. If you could connect all the dots and examine the patterns, you could identify the patriarchal forces that were keeping women down. They wanted to talk about everything from rape as a tool of male domination to the habit younger men had of referring to younger women as "chicks." Could a husband and wife really be equal partners or was marriage just a romantic form of serfdom? Was motherhood the most fulfilling role possible or a tool of male domination? Did high-heeled shoes remind anybody of foot binding?

American women were about to experience an extraordinary period of change that would undo virtually every assumption about the natural limitations of their sex. It was going to be a journey of many parts—terrifying and exhilarating, silly and profound, a path to half-realized dreams, unexpected disappointments, and unimaginable opportunities.

"Cool down, little girl."

The women who had been in their early teens in 1960 when *Mademoiselle* worried they might be too conservative to do anything interesting had wound up frolicking nude at Woodstock, shutting down college campuses to protest the war, and running off to the Summer of Love in San Francisco with flowers in their hair. They had come of age at a time of constant public turmoil. Those who had been freshmen in high school when President Kennedy was assassinated were freshmen in college when Robert Kennedy and Martin Luther King were murdered. There were 167 urban riots in 1967 alone, and the next year, when Dr. King was killed, the nation's cities seemed to be burning from coast-to-coast. They had watched the war in Vietnam go sour on the evening news, and the draft made it extremely personal. "One of the things I remember most vividly from my college years was sitting in front of the television set the first night they had the draft," said Laura Sessions Stepp. Picking dates by lottery, the Selective Service System revealed which young men's birthdays would doom them to be called up first and which would have numbers so high they were unlikely to be drafted at all. "They would read off the number, and I remember this guy Steven— his number was one of the first, and it was like, oh my God. And he just sat there. He was actually picked while we were watching TV. And there was a lot of sobbing and crying and it was horrible."

College campuses were hyperpolitical in the late 1960s, the scene of strikes and marches, sit-ins and "teach-ins" on behalf of civil rights, student power, and above all opposition to the war. The young women who would become part of the feminist second wave were almost all products of that passionate period. But they had often wound up sitting silent in political meetings or trying to speak and being ignored. In general, women had no more clout in leftist student politics than they had in Congress or on Wall Street. Just a few months before the Jeannette Rankin march, some of them had attended a New Politics conference in Chicago and proposed a resolution on women's rights. "By today's standards it wasn't very radical—equal pay for equal work, abortion on demand—but in those days it seemed very daring," said Jo Freeman. The committee in charge of vetting resolutions refused to let them bring it up for discussion. When they tried to challenge the ruling on the floor of the convention, they were completely ignored. One of the women, Shulamith Firestone, rushed to the podium in protest, Freeman said, and the chairman "literally patted her on the head."

"Cool down, little girl," he said. "We have more important things to do here than talk about women's problems."

After that meeting, some of the women got together and "talked about the contempt and hostility that we felt from the males on the New Left and we talked about our inability to speak in public," said Naomi Weisstein. "Why had this happened? All of us had once been such feisty little suckers."

It reminded them of the way their mothers had been treated at 1950s dinner parties, when all the questions and responses were directed toward the husbands. Women who were accepted into the leadership of the New Left tended to be the wives or girlfriends of the male leaders, just one breakup away from ostracism. Those in the rank and file could most frequently be found typing, copying, or fetching coffee. "I'll tell you, I was a whiz with a mimeograph machine. I can collate up a storm," said Margaret Siegel, who belonged to a chapter of the Students for a Democratic Society (SDS), the lead organization in the student antiwar movement. In a famous remark about a 1965 SDS meeting, one male attendee said that the "women made peanut butter, waited on tables, cleaned up, got laid. That was their role." Seattle women were stunned when a visiting SDS organizer from Chicago—who had been trying to develop revolutionary fervor in a white working-class neighborhood—explained that in order to relate to the young men in the community, "sometimes we all get together and ball some chick." The women demanded to know "what did that do to the chick's consciousness?" and the speaker eventually admitted that he had made up the story in order to appear tough. But the remark quickly took on the status of legend.

Antiwar protesters urged young men to resist the draft, chanting, "Girls say yes to boys who say no!" In previous American wars, from the Revolution on, legends rose up about patriotic young women who vowed never to give their hand to a man who failed to volunteer to serve his country. In the '60s the message was reversed, but the role assigned to women was pretty much the same.

It was a continuing complaint in the youthful counterculture. Hippie men were keen on getting in touch with their feelings and eliminating macho hang-ups about crying or showing their sensitive side. But there was a strong sentiment that women could reconnect with *their* most profound impulses by being domestic—nurturing others and cooking dinner. "What I have seen is a lot of very boorish men on some very heavy ego trips," wrote a woman who called herself Vivian Estellachild, in a report on ten months of living in two different communes where women were expected to do all the housework. Hippie men, she concluded, "act like suburban studs who look good but are selfish and rarely know how to do anything more than gain a little pleasure for themselves. Hippie women over 30 have that lean and desperate look." The Yippees, who were supposed to be the lighthearted side of the New Left, liked to suggest that men "shake a chick's tit instead of her hand."

The New Left was only a small sliver of America's young people, and the men who behaved so boorishly—like what would soon be known as "male chauvinist pigs"—were only a sliver of the sliver. But they had a profound impact on the cul-

ture of the women's liberation movement. It was probably no accident that the movement leader with the least confrontational style was Gloria Steinem, who had been born in 1934. "It's true that the women who were five to ten years younger than I had come out of a particular part of the male left that was very hostile and aggressive," Steinem said. "That had been their training ground. It probably took a while for that to go away."

When the women became more outspoken, some of the men reacted with a stunning rage. At the antiwar demonstrations in Washington during Richard Nixon's inauguration, the women decided that while the men were burning their draft cards, they would burn their voter registration cards to demonstrate that even though they were not subject to the draft, they felt disenfranchised. (A few reached out to Alice Paul, still living in the brick house in Washington, and suggested that she might want to join their protest. Paul, who had been jailed and had undergone force-feedings during a hunger strike in order to get the right to vote, said she would rather not.) At the Washington rally, Marilyn Webb was scheduled to give a speech announcing the women's plans. She framed her remarks mildly, assuring the crowd that "this isn't a protest against movement men." But the men were either bored or offended. "Take it off!" some of them cried. "Take her off the stage and fuck her!"

The women's movement would have arisen even if every single male activist had been as sympathetic as humanly possible. (And in fact many of them were.) But the bad behavior certainly helped to speed things along. "Was it my brother who listed human beings among the *objects* which would be easily available after the Revolution: 'Free grass, free food, free women, free acid, free clothes, etc.'?" asked Robin Morgan in a famous diatribe called "Goodbye to All That" which triumphantly announced, "WE ARE THE WOMEN THAT MEN HAVE WARNED US ABOUT." It was an essay that was reprinted everywhere there was a college campus and passed around women's groups all over the country. "Was it my brother who wrote 'Fuck your women till they can't stand up' and said that groupies were liberated chicks 'cause they dug a tit-shake instead of a handshake?" The final straw, Morgan said, was the male counterculture prediction that "men will make the Revolution—and make their chicks."

"Not my brother, no," she concluded. "Not my revolution."

"EVERY SINGLE WOMAN HATED HER BREASTS."

In Baltimore, a little community of antiwar activists had settled in a working-class neighborhood of brownstone houses. A few of the women went to Washington for the Jeannette Rankin march and came back bursting with news about the New York women and their coffin, and ideas for starting a women's consciousness-raising group. "That really was a big boost for us," said Vicki Cohn Pollard, a member of the community. "We really got fired up."

The consciousness-raising group was the central tool of the women's movement, and it was as simple as a handful of people sitting down together once a week to talk about being women. "One woman wanted us to talk about how we felt about our breasts," said Pollard. "We went around, and of the ten or twelve women, every single woman hated her breasts. They were too big or too small or too droopy or too perky. Everything you could imagine. We were all just astonished and felt so deeply the body hatred that represented. It was like— whoa, what was that all about in terms of the bigger picture?"

The idea, initially, was that the discussions would help women to discern patterns that would eventually create a portrait of the political, cultural, and economic forces that had kept their sex in such a secondary position. But the groups actually became whatever their members wanted them to be. At least one in New York sent shock troops out to confront members' unsatisfactory husbands. Six stormed into the office of a spouse who worked at *Penthouse* magazine, said Rosalyn Baxandall, "and

demanded he resign from the sexist rag. To our surprise he did." In many more groups, the women encouraged one another to "go for it," whatever the "it" of their dreams might be, and created a safe atmosphere for poking into painful areas such as body image or low self-esteem.

Sitting and talking with the other women in her group, Vicki Cohn Pollard mentally revisited her mother, who had seemed so harsh and hard to live with when Vicki was a child. Pollard, who had little talent for domesticity herself, tried to envision what it would be like to be restricted to a life of child-rearing and housekeeping. "I began healing with my mother in a way that is one of the most treasured things in my life…She was so suppressed and so angry because there was no place for her in the world. She wasn't a natural mom and she was stuck doing something she felt horrible about. My heart totally opened to her." Although Pollard never shared her insights with her mother, and her mother never examined her own feelings about the life she had led, "it was my shift that mattered," Pollard said. "We spent the rest of her life very, very close."

The conversations also raised the members' sensitivity to their common history as American women. They had almost all grown up in the United States in the postwar era, had watched *Bonanza* with its massive female mortality rate or *Father Knows Best* with its lessons about the inadvisability of competing with boys. They had seen movies such as *Gidget,* where the heroine learns that the highest calling of a woman "is to bring out the best in a man." They had been discouraged from taking math and science courses, and most had come of age without ever having met a female doctor or lawyer. They had spent their adolescence waiting by the phone for a boy to call, because a woman never ever made the first move. If they let their boyfriends dominate them, if they were hesitant to speak up or take the lead, it was not all because of sexist men. They were carrying a great deal of baggage that had been on their backs long before they started being ignored at political meetings.

"WE TAKE THE WOMAN'S SIDE IN EVERYTHING."

Virtually everyone who spent any time in a consciousness-raising group experienced what the writer Jane O'Reilly called a "click of recognition"—"that parenthesis of truth around a little thing that completes the puzzle of reality in women's minds." It was the moment when a woman realized how the men in her life really saw her, or what her place in society really was. O'Reilly offered up a story from a friend who had been invited for lunch at the executive dining room of a company for which she was doing some work. Later, when she told her husband about her day, she described what she thought was a funny scene of pompous men around the table in a stuffy room. But her husband started laughing before she got to the punch line. "Ho, ho," he chortled. "My little wife in an executive dining room."

"Everybody had had those moments, and you could remember when yours had been," said Nora Ephron. "One of my earliest was when I worked my summer internship in the White House. My fiancé at the time had come to visit and I walked him through, past one fabulous room named after what color it was painted after another. And at the end of the tour he looked at me and said, 'No wife of mine is going to work in a place like this.' And it was so funny because—I hadn't exactly shown him a sweatshop. It was the White House! But he thought he could say where I was going to work. Those things happened for quite a while before anybody added them up and said, 'Ka-ching! This isn't right.'"

Catherine Roraback was 49 when she went to a meeting of the National Lawyers Guild, an organization of civil rights attorneys, in 1969. The younger women at the gathering organized a women's caucus that Roraback remembered as "really a consciousness-raising session." As she sat listening and feeling much older than the rest of the people in the room, she thought back over her life and realized for the first time the compromises she had made in order to deal with the virtually all-male world of the courthouse, the raw jokes and sexist remarks she had simply smiled at or ignored. "It was as though I had scars on me and people were pulling the scars off of me, leaving the exposed tissue, you know? It was a terrible experience, but a very healthy one."

Some groups turned outward, inspired to public protest—a sit-in at a department store with a male-only dining room or a letter-writing campaign to a newspaper that allowed only boys to have its delivery routes. And others found themselves transformed into the movement's revolutionary vanguard. "The history we learned, the political sophistication we discovered, the insights into our own lives that dawned on us!" wrote Robin Morgan. "I couldn't believe—still can't—how angry I could become from deep down and way back, something like a five-thousand-year buried anger. It makes you very sensitive—raw even—this consciousness. Everything from the verbal assault on the street, to a 'well-meant' sexist joke your husband tells, to the lower pay you get at work (for doing the same job a man would be paid more for), to television commercials, to rock song lyrics, to the pink or blue blanket they put on your infant in the hospital nursery...everything seems to barrage your aching brain, which has fewer and fewer protective defenses to screen such things out."

Women like Morgan began to take their newfound perceptions public, writing essays, staging protests, causing trouble. But they did not have one unifying theory about the sources of oppression. Was it all men or only some? Capitalism? The ageless tradition of patriarchy? "The dogma is that dogma is a mistake," said Gloria Steinem. "So if there was dogma it has to come out of experience. You listen to women's experience and take what is the most shared and build from there."

What some women built was a call to sexual warfare. "Women are an oppressed class," announced the group Redstockings. "Our oppression is total, affecting every facet of our lives. We are exploited as sex objects, breeders, domestic servants, and cheap labor...We identify the agents of our oppression as men ... *All men* have oppressed women ... We do not need to change ourselves, but to change men ...."

"We take the woman's side in everything," said the first principle of New York Radical Women.

Some, such as Shulamith Firestone, envisioned an end to marriage and nuclear families—Firestone hoped that in the future, babies could be conceived and grown in incubators. Some adopted "freedom" names like Warrior or Sarachild and tried to rid their lives of the taint of patriarchy. Meanwhile, back in the reform wing, people like the NOW founders believed both sexes could work together to create something new and fairer, and tried to express their ideas in terms that moderate housewives could relate to.

Since the women's movement was generally opposed to structure or leaders or spokeswomen, there was no way to decide which of the many contradictory theories was right, which of the threads was the most important. "No one article is meant to be 'representative' of anything other than some part of all women. The women's movement is a non-hierarchical one. It does things collectively and experimentally," Morgan wrote in the introduction to *Sisterhood Is Powerful*. In the end, whatever turned out to happen would be ... whatever turned out to happen.

"PEOPLE WOULD END UP LYING ON THE FLOOR."

The heroines of the battles of the mid-'60s, such as Betty Friedan and Pauli Murray and Muriel Fox, were a little shocked to realize that the younger generation regarded them as timid and perhaps passé. Granted, they had come of age long before the era of sexual/cultural/political revolt. ("I have some pictures of the early NOW meetings. We wore hats," said Muriel Fox.) And because they were working for specific political and legal goals, they had a keen eye toward public relations and how things would be portrayed in the media. But they did not think of themselves as conservative in any way—or at least not until they heard what the newcomers were saying.

In March 1968 Muriel Fox picked up the Sunday

New York Times and found an article on the "Feminist Wave" that quoted Ti-Grace Atkinson, the new 29-year-old president of New York's NOW chapter, comparing marriage to slavery and predicting that once women were really liberated, "people would be tied together by love, not legal contraptions. Children would be raised communally." That came as quite a surprise to many NOW members, who believed no such thing. Atkinson was a relatively new face in the movement. She was a wellborn Louisianan who was studying at Columbia. Betty Friedan had championed her as a NOW leader, at least in part in the hope that Atkinson, with her elegant Southern manner, would be good at fund-raising. "Betty and I were delighted to have this beautiful socialite be active in the movement," said Fox. Ti-Grace did bring a wealthy suitor to the Fox home for dinner once, Muriel remembers, and "it was a pleasant evening," but no donation came from it.

NOW was still a relatively small organization—the *Washington Post* put its membership at about twelve hundred, with a third in New York. But it was, for several years, the only game in town for the feminist movement. Women of every conceivable ideological stripe flocked to it. At the meetings of New York NOW, Fox began to notice a great number of new faces. Her husband, Dr. Shepard Aronson, was chairman of the board—an example of NOW's long-standing commitment to welcoming male members—and that *Times* article marked the beginning of what Aronson always referred to as "the worst year" of his life. In the summer, 28-year-old Valerie Solanas, a disturbed hanger-on in the New York art scene, shot artist Andy Warhol on behalf of what she called SCUM (Society for Cutting Up Men) and issued a manifesto calling for the elimination of the male sex. When Solanas was arraigned, Atkinson showed up with a crowd of supporters in court, while Solanas's lawyer, Florynce Kennedy, described her client as "one of the most important spokeswomen of the feminist movement."

This was not a thought that many other people shared. Jacqui Ceballos, another NOW leader who often sided with the radicals, remembers being at a meeting in a basement apartment when Atkinson asked for support "in getting NOW to take the Solanas case and declare Solanas the first martyr of the movement." Atkinson handed out copies of the SCUM manifesto, which Ceballos said she read while "howling with laughter" on the bus afterward. The whole episode horrified Marguerite Rawalt, who found herself being horrified with disturbing regularity. "While I am for having university women in our midst...I do not want to see NOW in the midst of student rioting on campuses, or quoted as supporting some of the leftist doctrines read every day," she wrote to Betty Friedan.

"The battles!" Fox recalled. "You had to go to every board meeting because you didn't know what was going to be passed." Many of the gatherings were held at the Fox apartment and went on endlessly. It was, Muriel understated, a very intense time. "People would end up lying on the floor. Not only from sleepiness but from total stress." Among other things, Atkinson and her supporters wanted to eliminate conventional officers and choose leaders by lot, with a great deal of rotation. It was part of a growing sentiment in the radical side of the women's movement that there should be no leaders, no "stars," and that every person's opinion had equal weight. When their proposals were rejected, Atkinson led them off to establish a group of their own.

In December of that "worst year," Fox picked up the newspaper and found that the *Times* had, after years of resistance, eliminated its separate male and female help-wanted ads. The original NOW agenda, she was reminded, had been moving briskly along. "I said. 'Okay, I guess it was all worth it.'"

"WOULD YOU BELIEVE A BRA BURNING?"

The nation as a whole had little inkling that anything new was going on with American women until September 1968, when Robin Morgan, whose experience as a former TV child star made her a creative feminist event planner, came up with an idea for a Miss America demonstration.

The Miss America pageant in Atlantic City had been the most-watched program on television in the early 1960s. The cultural upheaval of the decade had begun to dent its appeal a bit, but Miss America was still regarded by many as the icon of youthful beauty and grace—"the queen of femininity," as its theme song went. It was the one program that President Nixon said he let his daughters, Julie and Trisha, stay up late to watch. The entrants were judged for their beauty in swimsuits and evening wear; for their talent in a much-satirized competition that usually included both classical singing and flaming baton-twirling; and for their poise in answering questions such as "What do you think is the secret to attaining world peace?"

Waving placards saying NO MORE BEAUTY STANDARDS—EVERYONE IS BEAUTIFUL! and leading a sheep that was supposed to represent the contestants, the demonstrators indulged in some guerrilla theater while photographers—delighted at a break from the usual scripted activities—took endless photos. "We protest," read the leaflet prepared by New York Radical Women, *the degrading Mindless-Boob-Girlie Symbol. The Pageant contestants epitomize the roles we are all forced to play as women. The parade down the runway blares the metaphor of the 4-H Club county fair, where the nervous animals are judged for teeth, fleece, etc., and where the best 'Specimen' gets the blue ribbon."* Female passersby, Morgan said, seemed amused, while a group of men gathered across the police barricades, yelling, "Dykes! Commies! Lezzies." A few demonstrators managed to make their way into the front row of the auditorium balcony, where they unfurled a banner reading WOMEN'S LIBERATION and released what police said was a stink bomb but what the demonstrators claimed were just the ingredients from Toni Home Permanent, the sponsor.

Since the Atlantic City Fire Department had refused to provide a permit, the protesters skipped over their plans to light a ceremonial bonfire in which they would burn some implements of fashion-torture such as girdles and hair curlers. However, a sympathetic reporter for the *New York Post,* Lindsy Van Gelder, was working off the original program when she wrote a preview story: "Lighting a match to a draft card has become a standard gambit of protest groups in recent years, but something new is to go up in flames this Saturday. Would you believe a bra burning?" It would turn out to become critics' favorite byword for the entire women's movement. "I shudder to think that will be my epitaph — 'She invented bra burning,' " Van Gelder said later.

The Atlantic City demonstration was, in retrospect, a huge success — after all, we're still talking about it now as the moment when the women's movement made its debut on the national stage. But when it was over, some of the protesters expressed regret about the tone of the event and said they should have been expressing solidarity with the sisters who were being paraded around in their bathing suits, not making fun of them. (Morgan herself called the sheep "not my finest hour.") And everyone quickly grew to despise the term "bra burning." The demonstration captured traits that would come to define the movement. It was didactic and playful, smart and sometimes sophomoric. The women who participated succeeded beyond their wildest dreams, then disagreed about whether or not the message was appropriate. But one thing was certain: the protesters got more coverage in the national media than the new Miss America — Miss Illinois, a blond physical-education major who wowed the judges with her talent on the trampoline.

"IT MADE ME FEEL NORMAL."

By late 1969, what was up with women had become a huge national story. NOW was racking up legal and political victories, while the younger, more colorful feminists fascinated, thrilled, and appalled the nation. Newspapers, magazines, and television networks all ordered up features. Every time one

appeared, a new flood of letters would pour into any group or person or address that was mentioned. "Heartfelt and handwritten on pink or blue notepaper, they basically asked the same question, 'How do I find a Women's Liberation Group near me?' " said Susan Brownmiller, a member of New York Radical Women. "Most of the letters went unanswered. The new movement was swamped." Responding would have required an army of women with Marguerite Rawalt's letter-writing skills or technology that was yet to be invented. Women's liberation, Brownmiller noted, was "the last American movement to spread the word via mimeo machine." Rosalyn Baxandall, looking back, thought, "If we only had computers, what we might have done!"

By the end of 1970, when four out of five Americans told pollsters that they knew something about the movement, women all around the country had figured out how to organize themselves without direction from the feminist celebrities. Barbara Epstein, a graduate student in California, watched the movement spread "with an astonishing pace" through 1968 and 1969. "In Berkeley, women's consciousness-raising groups sprang up everywhere; when Women's Liberation…held a public meeting, it was difficult to find a hall big enough for the crowd." By the end of 1969, one count found thirty-five women's groups in San Francisco, thirty in Chicago, twenty-five in Boston, and fifty in New York.

Nearly every group found plenty of things to challenge in their own backyard. "We were considered really radical in Dubuque," said Ruth Cotter Scharnau, describing her group's fight to open up elementary school patrols to girls. ("The principal of one school said it was 'too cold' outside and that girls had other jobs: 'They wipe the tables after lunch and take care of the kindergarten children once in a while.' ") In a more fanciful effort, feminists at the Iowa State University town of Ames cast a witch spell on the university football stadium, in opposition to the money spent on men's sports. "The stadium which was under construction, did indeed collapse and had to be restarted. We just loved that, of course," said Irene Talbott, a president of Des Moines NOW.

Very little happened in the movement that didn't wind up being written down. "Any time a group of more than two or three feminists came together, they seemed to produce a newsletter at least, if not a newspaper or journal," said Mary Thom. In 1972 Thom was part of a group, led by Gloria Steinem, that founded the monthly *Ms.* Glossy as a traditional women's magazine, its first issue sold out in eight days and generated more than 20,000 letters—along with 26,000 subscription orders. In Baltimore, Vicki Cohn Pollard's group began *Women: A Journal of Liberation*, which grew to a circulation of more than 30,000 and lasted for twenty-five years. It was unusual in its success and duration but typical in that its creators were all dedicated to the point of obsession. "It was beautiful," Pollard said proudly. "We typed it up. We laid it out. We did absolutely everything to put that magazine together. We were up all night long. We were impassioned. My husband and I with our little baby went to Cambridge to hawk it on Harvard Square. Many hours standing in Harvard Square. And we sold a lot." To underwrite the costs, one of the founders refinanced her house. Pollard recalled the "wonderful thinking and tremendous heart" that went into their efforts, as well as their over-the-top rhetoric. Her own essay for the first issue was about childbirth, and it had one sentence that decreed: "All doctors are the enemies of women." The other editors suggested that "most doctors" or perhaps even "many doctors" might be better. "But I adamantly refused," she recalled wryly. "*All* doctors were the enemies of women."

All across the country, millions of women who never took part in a demonstration or joined a consciousness-raising group watched what was going on and had flashes of recognition. "I loved it. I loved it," said Georgia Panter, the flight attendant. "Oh, I wanted to be there—I was off somewhere and I wanted to be there when they were marching in the streets, with Gloria Steinem. I saw pictures of those little old ladies with gray hair—I thought, oh, I wanted to be part of that." Madeleine Kunin, the would-be journalist who was raising a family in Vermont and thinking about trying for a seat in the state legislature, felt as if the women's movement was "a timer, set years ago, which had gone off, telling me to run." Without it, she thought, she would have felt obliged to wait until her children were grown. And, Kunin said, the women's movement had a second effect: "It made me feel normal."

"WE CAN DO IT. HE'S SMALL."

In March 1970 about one hundred women took over the office of John Mack Carter, the publisher and editor of *Ladies' Home Journal*. At his side during the long day of confrontation was Lenore Hershey, the only woman in management, who demanded to know how many of "you girls" were married. The protesters unveiled a long list of demands, including free day care for all employees, no more "advertisements that degrade women," and an end to the popular "Can This Marriage Be Saved?" column. The protesters also wanted to eliminate all celebrity articles, "all articles oriented toward the preservation of youth," and "slanted romantic stories glorifying women's traditional role"—a litany that pretty much did away with the entire table of contents. They also demanded Carter turn the magazine over to the movement for one issue. In what was perhaps the more exciting moment of the confrontation, tiny Shulamith Firestone jumped on Carter's desk, intent on deposing him by force. "We can do it. He's small," she said, diving at the editor. One of the other women, Susan Brownmiller reported, "grabbed Shulie's arm and expertly flipped her off the desk and out of danger."

Like the Atlantic City demonstration, the *Ladies' Home Journal* takeover was a small and exceedingly colorful protest about a very serious issue. Americans saw virtually everything through the lens of the mass media, and the newspapers, magazines, and television stations that did the communicating hired very few women, promoted even fewer, and broadcast a vision of what the American woman ought to be that was both trivial and stultifying. In the end, Carter—who impressed the protesters by lasting through an eleven-hour siege without ever going to the bathroom—agreed to give the women an eight-page supplement. It appeared in August 1970, and the magazine said 34 percent of its readers liked it, while 46 percent gave thumbs-down and 20 percent had a mixed response. The women thought Carter had stacked the numbers, but the supplement definitely did have the flavor of something written by a committee. Nora Ephron, who was supposed to do some of the editing, remembered sitting in "a gigantic circle" with twenty-four other women while the submissions were read out loud. The pieces, Ephron recalled, were for the most part "polemical and humorless," but the editors were "not allowed to be critical in any way" since the code of the movement was to always offer support to other women's efforts. And when the supplement was finally put together, the layout involved "just bundles of type next to one another. So if you wanted to read it, it was the unfriendliest layout imaginable and God help you."

Looking back, Ephron thought that the real victory had been not the supplement but the demonstration itself. "They had gotten all this publicity, and it was really kind of great." It was the pattern that would continue throughout the movement's course. Things that seemed critical at the time, from the Commission on the Status of Women to the *Ladies' Home Journal* supplement, would turn out to be important not in themselves but for the way they changed the women who worked on them, and the country that watched it all happen.

In what was perhaps the ultimate compliment to its growing influence, the women's movement got an FBI tail in 1969. When field officers suggested that there might be better uses for the agents' time than hanging around what the bureau liked to call the WLM, director J. Edgar Hoover responded, "It is absolutely essential that we conduct sufficient

investigation to clearly establish subversive ramifications of the WLM and to determine the potential for violence presented by the various groups connected with this movement as well as any possible threat they may represent to the internal security of the United States." One FBI report from the early '70s announced that "the so-called Women's Liberation Movement had its origins in Soviet Russia," and offered a "look at the red-hot mommas" of the movement leadership. "Most seemed to be making a real attempt to be unattractive . . . One of the interesting aspects of the delegates' dress was the extreme fuzzy appearance of their hair."

"You're not wearing a bra, right?"

Maria K. was initially pleased with all the talk she heard about a women's rights movement, but then she felt that, "as often happens with good things, people got carried away." When she and a friend went to New York City in the early 1970s, the women they stayed with, who had decorated their apartment with feminist posters, criticized Maria for wearing makeup. She lost interest in the cause when it appeared to equate trying to look attractive with subservience. "Of course I wanted more money and I didn't want the director to have the right to slap me on the butt when he walked by, but at the same time, I really didn't understand why I shouldn't wear a bra."

The declining popularity of foundation garments such as bras and girdles had as much to do with the general trend toward comfortable clothing as it did with feminism. But like the controversy about women in pants, the idea of women not wearing bras struck a deep chord and roused more public interest than many of the larger theories about equality of the sexes. "I remember walking down the sidewalk," said Wendy Woythaler. "I was by myself and there was this couple coming toward me and I'm walking along and all of a sudden they said, 'Would you stop just a minute?' and the man goes, 'You're not wearing a bra, right?' And I was like, 'No, I'm not.' I think he was trying to make a point to his girlfriend."

The term "bra burners" stuck like a burr. Betty Friedan once claimed that the story about bra burning at the Miss America contest was "the work of agents provocateurs" who wanted to undermine the movement. (Friedan was not above using it herself when provoked. She was quoted in 1970 telling college students not to fall into "the bra-burning, anti-man, politics-of-orgasm school" of women's liberation.) People could point out every day that no bras had ever actually been burned, but it still resonated. To many women, going braless suggested a deeply personal kind of liberation—literally not being tied down. To others, it simply meant sloppy, and they equated feminism with unattractiveness. "I didn't know what to make of them at first because I thought they were so militant and so unfeminine and so... too radical. Because it was, like, from one extreme to the other," said Sylvia Peterson, a hairdresser in New Hampshire. "The only one I admired was Gloria Steinem because she kept her femininity... but at the same time, she had the fight, she did something."

Gloria Steinem was the person America would come to identify most closely with the women's liberation movement, and she was a relatively late arrival. She had been a successful journalist in the 1960s, best known for that exposé in which she went undercover as a Playboy Bunny ("New York's Newest Young Wit," announced *Glamour* magazine). She was a striking woman, with spectacular long hair and a great figure. ("The miniskirted pinup girl of the intelligentsia," said a *Washington Post* columnist.) She dated some of the most attractive men on the intellectual side of the celebrity circuit. "She was so beautiful and smart and funny and went out with one amazing person after another," said Nora Ephron. "If there was anyone in the world you wanted to go out with, she had gone out with them and they all had been in love with her." When Steinem began to gravitate toward the women's movement—first through journalism and then as a nearly full-time activist—she was the

spokesperson every television show wanted to book. Betty Friedan, who was older, sharp-featured, and less charming, was overshadowed.

"Gloria is a very nice person, and of course beautiful and articulate," said Muriel Fox. "So when the media latched on to her, they really did drop Betty. And of course Betty was furious. And it really was unfair because Gloria was not a founder, although she was a wonderful philosopher of the moment. But Betty was the one who had the vision, and the energy and drive that got us going."

Looking back, it's clear that the movement needed them both. Friedan had been the outspoken standard-bearer who got angry on behalf of a generation too constrained to make itself heard. Steinem translated the sometimes raucous and disturbing language of a movement in full bloom in a way the nervous nation could relate to. For instance, on the extremely touchy issue of childbearing, which Ti-Grace Atkinson called "the function of men oppressing women," Steinem would say that every woman did not need to be a mother any more than "every person with vocal cords needs to be an opera singer." It was a comment that attacked the idea of motherhood as women's universal destiny while also complimenting the mothers. (Being an opera singer, after all, was something really special.) Her approachable style drew people to her; she made women feel that they were in the fight together. "I knew that if I ever met Gloria Steinem we would be best friends," said Jan Schakowsky, a housewife who found herself feeling "totally trapped" by the long days alone with two small children.

Steinem's soothing aura may have been a product of a childhood taking care of her mentally ill mother. She spent an eighth-grade Thanksgiving vacation reading *A Tale of Two Cities* for school while she hung on to the hand of her delusional parent, who believed there was a war outside the house and had "plunged her hand through a window, badly cutting her arm in an effort to help us escape." It was the kind of upbringing that kills you or makes you very strong, and Steinem became both strong and self-contained—a unique figure who could constantly support other women activists while remaining a little removed from any particular cadre or faction.

While Steinem was courted by the media, she was also battered by the kind of dismissive treatment that is often meted out to beautiful women who insist on being something more than decorative. "What Gloria needs is a man...," said talk-show host David Susskind. "The whole thing is so boring—and ridiculous. Gloria comes on with that flat Ohio accent and goes on and on about women's oppression—you feel like either kissing her or hitting her. I can't decide which." And her extreme visibility poked at a particularly sensitive issue. The radical arm of the women's liberation movement, which wanted to go far beyond reforming laws into the realm of changing the basic rules of human relationships, had a natural concern with the question of appearance. There was obviously nothing more unjust than the fact that the shape of a young woman's nose, the size of her waist, and the thickness of her hair were the things on which so much happiness and fortune hinged. Some women's groups tried to call a halt to unfair, superficial standards by rejecting the entire tool kit of the beauty industry. They banished makeup, wore formless clothes such as overalls and men's shirts. They not only tossed out their uncomfortable high heels but rejected feminine footwear altogether, showing up for television interviews in work boots. J. Edgar Hoover to the contrary, they did not strive for fuzzy hair, but they avoided any style that required an effort beyond washing and combing.

The sense that feminists were all homely had dogged every struggle for women's rights in American history. (In 1927 a *Harper's* essay said the very word "feminist" suggested people "who wore flat heels and had very little feminine charm.") Angelina Grimké, the early-nineteenth-century crusader, thrilled her supporters by marrying the dashing abolitionist Theodore Weld, thus demonstrating that it was possible to both be a feminist and land a husband. "I did not agree with the message some were trying to push—that to be a liberated woman you had to make yourself ugly, to stop shaving under your arms, to stop wearing makeup or pretty dresses or any skirts at all," said Betty Friedan, who turned out to be the chief standard-bearer for the personal-appearance wing of the movement. She urged her followers to be "as pretty as we can. It's good for our self-image and it's good politics." Roxanne Dunbar, a radical feminist from Boston, said that when she and Friedan were guests on a TV show, Friedan harangued her from the moment she refused to let the makeup woman apply powder and lipstick. "I was dressed in my very best Army surplus white cotton sailor trousers and a white man's shirt. She said that I and 'scruffy feminists' like me were giving the movement a bad name," Dunbar said.

Steinem never got into the fight, and she seemed uncomfortable when the issue of appearance came up. She loved wearing miniskirts and high heels—the heels, she admitted, were indeed a bit like the old Chinese practice of foot binding, but she felt that if men could wear something as meaningless and uncomfortable as ties, women might be forgiven for enjoying the feeling they got from wearing sexy shoes. Still, she worried that she would not be taken seriously because of her appearance. (And traditional women, she feared, might dismiss her because she did not have a husband or children.) Trapped in an interview on a local television station in New York with a host who called her "an absolutely stunning sex object," Steinem responded irritably, "Well, I should comment on your appearance, but I don't have time."

Like Angelina Grimké and her wedding, Steinem served as a symbol—whether she liked it or not—that women could be both militant and sexually appealing. Other movement leaders rolled their eyes when the media reported on her lifestyle—camping out in the Badlands of North Dakota, being photographed at an A-level movie screening in Manhattan, then sitting in a circle of sari-wearing peasant women at a conference in New Delhi. But it was exactly the way millions of young women around the country felt that they, too, would like to live: standing up for their sisters and fighting for equal rights in a manner that also involved having adventures in exotic places, plus dates with unusually smart football players and unusually attractive playwrights. "Every so often, someone suggests that Gloria Steinem is only into the women's movement because it is currently the chic place to be," wrote Nora Ephron. "It always makes me smile, because she is about the only remotely chic thing connected with the movement."

"BLACKS ARE OPPRESSED . . . WHITE WOMEN ARE SUPPRESSED."

The younger and more radical women dismissed NOW and the reformist generation as middle-aged, middle-class white people, out of touch with the needs of poor and minority women. (Ti-Grace Atkinson's breakaway group from NOW described themselves as "the young, the black, and the beautiful.") But in fact the older reform movement was far more integrated. It had focused on justice in the workplace—something black women cared very much about. The more complicated social and personal demands left many of them cold. "I'm not hung up on this thing about liberating myself from the black man," said Fannie Lou Hamer. "I'm not going to try that thing. I got a black husband, six feet three, two hundred and forty pounds with a fourteen shoe, that I don't want to be liberated from."

Black critics said the women's movement was too focused on the problems of suburbs and college campuses rather than on the issues of poverty and exclusion. "Blacks are oppressed . . . white women are suppressed . . . and there is a difference," said Linda La Rue, a black commentator. And the traditional black press stressed that the important thing was for women to shore up the men, not to compete against them. *Essence* magazine in 1970 told its readers that, once wed, "you have discarded your

independence and you must rely on him. Even if you don't feel that way in the beginning, show him that you do. Make him feel ten feet tall!" (A decade later, *Essence* apologized.)

As Ella Baker had predicted, once people started talking about black women's need to defer to their men, the women soon became regarded as part of the problem. In 1965 Daniel Patrick Moynihan, the future senator who was then a counselor to President Nixon, issued a report on "Black Families in Crisis" in which he blamed many of the economic and social problems of poor African-Americans on female-dominated families, where men were either absent or undermined. While Moynihan made it clear that he blamed the legacy of slavery, not the poor themselves, for their dire economic straits, a reader would have been hard-pressed not to conclude that he also blamed black women. "Both as a husband and as a father the Negro male is made to feel inadequate," the report quoted the civil rights leader Whitney Young as saying. It expressed alarm over the fact that black girls were doing better in school than their male peers, and suggested that black mothers were favoring their daughters over their sons.

Meanwhile, the black power movement in some cities was veering into outright misogyny. Women were outraged and insulted, and they began to speak out about the sexism they encountered within their community. "As a black person I am no stranger to prejudice. But the truth is that in the political world I have been far more often discriminated against because I am a woman than because I am black," Shirley Chisholm said. "I knew I would encounter both anti-black and anti-feminist sentiments. What surprised me was the greater virulence of the sex discrimination." Chisholm, who became the first African-American woman elected to Congress in 1968, ran in a district in Brooklyn where both the voters and the political power structure were black. Her opponent was James Farmer, the former Freedom Ride leader, who ran stressing the need for a "man's voice" in Washington.

"THANK THEE, LORD, THAT I WAS BORN A WOMAN."

In 1970 Betty Friedan stepped down as head of NOW. In her farewell speech—which her friends suspected she had never wanted to make—she surprised everyone by calling on "every American woman" to stop working for men and take to the streets on August 26, the fiftieth anniversary of the passage of the Nineteenth Amendment. "I propose that the women who are doing menial chores in the offices cover their typewriters and close their notebooks, the telephone operators unplug their switchboards...and everyone who is doing a job for which a man would be paid more—stop. Every woman pegged forever as an assistant, doing jobs for which men get credit—stop," she orated. While it was impossible to say how many women would join in "our day of abstention," Friedan said confidently, "I expect it will be millions."

Almost no one imagined that women would really risk losing their jobs in a mass walkout or that even if they were willing, such an event could be organized fast enough. But the strike morphed into an anything-goes "action" in which women in every city and town were encouraged to do what they felt best to mark the moment. On Strike Day itself, Friedan recounted over and over in later years, she was almost late to the Central Park start-off point of the New York City march because the traffic was unexpectedly heavy. Then, as she rounded the last corner, she saw "not hundreds but thousands of women and men and babies and grandmothers beginning to mass." The marchers had been ordered to stay on the sidewalks, but when Friedan saw how many there were, "there was no way we were about to walk down Fifth Avenue in a little, thin line. I waved my arm over my head and yelled, *Take to the streets!*' What a moment that was."

Later, at the postmarch rally, Friedan told the crowd, "In the religion of my ancestors, there was a prayer that Jewish men said every morning. They prayed, 'Thank thee, Lord, that I was not born a woman.' Today I feel, feel for the first time, feel absolutely sure, that all women are going to be able to say, as I say tonight, 'Thank thee, Lord, that I was born a woman for this day.'"

The strike for equality, which was marked by parades and demonstrations in cities around the country, drew the kind of bemused tone of superiority from male commentators that the women had come to expect. A West Virginia senator got massive coverage for his description of the marchers as "a small band of braless bubbleheads." On ABC, Howard K. Smith quoted an old saw about three things that were difficult to tame: the ocean, fools, and women ("We may soon be able to tame the ocean, but fools and women will take a little longer"). Nevertheless, it had been a glorious day, and it marked something important. American women understood that a seismic shift in understanding was taking place. Things they had always done in emergencies—such as working in defense factories during the war—and things that only a few unusual "women lawyers" or "women engineers" had done, were now going to be recognized as part of the normal deal. The world had turned, and the conviction that what women needed most was protection had given way to a call for an equal playing field. Relations between men and women were changing in thousands of major and minor ways. The household chores, if not divided, had at least been brought up for discussion. The idea that the most desirable girl was a demure thing who always lost at chess or tennis was slipping away. Young women plotting their futures were not feeling compelled to go for the least-adventurous option. Some people, of course, balked at the swiftness of the change, and others preferred not to pay attention. ("It's the funniest thing. I don't feel there's any discrimination. I know my husband feels that way," said Pat Nixon when NOW began picketing the White House in support of the Equal Rights Amendment.) But the nation's consciousness was quickly, and sometimes painfully, evolving.

"WHO'D BE AGAINST EQUAL RIGHTS FOR WOMEN?"

In 1970 Jo Freeman had to fly from Chicago to Washington, with a choice between a puddle jumper that made several stops along the way and a direct flight with United. She chose the puddle jumper and later wrote United a letter, saying she had picked the less-convenient flight because she was boycotting the airline that ran those men-only "executive flights" between New York and Chicago.

"A year later they changed the policy," Freeman recalled. "And they sent me a telegram."

Politicians, keenly aware that the new special-interest group they were courting represented half the population, rolled out reforms. In the early 1970s, Congress passed a bill equalizing benefits for married employees, an Equal Credit Opportunity Act, and the famous Title IX prohibiting sex discrimination in federally aided education programs. "We put sex discrimination provisions into everything," said Representative Bella Abzug. "There was no opposition. Who'd be against equal rights for women?" Meanwhile, Attorney General John Mitchell sued to end discrimination against women in large corporations, and the Nixon administration forced two thousand colleges to submit to an investigation of whether they were discriminating against women in hiring and salaries.

The states followed suit. Roxanne Conlin, who was assistant attorney general in Iowa, wrote a bill eliminating all references in Iowa law to man, woman, girl, boy, lady, gentleman, etc. The massive reform of the state code produced a huge protest from...barbers. Ever watchful of their perquisites in every part of the country, the Iowa barbers staged a huge fight against allowing men to have their hair cut in beauty parlors. That was fine by Conlin, "because nobody noticed the rest of it, such as equalization of pensions."

In 1972 the members of the National Woman's Party walked out of their headquarters and up Capitol Hill to watch the passage of the Equal Rights Amendment. At 85, Alice Paul was still in Washington, trying to orchestrate everything. Amelia Fry, a historian who had volunteered to assist with the lobbying, felt Paul's intensity like "a single beam of strong light." When an exhausted Fry finally escaped for a lunch where some topic other than the ERA might be discussed, she was conscious that "a mile away was Alice in the one hundred eightieth day of the forty-ninth year of telephoning, assigning tasks, getting advocate statements written, and running her small army."

The Equal Rights Amendment had become increasingly more popular as legislatures and courts abolished the discriminatory practices the amendment was meant to reverse. By the early 1970s, its passage in Congress was being held up by only a few very powerful and determined committee chairmen. Martha Griffiths took the unusual—and extremely difficult—route of getting a majority of House members to force the bill to the floor through petition. The signatures came with a great deal of help from Marguerite Rawalt, who was attending a convention of the Business and Professional Women in Hawaii. Every night, Griffiths would phone to tell Rawalt which representative needed pressure, and Rawalt would pass on the message to the delegates, every one a woman used to a great deal of letter writing.

Once the bill was released, it passed 352 to 15 after only an hour of debate—the first time the House had acted on it since its introduction in 1923. The Senate held out for another two years, thanks to Sam Ervin of North Carolina. ("Keep the law responsible where the good Lord put it—on the man to bear the burdens of support and the women to bear the children.") But in 1972 resistance gave way and the bill passed quickly. The Hawaii legislature, waiting expectantly, became the first state to ratify the amendment minutes later. At the same time, Marguerite Rawalt walked into the Capitol lobby, where a bust of William Blackstone, the famous legal scholar who once described women as "chattel," stands. Rawalt approached the stony Mr. Blackstone and draped her black scarf over him.

Keepsake Pages

When did you first hear about women's liberation? Did it strike any chords?

_____

_____

_____

_____

_____

_____

_____

Do you remember the time when guys called women "chicks"? How did you feel about it?

_____

_____

_____

_____

_____

_____

_____

Do you remember Woodstock? Did it seem like a big deal at the time?

_____

_____

_____

_____

_____

_____

_____

Beauty standards changed in the late '60s and the '70s. How did that strike you? Did you think women were going too far on the antiglamour line? Or did you just feel liberated from girdles and hair rollers? And what about bras?

_____

_____

_____

_____

_____

_____

_____

_____

_____

Gloria Steinem. How do you remember her?

_____

_____

_____

_____

_____

_____

_____

_____

_____

More Thoughts and Memories

More Thoughts and Memories

PART III

Following Through

Phyllis Schlafly, head of the "Stop ERA" movement, with a young fan. *(AP Images)*

Anita Bryant, leader of the gay rights opposition movement. *(AP Images)*

Betty Friedan reacts to an Equal Rights Amendment defeat in 1977. *(AP Images)*

Television's willingness to show women doing something besides housework began to evolve with Marlo Thomas's *That Girl* in 1966. Thomas portrayed an unmarried woman who lived on her own while pursuing an acting career, but her worried parents were never far away. *(© American Broadcasting Companies, Inc.)*

In 1970 Mary Tyler Moore's Mary Richards arrived and became a real grown-up whose claim to happiness was much more about work and friends than finding the right man. Moore is shown here with Valerie Harper, who played her best friend, Rhoda. *(CBS / Landov)*

Billie Jean King is carried onto the court for her "Battle of the Sexes" with Bobby Riggs in 1973. *(© Bettmann / Corbis)*

Bella Abzug first began wearing her trademark hats because her mother told her it would send people the message that she was not a secretary. Abzug marches here at the National Women's Conference in Houston in 1978. Billie Jean King is on the left, and Betty Friedan is on the right. *(Teresa Zabala / New York Times)*

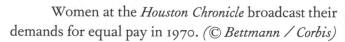

Women at the *Houston Chronicle* broadcast their demands for equal pay in 1970. *(© Bettmann / Corbis)*

Phylicia Rashad and Bill Cosby played the Huxtable parents in the '80s hit *The Cosby Show*. Clair Huxtable seemed to manage a law career, a large family, and a home with effortless grace, and American women hoped that they could Have It All—just like Clair did. (*NBC Universal Photo Bank*)

Mary Beth Whitehead agreed to be inseminated with the sperm of a childless biochemist whose wife had health problems. But when the child was born, Whitehead wanted to keep the infant, sparking national debate and a long court suit. (*Fred R. Conrad* / New York Times)

Sandra Day O'Connor with her husband, John, just after President Ronald Reagan announced he had nominated her to be the first woman on the Supreme Court. (© *Bettmann* / *Corbis*)

Lori Piestewa was the first American woman to die in the Iraq conflict. (*Rudy Gutierrez* / El Paso Times)

9 · Backlash

In 1977 Alice Paul was living in a small Quaker nursing home in New Jersey, having suffered a stroke that left her confined to a wheelchair. "She's 92. She ought to have her amendment before she dies," said the coordinator of an Alice Paul birthday salute. Paul was very frail, and her caregivers talked about her as a sweet old lady who loved lavender water and who would occasionally ask to hold the many medals she had been given over her long and extraordinary career. But when a delegation from the local YWCA's Center for Women came to deliver a birthday proclamation from the town council, the old Alice Paul popped right back up. "I read the proclamation I had painstakingly written," recalled Janet Tegley. "When I finished, Miss Paul immediately said, 'That's not right! You have the chronology wrong!'"

In a birthday interview, Paul told a reporter that while suffrage had been the great victory of her life so far, the Equal Rights Amendment would be the next. The women were bound to get the last four states they needed to ratify, she said, "because the volume of support exceeds what I dared hope for." Asked what she would do if she had time for yet another campaign, Paul told the reporter to read the short, succinct text of the ERA, which was dubbed the "Alice Paul Amendment" when it was rewritten from her original version in 1943: *Equality of rights under the law shall not be denied or abridged by the United States or by any state on account of sex.*

"It sounds to me kind of complete," she said.

⤞ ⤝

If, in 1972, you had told ERA supporters that the amendment wouldn't be ratified by 1977, they'd have been surprised and alarmed. Once it had finally gotten past the long-standing roadblock of Senator Sam Ervin, the ERA passed by overwhelming margins in Congress. Within two days it had been ratified by six states, all by unanimous votes. Twenty-four more had followed, virtually in lockstep. It felt as though the women's movement had become an unstoppable wave. The whole country was humming Helen Reddy's megahit, "I Am Woman (Hear Me Roar)." "I am strong. I am invincible. I am wooooman!" sang Reddy, who won a Grammy for her performance and thanked "God because She makes everything possible."

But the backlash was already building. After a few more states acted on the ERA in the mid-1970s, support dwindled off completely, three states short of the thirty-eight needed to put equal rights for women in the Constitution. What had been, in 1972, a kind of feel-good celebration of women's progress and the promise of even better things to come had turned into a vicious battle that would mark both the end of the women's liberation movement as a social uprising and the ascension of the New Right, whose culturally conservative troops would take over the Republican Party and realign American politics.

While conservative politicians would make use of the backlash for their own purposes, the fear and resentment underlying anti-ERA sentiment was genuine, particularly on the part of traditional homemakers. Those women had been born in a country where housewives had always been celebrated. To work outside the home was, in general, a sign of failure: your husband was not successful enough to support the family on his own. Their skills for mothering, cooking, running an efficient house, and keeping a man happy had been praised endlessly in magazines and newspapers. Even on television, while the role of the housewife might not have been portrayed as central, the scripts always made it clear that she, of all women, had chosen the best path.

Then the job abruptly lost prestige. Women started working outside the home not because they had to but because society seemed to have suddenly decided that being a housewife was not enough. Married women with a college education or with an above-average family income were becoming the most likely to have outside jobs. To be a stay-at-home was no longer a sign that you had succeeded—by winning a husband who could support the family without your assistance. It almost suggested that you were *unemployed,* unable to do anything better. "I never saw myself as a stay-at-home mom," said Kathy Hinderhofer, who was finishing college in the early 1970s. "Not to say that was a bad thing, but at that time it was almost—stay-at-home moms were looked down upon." And all the talk about husbands' responsibility to share the domestic chores seemed to suggest that there was nothing special in what women did at home. It was something anybody, even a man, could handle.

It would have been a miracle if many of the traditional housewives had not felt bitter.

"To me, being a wife and a mother is probably the best thing a woman can do, and with women's lib came the idea to a lot of women that they have to 'find themselves,' and being a mother was demeaning," said Louise Meyer Warpness, the Wyoming housewife, now widowed and remarried—still proud of the role she had been filling since the days she pressed the family clothes with that flatiron. "Women's lib was not a good thing. Well, it did do good in some ways, because if a woman had to work I think it's only fair that she receive equal pay, and I realize that some women do have to work, but there was a lot of women who didn't, and for them it was an excuse to get away from their children."

Housewives were not necessarily being paranoid

if they felt that the women's movement was looking down on their choices and repudiating the things they valued most. The young female revolutionaries who argued ideology and competed to make themselves heard in places such as New York and Chicago and Washington in the late '60s and early '70s had thrown around a lot of theories. Some had, indeed, compared housewives to prostitutes or slaves. Some had described childbearing as a curse that might someday be lifted with the help of artificial wombs. And quite a few had dismissed the idea that anybody could be happy taking care of a house and children full-time. "Mothers are the immediate enforcers of male will, the guards at the cell door, the flunkies who administer the electric shocks to punish rebellion," wrote Andrea Dworkin as she explained why girls did not want to become "like their mothers, those tired, preoccupied domestic sergeants beset by incomprehensible troubles." ERA opponents reprinted one of the NOW handbooks that informed American women who had proudly devoted time to their community schools, hospitals, and social services that volunteering was "yet another form of activity which serves to reinforce the second-class status of women." It appeared that to volunteer for NOW was a sign of liberation, while volunteering for your children's school was a sign that you were second-class.

"INTEREST IN IDEAS WAS LIMITED TO HOW IT WOULD AFFECT LANDING A GOOD, SAFE JOB."

Meanwhile, the economy started tanking. The gorgeous American money machine that had propelled the bulk of its citizens into a living standard higher than the planet had ever before witnessed began to falter. The warning signs were evident from the beginning of the decade, but the real crunch began in 1973, when the oil-producing nations started flexing their muscles, leading to a doubling of the price of gas. Bad weather and crop blight sent the cost of food soaring. By 1974 a consumer's dollar purchased only about two-thirds as much as it did in 1967. The unemployment rate, which was under 5 percent in December 1973, rose to 8.3 percent by June 1975. By the end of the decade, people felt they were living in an economic nightmare. Gas shortages in 1979 left drivers waiting in gas-station lines for hours, worried that they would hit empty before they made it to the pump. Inflation hit 13.3 percent.

Many of the young people graduating from school in the mid-1970s had grown up with the expectation that they, like their older siblings, could either get a good job and start a family as soon as they wanted or float through their twenties, working little, living cheaply, and devoting their energies to finding themselves. They were brought up sharp. The combination of rising inflation and slumping economic growth created a frightening new world where they not only would fail to get the enviable choices of their older brothers and sisters but would be hard-pressed to ever match the standard of living of their mothers and fathers. Anselma Dell'Olio, who spent much of her time speaking about women's liberation on college campuses, found that by 1975, the spirit of the gatherings had changed. Instead of eager crowds of women who were ready to sit up all night, swapping stories, the students seemed "quiet and passively attentive." The teachers told her she was right: "Interest in ideas was limited to how it would affect landing a good, safe job."

To keep family finances afloat, more wives went to work. By the end of the decade, for the first time, more than half of adult women had jobs outside the home. Although they got lower pay than men—less than 60 percent as much, on average—women found it easier to get work, since the growth sectors, such as health care and the service industries, were the ones that traditionally used a lot of female employees. The jobs men had taken—particularly those high-paying unionized factory jobs—were beginning to migrate overseas. The median income of families where the husband was under 30 fell 27 percent between 1973 and 1986. Young men, the latest hired, were terrified of layoffs, and inevitably, women moving up collided with men struggling to avoid falling down.

Patricia Lorance worked at a plant that made AT&T telephone circuit boards in the beleaguered blue-collar town of Montgomery, Illinois. Although the majority of the workers were women, the most lucrative work, which involved testing the finished product, almost always went to men. In 1976 Lorance, who had been helping to support her mother and four siblings, decided she wanted to qualify as a tester. She switched to the five a.m. shift, enrolled at a community college, and successfully completed sixteen courses in subjects such as electronics and computer programming. Armed with her credentials, she applied for the next vacancy. "I went on vacation, and when I got back, the position they told me I would have was gone," she recalls. "They said it was a cutback. And lo and behold, what do I see—somebody who had gone to school with me." The job had been filled by a man from her community college class.

But she finally got the tester's job, and three decades later, Lorance still remembers with pleasure how surprised her supervisors were at the quality of her work. "I'm going to brag on myself. I was very good during my whole working time. I was fixing things they gave me, and I think I kind of amazed them," she said. By 1979, 14 other women had joined her and the 185 male testers, while another 12 women were signed up for the community college courses. While some of the men were helpful, others resisted. They posted a picture of a fat woman with money spilling out of the top of her rolled-down stockings. "Today I are a tester," someone had written on the bottom. Lorance felt she got the worst products to test. "Sometimes things were picked over and what was left for me was really bad. But I'll put it this way—they got fixed." She was quickly upgraded to a higher-paying position.

While some of the harassment was pure sexism, the younger men had practical reasons to resent the newcomers. The women had become testers after spending years working at the low-paying bench jobs. Their seniority would put them ahead of many male workers when it came to opportunities for promotion, or protection of their current jobs during layoffs. The male testers proposed a new seniority system that discounted the women's prior experience. At the meeting where it was debated, people argued bitterly about who needed good jobs more—the men, who often had wives and children, or the women, who were often single mothers. Given their superior numbers, the men won the vote, but the company officials assured the women the new system would be used only to chart advancement, not when it came to layoffs. Nevertheless, when layoffs came, Lorance was downgraded to a post at lower pay and written up for a reprimand when she asked for a reason. She and two other women sued the company, which argued that they had missed the legal deadline for filing a complaint. That was true—if you counted from when the new seniority system was adopted rather than from when the women first learned about details in the rules that had been kept secret and that would cost them their jobs. The judge threw out the case on that technicality. By the end of the decade, Lorance was laid off entirely.

"IT IS MORE IMPORTANT FOR A WIFE TO HELP HER HUSBAND'S CAREER."

The American public had been through a lot, facing up to the national shame of racial segregation, the failure of the war in Vietnam, and economic disarray, as well as the news that age-old rules about the appropriate roles of men and women were wrong. The country was in a kind of digestion period that did not produce perfect consistency. Men told surveyors for one poll that they favored "an equal marriage of shared responsibility," and they told surveyors for another that they disliked changes in women's roles because it meant that the men had to spend more time on household chores. A National Opinion Research Center survey in 1977 found

wide support—in theory—for the ERA. But it also found wide agreement with the statement that "it is more important for a wife to help her husband's career than to have one herself." When the question came down to what sounded like *fairness*— the ability of women to get a credit card or to win a job or a berth in graduate school—polls showed that most people approved. But on other issues involving men's and women's roles, the public was much more conservative.

When the Equal Rights Amendment came under attack in the mid-'70s, its supporters needed to explain, in the most concrete terms possible, how it was going to make things fairer. The problem was that there weren't all that many good examples. When Alice Paul had first proposed the ERA, and even when the second wave of feminists had reclaimed it as their cause in the 1960s, it was unimaginable that all the state, local, and federal laws that discriminated against women in everything from credit to jury duty to the ability to work overtime could be gotten rid of one by one. But by the mid-'70s, between the courts and the legislatures, most of the laws that the ERA was intended to vanquish had already been eliminated or neutralized. One of the reasons the amendment was such a feel-good cause in 1972 was that it seemed unlikely to have much impact beyond the symbolic.

Feminists felt the need was still real. They pointed to the fact that women were so far behind men in earning power as proof that things were far from equal. And those court rulings were not as sweeping or consistent as they needed to be. Besides, what the courts and legislatures had given, they could take away without the protection of the Constitution.

All that was true but a little vague. Once politicians began getting caught in the middle of the Equal Rights war, many decided that the practical consequences of defeating the amendment were not dire. And the states where the fight was being waged were the hardest sells: the Deep South, Southwestern and border states, and Illinois, which required a three-fifths majority to ratify a constitutional amendment. The decade of annual ERA battles in Illinois, with the endless near misses, botched strategies, and thudding collisions between the aging New Left and the insurgent New Right, would become fodder for a generation of doctoral dissertations.

All these problems still probably wouldn't have killed the amendment's chances if it had not been for a single woman. It's not often in this story of large economic forces and roiling social change that any one person makes the difference. But in this case, it's unlikely that all the simmering discontent among traditional women, working-class men, and conservative churches would ever have been channeled and mobilized in time to stop ratification if it hadn't been for Phyllis Schlafly.

"I WAS GIVING SPEECHES FOR BARRY GOLDWATER AND IN NOVEMBER I HAD A BABY."

Schlafly was an extraordinary person. A brilliant debater, she could dish it out mercilessly and then stand serenely while her sputtering opponents tried to give it back. A tireless speaker and organizer for conservative Republican causes, she counted up ninety-eight public appearances in 1960, which was not one of her most demanding years. She was also a wife — a traditional one, by her own lights — and the mother of six children, who were very young at the time she was at the peak of her political activity. "I'd drive out to give a speech and sometimes I'd bring a nursing baby with me," said Schlafly, who breast-fed each child for six months. "There was always someone outside willing to take care of a baby rather than listen to a long lecture." (She also taught her children to read and write, so they were ready to begin school at the second grade when they turned 6.) In the middle of the anti-ERA crusade, she stunned her family with the announcement that she had decided to go to law school — which she did, at 51, graduating three years later in the top quarter of her class. "I think what Phyllis is doing is absolutely dreadful. But I just can't think of anyone who's so together and tough," said Karen DeCrow, one of the NOW leaders whose life Schlafly made absolutely miserable. "I mean, everything you should raise your daughter to be...she's an extremely liberated woman." Robin Morgan claims that whenever she had private conversations with Schlafly — mainly in studio greenrooms, waiting for TV debates to begin — Phyllis readily admitted that without the doors opened by the women's movement, she would never have been able to achieve so much. "But she would never repeat that in public," Morgan said.

Raised in a struggling, Depression-era middle-class family in St. Louis, Phyllis Stewart won a scholarship to a Catholic college but decided that the curriculum wasn't challenging enough, opting instead to work her way through Washington University in St. Louis — with a forty-eight-hour-a-week defense job on the overnight shift, firing guns and testing ballistics at an ordinance plant. After graduating Phi Beta Kappa in three years, she raced through a graduate program in government at Radcliffe. She returned to the Midwest, became very active in Republican politics, and married Fred Schlafly, a lawyer fifteen years her senior. They started a family in Alton, Illinois, with children arriving so quickly that Phyllis had three babies in diapers at one time.

In 1952, not long after their first son was born, Phyllis agreed to run for Congress as the Republican in a heavily Democratic district. She posed for her campaign pictures in an apron, cooking the family breakfast, but she was anything but a demure and deferential politician. Schlafly proved to be a ferocious candidate, bombarding the district with press releases attacking the incumbent, Melvin Price, for his position on foreign affairs, taxation, and — her favorite topic — the Communist conspiracy. (Nevertheless, Price won reelection rather easily.) Like many members of the Republican right, the Schlaflys gave their hearts to Senator

Barry Goldwater of Arizona. To support his presidential bid in 1964, Phyllis wrote a small book, *A Choice Not an Echo,* describing how, as she saw it, the establishment power brokers were trying to keep Goldwater and the forces of anti-Communism down. It sold millions of copies and was read by virtually every delegate to the Republican convention, where Goldwater won the nomination. Many years later, Schlafly said 1964 was "the most productive year of my life. I was running the Illinois Federation of Republican Women; I wrote *A Choice Not an Echo;* I self-published it; I went to the Republican convention; wrote a second book, *The Gravediggers*—now we're in September—I was giving speeches for Barry Goldwater and in November I had a baby."

Goldwater, Robert Taft, and the other conservative heroes of the '50s and '60s were focused on beefing up the military and reducing the role of the federal government in everything except national defense. They had no desire to get involved in social issues such as abortion or gay rights. "The conservative movement is founded on the simple tenet that people have the right to live life as they please as long as they don't hurt anyone in the process," said Goldwater, who had a gay grandson. Women's rights had traditionally been a Republican issue, and one with which many conservatives sympathized. It had been the Democrats, with their base in heavily Catholic urban districts and the South, who were more likely to resist anything that encouraged women's independence from the home. But both parties were changing, and the passage of the ERA by those huge congressional majorities in 1972 might be a good marker for the point when the Democrats and Republicans crossed paths on women's issues, one moving toward the cultural left while the other moved right.

Schlafly came late to the anti-ERA cause. In 1972, when a conservative forum invited her to take part in a debate about the amendment, she pleaded ignorance and proposed that they talk about defense policy instead. But when the sponsors insisted, she

started studying and quickly decided that the Equal Rights Amendment was another big-government plot, and one that would undermine the historic protection given to women—particularly mothers—through the "Christian tradition of chivalry." Schlafly wrote an essay called "What's Wrong with 'Equal Rights' for Women?" for a newsletter she published. Not long after, one of her subscribers called to say that it had been a crucial weapon in the defeat of the ERA in the Oklahoma state legislature.

The battle was on.

"DR. SPOCK WAS TRULY 'LIBERATED' FROM TRADITIONAL RESTRAINTS."

While the ERA supporters often had only vague explanations for what good the amendment would do, the opponents drew dramatic pictures of the terrible things that could follow passage. Maybe the Boy Scouts and Girl Scouts would have to be merged. Would child support become unconstitutional? What about unisex bathrooms? Since the language was so general, opponents felt free to argue that it could mean anything.

In speeches, books, and essays, Schlafly connected the amendment and the women's movement (the two were generally interchangeable to the anti-ERA forces) to all the economic and social changes that were making the traditional housewife feel threatened, including rising divorce rates. Dr. Benjamin Spock eliminated sexist language in his baby books, she noted, and he also "walked out on his faithful wife, Jane, to whom he had been married for forty-eight years, and took up with a younger woman: Dr. Spock was truly 'liberated' from traditional restraints." She claimed that the amendment would free husbands from having to support their families and that gender-neutral divorce laws might require that all wives go to work and provide half the family income.

It was a mixture of wild exaggeration and real problems that had nothing to do with the ERA. Few divorced women had ever been awarded adequate child support, and men seldom paid even the minimal amounts required by the courts. New divorce laws had made it easier for an unhappy husband (or wife) to end a marriage, but these were the product of reformist lawyers' groups, not the women's movement. And it was hardly the fault of the Equal Rights Amendment that more and more middle-class women were being pushed into the workforce—whether they liked it or not—to help support their families and pay their fast-rising mortgages. But the ERA was an extremely handy target for all the genuine anxiety and frustration.

Schlafly's bottom line was that women were not really discriminated against. During one debate, the psychologist Joyce Brothers emotionally recounted how her mother had been an attorney, and the only job open to her was practicing with her husband. Schlafly flatly denied women had ever suffered any bias in the legal profession. "I was invited to attend the Harvard Law School in 1945 and there was absolutely no discrimination then," she said assuredly. As her biographer Carol Felsenthal noted, that was five years before the law school dropped its ban on admitting any women.

One thing both sides did agree about was that the Equal Rights Amendment would make young women subject to any future military draft and that they could be sent into combat. It was an admission the ERA supporters could have dodged—the military probably had the power to set its own rules for who was drafted and where they were assigned. But most felt equal rights had to be coupled with equal responsibilities. And they were offended by arguments that young women were too fragile to stand up under the pressure of military training.

It was an admirable principle but a tactical disaster. The draft had just been abolished in 1973, and people could easily imagine it returning. Polls showed that only about 20 percent of Americans approved of the idea of drafting women or allowing them to take jobs that put them in combat. When Alan Alda, the popular star of *M*A*S*H*, testified in support of the ERA in Illinois, he was asked whether he would expect to see his own daughters conscripted if there was another draft. Alda's answer—that he would but that he would also expect them to be conscientious objectors—probably did not win the hearts of any conservative lawmakers who were sitting on the fence.

"I'D LIKE TO BURN YOU AT THE STAKE."

The ERA supporters kept pointing out, with rising frustration, that Schlafly herself was the farthest thing imaginable from the stay-at-home moms she was championing. While she liked to start speeches by thanking her husband for "letting me come"—because, she said, it drove the "libbers" crazy—even her conservative audiences understood this was a joke. Mr. Schlafly, who could not even dissuade his 51-year-old, manically overscheduled wife from going to law school, did not seem to be an overempowered head of the household.

In fact, Schlafly never argued that women shouldn't have careers. While she celebrated the full-time housewife, her underlying attitude toward the job in an age of automatic washing machines and dishwashers seemed just as dismissive as Betty Friedan's: "Household duties have been reduced to only a few hours a day, leaving the American woman with plenty of time to moonlight in full- or part-time jobs or to indulge to her heart's content in a wide array of interesting educational or cultural or homemaking activities." Still, she assured her followers that it was only motherhood and domesticity that could make women really happy. If they wanted careers, too, and they could manage to balance both, fine. But if they couldn't, they should quit their jobs, stay home, and stop whining. (Schlafly never followed a particularly consistent train of thought when it came to what she regarded as proper feminine behavior. Despite her defense of traditional marriage, she extolled Katharine Hepburn, who devoted much of her life to an affair with the married Spencer Tracy, as a Positive Woman who "had enough self-confidence that she could afford to accord to her man a preeminence in their personal relationship.")

She drove the pro-ERA forces crazy. They were used to thinking of themselves as the voice of American women, allied against the enemy: chauvinistic men. Having to fight against other women who depicted themselves as the *true* voice of their sex threw them off balance. And, of course, the fact that Schlafly was winning made it worst of all. "I'd like to burn you at the stake," Betty Friedan snarled to her at one debate. Another ERA supporter mused, in public, about how wonderful it would be to run over her with a car. Still another said she wished somebody would slap her. And while none of those things ever happened, ERA supporters did hire someone to throw a pie in Schlafly's face.

It was one of those awful fights in which each side believed it was battling for the forces of good and in which no compromise was possible. Legislators in swing states grew exhausted with the issue, as well as with its advocates and opponents. "These people pull at you, yank you, yell, scream, threaten, they all look wild-eyed to me," complained one female legislator in Illinois.

"LET'S TERMINATE THE PREGNANCY AND START AGAIN NEXT MONTH."

The final nail in the ERA's coffin was the suspicion that it was a vehicle for abortion and gay rights. While supporters of the amendment doubted that was true, most would have been happy if it was. The women's rights movement had become deeply invested in the abortion issue and in the fight for gay equality. The new political forces that had risen up to challenge the ERA were opposed to both. In fact, many cared much more about fighting abortion and homosexuality than they did about constitutional amendments of any stripe.

The abortion debate really first went public in the United States in 1962, with a story about the host of a children's television show in Phoenix. Sherri Chessen Finkbine was Miss Sherri on *Romper*

Room, and she remembers it as "probably the best job in the universe—you were on the air for an hour a day. You get to drink milk and eat cupcakes and you only have to take care of six kids." The program was a kind of franchise—with local *Romper Room*s directed out of a central office in Baltimore. At 29, she followed the directive of the day, including one memorable Soapsuds Fun Friday in which she was supposed to demonstrate how to mold a make-believe vase out of thick Ivory soapsuds and realized, halfway through, that she had inadvertently created a very realistic phallic symbol. "It couldn't have been more graphic," she laughed. "People from all the different departments were coming in to watch." More than forty years later, she was still running into people who used to work at the NBC station in Phoenix who would joke, "Miss Sherri, how about a little Soapsuds Fun?"

She was also the wife of a high school teacher and the mother of four children under 7. The family struggled a bit financially, and Bob Finkbine made some extra money by escorting high school students on summer tours of Europe. During a particularly stressful trip, he went looking for medication to help him sleep and obtained some tranquilizers in England. "He took a few, and when he came home I can remember him putting them way up high in the kitchen cupboard. Above the sink," Sherri said. She was pregnant with their fifth child, struggling with morning sickness and insomnia, and intent on staying in her job as long as possible, when she thought of the pills. She can still visualize herself crawling up onto the sink and taking them out.

It was only a few weeks later that Sherri saw a story in the local paper about a tranquilizer, never approved in the United States but popular in Europe, named thalidomide. It had been linked to terrible birth defects, babies born without arms or legs. She called her doctor and told him, "I think I took some of that awful medicine." Tests showed the pills did contain thalidomide, and she had taken it at the worst possible time, during the early stages of pregnancy, when the fetus's limbs were forming. The doctor told Sherri and Bob to come in for a consultation—on Saturday, when none of his other patients would be around.

"If you were my wife, I'd give you the same advice," the doctor told her. "Let's terminate the pregnancy and start again next month."

Sherri had barely heard of abortion, and the doctor's suggestion sounded simple and practical. She got pregnant easily, and there was no question in her mind that if she just "started over," everything would turn out well, with another healthy new baby to add to the family, just as planned.

Abortion was illegal in every state, but Arizona permitted hospitals to perform them when the life of the mother was in danger. Doctors used that regulation loosely when it came to well-connected middle-class families, and Sherri was scheduled to have a quiet procedure that no one needed to know about. It would have happened just that way if she had not felt compelled to warn other women about the drug. She called the editor of the local paper, whose daughter had been with Bob Finkbine on the European tour. It turned out that their reporter was working on a story about thalidomide at that moment.

"He won't use my name, will he?" Sherri asked.

On Monday morning, the paper arrived with the story in a black box on the front page. As promised, her name was not used. But there was enough about her husband's occupation, the way that the drug had come into her possession, and other details to make it all pretty clear. "They did everything but give my address," she said. That morning, while she was working at the TV studio, the hospital called and canceled the abortion. The Finkbines sued, and the case quickly became an international story. Sherri can still remember the TV reporter from her station "practically crying" when he came to her house to do the story. But she didn't attempt to avoid being interviewed: "I was never the kind of person who said, 'No comment.'"

When it became clear the lawsuit would never succeed, the Finkbines went to Los Angeles to pre-pare for a trip to Japan, where abortion was legal. But the Japanese, wary of the controversy, refused to give them visas. Meanwhile, the family was under siege at home. Death threats arrived in the mail, including one that promised to do to the four Finkbine children what their parents were planning to do to the fetus. Finally, with the kind of publicity that might normally be reserved for natural disasters or the opening of the Olympics, the Finkbines went to Sweden, where the abortion was performed.

Sherri never returned to *Romper Room*. "An executive from NBC in Phoenix called and said, 'We think you're unsuitable to handle children,'" she recalled. The station did give her a fifteen-minute talk show, which she kept until she became pregnant once again. Since pregnant women never appeared on television in that era, it was the end of her TV career. But she did hear from the NBC executive who fired her from *Romper Room:* "Darned if about a year later he didn't call me because his daughter needed to abort a pregnancy."

"AND YOU KNOW, I WOULD HAVE HELPED HER."

Early in America's history, abortion was regarded as a form of birth control, and the general presumption was that a fetus became a human being at the "quickening"—the moment that a woman began to feel it moving around in her body. That had changed in the nineteenth century, and many Americans had been taught from childhood that abortion at any stage was the same as murder. Most people found the whole idea of abortion, at minimum, disturbing. But they often had more sympathetic attitudes when the pregnancy involved a fetus that was seriously deformed. (Some polls showed that half of the Americans questioned supported Sherri Finkbine's decision to seek an abortion.)

Women had been having illegal abortions for far more pedestrian reasons—because they were unmarried or because they could not afford to raise another child—and many people knew someone who had had a pregnancy terminated. Anne Wallach remembered that when she was a student at Radcliffe in the late '40s, she accompanied a friend who was given an abortion by a dentist. "It was terrible," she said. "It was dirty, and the girl was in a lot of pain, there was a lot of bleeding. I spent the weekend with her in her dorm room. It was not a happy experience by any means."

The memories of those traumatic abortions made the issue an emotional one for the young activists in the women's movement. "For my first abortion in 1960 I took the Cuba option...," wrote Susan Brownmiller. "Here's what I remember: Banging on a door during the midday siesta in a strange neighborhood in Havana. Wriggling my toes a few hours later, astonished to be alive. Boarding a small plane to Key West and hitchhiking back to New York, bleeding all the way." But very few women discussed the issue publicly. Then, in March 1969, the feminist group Redstockings staged a public speak-out titled "Abortion: Tell It Like It Is" at a church in Greenwich Village. *New York Magazine* sent their young star writer, Gloria Steinem, to cover it. Listening as one woman after another got up to tell her experiences with an illegal abortion, Steinem felt she had reached a turning point. "I had had an abortion when I was newly out of college, and had told no one," she wrote later. "If one in three or four adult women shares this experience, why should each of us be made to feel criminal and alone? How much power would we ever have if we had no power over the fate of our bodies?" It was the moment, Steinem said, when she stopped being a journalist standing on the sidelines and became a committed activist.

In 1970 Hawaii approved a law permitting abortion on demand, with a lengthy residence requirement, but the change had little impact on the mainland. New York, however, was a different matter. The state was considering a bill that would simply leave abortion in the first six months of a pregnancy up to doctors and their patients. It was sponsored by

Constance Cook of Ithaca, a Republican who was one of four women in the 150-person lower house of the legislature. The debate began in the all-male senate, where the legislative secretaries—virtually the only women who worked in the capitol outside of the cafeteria staff—lined the walls of the chamber to listen. Clinton Dominick, who the *New York Times* called one of the senate's "most respected members," told his colleagues that he could best relate to the issue through his wife, the mother of five who told him that if she'd found she was pregnant again at 48, she would have sought an abortion.

"And you know, I would have helped her," he said quietly.

Supporters of the bill from poor districts angrily pointed out that their constituents were the ones most likely to die from botched illegal abortions. But opponents retorted that it was unborn children who were in danger of dying. "This is murder," said a Democrat from Brooklyn. A Republican who was the father of a child with Down syndrome described the pain he felt at hearing people say that abortion was justified if there was a danger the baby would be like his beloved boy. The bill finally passed the senate, 31 to 26, after five hours of emotionally fraught debate.

In the assembly, Cook thought she saw her bill going down to defeat when several former supporters voted no. A Bronx Democrat, Anthony Stella, said he originally thought his heavily Catholic district would feel it was "not my job to legislate morality." But they had been telling him different in no uncertain terms, he said. Others reported that they had been denounced from the pulpit or in church newsletters. Cook made her usual pragmatic argument for putting the whole issue "into the hands of a doctor" rather than the politicians. But her male colleagues were hardly as calm. "I point the finger at every member who votes for this bill and say, 'You, sir, killed these innocent children,'" said one. When the final vote came, it was a tie—the equivalent of defeat.

Suddenly, amid the hubbub, 60-year-old George Michaels, a ten-year veteran from a conservative upstate district, rose, his hands trembling. He had opposed the bill all along, he said, because his constituents opposed it. His voice breaking, he told the House, "My own son called me a whore for voting against this bill." His other son, a theology student who had served as an assembly chaplain, had begged him not to let his vote kill the measure. "I realize I am terminating my political career, but I cannot in good conscience sit here and allow my vote to be the one that defeats this bill," he said. "I ask that my vote be changed from no to yes." The legislative secretaries, the *Times* reported, broke into applause, and New York became the first mainland state to legalize abortion. Later in the year, the Democratic Party in Michaels's district refused to endorse him for reelection. He lost the primary while he was hospitalized after a car accident, and he lost in November, when he ran as a third-party candidate. Senator Dominick, who had told the story about his wife, was defeated as well.

"I'm going to the ladies' lounge and read a book."

By the end of 1970, three states—Hawaii, Alaska, and Washington—had passed laws permitting abortion on demand for state residents. And New York's law, which had no residency requirement, made legal abortion readily available to any woman who lived in the East and had access to a bus station. (In the first year the new law was in effect, about 55,000 New Yorkers ended their pregnancies, along with almost 84,000 nonresidents.) In California, the rules were loosened to the point that any woman who could pay for an abortion could usually qualify for one under the increasingly flexible "mental-health" criterion.

Meanwhile, a series of cases challenging state anti-abortion laws were making their way toward the Supreme Court. The one that would finally arrive there began in Texas, where a young lawyer named Sarah Weddington was put in touch with Norma McCorvey, an unmarried hard-luck woman

who wanted to terminate her pregnancy. Weddington was only 25 and McCorvey was 21, "a pregnant street person," as she later described herself, so uneducated she had walked away from a clinic where she had gone for a pregnancy test when the doctor requested a urine sample, because she had no idea what "urine" was. The happier parts of her childhood had been spent in reform school, the worst living as a 15-year-old boarder in the house of a man who raped her every night. She had married at 16, and her husband beat her when he found out she was pregnant. She sought shelter with her mother, who later took the baby to raise as her own. By then McCorvey had begun living with another woman, and her mother threatened to tell the police she was a lesbian unless she gave up her rights to her daughter.

It took, as McCorvey would later admit, an extraordinary degree of disorder for a woman who was living as a lesbian to have three unwanted pregnancies. She had never seen the second baby, which she gave away at birth. She discovered she was pregnant again when she was working as a carnival barker and was astonished when a friend told her about abortion—she had never heard the word and had to look it up in a dictionary. Her search for a way to get one led her to Weddington, who was looking for a pregnant woman who would be willing to challenge the Texas anti-abortion law. McCorvey believed the suit would lead to the desired abortion, and while she waited, "I discovered that if I smoked enough dope and drank enough wine, it was possible to not think about being pregnant." When, inevitably, the case dragged on and McCorvey's pregnancy was in the sixth month, she was finally told that it was too late to terminate. She unsuccessfully tried to kill herself, and gave the baby up for adoption when it was born.

Meanwhile, Weddington and her associate, Linda Coffee, argued what would become one of the best-known and most controversial Supreme Court cases in American history. Their combined ages were not equal to that of any one of the justices. Their client, McCorvey, was disguised as Jane Roe and never made an appearance in court. But they were stunningly successful. In January 1973, the Supreme Court ruled, 7 to 2, in *Roe v. Wade,* that any attempt to interfere with a woman's right to abortion during the first three months of pregnancy was a violation of her constitutional right to privacy. Justice Harry Blackmun, a Nixon appointee who wrote the decision, said the state's right to regulate abortions during the second trimester was limited to rules aimed at protecting the woman's health and safety. Abortions could be prohibited during the third trimester, he said, except when they were required to protect the health or life of the mother.

While abortion rights had been an ongoing controversy in some states before the *Roe v. Wade* decision, in others it had barely scraped the surface of people's consciousness. The sudden announcement that the Supreme Court was making abortion legal came as a shock, and the Americans who were most distressed turned against "activist judges" and everything else they connected with *Roe,* including the women's movement. By the end of the 1970s, the National Right to Life Committee claimed more than eleven million members.

The abortion fight ran side by side with the battle over the Equal Rights Amendment. People who believed change hadn't happened fast enough or gone far enough lined up against people who felt the nation had lost its moral bearings and needed to turn back. All this was happening at a time when the economy was betraying working-class families who had not gotten far enough up the ladder to protect themselves when the great postwar boom ended. The entire political texture of the nation was changing, and the Republican old guard, which had been conservative about economics but liberal on social issues, was sinking fast. Mary Crisp, the cochair of the Republican National Committee in 1980, said her party was "about to bury the rights of over a hundred million American women under a heap of platitudes" when the presidential nominating convention ended Republican support of the ERA and added a plank to its platform calling for a constitutional amendment against abortion. She

wound up going home midconvention, her name erased from the program.

Anti-abortion feminists went through an equally painful losing battle. One of the NOW founders, Betty Boyer of Ohio, had resigned from the board in 1968 after what she called a "shouting match" over the issue. Some NOW chapters divided themselves into separate local and national organizations so members who opposed abortion could give their dues solely to local activities. "Abortion was about fifteenth on our list of priorities," said Bev Mitchell of Cedar Rapids. NOW's national leadership, she said, "got so domineering that according to them, there is just no room in the feminist movement for women who do not believe in abortion."

The reaction against *Roe* in Washington began quickly. In 1976 Congress voted to cut off federal funding for abortions except in cases when a woman's life was in danger. The debate, Representative Barbara Jordan said later, "was awful…the people who got up and sermonized. It was a super mess. We, the sixteen women in the House, were trying to orchestrate the whole thing, and we had these clowns on the floor talking." One of them, she said, put a pillow under his jacket so he'd look pregnant. "He was ranting around…and I couldn't take any more of it. I told one of my female colleagues, 'I'm going to the ladies' lounge and read a book, and if you need me in this debate that's where I'll be.' And I just left."

"AS SOMEONE WHO HAS LOVED MEN TOO WELL…"

In 1977 the International Women's Year Conference was held in Houston (with a competing Pro-Family Rally sponsored by Phyllis Schlafly across town). A resolution supporting abortion rights passed easily, but sponsors were a little more concerned about one being offered on behalf of gay rights. Speaking in support, to many people's surprise, was Betty Friedan. "As someone who has loved men too well, I have had trouble with this issue," said the recently divorced Friedan. "Now my priority is passing the

ERA. And because there is nothing in it that will give any protection to homosexuals, I believe we must help the women who are lesbians."

Friedan was delivering two messages: one was in favor of the resolution (which passed), and the other was to remind the world that the Equal Rights Amendment was not about gay liberation. The idea that it was had crippled progress for the ERA in those critical final states. "I thought we had it made until Phyllis Schlafly came into the state with those films of the San Francisco gay parade," said Minnette Doderer, the former president pro tempore of the state senate in Iowa. "She spent twenty-five thousand dollars to put those on television and to say, 'This will happen in Iowa if you get the Equal Rights Amendment.'"

The women in Houston had already watched the antigay forces flex their muscles in Florida. Miami-Dade County had been in what the *Miami Herald* called "hysteria more appropriate to the seventeenth century than the twentieth" over an ordinance banning discrimination against homosexuals in housing and employment. The improbable leader of the opposition was Anita Bryant, a 37-year-old former Miss America runner-up who was best known as the spokesperson for the Florida Citrus Commission, chirping, "A day without orange juice is like a day without sunshine," on TV commercials. Suddenly, there she was on the barricades, warning Floridians that gays were out to seduce their kids into a decadent lifestyle: "Since homosexuals cannot reproduce, they must freshen their ranks with our children. They will use money, drugs, alcohol, any means to get what they want."

Bryant sang, quoted the Old Testament, and hinted that Florida's ongoing drought might be a punishment from God. One interesting part of the controversy was the low profile of gay women. "Most of the time, Bryant has concentrated her fire on male homosexuals, rather than lesbians, partly because her biblical texts deal with men," wrote *Newsweek*. "In addition, lesbians seem less of a threat to the foes of gay rights. Fewer in number than male

homosexuals, lesbians are generally less visible in Miami and other cities—and they are playing only a modest role in the gay coalition that [leader Jack] Campbell has assembled." It was not unusual for gay women to be left on the fringe of the early gay rights movement. Many women claimed that homosexual men behaved like men first and fellow gay rights activists second, and marginalized women when they tried to work together. However, the fact that gay women weren't seen as a major target of Bryant's crusade did not mean they were not affected. After the antidiscrimination ordinance was defeated by an enormous margin, *Newsweek* reported that a lesbian who had worked as an executive secretary in the county government for fifteen years lost her job the morning after the vote. And with Bryant's help, the antigay alliance successfully lobbied to bar gay Floridians from adopting children.

While other towns followed Miami's lead, a backlash against the backlash was also under way. Voters in Seattle refused to repeal their city's gay rights ordinance, and California voters defeated an initiative that would have led to the firing of gay teachers. Bryant's career, which had been based on her pleasant persona more than any extraordinary talent, floundered. A few years later, she divorced her husband and told the *Ladies' Home Journal* that she felt a new kinship with feminists: "I can see how women are controlled in a very ungodly way." As far as homosexuality went, Bryant said, "I'm more inclined to say live and let live."

"THIS WASN'T GOING TO BE THE WHOLE THING, WAS IT?"

The women's movement that was fighting for the Equal Rights Amendment at the end of the 1970s was much different from the one that carried the banner at the beginning. Activists who had cheerfully deferred all thoughts of jobs or money or security in order to devote themselves to the cause were suddenly confronted with the need to think about salaries and pensions and housing costs. "It became much more difficult to live on virtually nothing—the lifestyle that had prevailed in the movement," said Barbara Epstein, who had been active with California leftist and feminist groups.

Great social uprisings have a short life span. "Essentially it's a stage of naming reality," said Gloria Steinem. "It's the great 'Aha!'" Fixing the reality, of course, takes longer, and the women's movement would continue in many forms—from national groups such as NOW, to local battered women's shelters or antirape programs, to women's bookstores and women's history departments. But there was no longer that ecstatic sense of being part of a united force mobilized to change the world. Just as some of the young people who had worked in SNCC in the South never got over the sense of loss when the Beloved Community evaporated, women who had come of age in their movement experienced an emptiness. "Life felt good then...," wrote the essayist Vivian Gornick.

As long as I had a roomful of feminists to come home to I had built-in company for life. I'd never be alone again. The feminists were my sword and my shield—my solace, my comfort, my excitement. If I had the feminists I'd have community... Then the unthinkable happened. Slowly, around 1980, feminist solidarity began to unravel... One day I woke up to realize the excitement, the longing, the expectation of community was over.

"I CAN'T PREDICT PASSAGE NOW."

The Equal Rights Amendment had been the cause that held the fraying movement together for most of the 1970s, but by the end of the decade, the time limit on ratification was running out, while some state legislatures were attempting to withdraw votes they had made earlier in favor of putting the ERA in the Constitution. In New York and New Jersey, where the state legislatures had approved the ERA long before, supporters pressed for similar amendments to their state constitutions, which would require voter ratification. The show of popular support, they presumed, would give a boost to the national drive. But both amendments, stunningly, went down in defeat. In New York, the results weren't even close. The amendment lost by more than 400,000 votes. "There was such anxiety," said Carol Bellamy, a state senator from Brooklyn. "So many women I talked to had a sense that we wanted to take something away from them, some privilege or benefit that in most cases they don't really have." One widely distributed flyer in the state claimed the ERA was the product of a "militant women's group" that wanted to "make it difficult for the wife to remain home with the children and instead push her into the work market."

In state after state, polls showed that the public favored the amendment, but voters who went to the polls rejected it. There were different explanations in different places, but it was apparent that anxiety was triumphing over hope. Although Congress granted an extension until 1982, the cause had simply run out of steam. Advocates could only theorize that things would improve in the future.

"I can't predict passage now," admitted Ruth Bader Ginsburg in 1978. "But I can predict passage by the year 2000."

Keepsake Pages

The 1970s were a period of huge transition, particularly when it came to women's roles. (Suddenly we were liberated to both apply to law school and refuse to shave our legs.) Did you ever feel it went too far? Or that it wasn't going far enough?

_____

_____

_____

_____

_____

_____

_____

_____

Do you remember the fight over the Equal Rights Amendment? Why do you think it stalled and died?

_____

_____

_____

_____

_____

_____

_____

_____

When was the first time you heard about abortion? Did you know any women who had abortions when it was still illegal?

_____

_____

_____

_____

_____

_____

_____

_____

_____

_____

Do you remember Anita Bryant and the controversy over gay rights in Florida?

_____

_____

_____

_____

_____

_____

_____

_____

_____

More Thoughts and Memories

More Thoughts and Memories

10. "You're Gonna Make It After All"

"You walk into a meeting ... and now there's another woman."

In September 1970 Mary Tyler Moore—the actress who had broken television's no-pants rule on *The Dick Van Dyke Show*—returned with a new show in which she played Mary Richards, a thirtysomething single woman living alone and working for a local TV station. In the first episode, she fled from a broken engagement, driving tearily down the highway to Minneapolis, renting an apartment, and meeting neighbors and fellow workers who would become her surrogate family in the years to come. "You might just make it after all," the theme song promised. (It was changed after the first season to the more optimistic "You're gonna make it after all.") The show became one of the best-loved situation comedies of all time, and it ran through the decade. Mary, who spent much of the first year sitting around with Rhoda bemoaning their single state, became more assertive as time went on, proficient at her job, comfortable with her life, and more clearly engaged in sexual relations with her various boyfriends—who came and went without making any long-term impact. In a fractious decade, she became a cheerful symbol of the fact that a woman did not require a husband or children or a glamorous career to be happy, as long as she had people and work to care about and a healthy sense of humor.

The Mary Tyler Moore Show was, of course, only one program. TV in general was still a man's world—three-quarters of the characters in prime-time dramas in 1973 were men, and the women who did show up on the screen usually seemed to be in charge of answering telephones. But it's interesting to chart the difference between *The Mary Tyler Moore Show* and an earlier television series about a single woman living on her own. In 1966 ABC had unveiled *That Girl*, starring Marlo Thomas, which

followed an aspiring actress named Ann Marie through her adventures in New York City, many of which involved funny jobs (Ann wears a chicken suit, Ann is a meter maid) or mistaken identities. Ann lived in a residential hotel—one step beyond a college dorm—while her parents hovered in a nearby suburb. She spent an inordinate amount of time explaining to her worried mother and father that despite evidence to the contrary (dual hotel-room occupancy, pants in her closet), she was certainly not sleeping with her boyfriend, Donald. Ann was spunky and good-hearted, but she was not really a grown-up.

Like Mary Richards, American women in the 1970s were figuring out how to use their new powers to craft a good life. When viewed from above, it might have seemed that the big story was the backlash against the women's liberation movement. But on the ground, things looked much different. It was in the 1970s that American women set off on a new course. They went to college thinking about what work they wanted to do, not what man they wanted to catch, and flooded professional schools with applications. After graduation, they no longer marched right off to the altar, and the median age of marriage rose rather dramatically—particularly for women with college diplomas. No matter what their political perspective, they could feel new possibilities. "You walk into a meeting in one of the departments and now there's another woman," said Congresswoman Barbara Mikulski in 1978. "You see each other, maybe you wink, and you know you're both glad to see each other there."

"Do you prefer them actually?"

At a presidential bill signing in 1973, Richard Nixon turned to Helen Thomas, the veteran wire service reporter. "Helen, are you still wearing slacks?" he asked. "Do you prefer them actually? Every time I see girls in slacks, it reminds me of China." The remark may have been intrusive, but it was still an improvement from Washington a decade or so earlier, when Ruth Bader Ginsburg applied for a Supreme Court clerkship and Justice Felix Frankfurter rejected her after asking, "Does she wear skirts? I can't stand girls in pants."

The clothes women wore to work had changed dramatically, and that was no small matter for a generation that had grown up wrapped in heavy girdles and fragile nylons. The arbiters of fashion were suddenly "making it easier to be a woman," wrote Susan Brownmiller. "Lipstick color had lightened to a mere touch of gloss. Thanks to the wonders of Lycra, panty hose and a bra slip had replaced wires, garters, and girdles, allowing me to breathe normally for the first time since high school. Wobbly heels, the bane of my existence, were 'out' and flats were 'in.' Nails were permitted to be short and unpolished, hair didn't need to be teased and lacquered, the pantsuit had come into vogue, and skirts were completing their startling climb from below the knee to mid-thigh." Jane O'Reilly, recalling the first time she "stepped out on the streets of downtown New York City wearing blue jeans," said, "To my astonishment, no lightning bolt struck me down because I was not 'dressed for town.' The world had changed. I could put away the dark cotton, white gloves, and black pumps. The era of pin curls, waist cinchers, and girdles had ended."

Shoes were a feminist issue for some women, who loathed stiletto heels for their artificiality and discomfort. A "Stamp Out High Heels" movement blamed them for everything from "leg ache" to "inability to run from rapists." During the '60s the shoe reformers seemed to be getting their wish, as chisel-toed shoes with modest heels and thigh-high boots became the favored style for dressy occasions. (A fashion report in 1966 had announced that one of the loftiest shoe designs of the season was a "Pilgrim-buckled pump with a one-inch heel.")

However, by the early '70s younger women had embraced another style that was an outright invitation to leg fractures: platform shoes with enormous soles that could reach four inches or more. And by the end of the decade, the high heel had inched back, although politically sensitized designers suggested that women wanted to wear them "to please themselves, perhaps, rather than to attract attention from men, as in the past."

"GET THE HELL OUT OF MY RACE."

For all the moments that symbolized the changes for women in the 1970s, one of the most famous was also one of the cheesiest—the tennis match between Billie Jean King and Bobby Riggs in 1973. It was on one level a totally meaningless contest to settle the question of whether one of the world's greatest athletes in her prime could beat an out-of-shape 55-year-old man. But it was also a master course in how to disarm the most powerful weapon against women's fight for equality—ridicule.

Americans had always been uncomfortable with the idea of women athletes, although they had, on occasion, fallen in love with an exception. When Gertrude Ederle swam the English Channel in 1926, and did it nearly two hours faster than the five men who had gone before, she got a ticker-tape parade in New York City—and ears so damaged by the swim she was deaf at 27. In 1932 Babe Didrikson, an Olympic gold medalist in track and field, was also a professional baseball player, a star at tennis and swimming, and, most spectacular of all, a golfer who won her third U.S. Women's Open after cancer surgery had forced her to play with a colostomy bag. Esther Williams was a member of the U.S. Olympic team that never got to compete when the war canceled the 1940 games, and she wound up instead swimming through some very silly and extremely popular MGM movies.

Wilma Rudolph, a poor black girl with a left leg partially paralyzed from polio, spent her childhood shuttling from her small hometown of Clarksville,

Tennessee, to physical therapy in Nashville, while learning the brutal truths about what it felt like to be consigned to the back of the bus. She was finally allowed to play basketball for her high school team—and walked onto the court to score thirty-two points in her first game. She took up running for "pure enjoyment" and went off to college to become a world-class track star. She won three gold medals at the first Olympic Games that Americans were able to watch on television. "There was no doubt she was the fastest woman the world had ever seen," said *Time*. Rudolph was congratulated by the pope and the president and, in what must have been the sweetest moment of all, given a banquet in her hometown that marked the first time "in Clarksville's history that blacks and whites had gathered under the same roof for the same event." But for all her celebrity, Rudolph could not make a career out of her talent. There was absolutely no room in American culture for a woman professional athlete. She wound up teaching school and coaching.

In the Victorian era—when Americans disliked the idea of women moving around much at all—reformers brought physical education into girls' schools under the guise of health classes. At the start of the 1960s, most people still regarded athletics for women as being all about fitness, not competition. Altha Cleary, who attended Indiana University in the 1950s as a physical education major, said women students who got caught taking part in actual athletic contests were tossed out of the program. "Our department chair there said…girls were psychologically unfit: we would cry all the time if we lost."

The idea of mixing the sexes in sports was regarded as particularly improper. In 1950 Kathryn Johnston, 12, broke into the Corning, New York, Little League disguised as a boy named "Tubby." She was good enough that when she confessed, the team decided to keep her on the field anyway. But the next year the Little League instituted a new regulation barring girl players. It was informally known as the "Tubby Rule." In 1966 Roberta Gibb hid in the bushes by the starting line for the Boston Marathon, jumping out to join the other runners when the gun went off. Gibb had been training for the race in Vermont by running alongside the horses over a two-day, sixty-five-mile equestrian event, but her application for the marathon had been rejected on the grounds that women were not built to run long distances. As an unofficial entrant, she finished one hundred twenty-sixth out of four hundred fifty runners, but the ban on women continued to hold. The next year, Kathrine Switzer, a Syracuse University junior, got an official number in the marathon by entering as "K. V. Switzer." About three miles into the race, she was attacked by an official, Jock Semple, who tried to tear off her number, yelling, "Get the hell out of my race."

The Boston Marathon would finally allow women to run in 1972, and the Little League would integrate the following year, after a series of court cases filed by the angry parents of athletic little girls. In professional sports, the women's fight for recognition was fiercest, and most successful in tennis. Much of that was due to Billie Jean King.

"LITTLE GIRL, YOU CAN'T BE IN THE PHOTO."

The story begins with another fight over pants—or in this case, tennis shorts. "Little girl, you can't be in the photo," an official told the 11-year-old Billie Jean Moffitt when she joined the group for the team picture at her first tournament. "You're not wearing a skirt or tennis dress." It was a moment of humiliation she always remembered. The shorts were not a matter of rebellion. Billie Jean's lower-middle-class family did not know anything about the dress code at the posh Los Angeles Tennis Club, where the competition was being held. The shorts had been carefully sewn by her mother in what the Moffitts thought would be the right look for the big game.

By the time she went to college, Billie Jean had

already won the Wimbledon doubles championship, but she was working her way through Los Angeles State as a playground attendant. Athletic scholarships for women were virtually nonexistent. Larry King, the aspiring lawyer who she would soon marry, kept pointing out to her that he was "the seventh man on a six-man team" as a tennis player and still got money from the school, while she was the best-known athlete on campus and got nothing.

After she committed herself to a career as a professional athlete, Billie Jean Moffitt King began to rebel against the difference in prize money for men and women players. In 1970 the Pacific Southwest Open became the last straw—the male winner was scheduled to get $12,500, and the woman $1,500. The promoter was adamant that he would not go higher, so King and eight other top female players boycotted the event, playing instead at a hastily organized tournament in Houston sponsored by Philip Morris. It was the beginning of the Virginia Slims women's tennis tour, the increasing popularity of women's tennis, and a corresponding rise in purses. (King, always grateful for the cigarette maker's support, would never criticize Virginia Slims' marketing, which featured a jingle that announced triumphantly, "You've come a long way, baby, to get where you've got to today. You've got your own cigarette now, baby. You've come a long, long way!") As the marquee name who had made it all happen, Billie Jean was on the cover of *Sports Illustrated* as athlete of the year in 1972—the first time the place of honor had been given to a woman.

The idea of all this money and attention going to female tennis players was supremely irritating to some of the men, who regarded women's tennis as far inferior to the game they played. "Women belong in the bedroom and kitchen, in that order," said Bobby Riggs, a 55-year-old over-the-hill pro and natural-born hustler who quickly realized that he could get more attention, and money, as the champion of male chauvinism than in his previous

incarnation as champion of the tennis senior circuit. Women's tennis "stinks," he said; their play was so bad that even an old man like him could beat the very best the women had to offer. He challenged the top female players to prove him wrong, and Margaret Court leaped at the chance to make $10,000 for what she seemed to think was an ordinary exhibition match. (Court, who would later become a conservative preacher, had little enthusiasm for women's rights issues.)

King was horrified at the possibility of an embarrassing defeat. If Court insisted on playing, King told her, she had to win: "You have no idea how important this is." The match was held on Mother's Day, and Riggs presented Court with a bouquet of roses. Taken aback, she curtsied politely. (It was at that point, King said later, that she knew Court was doomed. "She should have smacked him over the head with them. She didn't get it.") Riggs's slow, peculiar game threw Court off completely, and she was trounced, 6–2, 6–1. The triumphant Riggs wound up on the cover of *Time*, and he told anyone who would listen that King was next. "I want her. She's the Woman's Libber Leader," he said.

King felt she had to accept the match. ("She won't admit it, but I can see her coming apart at the seams already," Riggs told *Time*.) The Court defeat had convinced a great many people—including some of the women tennis players—that Riggs was right and the women's game was "so far beneath men's tennis" that their best could not beat men's deeply mediocre. King threw herself into training and understood that she had to win the battle of the hype as well. Whether women had strong backhands was secondary to the question of whether they could stand up to people who wanted to make fun of them. She had to give as good as she got even during a weird, unpredictable event that was going to be watched by more people than any tennis match in history. (ABC paid $750,000 for the broadcast rights at a time when NBC was paying $50,000 for the rights to Wimbledon.) When—

just a half hour before the game—a promoter showed King a glitzy, chintzy Egyptian-style litter, held up by six underdressed young men, and hesitantly asked if she would consider riding in on it, she instantly said, "God, that would be great." It made for a perfect demonstration that she saw the event for precisely what it was. King satirized the spectacle while literally beating Riggs at his own game. As forty-eight million people watched on TV, she sent him running after her returns until he was winded. The final score was 6–4, 6–3, 6–3. "I underestimated you," Riggs told her.

"I thought it would set us back fifty years if I didn't win that match," King said. Her triumph was unalloyed, and fans of the game began to think it transcended the event's frivolous roots. "Because of Billie Jean alone, who was representing a sex supposedly unequipped for such things, what began as a huckster's hustle in defiance of serious athleticism ended up not mocking the game of tennis but honoring it. This night King was both a shining piece of showbiz and the essence of what sport is all about," wrote *Sports Illustrated*. It was the moment—at least, as many Americans remembered it—when women's sports arrived. Billie Jean King became one of the most famous athletes in the world, the most admired woman of her day. It was the ultimate repudiation of the *Father Knows Best* theory on the importance of losing to boys if you want to be popular.

"Second-class citizenship sounds good."

Young women watching the King-Riggs match might have started dreaming of becoming the next female athletic superstars. But they weren't getting much encouragement at their schools. Across the country, girls' sports were given such short shrift it was amazing that their taxpaying parents never rose up in arms. In Cedar Rapids, Iowa, where girls' sports got 9 percent of the athletic budget, the boys' tennis team had courts, and the girls played

on the school driveway, stopping the game whenever a motorist needed to get through. The women at the University of Kansas had to drive overnight to get to some of their track meets, and when they arrived, they slept on wrestling mats in the gym. (The male athletes were put up in hotels and transported at the university's expense.) The public school system in Waco, Texas, had $1 million in athletic facilities and equipment, but girls had use of only the tennis balls. Jane L., a ninth-grade basketball player, wrote to *Ms.* magazine in 1973 to say that she and her teammates had to play their matches in their gym suits, while the school provided the boys with expensive new uniforms. When Jane asked if the girls could have uniforms as well, she was told "to earn the money through car washes, dances, and bake sales." Billie Jean King's inability to get a scholarship for her athletic talents was not unusual—the sum total of women's athletic scholarships for the entire nation in 1972 was $100,000. Some public universities spent nothing whatsoever on women's sports.

All that began to change after 1972, when Congress passed the law that is universally known as Title IX. The bill, sponsored by Patsy Mink and Edith Green in the House, banned discrimination on the basis of sex in schools that receive federal funds—which meant virtually every school in the nation. (When the prickly Green retired, Senator Daniel Patrick Moynihan wrote wryly that she "did not suffer fools gladly—including this one" but added that she should be remembered for having "presided over the enactment of the most important education legislation in the history of the Republic.") At the time of its passage, most people who were paying attention thought Title IX was aimed at things such as opening up access to law and medical schools—which it certainly was. But in 1974 the federal agency tasked with coming up with regulations to implement the law said it also required schools to give women students comparable athletic opportunities.

Since an average Big Ten university invested

thirteen hundred times as much money on the average male athlete as on the average female one, this was obviously going to mean huge changes—to the men's disadvantage. (When Congresswoman Pat Schroeder visited a high school in her Denver district after the bill passed, the basketball coach told his team, "Show Mrs. Schroeder what you think of Title IX," and the boys turned around and mooned her.) There were dire predictions that schools would have to give up football and spend all the money on field hockey. In fact, the government was not requiring equal spending—just equal opportunities. That did not mean giving volleyball the same amount of funding as football, but it did mean that the volleyball players would no longer have to change clothes in the women's bathroom and that the men's coaches were going to have to share their training facilities, money for scholarships, and playing time on the fields and in the gyms.

Thanks to Title IX, by 1984 there were ten thousand athletic scholarships for women and thirty different national women's collegiate championships, compared to none in 1970. The number of girls playing sports in high school and college quintupled. The Cedar Rapids Women's Caucus quietly helped negotiate an agreement that got the girls off the driveway and onto the playing fields. "We got a lot more done than we'll ever get credit for, but credit is something you can trade," said Bev Mitchell, one of the caucus leaders. "You don't care what history says if the important thing is to get the girls a place to play tennis off the street before they get hit."

Critics questioned whether it went far enough—while the budget for women's sports went up, spending on men often went up even faster, and there was certainly nothing approaching parity. It all depended on your perspective. "Second-class citizenship sounds good when you are accustomed to being regarded as fifth-class," said Doris Brown, a former Olympic runner.

"YOU GOT MARRIED AND YOU NEVER TOLD ME."

By the mid-'70s, anyone who was unaware that there was a women's movement was living under a rock, and for all the controversy over the Equal Rights Amendment and abortion, there were large parts of the women's agenda that had overwhelming national support. Even an ardent traditionalist was likely to say that women deserved the same access to mortgages and credit cards as men. But American financial institutions didn't respond of their own volition. Women were still being asked whether they planned to have children when they applied for a car loan. In 1974 Kathryn Kirschbaum, the mayor of Davenport, Iowa, was told she could not have a BankAmerica card unless she got her husband's signature. Billie Jean King was the winner of three Wimbledon titles in a single year and was supporting her household with the money she made from tennis. But she could not get a credit card unless it was in the name of her husband, a law student with no income. Letters urging Larry King to apply for credit cards arrived in the mail regularly, "and I'm the one getting him through school. I get zip," she recalled.

Congress finally passed a ban on sex discrimination in lending in 1974, under the mysterious title of the Depository Institutions Amendments Act. By 1980 single women were buying one-third of all condominiums and one-tenth of all homes, according to the National Association of Realtors. One of them was Sylvia Peterson, the hairdresser in New Hampshire who had such conflicted feelings about the women's movement. "I thought that their values were mixed up. But at the same time, if it wouldn't have been for them, I wouldn't have been able to buy a house on my own," she said. Peterson was 30 at the time, and she had a struggle with the local bankers, who "didn't even want to talk with me . . . even one that was my age that I went to high school with." But she finally did an end run around them and applied to the government for an FHA loan. "I said, 'There's more than one way to skin a cat,'" she remembered with some satisfaction.

A little while later, Peterson noticed that one of her regular customers was starting to cold-shoulder her. "She would come and have her hair done every week and she would hardly speak to me...So finally I said, 'Did I hurt you in any way, or did I offend you?'"

"Yes, you did," said the customer. "You got married and you never told me."

"What makes you think I got married?" Peterson asked.

"Well, you bought this house," her client retorted. "You can't buy a house without being married."

Recalling the story recently, Peterson said that the conversation occurred in 1980 and that her client was not "the only woman who thought that way."

"Weird, huh?" she concluded.

"Nobody offered to scrounge up another chair."

The Ninety-second Congress (1971 to 1973) had only thirteen women in the House, and one of them was a congressman's widow sent to Washington by sympathetic voters for one year via a special election. There were two women in the Senate, one of them appointed by the governor of Louisiana, who happened to be her husband. The redoubtable Margaret Chase Smith was coming to the end of her career, and by 1973 the Senate would be all male. But if the quantity was disappointing, the quality was something else. The dozen women members of the House at the beginning of the decade included Martha Griffiths as well as Edith Green and Patsy Mink, who were about to sponsor the Title IX legislation. (Mink, a relatively new arrival from Hawaii, made news during her first year in Congress when she and two other women members tried to crash the men-only congressional gym.) There was Ella Grasso of Connecticut, who would soon become the first woman to be elected governor in her own right, and Margaret Heckler of Massachusetts, a champion of quality child care who had taken on a forty-two-year incumbent to win her seat. (In 1972, in a good demonstration of the way history repeats itself, Heckler made headlines with her discovery that the body armor being sent to American soldiers fighting an unpopular and frustrating war overseas was defective.) There was Shirley Chisholm, who would soon take on her Democratic Party by running for president.

And, of course, there was Bella Abzug, who had been a liberated woman long before there was women's liberation. She had worn her big, colorful trademark hats since she was a young woman, when her mother told her that a hat was a surefire sign that she was not a secretary. People tended to see Abzug as the ultimate representative of the women's movement — whether you believed that meant brash bossiness, or passion, energy, and bravery. Gloria Steinem remembered Abzug as the first woman she had ever met who succeeded in a male-dominated world without ever adopting the traditional ladylike trappings: "She expanded the way women can come to the public."

As a young lawyer in 1950, Abzug worked for civil rights in Mississippi — long before that kind of commitment was anything but immensely controversial and terribly dangerous. She was once threatened with lynching for defending a black man accused of raping a white woman. In Congress, she felt no need to spend her first term observing the traditional quiet deference of freshmen legislators, who were supposed to listen and pass minor proposals to rename buildings for departed politicians. On Abzug's first day, she introduced legislation demanding the withdrawal of all American troops from Vietnam.

Most of the new generation of congresswomen came equipped with a high degree of outspokenness. When Chisholm was appointed to the powerful

Rules Committee in 1977, she noted that the presiding officer, Representative James Delaney of Queens, called her "Shirley" while every other member was referred to as "Mr."

When she objected, Delaney asked, "Shirley, what's the matter? You and I have been intimate for years."

"Jim, we don't have to let the public know it," she retorted. She was "Mrs. Chisholm" from then on.

As the decade went on, the still-tiny House women's caucus would include Millicent Fenwick, the inimitable pipe-smoking WASP who surprised herself with her decision to run for office—the Equal Rights Amendment, she concluded, might have "affected me more than I realized." (It may be an indication of how much the nation's attitude toward age has evolved—or how different the attitude was regarding age in men as opposed to age in women—that when Fenwick was first elected at 64, the media called her victory "a geriatric triumph.") A principled, idiosyncratic politician, Fenwick drove her staff crazy by answering the office phones herself. When the caller would ask for a member of the staff, Fenwick often said, "They are too busy. Talk to me."

There was Geraldine Ferraro, the representative from Queens, who would make history later when she was chosen as Walter Mondale's running mate in 1984. Yvonne Braithwaite Burke became the first member of Congress ever to give birth; her daughter Autumn became a veteran flier before she could talk, as she and her mother shuttled between California and Washington. Burke, who had gotten married during her congressional campaign, wanted to start a family quickly without shortchanging her constituents. She managed to have the baby on the day after Thanksgiving, "which gave me until the session started on January fifteenth to adjust."

Barbara Jordan, who arrived in 1973, was already famous in her home state of Texas. Only the third black woman lawyer in Texas history, she became the first African-American to work in her county's courthouse in any job other than janitor, and the first black state senator since Reconstruction. In a giddily joyful moment in 1972, Jordan, who had been elected president pro tem of the chamber, became governor for a day under an old annual Texas tradition in which the governor and lieutenant governor both leave the state and put the legislators in charge. Diagnosed with multiple sclerosis the same year she arrived in Washington, Jordan would serve only three terms. But she impressed herself into the nation's consciousness as a great speaker. No one who watched the Judiciary Committee hearings into the Watergate scandal and the impeachment of Richard Nixon would forget Jordan's deep, precise voice as she recalled how, when the Founding Fathers wrote "We the People" at the beginning of the Constitution, she was not included.

But through the process of amendment, interpretation, and court decision I have finally been included in "We the People." Today, I am an inquisitor...My faith in the Constitution is whole, it is complete, it is total. I am not going to sit here and be an idle spectator to the diminution, the subversion, the destruction of the Constitution.

Molly Ivins, the great chronicler of Texas politics, remembered the trajectory of Jordan's political career—from her arrival in the state senate, where a few of her colleagues privately referred to her as "that nigger bitch" or "the nigger mammy washerwoman," through their growing respect, to the night of the impeachment speech, when all her old colleagues clustered around a television set. " 'Give 'em hell, Barbara!' they crowed," Ivins wrote. "As she lit into Richard Nixon, they cheered and hoorahed and pounded their beer bottles on the table as though they were watching U.T. pound hell out of Notre Dame in the Cotton Bowl."

The range of talents and intensity of the personalities of the handful of women who served in Congress in the 1970s made many of them national celebrities. "The whole world adopted you as their spokesperson," said Pat Schroeder. "You represented *all* the women. You got so much mail and so many requests and everybody who came to Washington wanted to see you. They would bring in baskets of mail from all over the country." Schroeder, who became another one of the best-known women politicians of the decade, was recruited by a group of liberal Denver Democrats—including her husband, Jim—to run against the local Republican congressman in 1972. It seemed like a hopeless race, and when Schroeder stunned everyone by winning, the family bought a house in Washington over the phone, had it furnished with whatever they could get delivered quickly, and "ended up with bright-red shag carpet throughout the house and avocado kitchen appliances."

The institution she was entering turned out to be astonishingly up front about its sexism, a liberty its male members had awarded themselves by exempting Congress from the antidiscrimination laws they had been passing. Given the small number of women in Congress, it was perhaps not surprising that so many members thought Jim Schroeder was the newly minted representative from Denver. But it seemed a bit excessive when, upon discovering that he was the congressional spouse, some retorted, "Why didn't *you* run?" The Schroeders were given tickets to a black-tie dinner at the prestigious Touchdown Club, then stopped by a guard who told them no women were allowed and that if she didn't leave quietly, "You'll be carried out." The worst part, she wrote later, was seeing the faces of her House colleagues "laughing as we were shown the door." When Schroeder got her hoped-for slot on the Armed Services Committee, the despotic chairman, F. Edward Hébert, was so outraged that he decreed Schroeder and Ron Dellums, the second-term black congressman from California, would have to share a chair since they were worth only half of a "regular" member. When she and Dellums were forced to

each perch on one side of the same seat, Schroeder said, "Nobody else objected and nobody offered to scrounge up another chair."

"They're legislators . . . and they're lovely."

The fact that the makeup of Congress didn't reflect the increasing political involvement of women in the 1970s isn't surprising. A seat in Congress is a big political prize, and the men who had been waiting for a chance to win one weren't likely to just step aside in the name of gender equity. Most of those congressmen-in-waiting had earned their places in line by winning elections on the state and local level. To elbow them out of the way, women were going to have to join the same farm team. That was the problem. In 1971 there were only forty-six women serving as state senators, and three hundred in state houses—fewer than 5 percent of the total. No woman had ever been elected governor in her own right. (Early in the century, two had been elected as stand-ins—one for a husband who had died suddenly and one for a spouse who had been impeached.) When it came to other statewide offices—often the best stepping-stones to the U.S. Senate—only three women had ever held jobs such as secretary of state or lieutenant governor. None had ever served as state attorney general.

The numbers were about to change, and by 1991 women would be edging toward 20 percent of the total number of state lawmakers. That was hardly earthshaking, but it was still significant progress in bodies that tended to have very little turnover. Another 323 women had won a statewide elective office, including ten who had become governor in their own right.

Like the women in Congress, the female newcomers on the state level weren't necessarily made to feel welcome. Many of them were pioneers in hostile territory, struggling to carve a place for themselves in political cultures that made Congress look idyllic. When Diane Watson was elected to California's state senate in 1978, she was not only the first African-American woman but the second *woman*. The first, Rose Ann Vuich, had arrived just two years before and had become famous for sitting through senate debates with a little bell, which she would ring every time a speaker addressed his colleagues as "Gentlemen."

Vuich, a conservative from an agricultural district near Fresno, and Watson, a former school board member who had been the point person in integrating the Los Angeles school system, had little in common politically. But they shared stony resistance from their colleagues. "They'd say, 'You're taking the seat of a man. There should be a man in that seat,'" Watson said. (The sole African-American man in the senate, Watson said, "was the first to say we had nothing to talk about.") The two women presented a united front when they discovered that a $40 million renovation of the capitol that was under way did not include a women's restroom off the senate like the one the men had always had. "We pointed it out to the architect, and he said, 'My gosh, I forgot all about it,'" Watson recalled. The women's room was added on and named "The Rose Room" in Vuich's honor. For a while, the senators seemed to be taking the name literally. "I had to go to Rose to get the key," said Watson.

Madeleine Kunin, who was living in Burlington, Vermont, with her husband and four children, followed the threads of new possibilities. She joined a small women's political caucus that was formed to get the state to ratify the Equal Rights Amendment. (The ERA's lasting impact, at least in the twentieth century, would turn out not to be on the Constitution but in its effect on the generation of political women who fought for it.) One afternoon in 1972, when Kunin and another member were talking about how to get more women to run for public office, "Esther and I looked at each other, laughed, and exclaimed, 'Why don't *we* do it?'" That November, she was elected to the Vermont senate and I

was elected to the Vermont house." Arriving at the capitol in Montpelier as a newly minted legislator, Kunin felt for the first time that she was herself rather than someone's wife, mother, sister, or daughter. But she and her female colleagues still struggled against the perception that they were unusual creatures—not regular legislators but women-lawmakers. When some of them were invited to appear on public television to discuss weighty topics from drug laws to highways to juvenile offenders, Kunin and the other women got together to view the program with a certain amount of excitement. After their part was finished, they watched as the host turned to the camera and concluded, "Well, you can see that brains and beauty do mix; they're legislators, they're ladies, and they're lovely."

The women sat in front of the TV in silence. Then the evening was saved, Kunin recalled, by a deeply refined Republican lawmaker, a retired schoolteacher, who got in the last word.

"Oh, shit!" she said.

"HELLO, GIRLS!"

In 1974 Kunin went to a midterm Democratic convention in Kansas City, traveling with another woman who was one of the state's Democratic leaders. Their governor was waiting to greet them when they arrived.

"Hello, girls!" he said cheerfully.

One of the most energetic reeducation efforts of the 1970s involved teaching men not to automatically refer to groups of two or more women as "girls," even if they happened to be grandmothers or lawyers or police officers. The difference between "girls" and "women" became the "Maginot Line of feminism," Kunin felt. It was particularly important in areas such as politics, where rather than being beaten down by resistance, the women tended to be drowned in paternalism.

Words mattered. It was an enormous victory in

1970 when Ben Bradlee, the editor of the *Washington Post*, told his reporters to stop using words such as "blond" or "divorcée" or "grandmother" to describe women in news stories. ("The juror, a blond schoolteacher...") At the *New York Times*, Barbara Crossette spent her years on the news desk running a rearguard battle against those same unnecessary descriptions: "Like 'a short, trim woman...' where you knew there would never be 'a tall, slightly overweight man.'" McGraw-Hill outlined an eleven-page policy in 1974 that warned editors about everything from use of the term "the weaker sex" to clichés about nagging mother-in-laws. But the longest, hardest battle involved the term "Ms." There were few things that more vividly reflected the philosophy that women were important only in their relationship to men than the fact that they had to be identified as either "Miss" or "Mrs." If a reporter didn't know whether a woman was married, it was necessary to ask—even if the person in question was lying dead of a gunshot wound or being awarded the Nobel Prize.

"Ms." had been employed in some business correspondence when a marital status wasn't known, and women lobbied to make it the one-size-fits-all equivalent of "Mr." But the *New York Times*, which many people saw as a particularly critical standard for language style, held out. "To our ear, it still sounds too contrived for newswriting," said the paper's language guru, William Safire, in 1984. (In the same year, the *Times* ran a story about Gloria Steinem's fiftieth birthday party that reported proceeds from the dinner "will go to the Ms. Foundation...which publishes *Ms.* magazine, where Miss Steinem works as an editor.)" In 1986 Paula Kassell, a veteran journalist, bought ten shares of *Times* stock and went to the annual stockholders' meeting to plead the "Ms." issue with the publisher, Arthur Ochs Sulzberger. (It was a measure of the importance Kassell put on the issue that she went to the meeting even though her husband had died the previous week.) Shortly after, Sulzberger wrote back,

thanking her for raising the question and informing Kassell she need not press further; the women had won.

"You see that maroon Malibu?"

Look back on a decade as fraught with change as the 1970s, and you can pick your own vision. Best of times or worst of times. Women who wanted to work often found it easier to get a job than men did, but the jobs they found still tended to pay much less. It was easier for them to end unsatisfactory marriages but sometimes harder to get spousal support. It was more difficult to keep life in balance but more possible to shoot for the stars.

Gloria Vaz had been through it all. She had been sexually abused by her mother's boyfriend as a child and had a baby out of wedlock back when it was so frowned upon that she made up stories about a mythical husband to tell the staff in the hospital when she delivered. She married a man who never told her he loved her. ("I told him a lot... He never said it back.") He cheated on her, and his family, who were West Indian, looked down on her because she was African-American. "He was the authority in the home. He really was. No ifs, ands, or buts," she said. "I didn't say a lot sometimes, but it was inside, and it manifested itself. I started getting psychosomatic illnesses—heart, dizziness, all kinds of nonsense that there was no explanation for." After years as a stay-at-home wife in New York, she got a job at a bank, and she had her first rebellion over the family car, which she loved and which her husband threatened to sell whenever he wanted to keep her in line. "Then something clicked in me...," she said. "I went out on my own and purchased a used car, without telling him... I said, 'Look out the window. You see that maroon Malibu? That's mine. All mine. So you can sell the car if you want to.'"

Years of struggle later, she got a job working for a nonprofit agency that recognized her abilities. "It was my blossoming time," said Vaz, who eventually became the acting director at the agency and, before her retirement, a director at the Fund for the City of New York.

>> <<

AFTER A CHILDHOOD on Cherokee lands in Oklahoma, Wilma Mankiller and her family moved to San Francisco when she was 10, living in a housing project near the shipyards. None of them had ever used a telephone before or seen an elevator. "There were never any plans for me to go to college," she recalled. "That thought never even entered my head. People in my family did not go to college. They went to work."

After high school she took a clerical job and met a handsome young college student whose family had emigrated from Ecuador. "I thought perhaps if I married Hugo all my problems would disappear," she said. She became pregnant on their honeymoon. Before she was twenty-one, she had two daughters and an undefined restlessness. While her husband pulled toward traditional married life, Wilma pushed in the opposite direction. She started taking college courses. He took her to look at houses in the suburbs and bought her a washing machine. She got deeply involved in the Native American movement and began taking her daughters to tribal events throughout the area.

Finally, Hugo told her she could no longer use the family car. Wilma went out and bought one of her own.

"THEY WERE JUST THEMSELVES, STARTING OUT."

Catherine Roraback had gotten used to being the only woman in the courthouse during her first two decades of legal practice. Then, in the '70s, that began to change. Women lawyers were becoming less unusual. Whenever Roraback saw one enter the courtroom, "I was so excited, I'd go over and talk to them. They didn't have any idea how excited I was." She laughed. "They were just themselves, starting out."

American history had been full of stories of amazing women who managed to become a doctor or lawyer or business executive against all odds and prejudices. But the new stories were different because they did not stop with a single heroic but lonely figure. This was the critical moment when the doors were opened for good. A small population of women working in traditionally male occupations pushed until there was room for a whole generation to walk through. The number of women in professional schools began to grow steadily. By the end of the '70s, a quarter of the students in medical school were women, and a third of the students in law school. That first big wave was not always made to feel particularly welcome. In law schools, professors often refused to call on female students except on an annual Ladies' Day, when women were supposed to answer all the questions. "In my criminal law class, the relatively young professor ... announced that on his Ladies' Day we would be discussing rape," recounted Brenda Feigen, who went to Harvard Law in the late '60s. "And when that day rolled around, the specific question for us women was: How much penetration constitutes rape?"

In the 1970s women also began to apply for acceptance in the skilled trade unions, where the pay was often more than three times what they could make at a nonunion job. "I liked it right away," said Brunilda Hernandez, who discovered that a local branch of the International Brotherhood of Electrical Workers had opened its ranks to women in New York City and quickly signed up. "It was working with your hands. It was using your brain as you were doing these formulas and you were figuring out how electricity worked and how to hook up panels — just how it all worked." The male union members, however, weren't enthusiastic. When Hernandez began her four-year apprenticeship, she said, "I got all these stares from these guys just sitting around. It was really nerve-racking." There were no bathrooms or changing rooms for women at her first construction site, and the men slapped up a makeshift plywood box for her in the middle of a line of toilets: "That was my little home, a toilet closet." On the job, she was paired with a hostile mechanic who put cinder blocks in front of the box to keep her from getting in. Evan Ruderman, Hernandez's best friend, worked at another site with an even more hostile partner. When she would leave her post to get something, he would urinate on the spot where she was working, "practically on my tools. Or I'd lay a ruler down when I was measuring pipe, turn around, cut it, turn back around—my ruler was gone."

Laura Kelber, another one of the first generation of female electricians in New York City, told her foreman that she was pregnant and was immediately transferred from a relatively light indoor assignment to a different site where the job involved heavy lifting, working in the cold, and no clean bathrooms. "It was the worst type of job," said Kelber, who tried to stick it out so she could qualify for full disability benefits at the end of her pregnancy. But she miscarried during her third month.

"I WAS SUCH A YOUNG NERD."

Sylvia Acevedo's great-grandfather on her father's side had been a wealthy man in Chihuahua, Mexico, who'd lost everything when Pancho Villa, the self-styled Mexican Robin Hood, rode into town. The family, impoverished, fled to El Paso. Meanwhile, Sylvia was told, her mother's relatives were one of the poor families who got a bounty of silver coins from Villa's loot. "I'm not sure how much of this is folklore," she says. "But there's a picture in the museum in Chihuahua of Pancho Villa and his right-hand man, which is my grandmother's cousin."

Her father was born in the United States, the beleaguered child of a disappointed woman who had watched her older siblings grow up in luxury that had vanished by the time she was ready to enjoy it. He became a chemist, but he never recovered from the trauma of living with a woman who took her endless anger out on her son. Acevedo's

mother, an immigrant, had only an eighth-grade education but boundless ambition for her children. She dressed Sylvia in gloves and hats and lace, none of which her daughter really enjoyed. "She kept saying, when you're 15, when you're 16, it's going to happen for you, and it didn't," Acevedo recalled. "But—I really love and honor this about her—she accepted me." When Sylvia was in high school, she bought the first issue of *Ms.* as soon as it came on the market: "I was such a young nerd. I really got into that whole Gloria Steinem thing."

It was a given that Acevedo would do well in school and go to college. However, when she looked carefully through all the catalogs and decided she wanted to be an engineer, her father's first comment was "But you have to be good in math and science."

"I thought, 'I've *always* been good in math and science,'" she recalled.

Her guidance counselor said, "Oh my goodness, you have to be really smart, really bright," so often that when Acevedo arrived with trepidation at the University of New Mexico's engineering school, she "thought I was going to be with Einsteins. And they were just the same guys I went to high school with."

"I HAD TO BE EDUCATED QUICKLY."

Suzan Johnson, who everybody called Sujay, had grown up in the Bronx, where her family was the first African-American household on their block. Her mother, a teacher, and her father, a motorman, came home from their day jobs and worked to build up a private security business in the evenings. They wanted not only to send their children to good private schools but to make sure that while they were there, they got all the trimmings—the tennis rackets, the summer trips to Spain, and everything else that would help them to fit into the virtually all-white world at the top.

Sujay responded by being an empowered overachiever who graduated from college before her twentieth birthday and embarked on multiple careers. She enrolled at Union Theological Seminary, vaguely contemplating the ministry, while hedging her bets by becoming a television producer and working at a public-relations job for Bronx-Lebanon Hospital. On the day she preached a sermon for a final exam at the seminary, she raced out of the classroom before the other students took their turns and jumped into her car to make two closely scheduled appointments—one to tape a television appearance for the hospital, and the other a job interview with *60 Minutes*. "And I got stuck on the 155th Street bridge." She laughed. Trapped in traffic as the minutes ticked away, she realized it was time to make a choice. "I was like, 'You can't do it all!' and I made a decision it was going to be full-time ministry." A year later, as she was doing her internship at the office of the American Baptist Churches, she was offered her own parish—Mariners' Temple, a church in lower Manhattan between Chinatown and city hall.

The church, which seated eleven hundred, had only fifteen members, and the Baptist leadership had privately been planning to shut it down and give the building to a Chinese congregation that was already sharing the space for its services. "I was supposed to do the final benediction, and it was going to be closed under my leadership. I didn't know that," Johnson said. She reached out to the residents of nearby housing projects, starting after-school tutoring sessions. She also began what turned out to be a hugely popular midday service for the people who worked in the courts, city offices, and police department nearby. "We'd have five hundred people at lunchtime," she recalled. "You'd see all these people converge, and the politicians were like, 'What's going on over there?'" She added on another job when the police department asked her to be one of its chaplains, and by her seventh year of ministry, she had been invited to be a visiting professor at Harvard Divinity School.

It was perhaps what Johnson had imagined when she was in the seminary but hardly what the male leaders of her church had planned. When she got to Mariners', "and they made all this hoopla about my being the first woman," she began to realize that the doors were not nearly as open as she had thought. That became even clearer when the women who had been her classmates started telling her they were unable to find positions as pastors or assistant pastors. "I really didn't know what the worldview was. I had to be educated quickly," she said.

The Hampton Ministers' Conference was helpful in the quick-learning process. The largest interdenominational gathering for black clergy, it attracted thousands of participants every year, and the first time Johnson attended, "there were, like, five women pastors" who were denied permission to get together for a meeting of their own.

"The first year some of the men tried to take me to bed. They didn't know how to relate to women," Johnson said. "I'm like, 'No, but I'll play basketball with you. I did the sports thing.'" She felt keenly unwelcome. She has a crystal-clear memory of going up to a prominent minister, putting out her hand, and introducing herself. "And he hit my hand like, 'I know who you are and I'm not even touching you.'" Humiliated, Johnson looked around to see who had witnessed her embarrassment. "I remember that moment. I remember where we were standing. He hurt my feelings really badly. But every year I'd come back and introduce myself again and say, 'How are you doing, Doctor?'"

"FLY ME."

While women were struggling to break into traditionally male professions, the flight attendants were fighting to prove that their jobs could be done by either sex. The attendants, who had been first at the door when the Equal Employment Opportunity Commission opened for business, were also among the first in the courtrooms. Their battles began with Eulalie Cooper, who had been working for Delta for nearly six years when the airline discovered she was secretly married and fired her. (To add insult to injury, the Louisiana Unemployment Compensation Board denied her benefits on the grounds that she had left her job "voluntarily.") Cooper sued, but a Louisiana judge agreed with the airline that serving food and ensuring safety on an airplane was a job that young single women were uniquely qualified to do, and therefore fell under the law's exemption for "bona fide occupational qualifications"—the loophole NOW once argued should be applied only to sperm donors and wet nurses. In another case in Miami, Pan Am brought in the psychiatrist Eric Berne, author of a bestselling book called *Games People Play,* to explain that an apprehensive male passenger would feel resentment if another man tried to tell him what to do—unless that man seemed gentle, in which case the passenger would feel homosexual panic.

While the flight attendants were fighting to establish their job as gender-neutral—including a war to get the airlines to stop calling them "stewardesses"—the airlines were going out of their way to make them international sex objects. Throughout American history, women who worked had to fight against the myth that because they were active in the public world, they were therefore promiscuous. Nurses had had a particularly difficult time, and the women who volunteered to serve during World War II suffered under malicious rumors that only a loose woman would willingly work in the middle of thousands of soldiers.

In the '70s it was the flight attendants' turn, but in this case it was their employer who was doing the mythmaking. In 1971 National Airlines began its "Fly Me" campaign, in which lovely young women in flight attendants' uniforms purred, "Hi, I'm Cheryl/ Donna/Diane. Fly me." Continental announced, "We really move our tails for you," and Southwest introduced itself as the "love" airline, where passengers would be served "love bites" and "love potions," otherwise known as snacks and drinks. Meanwhile the women who were dispensing the love bites, moving their tails, and (later) promising to "fly you like you've never been flown before"

were being dressed in miniskirts, vinyl, hot pants, and—in the case of TWA—paper clothes, such as togas, cocktail dresses, and "penthouse" pajamas, that were supposed to match the entrées.

Eventually, the same appeals court that had given Lorena Weeks her triumph over Southern Bell ruled that the business of an airline was getting people from one place to another and that men and women were equally capable of facilitating that process in the air. Finally, in 1973 a federal court in the District of Columbia wiped out the stewardess culture completely by ruling that Northwest Airlines had to do away with the appearance rules and any other restrictions that did not relate directly to safety duties.

"God, it was mean."

The National Press Club in Washington was the place where almost every prominent news maker who visited the nation's capital came to speak and be covered by the alleged cream of the American media. The male reporters were happy to invite their old colleagues who had become lobbyists or public-relations men to come as guests, have lunch, and listen to the big-name speakers. They even invited their golfing buddies or next-door neighbors. But they refused to allow a woman reporter to set foot in the place. In 1955, in what was regarded as a great concession, club officials agreed that on days when an important guest came to dine and speak, their female colleagues could stand in a narrow, hot, and crowded balcony and take notes for their stories. The women, of course, got no lunch. It was difficult to hear up there, and they were not permitted to ask questions. "In professional terms it couldn't have been meaner, it couldn't have been pettier. God, it was mean," said Bonnie Angelo, who had been the *Newsday* Washington bureau chief and a *Time* reporter in those days.

In 1971 one of the most outrageous instances of sexual segregation in the professions ended when the Press Club finally voted to allow women members.

The walls fell at a time when women were declaring war in their own newsrooms, wiping out the ancient journalistic traditions that had kept most of them stuck covering weddings and recipes for generations. *Newsweek*'s women led the way—which wasn't surprising considering the newsmagazine's famous system in which women became researchers and men became writers. In 1970, when *Newsweek* decided to run its big cover story on the women's movement, only one of the magazine's fifty-two writers was a woman—Lynn Povich, who had benefited from the fact that none of the men were willing to cover the fashion beat. Trying to find a writer to assign the women's cover to, the editors, after much churning and mind-changing, picked a freelancer, the wife of a staff member. They had figured out enough to know the article had to be written by a woman but not enough to realize their own female employees would be outraged that their bosses felt none of them were up to the job. "We thought, 'That's it,'" said Povich. "Being good media people, we knew the publicity would get them more than anything else." So, on the day *Newsweek* appeared on the newsstands with the big cover that read "Women in Revolt," the women of *Newsweek* announced they had filed a sex-discrimination suit against their employer.

It took endless negotiation, a memorandum of understanding that didn't work out, frustration, and threats of a second suit, but in 1972 *Newsweek* agreed to a plan that would not only open up writing jobs to women but also make sure a number of the researchers were men. The magazine promised to appoint a woman to a senior editor job, and in 1975 Povich became the first woman to enter the upper reaches of *Newsweek* management.

The saga of the *Newsweek* women inspired similar revolts at the TV networks and major newspapers. At the *New York Times*, the last straw came in the form of a memo from the publisher, announcing a series of top-level promotions and promising that there were more to come as the paper increased "the load of younger men who have demonstrated their capacity to carry it." After several years of organizing and negotiating with a seemingly sympathetic yet unresponsive top management, the women filed a suit against the paper for sex discrimination in 1972.

At the time, aside from those in the family/style department, the only woman holding any kind of editor's job was Betsy Wade, an editor on the foreign copydesk. Wade, who would become the first named plaintiff in the case under her married name, Boylan, had been a copyeditor since 1958—no small accomplishment, since the copydesk had always been considered a male preserve. On some papers, the copyeditors, like mine workers, claimed it was bad luck if a woman ventured into their territory.

It was a world Wade loved—like a lifeboat, she thought, "where you all had to pull on the oars and if one person didn't make it, nobody made it. There was this coherence." She had dreamed of working her way up to a top editing job. "I had finally opened this door no woman had passed through. I thought, 'Hell, I'm Miss America. I'm Queen of the May.'" It took a long time for her to process the fact that she was not moving anywhere. "People being broken in by me were being promoted beyond me," she recalled.

The fact that the *Times* suit had been filed was in itself a career-transforming opportunity—for younger women who had not been around for the battles. In 1973, 47 percent of the *Times*' new hires for reporters and editors were women, compared to 7 percent in the years immediately before. The newcomers got the jobs and promotions that the older rebels had missed out on. Wade remembers when the word arrived that several women had been brought in from other publications to work as editors at the *Times*.

"Someone came tearing in and said, 'For God's sake, look what we've done. They're hiring women from the outside,'" she recalled.

"You really didn't think it was going to do *us* any good?" one of the suit leaders retorted.

The women who had stood up to management

were hoping, of course, that the new opportunities they were creating might include some for themselves as well. Wade, at least, thought she would remain in place. "I thought I was going to slip through. I thought they'd find someplace, you know, maybe night foreign editor." But for the most part, the generation that took the risks, filed the suits, held the press conferences, and made the demands were not the ones who benefited. Some of them received settlements for discrimination, but the amounts were extremely modest. The women at *Reader's Digest* got an average of $244 each, those at NBC averaged $200, and the women at the *Times,* $454. And Betsy Wade Boylan wound up working as a writer in the quiet precincts of the travel desk.

Keepsake Pages

Do you remember the Billie Jean King versus Bobby Riggs tennis match? When you were in school, did girls play sports at all? Did you? How were the girls' teams treated—did they get the same kinds of uniforms, transportation, and crowds of supporters as the boys?

_____

_____

_____

_____

_____

_____

_____

_____

_____

When did you acquire your first credit card? Did you have any trouble getting credit when you were young?

_____

_____

_____

_____

_____

_____

_____

_____

_____

Who was the first female politician you identified with? Do you remember Bella Abzug or Shirley Chisholm? When Geraldine Ferraro was nominated for vice president, did that seem like a major event to you?

_____

_____

_____

_____

_____

_____

_____

_____

_____

How did you feel about using "Ms." instead of "Miss" or "Mrs." when the issue first came up? Do you remember the days when men called adult women "girls"?

_____

_____

_____

_____

_____

_____

_____

_____

_____

Do you have any memories of the way women were treated at work in the '60s and early '70s? Were you working then? Did you get the same salary as men doing the same job? Did you run into any other problems because you were a woman?

_____

_____

_____

_____

_____

_____

_____

_____

_____

Did any women file antidiscrimination lawsuits in your profession? Did you know them? Were you involved in any of the suits? If you came later, did you feel any specific benefits from them?

_____

_____

_____

_____

_____

_____

_____

_____

_____

More Thoughts and Memories

More Thoughts and Memories

11. Work and Children

There aren't many people born after 1960 who remember *The Adventures of Ozzie and Harriet,* an early situation comedy in which former bandleader Ozzie Nelson and his wife, Harriet, played a husband and wife with their real-life sons, David and Ricky. The show ran from 1952 to 1966 on television, but it doesn't appear in endless reruns like *"I Love Lucy"* or *The Jackie Gleason Show.* That's probably because it wasn't all that entertaining. The dialogue was stunningly bland. "They sure do taste good, Mom," said David in one episode as Harriet doled out the breakfast pancakes. "Yeah, they sure do, Mom," said Ricky, who the announcer would dub "the little guy with a twinkle in his eye." The action was nonexistent. (In the climax of the scene above, Ricky returns the pancake mix to the store and gets double the money back.) There was so little context to the plots—a chair is delivered to the wrong house, Harriet gets her hair done—that in fourteen years, the series never even revealed what the TV Ozzie did for a living. But the Nelsons were around so long that viewers—and the Census Bureau—came to think of them as the prototypical American family: breadwinner father, stay-at-home mom, and their kids, nestled in their comfortable suburban home, eating pancakes.

The Nelsons left the air just as the image was beginning to crack. In 1960, 62 percent of American households were made up of a breadwinner dad and stay-at-home mom with one or more children. By the middle of the '80s, only about 10 percent of American households were what people still referred to as "Ozzie-and-Harriet families." The model was not even working for the Nelsons. Ricky, the little guy with a twinkle in his eye, became a rock musi-

cian, and by the mid-'70s he was in the process of divorcing the mother of his four children.

The traditional family model that the 1950s had celebrated was being transformed—or undermined, depending on your point of view—by divorce, cohabitation, and unwed motherhood. People were staying single longer. The birthrate was plummeting, as women deferred marriage for work. And once children came, married women were discovering they could not afford to stay home even if they wanted to. The competition of baby boomers for housing in the 1970s and '80s tripled the cost of the average new home. In 1977 *BusinessWeek* said that a new house was "out of reach of blue-collar and nonprofessional, nonmanagerial heads of households whose spouses do not work." A new generation of young adults did the math and presumed that when they married, their family's future would have to be underwritten by two salaries. While in 1970 less than a third of women with preschool children worked outside the home, in 1976 it was 43 percent. In another decade it would be half.

"We were in this big change," said Walter Mondale, who was a U.S. senator from Minnesota, worrying about child-care issues. "Working wives had become a big thing in American life. It was sort of an unplanned change."

The divorce rate, which had been flat in the United States throughout the 1950s and early '60s, had started to skyrocket. By 1980 the government would note that the number of divorces was setting a record for the eighteenth consecutive year and was three times as high as it had been in 1962. There were a lot of theories about what made so many marriages collapse at once. The sexual revolution was one favorite culprit. It also seemed reasonable to assume that the rush to marry after World War II might be followed by a rush of divorces as the children left home. And a lot of people blamed the women's liberation movement. When Wilma Scott Heide, the president of NOW in the early '70s, agreed with her husband that it was time to divorce, Faith Middleton was one of the reporters dispatched to the Heide house to get an interview. "The editor's feeling was that this was an indication feminists were angry people, that they had bad marriages—that this was living proof," Middleton remembered.

And then there was the liberalization of divorce. In 1970 California became the first state to pass a no-fault divorce law that allowed couples to end a marriage by mutual consent. Over the course of the decade, all but three states instituted some variation on the no-fault theme. (Illinois, Pennsylvania, and South Dakota brought up the rear in the 1980s. Although New York liberalized its law, the state still had what were probably the most conservative rules, particularly if both parties did not mutually agree to end the marriage.) Defenders of the reforms pointed out that the divorce rates didn't seem higher in states that had made the change. But whether it was new laws, new kinds of women, or a new culture, by 1976 the number of divorces had gone well past one million a year—more than double the number a decade earlier.

And getting divorced was no longer a cause for shame. The creators of *The Mary Tyler Moore Show* originally intended to make their heroine a divorcée, but the networks felt viewers might not be able to relate to a woman with a failed marriage in her past. If the series had arrived a few years later, the original concept probably would have survived. By the mid-'70s it seemed almost every family had at least one member who was divorced. When Maria K. had her second baby, she moved to a larger city and told everyone that her boys were the product of a broken marriage. Once she had remade herself into "the gay divorcée" rather than a never-married mom, she said, "everyone loved me."

The women's rights movement had not been at the forefront of the drive to remake the divorce laws, but most feminists agreed that the idea of forcing unhappy people to stay married for the sake of propriety was outdated. And if you wanted equality, it seemed impossible to argue that women should automatically get custody of the children or that men should pay alimony forever to an ex-spouse who wasn't working to support herself.

Alimony had never been awarded in a large proportion of divorces, but under no-fault, it virtually vanished, except as a kind of temporary subsidy that could help ease the ex-wife back into the job market. That, too, seemed fair on its face. "It's healthy for the wife to become independent and self-supportive," the California attorney Ted Akulian told *U.S. News and World Report*. But a woman in her 40s who had spent twenty years taking care of the children and house was in no way capable of matching the earnings made by a husband who spent that same time developing a dental practice or accumulating seniority at a unionized car plant. "At that time we were so concerned with principle— that equality of right and opportunity had to mean equality of responsibility . . . that we did not realize the trap we were falling into," said Betty Friedan.

Younger women who might have embarked upon postdivorce careers were often hampered by the need to care for their children. In California, the average child-support award was barely enough to cover the cost of child care. Even that presumed the woman was part of the lucky minority whose ex-husbands actually paid. One study found that only a third of divorced men had alimony and child-support responsibilities that were greater than that of their car payments—and they were more likely to actually meet the car payments. In states where the laws called for a fifty-fifty split of community property, judges sometimes ruled that the family house had to be sold and the proceeds divided. That meant the mother had to move the children and pay for a new place to live. Minnette Doderer, who was a state senator when no-fault divorce was passed in Iowa, felt that in retrospect, the unfair old system had more virtues than people realized: "Women formerly used to use their kids to bargain for more money, or they bargained that they wouldn't give a divorce unless they got something out of it. Now they have nothing to bargain with." Doderer recalled one woman on welfare who told her that when she was married, "she had a husband who had a business. They had three cars and five kids. She said, 'Now I'm divorced and he has a business and he has three cars, and I have five kids.'" Lenore Weitzman, a sociologist at Stanford University who produced a much-quoted study on the effects of no-fault, said the new rules were great for "young childless divorcées of 25, but they are being applied to women of 55 who have spent their lives as housewives, helpmeets, and mothers."

The divorce surge and the no-fault laws combined to form a terrifying picture of husbands suddenly deciding that they were tired of their aging wives and walking out to start a new family with a younger woman. Men had been doing that for millennia without the help of liberal divorce laws, but there was something about the thought of a marriage being abruptly ended, just out of the blue, that haunted the era. The new idea that alimony was only a temporary subsidy was a pretty clear signal that all women had better be prepared to take care of themselves, and that ten, twenty, or thirty years of work as a full-time housewife was not seen as being worth very much at all.

Myrna Ten Bensel, the Minnesota doctor's wife who had made her own diapers when her four children were small, thought that "people were married forever" until her husband suddenly decamped. The family was living in a three-story Victorian house in 1977, in a neighborhood where Myrna presided over PTA meetings and was active in her church. "He came home one evening, the evening of my son's swimming banquet, and got us all together and said, 'I'm moving out. I'm divorcing your mother.' I did

not know anything about it. He didn't say the reason. I found out weeks later that there was another woman, which just destroyed me emotionally." There were at least three million women in America in the same position in the late '70s—full-time housewives who suddenly found themselves alone. Some estimates put the number at seven million. While Bensel's husband provided adequate support to allow her to go to law school and start a new life, most of these women were left at sea. By 1978 they had been given a name—"displaced homemakers"—and various state and federal training programs. None of the government-funded counseling, however, could put things back the way they were—to a way of life the women had counted on. "My rage centers around being so poor suddenly," said a middle-aged woman at a workshop on job hunting in New York City in 1979.

"You've got lots of company," said the moderator.

"WELL, I LOVE YOU, TOO, BUT I DIDN'T PROPOSE."

Maria K., meanwhile, met the right man. "I think he loved my children before he loved me, to be honest with you," she said. "God has sent me angels all my life, I swear that he has." He bought a house for Maria and her children, and gradually moved in. They were a family, but they never married.

"He was also Italian and I think at first he thought his mother and father would have difficulty with him marrying a girl with two children. And I'm sure he was right," she said. One night, "he told me he loved me, followed immediately by the words 'but I don't want to get married.' So we just went along that way." Later, while the two of them were at Mass, "he put his hand over my hand and he said, 'I really do love you. But I don't want to get married.'

"And I looked up at him and I said, 'Well, I love you, too, but I didn't propose.'"

The census-takers counted about a million cohabiting couples in 1977, although the experts suspected that the real figure was much higher. (They were right. In 1986 a government study on single women would determine that a third of them had at some point lived with a man they weren't married to.) In some parts of the country, unmarried partners were so common they were incorporated into the routines of daily life. At Harvard Medical School, Perri Klass reported that when the Married Students' Association shunned medical students who were living together, one of her classmates came up with a Living-in-Sin Potluck Dinner for "those of us who are sharing these special years with someone to whom we are less formally bound." The Bagehot program for journalists at Columbia University included dinners for the Bagehot fellows and their "spouse or spouse equivalents." The 1970 census began counting Persons of the Opposite Sex Sharing Living Quarters (POSSLQ), and CBS commentator Charles Osgood came up with a poem that began "There's nothing that I wouldn't do/If you would be my POSSLQ."

"I KNOW I REALLY WANTED TO HAVE A BABY."

Unwed mothers were no longer being forced to choose between abortion and adoption. They were keeping their babies. In black communities, where the birthrate for married women had dropped dramatically, the proportion of children born out of wedlock soared. In 1976, for the first time, more than half of African-American babies were born to unmarried women. Forty percent of black children lived in a family headed by women. "We have very, very strong women in my family," said Virginia Williams, the single mother and former post-office worker from New York, counting off her female relatives, from her aunts through her cousins to her daughter, who were left with the responsibility of supporting their children on their own.

Illegitimacy had historically carried a stigma—the children were branded "bastards," and it was not until 1968 that the Supreme Court began issuing a series of decisions that would make it clear

that they had the same basic rights under the law as children born in wedlock. Now it began to look routine in poor neighborhoods. Was that due to the increased availability of welfare, people asked, or the way welfare systems penalized families where the father remained in the house? As the trend continued, some experts wondered whether African-Americans were developing a different kind of family structure, an extended network of relatives rather than a nuclear family. Whatever the answer, black extended families did provide a critical safety net. Virginia Williams, who struggled mightily to support her daughter Denice, was constantly being helped by her relatives. "Even if you didn't want to hear their mouths, even if you didn't want to get the lecture, even if you didn't want to hear 'I told you so,' yes, you could depend on them," she said. "My cousin said, 'Sis, I'll watch your Denice for you,' and my aunt said, 'Well, Sis, with Denice being over here, why are you paying rent on that apartment? Why don't you move back?'"

→← ←←

GLORIA VAZ'S YOUNGEST DAUGHTER, Dana Arthur, was a shy, overweight child whose learning disability made her life at school difficult. The fact that her older sister, Adrian, was a good student made things worse—one day Dana heard her teacher tell Adrian's, "Oh, you have the good one and I have the bad one." Trying to fit in, Dana became "the class clown"; she "acted out and had some problems." That spilled over into her home, where her father would beat her if she received bad report cards or got in trouble for misbehaving. "My father was very moody and had a real mean streak, so I was his outlet," she recalled. "It was very obvious. He would come right at me, and he knew what my weaknesses were." The family wound up in therapy, trying to deal with the chaos at home, but Dana felt she was on her own. "My mom, she is an amazing woman, but at that point she wasn't really strong enough to come to my defense. She was dealing with her own stuff."

By the time she reached 14, Dana had begun drinking and having sex. She became pregnant when she was 15. "Not to say that I got pregnant on purpose, but I kind of wished it would happen," she said. She and her boyfriend Harry were both happy with the idea. She waited until the end of her first trimester before telling her mother. "I'll never forget. She just started crying. It was a sad thing. I was very upset because everybody was in mourning and I just couldn't understand it. We were happy... I mean, nothing else was going right for me, so I just felt like, wow, that would be cool." Gloria had become a Jehovah's Witness, but she left when the congregation ostracized Dana over her pregnancy. "I got disfellowshipped from church," Dana said. "'Disfellowshipped'—that's what they call it where you're not allowed to be spoken to...It's a whole process. You have to sit in front of the council and talk about what you did."

In 1975 Dana gave birth to her daughter, Lynnette. She was 16, living at home with her mother, and still seeing Harry, who proposed that they get married and that Dana work while he went to medical school. But the image of the displaced homemaker suddenly ditched by her successful husband had already filtered down to an unhappy working-class teenager in New York: "You have your stories of guys going to become a doctor and all of a sudden they've outgrown the woman who was drudging, keeping it together. I was like, 'Uh-uh, not me.'"

Perhaps her own home life gave her a bleak image of marriage or perhaps her childhood weight and school problems had given her a low self-esteem, but Dana never imagined herself as a bride—only a mother. "I never had girlie fantasies about wedding dresses. I just didn't...I wanted a baby, I know I really wanted to have a baby...I just loved children. Children and animals." Remarkably, Dana successfully finished high school and began studying theater at City College of New York, leaving Lynnette with a babysitter and picking her up in the evening. She took motherhood seriously, reading Dr. Spock's baby books and doing her homework while she tended Lynnette at night. "I really got into it. I was kind of shy anyway, and now I had a purpose."

"WE ALL CHIPPED IN...I LOVED IT."

The big problem for America was not that working wives and single mothers were replacing the stay-at-home spouse in so many households. The world has seen a lot of different family models come and go over the centuries, and there is no real way to demonstrate that a nuclear family like Ozzie and Harriet's is better than a small interknit tribe or a vast extended family. The problem was that the latest changes were taking place in a society where families tended to be far more isolated and autonomous than in the past. When the stay-at-home mother was removed from the scene, there was often nobody to step in and take her place.

By the 1970s Barbara Arnold had finished nursing school, married, given birth to a daughter, and moved to Massachusetts. When her husband developed a drinking problem, they parted, to her family's dismay. "Roman Catholics did not divorce," she said. "I was the first one to so sin...My mother really fought hard for me to stay in the marriage, that that was my duty...My friends got me through it. My neighbors, my coworkers, my Al-Anon friends, that was my support system." Arnold went to work at a hospice, and when she got an emergency call at night, one of her neighbors would come over to sleep on the couch and make sure her daughter was all right. "It was a truly wonderful neighborhood, they just helped me immeasurably. I never worried about Alex, I never worried about her...," she said. "And they really became part of my extended family. My neighbors across the street, there were three girls and they would come over and ask if they could take Alex for a walk when I got home from work...It gave me, like, twenty minutes to decompress and start supper."

That supportive neighborhood was, in a way, what everybody seemed to be looking for. Baby boomers had gone to college in record numbers, then discovered either that they lived far away from their parents and siblings or that the experience of being off at school and living on their own had changed them and made it more difficult to fit back into the family circle. Long before Hillary Clinton wrote *It Takes a Village*, or the first episode of *Friends* appeared on TV, young people were dreaming of creating their own villages—extended families, only perhaps without relatives.

In Baltimore, Vicki Cohn Pollard and her husband, Robert, lived within a few blocks of eight other couples who were all friends and fellow members of the antiwar movement. They wandered in and out of one another's kitchens and took care of one another's children. "It was an extraordinary time," Pollard recalled. "We created a free medical clinic, an alternative school, a women's bookstore. We were an amazing community." Most people never managed to find a circle of friends that productive, but there was a growing sentiment, especially among younger people, that it was really friends who should be counted on for support in a pinch. "My friends are my family," said the writer Jane O'Reilly. Television series such as *The Mary Tyler Moore Show* idealized a network of friends and coworkers in much the same way programs such as *Father Knows Best* had idealized the nuclear family for the previous generation. Viewers seemed to yearn to be part of a community in which everybody knows your name—and understands you, cares about you, keeps you company, and steps in when you need help.

For a while in the '60s and '70s, young people tried to formalize this kind of arrangement with communes. "I lived in this little hippie house," recalled Alison Foster, who stayed on in Yellow Springs, Ohio, after she graduated from Antioch. "We all chipped in . . . The rent was, like, a hundred dollars. We had one stereo, one TV. We combined our money to cook together, bought at the food co-ops. I loved it."

Vicki Cohn Pollard and her husband, Robert, had painfully scraped together enough money to purchase an old Baltimore row house, which they painted bright red. Eager to live out their belief that the nuclear family needed to be replaced by something larger, they invited another couple, Frank and Jean, to live with them and their 2-year-old daughter, Tanya. It was important to Vicki that Tanya not be raised by her mother and father alone. "I knew that I wanted her to be trusting rather than competitive," Vicki wrote in the magazine she and her friends were devoting vast amounts of time to nurturing into success. "I wanted her to be able to love many adults, not just her parents, and I wanted her to grow up mostly with her peers rather than with family. I became convinced that the nuclear family was destructive for everyone in it. I feel that the more responsibility any one person bears for raising a child, the more anger that person will have for the child."

The four adults worked conscientiously at figuring out ways to share every part of the little girl's upbringing. When the others pointed out that Vicki was always the one to put her to bed at night, the group decided that it should be everyone's duty in turn. (Looking back thirty-five years later, Pollard could still remember the trauma of ceding the chore.) "We have moved slowly, but wonderful things are beginning to happen now," she reported to her readers, detailing how Frank was reading books to Tanya and putting her to bed at night, while Robert "gets up with her, dresses and feeds her, and takes her to mini-school."

A great many young people had looked at the nuclear family and found it wanting. (Robin Morgan, living with her husband in Manhattan, referred to her house as a "two-member commune" in an attempt to convince herself and her friends that she wasn't part of a traditional couple.) "We were all so dedicated," Pollard said. "Really, we were giving our lives to what we believed in. Doing this living arrangement was a part of that . . . That's why the endless discussions, trying to figure it all out."

The estimates of the number of communes in the

country ran to about a thousand. But those were larger groups, such as the thirty-member New World Collective in Des Moines, which had a rule that women were allowed to walk out of a meeting en masse if any female member detected a whiff of sexism in the air. No one ever tried to count small efforts such as the Pollards' or the many, many less formal setups like Alison Foster's "hippie house." Young people were coming out of college with the idea that they wanted to live differently than their parents did, with less emphasis on material goods and more on personal relationships. Living together in groups of friends who shared resources and chores seemed like a logical step, particularly since it also solved the problem of how to find cheap housing.

The commune movement didn't last long, but it is of particular note for this story because it was one attempt to answer the practical problem of who was going to change the diapers and do the dishes once women got jobs in the outside world.

"WHAT WOULD SHOES BE LIKE IF EVERY MAN MADE HIS OWN?"

The question of what happened to housework and child care if women were not automatically available to do it was not new. It had been discussed since the Civil War era. Even some social planners who did not worry deeply about feminist issues felt that evolution toward a just and more perfect world ought to involve the gradual extinction of housework. At the end of the nineteenth century, a novel called *Looking Backward* by Edward Bellamy made a huge stir with its story of a man who falls asleep in 1887 and wakes up in the year 2000, when the United States has turned into a utopia. While Bellamy was most interested in describing how the economy could be reorganized to maximize personal happiness, his readers were fascinated with details of everyday life. In the perfect world of 2000, young people all spent a few years in the national "industrial army," which performed all the civic and domestic chores, while their elders dropped off their clothes at public laundries and dined in magnificent community halls where each family had its own dining room. "The meal is as expensive or simple as we please, though of course everything is vastly cheaper as well as better than it would be if prepared at home," explained the hero's guide.

The utopian writer who thought most about the housework issue was Charlotte Perkins Gilman, who made the simple but radical argument that every person should be employed at the job he or she does best. (Gilman, whose own single-parent mother had dragged her to nineteen different homes in her first eighteen years, probably appreciated better than most people that every woman was not naturally gifted in the domestic arts.) Only the people who really enjoyed cooking and were really good at it should cook, she said. The people with a natural bent for child care should take care not only of their own children but of the children whose own mothers were better at art or architecture or landscape design. "What would shoes be like if every man made his own?" she demanded. Her book *Women and Economics* became a bible for the female college students of the early twentieth century.

But Gilman's ideas never took hold, and women continued to be expected to perform virtually all the household chores, whether they had any aptitude for them or not. And the commune movement never caught on either. The Pollards' version did not last long before the second couple decided to split up and move on. Their own marriage was teetering, and they never tried to repeat the experiment. "I don't think we had any societal support for people who are trying to make those kinds of changes in their lives," said Pollard.

More than thirty years later, Alison Foster still thinks wistfully of the days when she lived in a house where everyone accepted the fact that there were other people better equipped to do the cooking than she was. "There's part of me that really misses that," she said.

"ONE OF THE IRONIES OF THE WOMEN'S MOVEMENT . . ."

While household chores were a problem, the biggest unanswered question was that of child care. Working women were patching together solutions as best they could. Maria K. joined forces with another mother who lived across the street. "She worked nights and I worked days, and she had two little girls. I had two little boys, so we took turns. She watched my children and I watched hers, and in that way we were able to make decent money."

Those who could afford it sent their children to as good a day-care program as they could find. The number of 3- and 4-year-olds in nursery school or kindergarten doubled between 1965 and 1970. Others hired help and undoubtedly came to appreciate why, when the first woman cabinet member, Frances Perkins, was honored at a testimonial lunch, she spoke warmly of her husband and daughter but reserved her most effusive praise for her nanny. Madeleine Kunin, whose political career had begun to get some traction, realized very fast that it was her babysitter that made her work possible. "Without her, my choices would have been much more narrowly circumscribed. At the very least, my political life would have had to wait until my children were older . . . One of the ironies of the women's movement is that women like me obtained our liberty because of other women who agreed to help us as our housekeepers, babysitters, and cleaning women."

Of course, most women couldn't afford to pay for help, and communities made up of friends tended to break apart or fail to meet all the needs of young mothers struggling to balance work and child rearing. In Baltimore, when the Pollards divorced, Vicki was left alone in the row house with Tanya and a small son. Despite that network of neighbors, she felt she was struggling alone. "I remember one time when my little son and I were both incredibly sick," she said. "I just didn't know what was going to happen. I couldn't imagine what was going to happen." She was deeply moved when a friend dropped by with some chicken soup. "It was one of the beginnings of our relationship," she said of the man who later became her second husband.

The poorer a woman was, the more fraught the child-care problem. "You learned how to manage, you learned how to scrape by," said Virginia Williams, whose little girl once became ill and had to be hospitalized. "I would go to that hospital to see my baby every day. I would leave the hospital; I'd go to work. I'd come home, I'd take a nap, I'd go back to the hospital," she recalled. "And they threatened me with taking my child away. They're saying, 'You don't spend enough time.' Well, hello, I work every day." The social worker, she said, insisted that she was neglecting her maternal duties, so rather than risk losing her child, Williams went on welfare for the only time in her life.

". . . THE SOVIETIZATION OF AMERICAN CHILDREN."

While a number of developed countries provide early child care the same way they provide kindergarten, most Americans take it as a given that they are on their own; that the government has never seriously considered offering anything more than a patchwork system to help the very poor. But back in the early '70s, a bipartisan group of U.S. senators and representatives actually *passed* legislation that would make child care available to every family that wanted it. "My idea was first of all that it would be national," Walter Mondale recounted. "Impoverished to middle class, and any others that wanted to participate. I was trying to avoid typing it as a poor person's program."

Representative John Brademas, a Democrat from Indiana who had a long-standing passion for education issues, was the chief sponsor in the House, but the bill had strong Republican support as well. "We had to recognize that more and more married women were continuing to work," said

Martha Phillips, who worked for the Republican Research Committee in the House. "Having been a working mother, I knew what day-care problems were like." The legislation aimed at establishing early-education programs in every community in the country, as well as after-school care for older children. The federal government would set standards and provide support services such as meals, medical and dental checkups, and counseling. There was money to train staff and acquire buildings. The services would be free for lower-income people, and most middle-class families would qualify for at least subsidized tuition. Households whose income was in the top 25 percent would be charged the full fee. No families were required to participate, but everyone would be eligible.

Congress passed the bill in 1971, after what the people working on it felt was a great deal of discussion and a large number of hearings. But the general public actually knew very little about it. "The news media pulled away from covering social issues of that nature," said Jack Duncan, who was the counsel for Brademas's education subcommittee. "They went for big things — Vietnam, Watergate." Actually, the child-care bill was pretty big in itself. It was budgeted at $2 billion for the first two years, the equivalent of about $10 billion today. That was a huge amount of money at a time when the economy was beginning to falter, but it was also far less than would have been required once the system was up and running. "We were hopeful," said Duncan. "The first step was to make sure there was a program." The bill passed the Senate easily and made it through the House by a narrow margin after fights over what kind of community groups should be able to participate. But there seemed to be far less disagreement about the basic concept. "It was the high-water mark for the notion that our country would be far better off if we gave children in the earliest years a chance to get the skills and emotional strength they need to make it later on," said Mondale.

The water receded very quickly. President Nixon vetoed the Comprehensive Child Development Act, claiming it "would commit the vast moral authority of the National Government to the side of communal approaches to child rearing" while undermining "the family-centered approach." It was a slashing message, denouncing the act as "radical" and likely to "diminish both parental authority and parental involvement — particularly in those decisive early years when social attitudes and a conscience are formed and religious and moral principles are first inculcated."

"I couldn't believe it," said Martha Phillips. "We all thought it would be signed. We had been working with the administration. They were helping draft it. There's this disbelief that your own team had done it to you."

Mondale had been consulting "almost daily" with Elliot Richardson, the secretary of health, education, and welfare, in an effort to get the White House's approval. It was generally known that Nixon had ordered up both a veto message and a signing message, keeping his options open until the last minute. But Congress was stunned by the president's tone, which seemed to suggest that the legislative backers of the bill were in cahoots with the Communists to destroy the American family. "It was one of the most irresponsible and demagogic veto messages," said Brademas, who kept the message in his office for a long time, along with the alternative one Nixon would have used if he had decided to sign the bill.

Few people believed the bill had been vetoed because of its cost — although the cost was high. "I don't think it was an entitlement issue," said Brademas. "It was a cultural issue, a values issue." Elliot Richardson said later that he believed Nixon, who was preparing to leave for his famous trip to China, wanted to throw a bone to the right wing of his party, which was outraged by his efforts to establish diplomatic relations with the Communist government.

The child-care bill was passed during the same period that the Equal Rights Amendment was approved with such overwhelming support — that moment when the two parties were changing sides on so many social issues and spent a brief time together in a place we might now define as a kind of establishment liberalism. The New Right was still in its infancy, but some of the people who would lead the culture wars later in the decade were on the White House staff, and the destruction of the child-care bill was one of their first big victories. The veto was actually the work of Howard Phillips, who was perhaps the most conservative member of the administration. Phillips, who would later run for president as the candidate of the U.S. Taxpayers Party, was gunning for the child-care bill, and he enlisted the help of Pat Buchanan, then a special assistant to the president. Buchanan recalls that they had to overcome the White House's preference to simply veto the bill on the basis of its cost. "We wanted to go at it philosophically. We didn't want this in the United States of America. The federal government should not be in the business of raising America's children. It was a political and ideological ideal of great importance," he said.

The goal was not just to kill the bill but also to bury the idea of a national child-care entitlement forever. "I insisted we not just say we can't afford it right now, in which case you get pilot programs or whatever," Buchanan said. The veto message was actually a toned-down version of what Buchanan had suggested—he wanted to accuse the bill's drafters of "the Sovietization of American children." But it did the job Buchanan and Phillips had hoped it would do. It delivered the message that it was much more politically dangerous to work in favor of expanded child care than to oppose it. Meanwhile, the other side was sending no message at all. There was no outcry about the veto from the electorate—virtually no talk about it at all. The child-care community, which would have had to lead the charge, was actually divided over the bill. Some groups worried that the huge Child Development Act would drain money away from programs such as Head Start—those set up for the poorest children who needed help most.

Among the people who were not giving up was Margaret Heckler, the Republican congresswoman from Massachusetts. Heckler was determined to put an early-child-care plank in the Republican Party's platform for the 1972 presidential election. One reporter noted, in wonder, that she "worked over a staggering total of ninety-six drafts on child care. For two hours she argued for the inclusion of a single word: 'quality.'" Heckler won the battle of the platform but failed to get the hoped-for bill in the next session of Congress. Supporters went underground, fearing another veto.

After Nixon resigned and Gerald Ford became president, Brademas and Mondale resurrected their plan in 1975, renaming it the Child and Family Services Bill in order to make it clear that they were in favor of families, and starting it off with a modest appropriation of $150 million for the first year. But the economy was growing worse, the new administration was demanding budget cuts, and in the summer the two sponsors sat down for breakfast and agreed that they should withdraw the bill and wait until after the 1976 presidential election, when a more friendly Democrat might be in the White House.

"What happened next," Brademas said, "was remarkable."

Members of Congress started getting thousands of near-hysterical letters demanding that they kill the already-moribund legislation. "Seldom does a bill that is going nowhere, by all informed accounts, arouse such stridency," reported the *Chicago Daily News*. Illinois senator Charles Percy, the story said, had gotten eight thousand letters in 1975. The writers appeared to believe that the Child and Family Services Bill would allow children to organize labor unions, to sue their parents for making them do household chores, and make it illegal for a parent to require their offspring to go to church. One letter writer said Brademas was trying to create "a breakdown in family order, increase in delinquency, and a godless Russian/Chinese type regimentation of young minds." Another said that he "should be deported to Russia."

Many of the letters had been inspired by a flyer, circulating around the Midwest and South, that confused the Child and Family Services Bill with a bill of rights for children that had been once proposed—but never seriously considered—in England, and which an opponent of Mondale's original bill had referred to darkly during the debate in 1971. The leaflets were also picked up by conservative editorial writers and radio commentators; they created such a stir that a reporter for the *Houston Chronicle* tried to trace them back to the source. He found a retired director of a Bible camp in Kansas who said he had written the leaflet based on a pamphlet a relative had received at a revival in Missouri. He said that he was "sort of sorry" he had distributed it, since he had learned that virtually everything in it was untrue.

Although Jimmy Carter did bring Democratic control back to the White House, with Mondale as his vice president, the new administration had little interest in creating expensive new government programs. Brademas, who had become part of the Democratic leadership in the House, was busy on other projects. And, as Jack Duncan said, nobody really "wanted to go through that again." Although Congress would keep fiddling with preschool programs to help poor children, there was never another serious attempt to create a national answer to the problem of who took care of the kids in an economy that now depended on women to work.

"I still hope we can get ourselves organized," said Mondale recently, not sounding all that hopeful. "I tried everything."

"People always think there will be another day," said Duncan. "Well, there might be another day, but not in my lifetime."

Keepsake Pages

Did you know any women who were divorced when you were young? Did it seem normal or sort of shocking?

_____

_____

_____

_____

_____

_____

_____

_____

How about single women having children? Did you know any when you were growing up? When girls got pregnant in your high school, did they expect to marry the father as a matter of course?

_____

_____

_____

_____

_____

_____

_____

_____

There was a lot of experimentation in the '60s and '70s about ways to replace the nuclear family. How did you feel about women who lived with their boyfriends? Did people talk about it as "living in sin"? Did you ever live in a commune or know other women who did? Was that something you thought sounded attractive or terrible?

_____

_____

_____

_____

_____

_____

_____

_____

_____

_____

What did working women do about child care when you were young? Have things changed much since then?

_____

_____

_____

_____

_____

_____

_____

_____

_____

_____

_____

More Thoughts and Memories

More Thoughts and Memories

More Thoughts and Memories

12. The 1980s — Having It All

"Way to go, Mom!"

The 1970s ended badly for June LaValleur, the wife of a gas-station owner who was raising three sons in a small town in Minnesota. Wanting work more ambitious than her job as a lab technician, she had qualified to become a physician's assistant but then lost her job. She and her husband were fighting all the time. Unsurprisingly, she felt depressed. "I went to a therapist. I felt like my whole world was caving in on me."

When she tried to envision a way out of her dark hole, one idea that kept coming up was medical school. Working with doctors, she had often thought, "You know, I can do what they do. I just need to get trained to do it." But it seemed like an impractical dream. It would take two more years just to get the necessary undergraduate credits. There was no medical school nearby, and even if she did somehow make it through, she would be 50 by the time she finished her training. Plus, her husband was totally opposed to the idea: "He thought it would ruin our marriage."

But, she told herself, the marriage was in trouble anyway. She felt compelled to try.

Since both her husband and her sons regarded cities as alien territory — "too many people and too many cars" — there was no question of their moving. Instead, June began a Herculean effort to become a doctor at the medical school in St. Paul, 120 miles away, while taking care of her family back home. "I would drive to Twin Cities either late Sunday night or get up at three a.m. and go down Monday morning, then work very hard during the week," she said. "I would go home on the weekends to be home with my family. I had a dual life. I just didn't talk about one when doing the other." On weekends, she tried to spend as much time as possible with her boys and do the household chores. "I did all the laundry, prepared food for the next week. I made pancakes and put them in bags so all they had to do was put them in the microwave. I made hot dishes that could be popped into the oven." She also hired a woman to do "day-to-day cleanup" and to be at the house between the time the boys came home from school and her husband's arrival from work.

"Randy didn't like that I was gone, but we didn't talk about it...I felt guilty. Terrible guilt," she said. On the plus side, the boys eventually learned how to wash their own clothes and look after themselves.

Three times a year, when final exams arrived, June would spend the weekend at school, studying "twelve, fourteen hours a day." The year her son Chris was in the sixth grade, she called home during a study break and listened to him tell her about what was going to happen at his last Sunday school class. Guilt-ridden, she told her husband she was "lonesome, feeling terrible," and he retorted, "Well, you knew what it was going to be like." She hung up the phone and began to sob. The hospital chaplain, who was walking by, stopped and patted her shoulder.

The first time Randy and the boys came to see June at her school was graduation. "I started walking to the middle of the stage, when my oldest son, John, who was at the time 18 or 19, stands up and hollers, 'WAY TO GO, MOM!' The audience was supposed to hold their applause, but everybody was applauding."

"The promise is dazzling."

In the 1970s the nation came to grips with the fact that most women were going to work outside the home. But it was in the 1980s that the country got used to the idea that women would not only make money to help support the family but also have serious careers. It was perhaps the decade when women were most optimistic about the possibility of merging husband, children, and major-league jobs. *Mademoiselle,* which had given its readers tips on manicures for the well-groomed typist in 1960, offered up an analysis in 1981 on whether "men will still love us as much now that we dare to love ourselves and our work as much as we love them." (The answer was yes.) A study prepared for the President's Advisory Committee for Women found that most Americans felt—or at least said—that it would be fine by them if their doctor, lawyer, mayor, or boss was female.

The number of women attending college crept past the number of men, and more women like June LaValleur started to set their sights on professional training for careers such as medicine and law. (A third of the law students in 1981 were women—up from 10 percent in 1971.) The stubborn gap between women's wages and men's narrowed dramatically. In 1979 the average working woman made fifty-eight cents for every dollar a man made. By 1994 she made seventy-two cents. Younger women with college degrees averaged eighty-three cents.

Cosmopolitan, in a welcome-to-the-'80s feature, announced, "The promise is dazzling—new-style egalitarian marriage, professional parity with men, full sexual self-expression sans guilt." The reality was somewhat less perfect. Some professions, such as construction, remained doggedly resistant to female incursion; most working women were still employed in traditionally low-salaried jobs, in clerical, sales, service, or factories. And in an ironic by-product of new opportunities, the great careers that had been open to women all along suffered a decline in prestige because they had, well, been open to women all along. Ellen Baer, an associate professor at the University of Pennsylvania School of Nursing, complained that she was constantly being introduced as "almost a doctor" by people who were trying to assure her that they thought of her as more than just a nurse. Randi Weingarten, the future president of the United Federation of Teachers, joked that "feminism killed teaching." While conditions in schools had always been poor, Weingarten felt, teachers had been buoyed by the company of terrific peers and the feeling that, despite bad pay, they were professional successes. Many saw educating the next generation as the most rewarding calling possible and would have taken the same path no matter how many doors were opened. However, once younger women started peeling off into other careers, the feeling of success began to dwindle a little. "We saw real disrespect for the profession," Weingarten said.

Still, there was a sense of great opportunity in the air. A Gallup poll showed 88 percent of younger American women were satisfied with their lives, with 83 percent believing they would meet their goals. Those goals almost all involved personal careers, not social change. The political conservatism heralded by the cultural wars of the 1970s had taken hold in Washington with the Reagan administration. Government grants for women's projects—especially ones that sounded radical in any way—dried up. The people who would have been applying for them five years earlier reinvented themselves as academics or entrepreneurs or journalists and made concessions that the traditional world seemed to require. "It really blew my mind that all of a sudden, everybody's shaving their legs, all these people who were very hairy and very proud of it," said one Ohio feminist who got a job as a university professor—and started shaving herself.

"WE WORE SUITS."

Women who wanted to succeed in business followed the men's lead in their clothing choices. "We wore suits," remembered Laura Sessions Stepp. "We wore blouses and those horrid little ties. You'd tie them in a little bow at your neck...I just look at them now and think that was so god-awful."

John Molloy, a "wardrobe engineer" who had written a bestselling book on how men should dress if they wanted to be successful, followed up with

The Woman's Dress for Success Book. Molloy said he had scientifically studied the reaction of bosses, colleagues, and underlings to women in different kinds of clothes, and he determined that the best route to the top was a "uniform": different variations of the same look every day, beginning with a dark-skirted suit and tailored blouse. The book also recommended a "feminine fedora," shoulder-length hair, a scarf tied around the neck somewhat like a necktie, and hems that ended slightly below the knee. According to Molloy, it was a look designed to give women an aura of authority and a sense of confidence. His readers seemed to agree. Sales of variations on the "uniform" soared, and six million more women's suits moved off the racks than in previous years.

Virtually every one of those suits and tailored dresses came with shoulder pads. A report on the 1985 fall fashion shows in Paris said top designers were featuring "clothes with shoulders so massive that the models appeared to have emerged from locker rooms instead of dressing rooms." Declaring "shoulders forever," the designer Claude Montana unveiled one coat with padding that extended the shoulder line six inches. While the padded shoulders undoubtedly sent a message of solidity and strength, their major attraction, in truth, was that they made clothes hang better and waists look smaller. But the pads also had a disconcerting way of slipping, and women spent a great deal of time realigning their shoulders. Friends gave friends a helpful tug on their jackets, and mothers drove daughters crazy by constantly pulling and poking at their shoulders.

At the same time, miniskirts had returned, to the dismay of many older women. "We're trying to be taken seriously, and professional women find it's a bad enough day-to-day battle without the mini," protested Nancy Clark Reynolds, the president of a Washington lobbying firm, when the hems rose in 1987 to heights they hadn't reached since the 1960s. And high heels were back with a vengeance. If anyone still wondered when American women were going to embrace sensible shoes, the '80s suggested the answer might be: never. "Shoes have become the most important accessory...Shoes are to the present generation what hats were to their mothers in the '50s," opined the *New York Times*.

Susan Brownmiller, who had converted to pants in the 1970s, was dismayed by the new developments. "When blue jeans became the emblem of hip sophistication, I didn't understand I was riding a very short wave," she wrote sadly. She had believed that women would never wear skirts again "in the way that friends of mine felt that the revolution was just around the corner. And here it is, well into the eighties, and a woman who wears nothing but pants is a holdout, a stick-in-the-mud, a fashion reactionary with no sense of style."

"...'TOP OF THE WORLD.'"

The return of the miniskirt was a reminder of a dramatic change that had occurred in women's attitudes toward their bodies. Worrying about getting fat had been a preoccupation for most of the century, but now women began to feel responsible not only for maintaining the right weight but also for sculpting their figures through exercise. The work that girdles and bras had done for previous generations was now a matter for the gym (and another set of responsibilities for working mothers to add to their schedules). Aerobics—and the whole concept of exercise classes—arrived on the scene and quickly became a mass movement. The return of the miniskirt, the invention of the term "thunder thighs," and the popularization of workout books and TV exercise tapes by Jane Fonda all occurred in the early 1980s.

Fonda, who was born in 1937, is given credit for linking the nation's beauty culture to its burgeoning health culture. She was a well-known actress by the early 1960s and an international sex symbol after she made *Barbarella,* an erotic science-fiction satire in which the heroine undresses in zero gravity before the opening credits finish rolling. She then became an icon of the antiwar movement whose visits to North Vietnam remained a sore point with conservative Americans well into the twenty-first century. Fonda had taken dance classes for years to protect her figure, and as she moved into middle age, it occurred to her that millions of other American women wanted to achieve the same effect her fellow ballet classmates did. The workout program she came up with became the bestselling videotape of all time. "If you want to trace the changes in American culture over the past twenty years, all you have to do is look at her," said the *Washington Post*. "She is a lightning rod for a generation whose rhetoric has evolved from Burn Baby, Burn to Feel the Burn."

The conviction that you could take things into your own hands, achieve your dream, be all that you can be, was deeply ingrained in the American psyche. But it was a relatively new idea to extend that can-do confidence to one's body. For those who failed to achieve perfection at the gym, there was now liposuction. Plastic surgery, which had been seen as an option for only the very rich or those whose livelihood depended on looking young and pretty, was repositioned as a tool for everybody. The American Society of Plastic and Reconstructive Surgeons announced in 1983 that there was good reason to believe that small breasts "are really a disease" since they create "a total lack of well-being."

This new expectation of physical perfection fell hardest, of course, on women. Anyone whose body or face didn't live up to the current standards was no longer simply unlucky. Now she was an underachiever who failed to make the proper effort. In 1982 the country heard about the travails of Peggy Ward, a 16-year-old drum majorette at Ringgold High School in Pennsylvania who was threatened with expulsion from the band unless she lost weight. Peggy, who was five feet four, had started the season at about 138 pounds. In another era, that might have been regarded as ideal. Peggy was, in fact, about the same height and weight as Marilyn Monroe, the ultimate sex symbol of the 1950s. But that

was then. Peggy's band instructor claimed that audiences at football games had been jeering at the drum majorettes, and set a limit of 100 pounds for girls who were five feet tall, with an extra five pounds for every additional inch of height. Later, after Peggy began skipping meals and taking diuretics to try to meet the limit, he raised the weight for five feet four to 126. But when Peggy came in at 127 pounds before the game with Aliquippa High, the nation was informed that she had been sent to the bleachers.

The average American woman weighed 143 pounds at the time. The difference between reality and ideal—and the expectation that everybody could bridge it—helped create an epidemic of eating disorders among young women. By the late '80s, there were estimates that 5 to 10 percent of teenage girls had conditions such as anorexia or bulimia. The nation first focused on the problem in 1983, when the singer Karen Carpenter died at the age of 32 from the effects of a long battle with anorexia. Carpenter, who with her brother, Richard, had cheery hits such as "Top of the World" in the 1970s, had begun to exhibit symptoms during the height of her career, and by the early '80s she was unnerving audiences with her wraithlike appearance. Her weight went as low as 80 pounds before she sought treatment, and although she began to improve, the stress on her body triggered a fatal heart attack.

"THAT WAS LIKE A RELIGIOUS EXPERIENCE."

By the 1980s TV series structured around hospitals, law firms, and police precincts—the staples of prime-time drama—featured women working with men in a manner that seemed more and more like business as usual. The first television drama with two female leads, *Cagney and Lacey*, debuted in 1982, with its stories of policewomen who arrested the bad guys while handling stresses of family, loneliness, and friendship. It put a significant dent in the presumptions about women's inability to carry long-running television series. So did the arrival, in 1988, of the hit comedy *Roseanne*, in which Roseanne Barr picked up the leading-woman baton that Lucille Ball had dropped so long ago. In another breakthrough, the film *Flashdance*, a huge moneymaker in 1983, featured a heroine who yearned to be a dancer but who made her living as a welder. However, the movie's major contribution to youth culture was to spark a fad for wearing dancers' leg warmers, not for construction work.

Madonna arrived on the scene in 1982, offering a whole new version of the strong American woman. She was the boss, totally in control of her work, her image, her sexuality, and she taught her female fans—to the despair of their mothers' generation—that they could flaunt their bodies the way a male peacock uses his garish tail as a symbol of power. Young women claimed the right to take to the dance floor by themselves or with their girlfriends, using the kind of aggressive, sexy moves Madonna would have approved of. "We dirty-danced to Salt-N-Pepa and all of those songs like 'Candy,'" said Camara Dia Holloway, laughing. "There was a group of us—and we all had our songs—that were girls. But also there were guys who would end up dancing with us. Two of us would sandwich one guy and rub all up and down him—just totally ridiculous and overtly sexual in a totally silly kind of way." Just as the Twist had heralded the era when girls were freed from having to follow the lead of a less-skilled boy when they were dancing, the '80s nailed down women's right to forgo the struggle to get a man to dance at all. "Even as adults you find yourself more often dancing with other girls," sighed April Chisholm, who was born in 1973. "I don't know what it is socially... boys and men just do not get up and dance. From being 6 years old to 32 years old, you dance by yourself or with other girls."

There has never been an era in America in which popular culture faced one direction for more than five minutes, and women who saw the '80s less optimistically pointed to programs such as *Dallas* and *Dynasty*—two extremely popular expressions of the decade that made Donald Trump a household word and "Greed is good" a popular slogan. Both told the stories of super-rich families who might have been descendants of the Cartwrights of *Bonanza*. This time the women got to survive past the final commercial, but their chief duties seemed to involve wearing extremely expensive clothes to dinner and trying very hard to produce an heir. *Dynasty* did, however, give women their defining fashion of the decade—those padded shoulders. Linda Evans, who played the beautiful, beleaguered Krystle, may not have had much power on the home front, but her dresses and suits gave her the aura of a lovely linebacker.

The biggest hit of the decade was *The Cosby Show*, and for black families, Yana Shani Fleming said, "that was like a religious experience. Every Thursday you had to watch *The Cosby Show*" as well as *A Different World*, which followed one of Cosby's TV children off to college. Growing up, Lynnette Arthur loved Bill Cosby and his handsome family, where "no one has any issues... I think the worst one was Vanessa got drunk. They never did an episode where, like, Theo decides to try crack. And then I loved *A Different World*, when Lisa Bonet did her spin-off. I used to love the beginning credits, where she'd be dancing with her friends. I would be like, 'Oh, I want to be older and live free and dance on trucks while my friend plays the piano in the back of the pickup.'"

"She was very fly!"

Clair Huxtable, the TV matriarch of the Cosby clan, was an attorney, but the audience saw very few signs of stress from the demands of holding down a job, raising five children, maintaining a large but warm and cozy home, and being an attentive, sexy wife. She was the embodiment of the ideal 1980s woman: She Had It All.

One of the best-known television ads of the era

was for Enjoli Perfume, "the new eight-hour perfume for the twenty-four-hour woman." Singing to the tune of "I'm a Woman," a gorgeous woman struts toward the camera in a business suit, announcing:

I can put the wash on the line,
Feed the kids, get dressed,
Pass out the kisses
And get to work by five of nine....

In the famous final stanza, a woman morphs from business suit to housedress to sexy night wear while singing:

I can bring home the bacon
Fry it up in a pan
And never let you
Forget you're a man....

It was a new vision of the good life for middle-class young women. Nothing their mothers had wanted had been subtracted. There was just more. Much, much more. In 1943 the sociologist Mirra Komarovsky surveyed sophomore women at one college and found that most of them said they did not want to work after marriage. When Komarovsky did a similar poll at the same college in 1979, only 5 percent said they preferred to forgo work and focus on "home and family." But their new attitudes toward work had not changed their attitudes about marriage. The idea of a career and single life appealed to only 2 percent of the respondents — the same number as in 1943. They wanted to have it all, like Clair Huxtable.

Striving for "it all" was not for sissies. Zoe Cruz, an up-and-coming executive at Morgan Stanley, maintained a work schedule that had her talking to the trading desk while she was in labor with her daughter. Although Cruz was at work by six every morning, *New York Magazine* reported, "she found time to do traditional motherly tasks. When her daughter needed to bring cookies to

school, for instance, Cruz got up at four a.m. and made them herself before going to the office." Linda Mason was executive producer of the CBS weekend news and doubling as the producer of the network's Sunday morning news programming while she and her husband were raising their daughters. "I was a mother and I was a producer, that's all," she said. "I gave a hundred percent to CBS and a hundred percent to my family." When her older daughter learned how to dial the phone, Mason encouraged her child to call her at work. "The instructions were, no matter what I was doing — talking to Walter Cronkite, Dan Rather — it didn't matter. It was always only about thirty seconds, but I felt she knew she was connected to me."

It was a little more frantic than Clair Huxtable made it seem on TV. While the Huxtables did not appear to have a maid or nanny, many women trying to mix high-powered careers with child rearing did. Camara Dia Holloway remembers her mother, who worked for the United Nations, as "probably a proto-idea of the superwoman of the '80s...because she worked full-time and wore hip little pantsuits — she was very fly! And she had kids and a family. We had a babysitter who took care of us in the afternoons into the early evening. And we had a cleaner who came into our apartment in Washington. So my mom managed to have two young kids, get a PhD, work full-time...but she had help."

Only a tiny sliver of the population had that option. Most women were working not because they were pursuing a career but because they had to make money to help support their families. One of the reasons women's wages were coming closer to those of men was because men were getting less. While pay for women working full-time rose 12 percent on average between 1979 and 1989, men's dropped more than 4 percent. And for men with high school diplomas but no college education, the average drop was a chilling 11 percent. For the first time, more than half of American women with children under 1 were working or looking for work.

"MY DAD WAS A GOOD BABYSITTER."

The most obvious answer to the overwhelmed working woman was a spouse who shared the chores and child care. Polls showed that people thought this was a good idea, but there's very little hard information on how much it actually happened. There was some indication that men began doing more at home in the 1980s, whether their wives worked or not. But that extra effort doesn't seem to have been very significant—about an hour and a half a week, according to one study. In her book *The Second Shift,* Arlie Russell Hochschild concluded that women suffered from a "leisure gap" of fifteen hours a week when it came to the amount of time they devoted to either paid work or household chores compared to what their husbands did. In one of the most optimistic conclusions, a professor at Wheaton College estimated that husbands did 30 percent of the work at home, up from 20 percent two decades earlier. "I don't predict that we'll be seeing fifty-fifty anytime soon, but a jump of ten percent in a national sample is a big change," said Joseph Pleck.

On the plus side, the era when men would routinely come home and expect to be waited on like weary warriors resting from the day's battles was pretty much over. June LaValleur's marriage ended after medical school, and when she was a hospital resident, she began a new relationship. "We bought this house together," she said. "He was the same age and had been divorced. We talked about marriage at one point. Then I came home one night at seven p.m. I had been on call since seven a.m. He was sitting in the chair with his feet up, reading the paper. I came into the room, and he said, 'What's for dinner?' That was it. I wasn't going to do that again."

In an increasing number of homes, fathers worked the day shift while mothers worked nights (or vice versa) so that one parent would be home to take care of the kids and keep the domestic front under control. In 1983, the *New York Times* told the story of Patricia Cremer, a reservations agent for Delta Airlines, who finished work in the middle of the afternoon, at almost exactly the same time her husband, Richard, a Delta mechanic, was arriving. Halfway between their home and the airport, the paper reported, the Cremers would rendezvous every day "for the changing of the guard—he would hand her the baby." No one knew how common that kind of arrangement was, but Harriet Presser, a professor of sociology at the University of Maryland, produced a study in the late 1980s showing that, among families where the mother worked part-time, two-thirds of the child care was done by the fathers in their wives' absence.

Jennifer Maasberg Smith, Louise Meyer Warpness's granddaughter in Wyoming, remembers that when she was young, her mother, Jo, would go off to school to teach while her father, a rancher, "would babysit us. She'd come home and we'd have the house torn apart and have built a fort. My dad was a good babysitter. When we ran out of Kool-Aid, he'd make Jell-O water." As fathers began taking more responsibility for their children, some mothers banged up against the issue of different expectations. If a husband was in charge of dressing the kids for school, did that mean the wife had no right to demand they wear matching clothes and not show up for the bus in plaid pants and striped T-shirts? In a great many households, plans to evenly divide the chores collapsed when women found themselves unable to compromise their standards. "My mom wanted a girl to wear dresses," said Jennifer. "I didn't want to wear dresses, but she made me, and I would insist on wearing my hiking boots with my dresses. Well, my dad thought that was just fine. So it would become a war when I was getting ready for school."

When the young activists of the '60s and '70s had imagined what life would be like for the liberated woman, they did not think of either the Enjoli Perfume model or the husband and wife living on different shifts. The vast majority might not really have expected that there would be a "revolution" in terms of a complete social and economic upheaval. But they did truly believe that the structure of society would change to accommodate their new ways of living. They thought the humanistic corporations of the future would offer flexible schedules so both the husband and wife would be able to pursue success on the job while having time to take care of the responsibilities at home. They expected that men would automatically do their share of household chores. And they believed the government would start providing early child care the same way it provided public education.

They had not considered the possibility that society might remain pretty much the same as always, and simply open the door for women to join the race for success while taking care of their private lives as best they could. Congress walked up to the line and decided not to make child care for working mothers anything approaching an entitlement. Economists who believed in the magic of the marketplace had predicted that once businesses realized how important child care was to working women, they would offer programs of their own to attract and retain good employees. But by 1987 the Bureau of Labor Statistics said only 2 percent of the 1.1 million American workplaces it studied offered child-care services to their employees, and only about 3 percent helped pay for it elsewhere. In fact, the bureau said, any kind of family-friendly options such as flexible leave, part-time work for mothers, work at home, and job sharing were exceptions to the rule. The columnist Ellen Goodman expressed a common sentiment about the way things were turning out: "The only equality she's won after a decade of personal and social upheaval is with the working mothers of Russia."

"LIFE WAS MESSY."

After six successful years in the legislature, Madeleine Kunin decided to run for lieutenant governor in 1978. (When she won, her local paper's headline was "She's Somebody's Wife, She's Somebody's Mother, and She's Our Lieutenant Governor.") When she moved up, she also moved from a part-time legislative job to a full-time political career. Kunin's husband, a doctor, became the family's gourmet cook, but she found herself making "long lists at night," with domestic and political chores all mixed in together. "Never did I get everything done. Always there were piles of paper to be sorted, lost socks to be found, dirty dishes to put in the dishwasher, and clean dishes to take out. Life was messy."

Women who got good jobs felt lucky to have them, and the ethos of the '80s called for them to make balancing home and work look easy. Twenty years earlier, Anne Wallach and her friend had vowed that their husbands would have all the comforts the men would have gotten with stay-at-home wives. Now, working women tried to give their employers the illusion that they had no concerns whatsoever except making them happy. They tried not to mention their domestic responsibilities and sometimes even refrained from putting family pictures on their desks, for fear they would be seen as less than serious professionals. "I never talked about it," said Linda Mason. "If I had a bad night, that was my problem." Elizabeth Patterson, who was working as a lawyer in Washington, DC, found law firms were particularly unsympathetic to the idea of families. She remembers a partner in one firm who invited the staff to a picnic with a memo ending, "No children and no dogs, please."

Patterson and her husband had two small children, and one weekend early in her career, she had to leave on Sunday to catch a plane to Minneapolis, where she and a male senior associate had a meeting first thing Monday morning. "I think Malcolm maybe was 9 months old and Sala would have been a little over 3 years old. I remember getting up in the morning while my husband stayed with the children; getting to the supermarket to be there by eight a.m. when the doors opened; doing the shopping; getting the food home. I may have cooked something before I left. And by the time I got on the plane, which was maybe one or two in the afternoon, I was absolutely exhausted." The senior associate was waiting for her, sitting and looking relaxed. "I asked him how his day had gone, and he said, 'Oh, I spent the morning reading the paper.' I wanted to strangle him. I was panting, you know."

Kunin, Mason, and Patterson had supportive husbands, but many who were trying to raise children and carve out a career were single mothers. Sherri Chessen Finkbine's marriage broke up in 1973, when the youngest of her six children was only 4. "I was supposed to get a hundred fifty dollars a month in child support, total," she recalled. "Some months, if I begged or cried enough, I would get it. Nobody helped me but me, myself, and I." With only $750 in her savings account, she left Phoenix and moved to La Jolla, California, with her youngest three children and rented a house on the beach. A woman she knew who was in real estate sales in town suggested Chessen, who had returned to her maiden name, try it, too. "I went with her company and started selling," she said. It all worked out, but looking back, Chessen can't quite imagine how. "I had more luck than sense, I guess."

Perri Klass, who'd had a baby while she was a 26-year-old medical student at Harvard, was called "Superwoman" by her classmates, but she was feeling anything but super. Klass was "totally frazzled, frequently irritable, chronically sleep-deprived... depending for my survival on the support and patience of others — Larry, especially, but also my parents." Larry, meanwhile, got praise for being the primary parent, "but frequently there was an undertone there, too, and it was, you miserable wimp...."

A life as an American working mother was hardly the planet's worst fate. Some women really did feel as if they were having it all. It depended on so many variables: the personality of the mother; the number, ages, and temperaments of the children; the helpfulness of the father; and the demands of the job. When it was good, it could be very good. Even as a divorced single mother, Tawana Hinton felt working as a speech pathologist and raising her daughter, Tiffany, made for a rewarding mix: "Coming home... I wasn't tired, it was exciting to see her and do what she needed." Tiffany still remembers how "she picked me and my friends up from school every day. She always had dinner ready at five o'clock... And I can see now, how the structure she gave me, how it helped me out."

Alison Foster, who got married a few years after college and quickly became pregnant, settled into a life in which job and family seemed to merge together seamlessly. She and her husband, a photographer, lived in a loft in downtown Manhattan, and while he worked out of their home, she brought the baby to her job at a studio that sold designer wallpaper for a California decorator. Since Foster ran the studio and the decorator was half a continent away, there was no one to object.

But when Justin was about 3 months old, the boss arrived in town, took a look around, and said, "You are breast-feeding a baby in a design studio!"

"I realized the writing was kind of on the wall," Alison said. "So I got my old portfolio together." She went job hunting and found an entry position at J. Walter Thompson advertising agency — her mother's old stomping ground. It was also her introduction to the frazzling routine of home, to day care, to work, to day care, to home.

"... Forever Single."

Rather than take on the burdens of being a superwoman, many women began to delay marriage. In 1980 half of American women ages 20 to 24 were unmarried — up from a little more than a quarter in 1960. The idea that it was fun to be single — so shocking when Helen Gurley Brown proposed it — had become conventional wisdom. The college where members of Muriel Fox's graduating class had been given corsages if they were engaged and lemons if they weren't had become the place where, the *New York Times* reported, a senior was introduced by her friends as "the only girl at Barnard who's getting married." The number of people who told pollsters that they thought those who failed to marry were somehow "sick" or immoral had dropped to about 25 percent.

Nevertheless, most women expected that their lives would eventually include a husband and children. And the media started to question whether women's search for self-fulfillment at work would wind up cheating them out of the chance. Betty Friedan, of all people, led the way. In 1981, in *The Second Stage,* Friedan raised the specter of "the insatiable demands of female machismo" that could leave the liberated woman alone in the bedroom with her computer, frightened and depleted. A raft of articles about spinster panic followed, most of them opening with an anecdote about a beautiful, lonely career woman. A headline for *New York Magazine* in 1984 asked, "Born Too Late? Expect Too Much? Then You May Be…FOREVER SINGLE." In it, Patricia Morrisroe introduced readers to people such as "Mary Rodgers," a beautiful 33-year-old executive who had been having terrible dreams and waking up in need of comfort, only to find that there was "no husband, no children, only me."

In 1986 a Yale sociologist told a newspaper reporter searching for a Valentine's Day feature that he had a study that seemed to show women with a college education were losing out in the "marriage market." Female college graduates who remained unmarried until 30, he said, had only a 20 percent chance of finding a husband. At 35, their chances dropped to 5 percent, and at 50, down to about one in a hundred. Things were even worse if she was black. It became the story heard round the world. *Newsweek* ordered up a cover on the plight of the unmarried career woman, and while it was being prepared, one of the bureau reporters began joking that an older woman had a better chance of being killed by a terrorist than of getting married. "The next thing we knew," the reporter told Susan Faludi, "one of the writers in New York took it seri-

ously and it ended up in print." Long before anybody in the United States really worried about being killed by a terrorist, conventional wisdom held that this scenario was more likely than an over-35 college graduate finding a husband. *Newsweek*'s cover showed a graph that looked like the slide on the world's most dangerous water-park ride, with the legend "If you're a single woman, here are your chances of getting married." Perhaps, the stories suggested, women were being too picky. *Newsweek* came up with a prize example: a 28-year-old Bostonian who said she wanted a husband "who likes all the things I like. Like if they hate sailing, that's really a deterrent. I like to experience everything in life. So if they hate sushi, I can't stand that." Readers undoubtedly started downsizing their own wish lists as they made their way through stories such as that of the 38-year-old pediatrician whose biological clock was "striking midnight," of the 30-year-old Chicagoan whose date taunted her about her dwindling chances, and of the 32-year-old real estate appraiser who said finding a man had "become an obsession."

As time went on, it would become clear that the marriage study was flawed. In fact, the career-driven '80s featured the smallest proportion ever of women ages 45 to 54 who had never been married — 5 percent. But the corrections never really caught up with the story. It was as if the world, having read all those surveys in which women said they didn't think you needed to marry to be happy, was intent on bringing them up short.

Sujay Johnson had a very clear memory of that *Newsweek* cover. By the time she was 33, she had built her own church congregation, taught at Harvard, and preached at Martin Luther King Jr.'s old pulpit in Atlanta when the Democrats came there for their presidential convention. She was still single, the veteran of a series of unhappy relationships that she had expected would lead to marriage but that had fallen apart in the homestretch. And the quality of the pool of prospects, she could see, was diminishing. At one point, Johnson said, she answered an ad in a magazine for black professionals that looked promising. The return letter had the address of a local correctional facility and began, "Dear Suzan, I'm accused of murder but I'm dying to meet you…."

After several more "Mr. Wrongs," Johnson was still looking. "I never felt like I wasn't going to get married—it was so much a part of what I needed to do to make me, me. I wanted a family too much," she said. Still, when 1991 rolled in, she decided to embark on a special fast before Easter and prayed, "Jesus, send me a husband or help me deal with the singleness." On Easter Monday, she went to Convent Avenue Baptist Church in Harlem to hear a friend preach. After the service she was preparing to go out to dinner with a girlfriend when she noticed a man working in the back of the church. "That's Ron Cook," said her friend. "Do you want to meet him? I think he's single." He joined them for dinner, and she discovered that Cook was an administrator at Convent Avenue and just finishing a fast of his own, during which he had been praying for a wife. They were married and had two sons. Sujay, not much changed by motherhood, successfully applied for a White House fellowship while she still had stitches from her first delivery.

"HAVING A BABY IS A VERY 1980s THING TO DO."

Children were the second big issue confronting women who threw themselves into their work with all the ardor of the most ambitious men. The national fertility rate leveled off at an average of 1.8 children per woman, less than half of the 3.8-children-per-woman peak in 1957. While there was a spurt of antichild sentiment among women who were getting tired of being asked when they were going to get down to the business of producing the next generation, for most, the expectation that sooner or later a baby would come never really changed.

Little girls practiced their maternal skills on Cabbage Patch Kids, soft baby-size dolls that were supposed to be "adopted" by their new owners (after their parents plunked down the "adoption fee"). Meanwhile, Barbies ran afoul of many conscientious mothers who worried about unrealistic body images and gender-typing. Ellen Miller and her husband, who had two young daughters in the '80s, banned the dolls from their household. "It was very upsetting," remembered her daughter Annie. "They were very clear on how they felt about Barbies…My sister and I wanted them anyway." Instead, Annie and her sister got long-maned My Little Ponies (which combined little girls' fascination with horses and hair) and early versions of the history-related American Girl dolls. But Barbies retained their popularity despite their sinking social status. Dana Arthur's daughter, Lynnette, had both a Barbie and a Cabbage Patch doll. She treasured the Cabbage Patch but followed what seems to be an extremely popular route of turning Barbie into a sex object. "When I did play with Barbies, it was, like, Barbie and Ken would be making out. They'd be in bed under the washcloth. The Barbie and Ken soap opera."

While women's expectations of having children hadn't much changed, their timetables had. Those who hoped to combine a career with a family were definitely waiting longer. The fertility rate for women ages 18 to 24 declined, while the Census Bureau reported a jump in the rate of childbearing for women in their early 30s. (Among women who graduated from Harvard/Radcliffe and had children, the median age for the first birth was between 31 and 32.) The women who pioneered the American suburbs in the 1950s had often completed their childbearing before they were 30. Now, 30 seemed more like the starting gun than the finish line—especially in urban areas where well-educated careerists congregated. When Perri Klass got pregnant at 26, she imagined that when a lecturer in one of her medical school classes mentioned teenage pregnancy, "my classmates were turning to look at me." Her friend, a corporate lawyer in New York, assured Klass that "having a baby is a very 1980s thing to do" but added, "You and Larry are much too young."

In 1982 *Time* had a cover story celebrating motherhood after 30, awash with anecdotes about actresses, doctors, writers, literary agents, having "it all" by adding a healthy baby to a list of achievements that already included professional success and happy marriages to supportive husbands who were eager to help with the child care. It arrived on the stands the same week the *New England Journal of Medicine* announced that a new study showed women's chances of becoming pregnant dropped more precipitously after 30 than experts had believed. Georgia Dullea of the *New York Times* interviewed a 32-year-old woman who complained darkly that building a career as a single professional was tough enough. "Now we're being told, 'By the way, you're over the hill.'" Medical experts responded soothingly that the odds were still not bad, but suddenly stories on infertility seemed to be everywhere. A government study reported in 1983 that three million married American women who wanted babies were physically unable to get pregnant.

Fertility clinics began to proliferate. There were 2 in vitro fertilization programs in the United States in 1980; by 1990 there were 192, offering increasingly elaborate options. Almost as quickly, a new cautionary tale arose in the form of Baby M, a blond, blue-eyed little girl who was the biological daughter of William Stern, a New Jersey biochemist, and Mary Beth Whitehead, the 30-year-old wife of a sanitation worker. Whitehead had signed a contract agreeing to be inseminated with Stern's sperm and carry a baby for him and his wife, Elizabeth, a 40-year-old pediatrician who suffered from multiple sclerosis. When word came that Whitehead was pregnant, William Stern, whose family had almost been obliterated in the Holocaust, turned to the stranger sitting next to him on a flight home and said proudly, "I'm going to be a father."

But once the baby was born, Whitehead decided she could not bear to give her up. She refused the $10,000 payment, convinced the Sterns to let her take the baby (who she called Sara) home for a short time, and then had her spirited off to Florida. When detectives found the child (who the Sterns called Melissa), both couples went to court for a seven-week trial, during which Whitehead's lawyer said the baby would do better with a full-time mother like Mary Beth rather than "a career woman" like Elizabeth Stern. The Sterns' lawyer played the tape of Mary Beth hysterically threatening to kill herself and the baby, and pointed to the Whiteheads' periods of separation and financial trouble. Outside the courthouse, Whitehead supporters displayed an empty crib. Mary Beth posed with a baby, holding a NOT FOR SALE sign.

The country debated the case, with Mary Beth's supporters arguing for the rights of motherhood and claiming class bias. "I will never feel quite the same about dyeing my hair now that Dr. Marshall Schechter, professor of child psychiatry at the University of Pennsylvania, has cited this little beauty secret as proof of Mrs. Whitehead's 'narcissism' and 'mixed personality disorder,'" said Katha Pollitt, who championed the natural mother in *The Nation*. The Sterns' supporters said they could offer a more stable home, and anyway, a deal was a deal. A New Jersey Superior Court judge agreed, calling Whitehead "manipulative, impulsive, and exploitive" and awarding the baby to the Sterns. Another judge later ruled that Mary Beth still had the right to visitation.

"Bill and I are very, very sorry that what started out as a very nice thing to end up like this," said Elizabeth Stern, who legally adopted Melissa years later when the girl turned 18 and had the right to terminate her relationship with her natural mother.

"WE HIRED THE PERSON YOU TRAINED."

Lillian Garland was raised by her great-grandmother, a former showgirl who had married a black man and ended up on a farm in Finleyville, Pennsylvania. "She had long black hair, a tiny little waistline, and she was built bigger than Marilyn Monroe. So when she married my — well, her husband, like I said, was black. Can you imagine her grief way back then before the '20s? So I'd be sitting on the floor and she'd be brushing my hair, and one of the things she would always say..., 'Remember that word.' And she would say it, she said 'nigger.' And she would point at me and she'd say, 'It only has as much power as you give it. It's only a word. Don't give it any power.' "

A tomboy who dreamed of being Annie Oakley, Garland grew up to be a pretty young woman who dreamed of being an actress. In 1976 she left for California with her eyes on Hollywood. But she wound up on the run from an abusive marriage, working as a security guard in Los Angeles. Things started looking up when she landed a job as a receptionist at a California Central Savings and Loan Association office. "I'm sitting answering phones, giving everybody messages, fussing at the bosses for not answering their wives' calls...I was having a ball, like I was mothering everybody." When she got pregnant, Garland trained someone to fill in while she was gone and returned after a three-month unpaid leave.

"We hired the person you trained...," she was told. "If something comes available, we'll give you a call."

Garland, who was searching for a new job with her baby in her arms because she couldn't afford a sitter, contacted the Department of Fair Employment and Housing, which told her that California had a law requiring employers to offer pregnant women unpaid leaves of up to four months. Her ex-employer challenged the law, claiming it discriminated against men, who could not claim such a benefit. By the time the court ruled in her ex-boss's favor, Garland had lost her apartment and custody of her daughter, Kekere, to the child's father.

As the appeal wound its way through the courts, her former employer offered to take her back, and her lawyer told her she had to accept in order to maintain her status as plaintiff. "They did things to

me — they stuck pins in my chair...They had me doing really demeaning things. They were putting in new computers, and they said, 'We want you to get on your hands and knees underneath all the desks on this floor and write down how many blue cables, white cables, and what the numbers are on the cables.' "

She told herself, "They want to force me to quit, because they figure if I quit this, I'll quit the case, too. But they don't know I'm my grandmother's granddaughter."

In 1987 Garland's case made it to the Supreme Court, which ruled 6 to 3 that states could require employers to provide job protection for pregnant women. *Time* wrote a big story about Garland, and she was invited to Washington, where President Clinton signed her copy of the magazine, and a security guard, recognizing her, asked to shake her hand. "He says, 'I gotta tell my wife that I met you. We just had twins. Because of you, she didn't lose her job.' " Later, at a dinner, Garland was seated next to Rosa Parks, who told her, "Young sister, I have been following this case for years, and I am so proud of you."

"I said, 'I'm sitting next to Rosa Parks, and you're proud of me?' And she started laughing and laughing."

"TOO OLD, TOO UNATTRACTIVE..."

Garland was hardly the only woman to come crashing up against a barrier she imagined had long been eliminated. And she was not the only one to go to court. Throughout the '80s, women in accounting and law firms fought to get a better chance to make partner — a status the top firms repeatedly argued was based on personal relationships rather than on any specific and quantifiable qualification. In 1982 Ann Hopkins was the only woman among eighty-eight candidates nominated for partner at Price Waterhouse, a giant accounting firm. Although she brought in more business than any other candidate, she was rejected. "It was only later, when we were in litigation, that I found out about the comments that I needed to go to charm school, that I was too macho, that I was overcompensating for being a woman," she said. The partners said she would have a better chance if she dressed "more femininely" and wore more makeup and jewelry. It took the rest of the decade, but in 1990 a federal district judge ordered Price Waterhouse to make Hopkins a partner and give her $400,000 in back pay.

In 1982 Christine Craft, of KMBC-TV in Kansas, sued her employers after she was demoted from anchor to reporter because she did poorly in a viewer focus group. The viewers, she was told, found her "too old, too unattractive," and not sufficiently deferential to men. Craft said she was told by her boss, "We know it's silly, but you don't hide your intelligence to make the guys look smarter... They don't like the fact that you know the difference between the National League and the American League." A 36-year-old California outdoorswoman, Craft said she was wooed to come to Kansas by the KMBC management, who assured her that they did not mind that she looked more like an "aging surfer" than a beauty queen. Once she joined the station, however, she was sent through makeup, clothes, and hair consultations that left her equipped with an endless supply of "polyester bowed blouses and blazers." The station claimed the focus group showed the makeover wasn't working, but testimony at the trial revealed that the consultant had opened up the focus group's discussion by saying, "Let's spend thirty seconds destroying Christine," and "Is she a mutt? Let's be honest about this." The jury awarded her $500,000 in damages. Then the judge tossed out the verdict, saying it was "the result of passion, prejudice, confusion, or mistake on the part of the jury."

The job of TV news anchor had particular significance since the person reading the evening news had always been a figure of authority in American culture. "I have the strong feeling that audiences are less prepared to accept the news from a woman's voice than from a man's," said Reuben Frank, the president of NBC News, in 1971. ABC made the first attempt to break the network men-only club in 1976, when Barbara Walters was hired to coanchor the evening news with Harry Reasoner. The pairing was not a success. "Harry Reasoner didn't want a partner and he didn't want a woman," Walters said years later. "He did not talk to me off the air." The on-air chemistry, unsurprisingly, was poor. Ratings did not go up, and eventually Reasoner and Walters went off to TV newsmagazines, while Peter Jennings claimed the anchor's chair.

While the networks would continue to wrestle with the anchorwoman issue for another quarter century or so, local news had less trouble adapting. In 1972 KING 5 in Seattle appointed Jean Enersen as evening news anchor, making her the first woman to hold that job permanently. (Her management had surveyed listeners and found the audience "very receptive" to the idea.) Others followed quickly, many of them women who would later become national household names: Judy Woodruff in Atlanta, Jessica Savitch in Houston, and Jane Pauley, who became the first anchorwoman at stations in Indianapolis and, later, Chicago. By the early 1980s, more than a third of local anchors were women. Only 3 percent of those women, however, were over 40, compared to almost half the men.

"THEY'RE NOT LISTENING TO YOU FOR THE FIRST TEN MINUTES."

When Sylvia Acevedo decided to become an engineer, she embarked on a life in which she would almost always be the only one of her kind in every room. During a college internship, she worked on a weapons-testing range in the Nevada desert. The first time she headed for the bathroom, she was stopped, "and they said, 'No—yours is over there.' It turned out they had had *much* correspondence over where I would go to the bathroom. And there was this brand-new Porta Potti that said HERS."

When she got to graduate school at Stanford, there was only one other Latina in the entire engineering program: Ellen Ochoa, the future NASA astronaut. "There weren't a lot of people like me. But I've always been a kind of social person, so I did sports, I hung out," Acevedo said. After a stint with the national space program, she went to work for IBM in Palo Alto. The office next to hers was occupied by a former football player from Purdue ("not the sharpest crayon in the box"), and Acevedo watched as his IBM mentors came in to tell him how to make a presentation, what to wear, and what to watch out for. "No one was doing that for me or the other women who were there. I began saying, 'I have to innovate.'" She carefully analyzed what skills IBM seemed to expect for the kinds of jobs she wanted to eventually have and then methodically went out to get the right résumé. When she discovered her many trips to Mexico didn't count as international experience, she booked a trip to Hong Kong at her own expense and befriended the local sales team.

Reflecting back on her IBM days, Acevedo recalled that she did have "one guy who was a good mentor," who advised her not to begin her presentations in the normal way. "You have to start with how you're like them," he urged. "You need to tell them you're a Stanford engineer and you've done this and that. Because they're not listening to you for the first ten minutes. All they're thinking is, 'What is this Hispanic female doing in front of us?'"

"THE WOMEN I SPEAK WITH . . . WANT TO KNOW THEIR PARTNERS."

At the height of the sexual revolution, college students were reading *The Harrad Experiment*, which described how the next generation could use free love to create an American utopia. By the late 1970s, they were reading *Looking for Mr. Goodbar,* which painted a picture of the new morality that was so dismal it's a wonder the entire generation didn't head for the convent. *Goodbar* was Judith Rossner's fictionalized account of the 1973 murder of Roseann Quinn, a 28-year-old teacher who spent

her days working with deaf children in the Bronx and her nights reading novels in a bar on the Upper West Side of Manhattan, where she picked up men for one-night stands that sometimes got rough. (Her accused killer, a drifter named John Wayne Wilson, hung himself in his jail cell.) The violent death of Rossner's heroine, Theresa Dunn, became a byword for the terrible consequences of anonymous sex. The reviewers of *Looking for Mr. Goodbar* made it clear that they felt both Quinn's murder and Rossner's book said something sweeping about the way young people's sex lives had gone astray. ("We know there are Theresa Dunns in our lives, in our offices.")

"The Revolution Is Over," announced *Time* in 1984. In fact, what was over was not the dramatic change in women's feelings about the double standard that had been at the heart of the sexual revolution. What ended was the to-the-nth-degree-ness of it—the group sex, the casual encounters at a rock concert or airport ticket line that led almost instantly to sex behind a tree or in a plane restroom. Swing clubs, where people came to trade partners, began to dwindle away. The legendary suburban cocktail hours where couples dropped their car keys into a hat and chose the keys of their partner for the night seemed to disappear—if many had ever really existed in the first place. "The difference now is that things are not so casual. The women I speak with seem to want to know their partners," said the director of the health center at Wheaton College.

While a religious backlash against sexual permissiveness undoubtedly played an important part in the new attitude, there were very profound practical reasons that women wanted to "know their partners." That brief window in which people could have sex at random without any serious safety concerns had closed. There was an epidemic of chlamydia, the "silent disease" that exhibited no symptoms but that led to sterility if it went untreated. By the mid-1980s, an estimated one-sixth of young women who were sexually active were infected. The disease hit hardest in the black community, and infertility rates in young black women tripled.

The decade also ushered in an epidemic of genital herpes, the first widespread incurable sexually transmitted disease since the invention of penicillin. It was, *Time* said, "The New Scarlet Letter." Although seldom life threatening, herpes caused painful sores that could erupt at any time, and it could be easily transmitted during unprotected sex. (Women suffered physically more than men, averaging more lesions with long-lasting pain.) The Centers for Disease Control estimated that twenty million Americans were infected, with up to half a million new cases each year. The media sounded the alarm with stories that usually centered around young women who were punished for promiscuity. ("They were just one-night stands, they deserved it anyway," said one infected man of his unwitting partners.) Some of the cases cited were so horrific that the unnamed victims seemed to have stepped out of a Victorian novel. "A schoolteacher in Los Angeles developed herpes blisters on her genitals and legs a month before her scheduled wedding," reported *Time*. "Her fiancé, who had given her the disease, walked out."

AIDS was identified and named in 1982, but it only really hit general American consciousness in 1985, when actor Rock Hudson announced the disease that was killing him was what people were beginning to call "the gay plague." It quickly became clear that AIDS could be spread by heterosexual sex, too. Near panic ensued, and by 1986 an expert from the federal Centers for Disease Control was predicting that up to 10 percent of the population would contract AIDS within a few years unless there were revolutionary changes in sexual behavior. When *Fatal Attraction* became one of the hit movies of 1987, feminists worried that the tale of how Glenn Close beds a happily married Michael Douglas and then turns into a murderous stalker of her ex-lover and his wife was a parable about the evils of the unmarried career woman. But many people saw it as a metaphor for AIDS and how the

classic one-night stand could become a death sentence not only to the casual adulterers but to their families as well.

"RAPE ME, LUKE!"

In 1981 *Newsweek* announced that *General Hospital*, a long-running afternoon soap opera, had suddenly become "Television's Hottest Show"—not only "the highest rated daytime show in the history of television, but a genuine pop culture phenomenon." In a pre-TiVo world, college students ditched classes and crowded in front of dormitory TV sets to watch, as did shoppers at department-store electronics sections and travelers in airport lounges. The drawing card was the romance of Luke and Laura, the fractious, sexually overcharged couple who were on the run from the mob, stranded on a tropical island with a mad scientist, and finally united in matrimony in one of the biggest events in the TV decade.

Only the die-hard feminists had any complaints, it seemed, about the fact that the young lovers first got together when he raped her. Laura (played by 19-year-old Genie Francis) was married and working for Luke (played by 34-year-old Anthony Geary) when he declared his passion and forced himself upon her on the floor of an abandoned nightclub to a disco beat. Astonishingly few people seemed to object. "Rape me, Luke!" cried a fan at a Texas shopping mall. Another woman presented Geary with a homemade award for "America's Most Beloved Rapist."

It was perhaps a moment of mass neurosis, but the fans should have known better. There had been a great deal of discussion of rape over the previous decade, beginning with Susan Brownmiller's *Against Our Will*, which had portrayed it as "a conscious process of intimidation by which all men keep all women in a state of fear." Rape, feminists said, was not about sexual desire but power. They began holding "Take Back the Night" marches to protest the way the threat of rape overshadowed their lives, keeping them trapped in their homes because they were afraid of walking alone after dark. Self-defense classes and rape-crisis centers sprung up around the country, particularly in college communities.

Many Americans living in the 1980s could remember a time when it was difficult—if not impossible—for a woman to bring rape charges against a man unless she had an eyewitness. In some states she had to prove she had been a virgin at the time of the attack. (Go back far enough in American history, and you will come to the point where people believed women could conceive a child only if she enjoyed the sex and that therefore there was no such thing as a rapist impregnating a victim.) In the '80s the country had moved toward a far greater sympathy for women who claimed to be victims of sexual assault, and states had begun to pass rape "shield laws" that restricted defense lawyers' ability to dredge up a victim's entire sexual history in order to portray her as a tramp who "asked for it."

The concept of date rape, however, was controversial. The idea that a woman could seem to lead a man on and then have the right to say "no" was a relatively new concept, particularly for people who had been brought up to believe that women were supposed to pretend to be reluctant to have sex even when they were in fact eager. Susan Estrich, a Harvard professor of sex-discrimination law, argued that sex became rape whenever it was against the woman's will, even if she had been tricked or bullied into it without the threat of violence. On the other side, "postfeminists" led by Katie Roiphe, a doctoral student at Princeton, retorted that by downplaying women's ability to hold their own against psychological pressure or the effects of alcohol, "rape-crisis feminists reinforce traditional views about the fragility of the female body and will."

There were plenty of events that encouraged further debate, including a series of celebrity-rape trials. William Kennedy Smith, a physician and member of the famous political clan, was acquitted of charges brought by a woman who he had met in a Florida bar and taken for a walk on the beach. The trial was televised, and much of the nation watched Smith and his accuser (her head a white blur to conceal her identity) tell their dramatic and divergent stories. In the 1992 Mike Tyson trial, an 18-year-old contestant at the Miss Black America contest in Indianapolis said she had accepted a late-night date with the former boxing champion, believing she was going to meet celebrities—she showed up at her hotel lobby carrying a camera. But Tyson took her to his hotel room, where they chatted for a while, until she went to use the bathroom and emerged to find him stripped to his shorts. Tyson's lawyers argued that the very fact that a young woman would go up to a man's hotel room in the middle of the night proved that, as the boxer testified, she was a willing participant in consensual sex. But the jury felt otherwise, sending Tyson to jail and effectively ending his boxing career.

→+ +←

LYNNETTE ARTHUR HAD A DIFFICULT CHILDHOOD. Her mother, Dana, had loved taking care of her as a baby but fell into a period of depression and substance abuse that left Dana incapable of raising the little girl. Lynnette lived for a long time with her grandmother, and when Dana reclaimed her life and brought her daughter back to live with her, the reunion was fractious. Lynnette was "hanging out with these two guys" one night, an angry 17-year-old sitting in the bleachers of a remote playing field in Brooklyn not far from her mother's apartment, smoking and drinking and arguing. Suddenly, one of the men turned on Lynnette and raped her. The men walked away together. Then the second—who Lynnette had actually been dating—stopped and went back. "I thought he was going to help me, but he just did it, too," she said.

As she stood there crying, the man she did not really know started saying, "Yo, let's kill the bitch." She ran home with her attackers in pursuit.

When she came in the door, her mother knew immediately what had happened, and when Lynnette tried to take a shower, Dana took her instead to a hospital, where the nurses took evidence. Lynnette picked the men out in a lineup, but after she had given a deposition, she decided not to press charges.

"The lawyer was saying it would be a rough trial for me because it would be my word against theirs," she said. "We were drinking...and their lawyer was definitely going to make me seem like I asked for it or I allowed it or something."

"I believe you and I believe a jury would believe you," her lawyer said. "But you have to understand this is what we're taking on." Lynnette decided not to go forward.

"Am I okay with that?" she asked herself afterward. Sometimes, she felt not. Once, she saw one of the men on the street. "I just remember my stomach kind of dropping and kind of feeling like—has he been punished enough?" There were no good answers. "I do believe in karma," she said. "What goes around comes around."

"...THE LAUGHINGSTOCK OF THE TRIBAL WORLD."

In that poll for the President's Advisory Committee for Women, the one that was so astonishingly positive about women having important careers, most people still said they did not believe the country was ready to elect a female president. Perhaps as a compromise, the majority said that the United States would probably be ready to elect a female vice president by the end of the century. In 1984 the Democrats tried to push the timetable ahead a bit faster, nominating Geraldine Ferraro, a congresswoman from Queens, New York, as the party's vice presidential candidate. (Ferraro, who was married to John Zaccaro but used her maiden name, helped the cause of "Ms." when she told reporters that if she couldn't be referred to as "Ms. Ferraro," she wanted to be called "Mrs. Ferraro" to reflect the fact that she was, indeed, a wife and mother. That was too much for the *New York Times* language columnist, William Safire, who couldn't countenance

"Mrs." in front of a maiden name but knew he couldn't demand that a vice presidential candidate change her professional name to Mrs. Zaccaro. "It breaks my heart to suggest this, but the time has come for Ms.," he wrote. "We are no longer faced with a theory, but a condition.")

It was the same year Madeleine Kunin was running for governor of Vermont, and Ferraro arrived to campaign with her. Thousands of people turned out to greet them. "Fathers brought their daughters to see us, carrying them on their shoulders, holding them in their arms, leading them by the hand. 'I want her to see this, to know this, so she'll remember,' a man said as he asked a bystander to snap our picture together: Gerry Ferraro, Daddy, the baby, and me." Kunin was elected that November. Ferraro lost. Her campaign had been dogged by questions about her husband's finances, but some said it had been a hopeless cause from the beginning, that her nomination had been a desperate Hail Mary pass for the Democrats, struggling against a popular president in Ronald Reagan with a qualified but hardly electric presidential candidate in Walter Mondale. Mondale's record as an advocate of early child care certainly did him little good. Championing the child-care needs of working mothers was then, and is now, something that pays very few dividends for politicians at the polls.

➤➤ ◄◄

WILMA MANKILLER HAD GOTTEN A DIVORCE and a college degree, and had moved with her daughters back to Oklahoma, where she began working for the Cherokee tribal government. By 1981 she had been named director of the Cherokee Nation's Community Development Department and met Charlie Lee Soap, the strong, quiet man she would marry a few years later. In 1983 the chief of the nation, Ross Swimmer, asked her to run for deputy chief on his ticket in the upcoming election. "Because our tribe is so large, running for tribal office is much like running for Congress or even a national political post," Mankiller said. "It is very much a mainstream process, complete with print and broadcast advertising, campaign billboards, rallies, and all that sort of thing." In this case it was also complete with rancor. Some of her fellow Cherokee claimed a woman running for such a high office was an affront to God. Others, she remembered, "said having a female run our tribe would make the Cherokee the laughingstock of the tribal world."

She was shocked. "Everybody liked me. I was the person who helped them get electric lines built, water lines built. I was the person who helped everybody... The female issue was very, very hurtful. Nobody seemed to be listening to the issues I cared about—housing, health care, services for children. They were more interested in debating whether a woman should be principal chief or not. People said some very hurtful things."

They did not, however, defeat her. She won the election, and in 1985, when Swimmer moved to Washington to head the Bureau of Indian Affairs under Ronald Reagan, Wilma Mankiller became the first Native American woman ever to serve as a chief of a major American tribe. At the next election, she easily won in her own right.

"It must be a secretarial position, is it not?"

Exit polls in the 1980 presidential election showed that 55 percent of male voters had supported the winner, Ronald Reagan, but that only 47 percent of the women had voted for him. Women—especially single women—were tending to favor the Democratic candidate, while men leaned toward the Republicans. The gender gap would widen during the Reagan years, then shrink when George H. W. Bush ran against Michael Dukakis, then widen again when Bush ran against Bill Clinton. The meaning of the gap would be debated over the next quarter century, but one clear factor was women's higher support for safety-net programs such as Social Security and Medicare, and for government spending in areas such as education and social services.

Reagan had noticed the gap from the beginning of his presidential campaign and, in an effort to reduce it, had promised to try to appoint a woman to the Supreme Court. In 1981, when Justice Potter Stewart decided to retire, then-president Reagan asked for a short list of female potential nominees. As a result, Attorney General William French Smith placed a call to Sandra Day O'Connor, a 51-year-old appeals court judge in Arizona, to tell her she was being considered for a "federal position."

"It must be a secretarial position, is it not?" she joked. O'Connor knew that Smith was from the Los Angeles law firm of Gibson, Dunn, and Crutcher—one of many she had applied to when she graduated from Stanford Law in 1952. The only job she was offered was as secretary. The attorney general pretended he hadn't heard her.

It was very typical that O'Connor never pressed the point. It was also typical that when Smith and his assistant, Kenneth Starr, arrived at her home to interview her, they found her "clearly prepared" as well as ready to serve them a salmon mousse lunch she had fixed before their arrival. Finally, it was very typical that O'Connor never mentioned that she was recovering from surgery, having just undergone a hysterectomy.

Sandra Day was a rancher's daughter, reared on an isolated cattle spread by a mother who treasured her subscriptions to *Vogue, House Beautiful,* and *The New Yorker,* and a gruff but doting father who had little tolerance for whiners. Her parents seemed to have no doubts that Sandra would go to college and no reservations about sending her on to law school. (Her father, who felt he had been tormented by lawyers all his life, liked the idea of having one in the family.) She was 19 when she started at Stanford Law, one of only five women in the class, but utterly uncowed by her position. She was a star student, a member of the law review, and also a perfect lady who, the men remembered, would draw them out about their accomplishments and interests without ever letting on that she had plenty of accomplishments herself.

It was at law school that she met and married

John O'Connor. She was sworn into the Arizona bar three days before their first son was born. After the family moved to Phoenix, she started a law practice, but when her second son was born, O'Connor faced the crisis every working mother dreads: her babysitter moved away. Unable to find a suitable replacement, she worked part-time from home and greatly stepped up her volunteer work in local politics. She was a Republican of the old school, enthusiastic about women's rights and disturbed that only 300 of the nation's 8,750 judges were women. She had written to Richard Nixon, urging him to put a woman on the Supreme Court, apparently unaware that Nixon had no intention of doing any such thing. ("I'm against it, frankly...I don't want any of them around," he told an aide.) When she was appointed—and then elected—to the Arizona state senate, one of her first successful pieces of legislation removed an Arizona statute prohibiting women from working more than eight hours a day. But she always dressed her beliefs—literally—in a manner her male colleagues found appealing. She never wore pants, and she made it clear she was not a militant. "I come to you wearing my bra and my wedding ring," she often told audiences. It took a while, one of her state senate colleagues recalled, to discover that "this pretty little thing carries a disconcerting load of expertise."

O'Connor beat out an incumbent judge for the appeals court post and was working there when she got the call from Smith. She seemed an unlikely possibility, since justices usually came from the federal court, but the shortage of Republican women on the bench had limited Reagan's options considerably. The liberal magazine *The Nation* congratulated the president for picking a woman when he released O'Connor's name but added that she seemed to have been chosen "almost entirely because of her sex and not on the basis of individual merit." And social conservatives angrily pointed out that O'Connor's record as a state senator suggested she supported abortion rights. But a Gallup poll found 86 percent of the public approved the idea of a woman justice, and virtually all of those who had an opinion about O'Connor thought she was a good candidate. She was confirmed 99 to 0.

O'Connor would live as a Supreme Court justice much as she had lived as an Arizona housewife and part-time lawyer—intensely. She took exercise classes three mornings a week with her female clerks (some of them under duress) and marched her staff, friends, and family through art exhibits, cherry-blossom-time picnics, and holiday celebrations while working six days a week. With her husband, she was a regular on the Washington social scene. She kept to her identity as a moderate and a former politician. Her opinions did not wow the legal world with their scholarship or theory, but as time went on and the division between the older liberal justices and the newer conservatives on the bench grew deeper, she was the person best equipped to knit together opinions out of fractious dissent. Eventually, she became the swing vote in a Court that was perpetually divided, 5 to 4. O'Connor employed her leverage to fashion a series of opinions on hot-button issues, such as abortion and affirmative action, that reflected her own pragmatic instinct for what made sense. The fact that she took her opportunity, shouldered it, and used it in a way that commanded so much respect turned the Supreme Court into the O'Connor Court and made Sandra Day O'Connor into a jurist so influential that the legal affairs writer Jeffrey Toobin called her "the most important woman in American history."

Keepsake Pages

In the 1980s people talked a lot about women "having it all." Do you remember that? What did it mean to you?

_____

_____

_____

_____

_____

_____

_____

_____

What did you wear to work in the 1980s? Did you have one of those blouses with a big bow at the neck?

_____

_____

_____

_____

_____

_____

_____

_____

Teaching and nursing used to be just about the only professions a woman could pursue. When other opportunities opened up, do you think respect for teachers and nurses dropped?

_____

_____

_____

_____

_____

_____

_____

_____

Do you remember *The Cosby Show*?

_____

_____

_____

_____

_____

_____

_____

_____

_____

Do you remember when people were saying that an older woman had a better chance of being killed by a terrorist than finding a husband? Did you worry about not getting married when you were in your twenties?

_____

_____

_____

_____

_____

_____

_____

_____

In 1976, ABC News briefly tried using Barbara Walters as coanchor on the evening news. It didn't last, and then it was a long time until Katie Couric became the first female solo evening news anchor. Do you remember following that? Did it seem important to you?

_____

_____

_____

_____

_____

_____

_____

_____

More Thoughts and Memories

More Thoughts and Memories

More Thoughts and Memories

13. The 1990s — Settling for Less?

"THE THINGS I FOUGHT FOR ARE NOW CONSIDERED QUAINT."

Lynnette Arthur's adolescence had been tumultuous, but she came out the other end as a strong and solid young woman. Her family, she said, "was like, 'Whew, thank God. We've got Lynnette back again.' But it was a better version of Lynnette." She was an heir to the women's movement of the 1960s and '70s, and even while she wrestled with family troubles, neighborhood troubles, and personal troubles, she never felt that she was constrained in any way by her sex. "I guess that was my generation's way of thinking...There's nothing intellectually that men can do that we can't."

The first generation of American women who had not been told that their only place was in the home had come of age. On TV, heroines such as Xena and Buffy the Vampire Slayer were saving the world on a weekly basis. To their young fans, the complaints and concerns of their elders sounded like ancient history. "I must have been about nine years old when my babysitter explained to me that feminists burned their bras," wrote AnnJanette Rosga, who was born in 1966. "Since this was also the first time I gave any thought to the *notion* of a bra, I was especially confounded by the image." Rosga was aware that there had been a time when young women saw no role models for themselves in the outside world, but it was nothing to which she could relate personally. "Before I went to college, I had a series of jobs — this was in the mid-'80s — in which my direct supervisors were *always* women; often, the highest authority in the workplace was a woman," she said. "I went to college from 1986 to 1990, during which time I believe I had a total of *three* male professors. During both college and graduate school, my mentors and advisers were

among the leading feminist scholars in this country. If I can help it, and I almost always can, I only go to women doctors...and it's never occurred to me at rallies to wonder where the women speakers are, because they're everywhere."

It was, in one way, exactly what their elders had been hoping for — American women who had grown up confident that they were entitled to all the educational and career opportunities that boys got, who played sports in school with as fierce a competitive spirit, and who expected to have success and love and adventure in equal measure. All that was a point of pride for the older generation. But there was also the disappointment of realizing that the younger women took it all for granted. "The things I fought for are now considered quaint...," the novelist Erica Jong told *Time*. "They say, 'We don't need feminism anymore.' They don't understand graduating magna cum laude from Harvard and then being told to go to the typing pool."

The young women often responded with impatience or mystification. "We don't feel we have to fight the battles women were fighting ten years ago, that *Ms.* still thinks we're fighting," said Claire Gruppo, an editor at *Savvy*. Talking with young Hispanic women, Sylvia Acevedo got blank looks when she brought up gender discrimination. "I'm saying, 'You guys just don't know what it was like!' But it's a moot issue." She shrugged. "It's like talking about dinosaurs." While surveys showed that young women believed the women's movement had helped — and was in fact still helping — to improve things for their sex, they shied away from calling themselves "feminists." ("Feminist" simply means someone who supports equal rights and opportunities for women. But there have been very few periods in American history when it didn't wind up being linked to images of cranky man-haters in unfashionable footwear.) While young women freely referred to themselves as "Ms.," they were more likely to take their husbands' names after they married than their older sisters had been.

When the new generation of women got into medical school or won a promotion, they were proud of themselves, but they did not think of it as a victory for their sex. Work was not something you fought for the right to do; it was something you just *did*. In 1991 two-thirds of married women with children worked, and the economics of family life made it inevitable that most of them would continue to do so. The two big-ticket expenses for middle-class families—home buying and a college education—were almost impossible to pay for without two paychecks. The cost of college was going up almost three times faster than household income. Married women who worked provided, on average, 41 percent of a family's income, and in almost a quarter of families with working wives, the woman earned more than the husband.

There was also the matter of self-preservation. Even if their husbands were capable of supporting the family on their own, younger women were, in general, clear about how fragile an institution marriage could be. "I always wanted the independence of being able to support myself and, if it ever came down to it, to be able to get away and take care of myself, having watched *Sleeping with the Enemy* too many times and having a divorced family," said Barbara Arnold's daughter, Alex Dery Snider.

"MY POINTS TOUCHED A RAW NERVE."

In 1989 Felice Schwartz, a consultant on women's careers, wrote an article for the *Harvard Business Review* on how companies could avoid losing valuable employees to motherhood. Along with familiar suggestions such as job sharing and flexible hours, Schwartz tossed another on the pile: corporations could divide their female employees into "career-and-family" women and "career-primary" women. The "career-primary" women could be put on the fast track, with the same demands as upwardly mobile men, while the "career-and-family" women would get a less-demanding schedule. No one would pressure them to work late or on weekends, and in return they would not pressure the company for big raises or promotions.

"My points touched a raw nerve," Schwartz understated.

By 1990, 60 percent of mothers with children under 5 were working—up from 30 percent two decades earlier. As more and more women tried to balance jobs and child raising, they became painfully aware that it was a whole lot harder than Clair Huxtable had made it seem on TV. Perhaps Schwartz's article would have gone unnoticed if the *New York Times* had not dubbed her proposal "the mommy track." The image of motherhood as a ticket to a slow ride to nowhere at work created an enormous, long-running controversy. A coalition of forty-four national women's groups quickly denounced the concept. They demanded to know why Schwartz assumed it would always be the *mother* who would want to work less and spend more time with the children. Why did everyone presume it should always be the woman—never the father or the employer—who would make the compromises?

It was a debate that would continue into the twenty-first century. Some women really did yearn for a less-demanding path, at least while their children were young, and found themselves downsizing their ambitions. Others figured out ways to juggle all the balls and make everything work. And some became angry—angry with their employers for expecting so much, angry with their husbands for helping so little, angry with themselves for not getting "it all" the way they had planned.

"I HATE RUG RATS."

Laura Sessions Stepp had every reason to think the sky was the limit in 1981, when she was working for the *Charlotte Observer* and won a Pulitzer Prize for a series of stories about lung diseases and textile workers. The *Washington Post* offered her an editing job; her husband, who landed a teaching post at the University of Maryland, encouraged her to go for it. "I was so ambitious," she recalled. "I thought I wanted to be a managing editor or an editor of a major newspaper in this country." But after she had a child, she began rethinking: "I looked around and I saw how much commitment it took to really be a top editor at a paper like that," she said. She was coming home exhausted at night and "going into the newsroom in tears because I missed my little boy so much that I wasn't doing anything very well."

She decided to give up editing and go back to writing, with its more flexible schedule. And while she says she's never regretted it, Stepp did feel for a while that she had let down the team, that it was her duty to shoot for the top, that "I had to do that for all women."

→ ←

FOR ALL ITS ACHIEVEMENTS, the women's movement had not managed to solve the work/family divide. "You second-guess yourself at work, you second-guess yourself at home, and you second-guess yourself in terms of your own personal time," said Kathy Hinderhofer, a Boston bank executive with two daughters. "That's one thing the women's movement may not have foreseen." The children themselves were generally not shy about expressing their opinions. Jo Meyer Maasberg says that when her daughters were growing up, they told her that "I spent too much time with other people's kids," teaching and grading papers. "They said they would never be teachers. So I guess I didn't know I was causing tensions, but yet I guess I did."

Those are the kinds of remarks that stay with a mother long after the children have forgotten uttering them. Jo's daughter, Jennifer Maasberg Smith, says now that she thinks things "worked out pretty good." Her mother was not, after all, far away in the little rural Wyoming school system. For six years, she taught Jennifer's class. "It was funny because she gave me this big speech . . . how I had to show her respect and call her Mrs. Maasberg and, you know, all on the same playing field as the other kids. But I couldn't call her Mrs. Maasberg. I called her Mom. So my whole class called her Mom."

→ ←

ALISON FOSTER HAD MADE HER FORAY into virtually every lifestyle arrangement on the map since her original, idyllic take-the-baby-to-work routine fell apart. She became a typical New York working mother, delivering her son Justin to day care via the subway. "And I would run to work and I'd always be late, and I'd work and at six o'clock I'd run back down and pick him up." She found the routine frazzling and isolating. "Advertising was definitely a singles business," she said. "There were men that were married, and they went back home to the suburbs, but not women." Once, at a meeting, a very successful advertising woman suddenly announced, "I'm turning 40 tomorrow and I don't have any children. I hate rug rats."

"She hates me because I have a child," Foster thought.

Eventually she and her husband moved to the suburbs, but she found the commute even more draining. Pregnant again, she quit and settled in to become a full-time housewife. "I just hated it," she said. She felt intimidated by the other mothers, who seemed to her to be doing things perfectly. ("I never had the right stroller.") And she missed working. "I loved *coming home* to my kids," she laughed.

The family moved to Europe for her husband's work. Living in a rather remote Italian village with the children while he traveled constantly, Alison was just as lonely as she had been in the suburbs.

"But at least I'm in Italy," she told herself.

"IT WAS BEFORE WASHING MACHINES."

In the 1970s, as we've seen, Congress bowed to pressure from social conservatives who believed a mother's place was in the home, and killed plans to provide early child-care programs for American families who wanted them. In 1996, under pressure from many of the same forces, it decided the government should not help support poor single mothers so they could stay home with their children.

A national debate over welfare had been raging for a quarter century by then. The least-popular woman in America was probably Linda Taylor of Chicago, although virtually no one knew her name. She was the model for the "welfare queen" that Ronald Reagan talked about endlessly during his 1976 campaign for president. Reagan never used that offensive term, but over and over, he told shocked audiences about the woman who had "eighty names, thirty-six addresses, twelve Social Security cards," and who used them to collect $150,000 in government benefits. The real Taylor was not nearly as good at milking the system as the one Reagan conjured up—she was eventually convicted of welfare fraud and perjury for using two aliases to collect $8,000. But she became an all-purpose emblem of a welfare system that average Americans were coming to hold in contempt.

The nation had been offering aid to poor women with children and no husbands since Franklin Roosevelt's New Deal, but the original recipients were mainly widows. By the last decade of the century, they were almost all unmarried mothers. Most women receiving money under the program, Aid to Families with Dependent Children, were white, and although the AFDC benefits were modest to impossibly stingy, depending on the state, many Americans seemed to envision recipients as black women who used their food stamps to buy cans of lobster and other luxuries struggling middle-class families never got to enjoy. Many people also believed that these women kept having more and more babies just so they could get higher benefits, even though the amounts they might gain were so small it would have been a suicidal strategy.

When Congress ended welfare as an entitlement, turning it into a short-term support system that could generally be extended only for the disabled, its backers predicted the change would reduce unwed motherhood. "When we started the current welfare program, two-parent families were the norm in poor families in America," said Senator Phil Gramm of Texas. "Today two-parent families are the exception." President Bill Clinton did not appear to share that theory, but he signed the bill into law in order to end a controversy that had left the Democrats connected, in many voters' eyes, with "welfare cheats." Clinton's expectations were the ones that held true. Welfare, once the hottest of hot-button political topics, quickly dropped out of the national political debate.

Like the divorce reforms of the 1970s that presumed ex-wives should go to work to help support their children, the 1996 welfare law was a blow to stay-at-home housewives. Whatever it did or did not accomplish, it was a public statement by the federal government that the nation did not put all that much value on full-time mothering. "When the original welfare program began, the family was seen as an arrangement where the husband went out to work and the woman stayed home and kept house and raised the children. It was before washing machines and refrigerators and vacuum cleaners," said Senator Daniel Moynihan, who had championed a less-drastic version of welfare reform. But now, he said, many "self-respecting" middle-class women were working to help support their families, and the American public had a right to expect poor women to work outside the home as well.

In truth, the social rule that mothers should stay at home with their children had seldom been applied to poor women. After the Civil War, white Americans in both the North and South denounced black families in which only the husband worked. And from the time there were factories in American cities, there were women, many of them mothers, working in the assembly lines. Still, it was ironic that some of the same people who drove down the Equal Rights Amendment, and argued ferociously for motherhood as an all-important calling, were making it their mission to send the mothers of the poorest and most at-risk youngsters into the workplace.

Rather than reducing illegitimacy—or creating a huge spike in homeless families, as some opponents predicted—the changes in welfare seemed mainly to save the government money. Nine million families, virtually all of them composed of single women and their children, left the welfare rolls. A great many women did go to work, but few managed to pull themselves out of poverty. There was some modest evidence that the children benefited if they wound up in day-care programs while their mothers were working, but only about one-seventh of the eligible children actually got day-care subsidies, and there were long waiting lists in at least twenty states. Jason DeParle, who had covered the welfare story as a *New York Times* reporter, followed three Milwaukee women to see what effects the changes would have on them and their families. Angie, the most ambitious, got a job as a nurse's aide, stitched together enough cash to pay for a used car, and then also hopefully signed up with a temporary-employment agency to make extra money. When she finished filling out her application, she discovered her car wouldn't start. Then it began to rain. Other commuters driving home for dinner, DeParle wrote, "had no way to know that the drenched woman trudging down the road was a welfare-to-work marvel trying to work two jobs." The high-paying temp service never did come through with enough work to make a difference, and Angie—who was caring for some of her cousin's children as well as her own—was often unable to get the utility bill paid before the lights went off. "On welfare Angie was a low-income single mother, raising her children in a dangerous neighborhood in a household roiled by chaos...," DeParle concluded. "Off welfare, she was a low-income single mother, raising her children in a dangerous neighborhood in a household roiled by chaos." Since Angie often had to leave home before

her five kids were awake, they became chronic class-cutters. Her teenagers began experimenting with sex, and her oldest daughter was resentful of being stuck with so much responsibility for the younger children. When DeParle asked Angie if her family was proud of her for holding down a job, she seemed puzzled. "I don't think the kids think about that. They'd like it if I'd just sit around with them all day," she said.

"LEGAL ONLY IN CERTAIN CIRCUMSTANCES."

In 1995 Norma McCorvey, the Jane Roe in *Roe v. Wade,* switched sides. She had been a pro-choice activist and written a book in which she described herself as "a poor, half-crazed, half-ordinary woman who had been picked by fate to become a symbol of something much bigger and finer than herself." But she was still subject to depression and bouts of heavy drinking. McCorvey was working at a women's clinic that offered abortions when she got to know people from the anti-abortion group Operation Rescue, who were picketing outside. After talking with them for a while, she claimed she could hear the sound of a baby's laughter in the clinic and began telling women who called to schedule an abortion that they were killing their child. She converted to evangelical Christianity in a baptism filmed for television and took a job in the Operation Rescue office. "My life has been restored to me, and now I have the privilege of speaking for those who cannot speak for themselves," she said at the National Memorial for the Unborn in 1997.

The pro-choice camp suggested McCorvey's change of heart had to do with a desire for attention. ("They could have been nice to me instead of treating me like an idiot," she told CNN.) Whatever lay behind the transformation, it did dramatize the constantly shifting feelings about abortion rights. The pro-choice movement had hoped the issue was settled after *Roe v. Wade,* but instead, opposition to the abortion decision helped precipitate the rightward turn of American politics in the 1980s and the alliance between the Christian right and fiscal conservatives that propelled George W. Bush into office.

For the majority of Americans, the idea of terminating a pregnancy was an uncomfortable one, yet most did not want to eliminate the option. When poll takers came calling, people jumped at any answer that suggested it was none of their business and was a matter between a woman and her doctor. When simply asked whether abortion should be legal or illegal, they tended toward anything in the middle—such as "legal only in certain circumstances." Even many of the women who told *New York Times* pollsters in 1989 that the nation still needed a women's movement to fight for them said they were opposed to abortion on demand—roughly half favored more restrictions than existed at the time.

The abortion rate peaked in 1981, when roughly 3 percent of all women of childbearing age in America terminated a pregnancy. It then began to decline slowly. In 2005, 1.2 million abortions were performed, or about 2 percent of women of childbearing age. But since most women weren't pregnant in any given year, that was still one out of every five pregnancies.

Americans were most likely to support early abortions, and nearly 90 percent of the procedures performed in the United States occurred during the first three months of pregnancy. By 2005 more than 60 percent would occur during the first eight weeks. The arrival of RU-486, a French drug that caused a fetus to abort without medical intervention very early in pregnancy, helped to propel the trend. But there was very little talk about any sort of compromise that would make early abortions easier to obtain and later ones more difficult. Political advocates on both sides tended to see the issue in terms of absolutes—a woman's constitutional right to control her own body versus the belief that the fetus had the full rights of a human being. (In South

Dakota, an antichoice leader said she rejected any suggestions about compromise because "I have to save as many children as I can.") On the farthest fringe, abortion opponents believed violence was justified if it was directed against people who were involved in what they saw as mass murder. Between 1993 and 1998, seven people were killed in attacks on abortion clinics or on doctors who performed abortions. That led, not surprisingly, to a decline in the number of doctors, hospitals, and clinics willing to provide abortion services. The decline would become more dramatic from 2000 on, leaving women in many parts of the country with few options, no matter how early their pregnancy or how desperate their situation.

"WE WANTED A PLEASANT OCCASION."

Sexual harassment in the workplace seems to have been around since the first female clerical worker. More than a century ago, *Typewriter Trade Journal* reported worriedly that employers were using "peculiar language" when advertising for a secretary—language like "a pretty blonde." Women who worked were always aware of the problem, but if the broader public thought about it at all, it was only in the classic terms of a boss threatening to fire a female employee unless she had sex with him. That changed in 1991, when Clarence Thomas, a nominee to the Supreme Court, was accused of tormenting a female subordinate with requests for dates and talk about pornography.

Anita Hill, a graduate of Yale Law School, had been only 25 when Thomas hired her as his chief aide in the Reagan administration's Department of Education. A native of Oklahoma, she was the youngest of thirteen children in a hardworking farm family so averse to scenes and confrontation that when Anita became the center of the biggest political controversy of the era, no one mentioned the matter when she returned home for Thanksgiving. ("We wanted a pleasant occasion," one of her relatives explained.) Hill had worked under Thomas in two federal agencies, including the Equal Employment Opportunity Commission, which, ironically, handled sexual harassment complaints, albeit without much enthusiasm. (*Time* reported that although complaints of sexual harassment to the EEOC had risen 70 percent between 1981 and 1989, most were dismissed without even being investigated.)

Hill said that after she agreed to follow Thomas to the EEOC, his behavior changed for the worse, that he claimed someone had "put pubic hair on my Coke" and began to talk very specifically about pornographic movies he had been watching, about "women having sex with animals and films involving group sex or rape scenes." When she was offered a job teaching law at Oral Roberts University, Hill accepted quickly, even though the law school was verging on losing its accreditation.

Nevertheless, Hill kept in contact with Thomas, and he may have been as stunned as the rest of the country when she eventually sent a statement describing his behavior to the Senate Judiciary Committee. Of course, it created a sensation. When she appeared to testify, Hill was called a liar, a lesbian, and sexually repressed. Changing planes in Houston on her way home, she was surrounded by hecklers yelling, "Shame! Shame!" A divided Senate approved the nomination 52 to 48, by far the narrowest margin ever for a Supreme Court confirmation. The White House swore in the new justice nine days ahead of schedule, out of fear that some other revelation would derail the installation. A poll found that 55 percent of men thought Thomas was more believable, and 49 percent of women.

But as time went on and the debate continued, voters—particularly women voters—became more likely to say they believed Hill. Perhaps that was because so many other tales followed. One involved Tailhook, an annual gathering of Navy and Marine Corps officers that had always featured mass drunkenness and boorish behavior. In 1991 in Las Vegas, the male officers' conduct was particularly shocking. Lieutenant Paula Coughlin told reporters from *60 Minutes* that she had been caught in a gauntlet of drunken officers who pawed her, tossed her from man to man, and put her in fear of being raped. The Navy made things worse by trying to cover up the complaints. A Pentagon report found that at one point the commander of the Naval Investigative Service, Rear Admiral Duvall Williams Jr., had "a screaming match" with a female officer in which he compared women pilots to "go-go dancers, topless dancers, or hookers." He also said, citing Coughlin's language, that "any woman that would use the F-word on a regular basis would welcome this type of activity."

And then, of course, in 1998, the beginning of the Clinton impeachment crisis over the Monica Lewinsky affair told Americans far more about the way employers could behave with female underlings than they wanted to know. Although Lewinsky was a willing participant, the president was very, very obviously more powerful than the humble intern, and some feminists claimed that along with his other offenses, he was guilty of sexual harassment. Others disagreed. The "commonsense guideline in sexual behavior that came out of the women's movement," Gloria Steinem wrote, was that "no means no and yes means yes." She argued that the case was not comparable to Clarence Thomas's, or cause for impeachment. But, she added, the allegations against Clinton might suggest the president was "a candidate for sex addiction therapy."

A side product of the Thomas episode was an increased interest in electing women to Congress. Their numbers had been creeping up very slowly through the '80s, but watching the Senate Judiciary Committee debate sexual harassment, people found it hard to ignore the fact that all those doing the arguing were men. Patty Murray, a state senator in Washington, decided to become part of the solution and won a Senate seat for herself by running as a typical "mom in tennis shoes." Barbara Boxer of California, who had been part of a delegation of Democratic women from the House of Representatives who had marched to the Senate to urge that

Hill's testimony be given more credence, won a Senate race as well. The 1992 elections raised the number of women in the House from twenty-eight to forty-seven and put six women in the Senate, creating the legend of the Year of the Woman. While reaction to the Thomas case might have had an impact, women candidates benefited much more from the reapportionment of congressional districts that took place before the election, creating more places where nonincumbents had a chance to win. Senator Barbara Mikulski, for one, hated the whole Year-of-the-Woman idea. It sounded, she thought, "like the Year of the Caribou or the Year of the Asparagus. We're not a fad, not a fancy or a year."

"AN OCCUPATIONAL HAZARD OF GOING TO WAR."

The suffragists might have imagined that women would someday have a significant presence in Congress, but chances are very few thought they would also become a critical part of the armed services. The military had traditionally welcomed women's participation only in times of crisis, and even then in very limited roles. Although Congress made women a permanent part of the armed forces after World War II, the number of female recruits was kept small. Besides being barred from combat, they were not supposed to serve on ships, and they could be discharged for getting married, getting pregnant, or having an abortion. The idea that the nation would come to depend on women in uniform did not really occur until after the war in Vietnam, when the military's prestige was low, its leadership was in disarray, and the new volunteer Army was finding it almost impossible to fill its ranks. Women who were willing to sign up had more education and tended to be better motivated than male volunteers.

In New Mexico, Sylvia Acevedo had dreamed of following her older brother to West Point when she graduated from high school in 1975. But she discov-

ered that "it was against the law for me. It wasn't 'No, you can't come.' I couldn't even apply." She was a year too early. The armed forces' increasing needs, combined with political pressure from the women's movement, forced the military academies to go coed in 1976, to the howls of the old guard. "Maybe you could find one woman in ten thousand who could lead in combat, but she would be a freak and we're not running the military for freaks," said General William Westmoreland. Women were still barred from "combat-related" jobs—a rule that was as big a constraint on advancement as the rules against overtime and lifting heavy objects had been on women in the private sector. Combat-related assignments involved more than firing guns at the enemy; they included everything from flying jets to support services. In fact, they counted for 73 percent of all possible military occupations in 1980. The military gradually relaxed the rules and ignored some of the ones that still existed. And once American troops began fighting in Iraq, the line between combat and noncombat roles virtually vanished.

By the first Gulf War in 1991, 7 percent of the people deployed to Iraq were women, and besides tending the sick, they flew helicopters, delivered supplies to the front units, and filled other jobs that put them in the line of fire. Twelve women were killed, and two were taken prisoner. In the most famous incident, a Black Hawk helicopter carrying Rhonda Cornum, a 36-year-old flight surgeon, was shot down behind Iraqi lines. Most of the other soldiers in the helicopter were killed in the crash. Cornum had a bullet in her back, two broken arms, and a shattered knee when the Iraqis found her. Her arms, she wrote later, "were swinging uselessly beside me like sticks tied to my shoulders with string." She was tied up and put into a truck, and as it was driven off, one of the Iraqis unzipped Cornum's flight suit and began to molest her. "I remember thinking, 'Hey, you could do better than this,'" she wrote. "I was not only repulsed by his advances, but amazed." Although the Iraqi kept fondling her breasts, she wrote, "My screams and the fortunate impossibility of getting me out of my flight suit with two broken arms kept the molester at bay" until the truck got to its destination. After she was released, Cornum tried to downplay the story. It was, she said, "an occupational hazard of going to war."

→→ ←←

DENA IVEY'S QUEST to find herself involved many different parts. She was born in Alaska to a Norwegian-American mother and a father who was part Yup'ik, a local Eskimo tribe. "My dad was ashamed of his Yup'ik heritage because he had to deal with a lot of racism growing up," she said. "So Mom pretty much bombarded us with Norwegian while Dad downplayed our Yup'ik side to protect us." She gradually came to embrace her identity as a Native American. She also realized she was gay. But her first romantic relationship was traumatic. "So I joined the military to get the hell away from her," Ivey recalled. She had dreamed of being an FBI agent. ("*The Silence of the Lambs* had come out at that time. I wanted to be Jodie Foster.") With that in mind, she enlisted in the air force and trained for the military police.

Most of the women Ivey met in the Air Force were heterosexual, "very focused on their husbands and boyfriends," she recalled. "These were tough gals…We were all working. We were doing a tough job. I wasn't trying to convert anybody or anything." Ivey said she was "paranoid" about telling people she was gay, and for good reason. The military's "don't ask, don't tell" rule could be enforced in an arbitrary and irregular fashion; it did not stop Ivey's supervisors from asking her about gossip that she had a relationship with another woman. In 2007 Pentagon statistics showed an extremely large proportion of the people discharged for being openly gay were women: 46 percent in the Army, where women made up 14 percent of the personnel, and 49 percent in the Air Force, where they made up 20 percent.

While many women resented the no-combat rule as a bar to their full participation in both the opportunities and the responsibilities of military life, Ivey thought some restrictions were a good idea—especially if they kept the sexes separate when soldiers were away from their home base. When her squadron was involved in war games, she fought for the right to keep her team in a different tent from the men's. "These guys were piggy. They were making all kinds of sexist jokes," she recalled. In the end, because of her protests, the nine women were indeed separated—and assigned to a leaky six-person tent of their own.

"BLACK AND WHITE KIDS RIDE TO THE DAIRY QUEEN TOGETHER."

In 1990 a Fox TV comedy, *True Colors*, showed a black man and his white wife in bed together. That was a little thing, but maybe not quite so little when you considered that in 1968, the white singer Petula Clark made headlines when she unthinkingly touched the arm of Harry Belafonte on her television special. (A representative of the sponsor, who was watching the taping, said his employer's car sales would be hurt if the shot aired and demanded a retake. Clark complied, then told a technician to erase everything but the original version.)

The idea of sex between a black man and a white woman was the source of unending racist hysteria in the segregated South, and it was illegal for blacks and whites to marry in most Southern states until the Supreme Court ruled in 1967 that the laws against interracial marriage were unconstitutional. Even in the North, Americans seemed to have a hard time accepting the idea. It was not until 1991 that Gallup first reported more Americans saying they approved of interracial marriage than disapproved. (The margin was 48 to 42 percent.) That was down from more than 90 percent disapproval in 1958.

If the country needed a reminder of how fraught

the issue still could be, there was Wedowee, Alabama, where in 1994 an unknown arsonist burned down the high school after the principal barred interracial couples from the prom. It was, in a weird way, actually in part a story about change. Alabama had been infamous in its resistance to integration, and it would be the last state to officially wipe its meaningless but symbolic laws against interracial marriage off the books in 2000. But for all that, interracial dating was not uncommon. "Black and white kids ride to the Dairy Queen together, they go to ball games, and most people don't think anything of it... The red lights don't all quit working when an interracial couple drives through town. This is 1994," said Terry Graham, the mayor of the small town of eight hundred residents. In fact, 17-year-old Revonda Bowen, whose plans to go to the prom with a white date helped spark the crisis, was the child of a marriage between a black woman and a white man.

➤➤ ◄◄

DANA ARTHUR WAS DATING A WHITE MAN in the late 1980s, much to her daughter Lynnette's dismay. "She was at that age when she was trying to fit in with everybody, and here's her mom in Crown Heights with this white boyfriend coming to see her. She was, like, 14. She was just not having it," said Dana. "She gave him a hard time, and he just hung in there." The entire neighborhood seemed unhappy about an interracial relationship. When Dana and Tony Monteleone would walk down the street in her almost-all-black neighborhood, she said, "young boys would say stuff like, 'Traitor!' and 'What are you doing with that white man?'... And they said things to him, trying to engage him in some kind of argument... It was weird, and Lynnette was very embarrassed by the whole thing."

Tony, who had pulled himself up from a difficult youth, was willing to stick it out. They dated for eight years and, Dana said, "eventually, after years, people warmed up to us—warmed up to him,

mostly—and didn't treat me like a traitor." When her relationship with Lynnette solidified, too, she felt it was time to move on to the next step. "We stayed engaged for a year and then we got married. We bought a house." Lynnette, who was 21, got to keep the old apartment—a prize jewel in New York's real estate–mad economy.

"AND YOU MIGHT FLOAT FROM DORM TO DORM."

Nora Ephron once joked that "the major achievement of the women's movement in the 1970s was the Dutch treat." But the matter of who paid for what on a date never did quite get worked out. The concept of sharing the bill may have hit its peak around the same time communal living did, then declined in popularity as time went on. (In 2005 Maureen Dowd would write with dismay that a younger woman told her sharing the cost of a date was "a scuzzy '70s thing, like platform shoes on men.")

What had perhaps changed the most was the dwindling of the whole concept of a date. Young people were much more likely to simply go out as a pack than have an organized night out at the movies or dinner as a pair. As a teenager, Alex Snider said, her crowd's chief recreation was to "drive from one end of town to the other, or call people and try to track down everybody, and once we did that, we'd realize there was nothing to do anyway and we'd end up at the movie-rental store ten minutes before it closed. So really, if we'd had cell phones when we were in high school, we wouldn't have had anything to do whatsoever."

In college, dormitories generally had open visiting privileges, and many were less like the barren cubbyholes of yore and more like small apartments. Camara Dia Holloway remembers life in college in the early '90s as a time when you didn't so much date as "hang out... You and a group of your girlfriends might go to another dorm, to a boys' dorm, and hang out with a group of guys, but you would really be scoping out somebody. And you might float from dorm to dorm."

"AND ONE DAY, IT HAPPENED."

After she broke up with her boyfriend of three years, June LaValleur was "wondering why I can't keep a relationship"—although perhaps she should have given herself more credit for that thirty-year marriage. It was at that point she met Jill, a lesbian, for whom she felt an immediate attraction. "I had never knowingly known anyone who was gay," she recalled. Growing up in the 1950s, LaValleur had not even been aware that women could be attracted to other women. When she was in medical school, though, she had learned "about the Kinsey model of hetero-homosexuality, where there's a continuum" and decided that she "was somewhere in between."

Jill, who was twenty-two years younger, was different from June in many ways. But on the things that were most important to June—from a willingness to share, to liberal politics, to being a nonsmoker—they matched up. "I knew she was a lesbian because she was open about it. She was at the time breaking up with someone. I guess you could say one thing led to another. We had dinner, movies, coffee. We were friends. And one day, it happened."

Being in a relationship with a woman, June found, was much different from being in a relationship with a man, "besides the obvious plumbing issues. That's just a teeny thing. Being in a relationship with a woman is a much more emotional intimacy. We talked more about things. I felt less vulnerable. Jill likes women who are of generous size, which is amazing given her ninety-eight pounds. We just shared everything. We were both rabid Democrats. We were both avid readers. We both loved to travel."

By the 1990s lesbianism was increasingly accepted, and in some parts of the country it seemed to be downright trendy. "What most lesbians remember

as a major opening volley occurred on October 23, 1992," wrote Lindsy Van Gelder and Pamela Robin Brandt in their book *The Girls Next Door*. On that night, *20/20* broadcast a segment on the lesbian community in and around Northampton, Massachusetts, with a teaser that announced, "Women are meeting, marrying, and raising families in the heart of New England!" After that, Van Gelder and Brandt wrote, "suddenly we were everywhere." In the *Washington Post*, Kara Swisher wryly noted that "the new improved lesbian is a party girl of much sex, lingerie, and sophistication...Straight women trendsetters like Madonna flirt with the lifestyle and make it chic. Travel to Santa Fe, dance with wolves, be a lesbian!" *New York Magazine* put K. D. Lang on the cover of a May 1993 issue on "Lesbian Chic." *Newsweek* followed with a lesbian couple on the cover the next month, and in August Lang was back, on the cover of *Vanity Fair*, being shaved by Cindy Crawford. Dee Mosbacher, the daughter of a cabinet member in the first Bush administration, came out in her college commencement address, leading the way for so many other lesbian daughters and sisters of prominent men that it began to seem that a gay female relative was a prerequisite for political success. (In a reverse case, Phyllis Schlafly's son John, who worked for her conservative Eagle Foundation, acknowledged he was gay in 1992. "He's a good lawyer and very helpful. He is not a proponent of same-sex marriage," said Schlafly, who made it clear this was not her favorite topic.)

For all the stories about lesbian chic, gay women could not give their partners the same rights and protections legally married spouses had, and if they had children from an earlier marriage, they had reason to worry about custody rights if their ex-husbands chose to make their sexuality an issue. (About 1.5 million lesbians were believed to be mothers, either from previous relationships or from artificial insemination.) In a famous case in 1995, the Virginia supreme court upheld a lower court ruling that Sharon Bottoms was unfit to have custody of her children. The fact that she was a lesbian would impose "social condemnation" on her child, the court said, as it gave custody to Bottoms's estranged mother.

Still, a new generation of gay women were confident that they had full rights to the world's opportunities. They had still been in school when Lang announced she was gay in 1992 and when comedienne Ellen DeGeneres came out in 1997, both in real life and as the heroine on her TV situation comedy. Diane Salvatore, a gay novelist who would become a successful editor at women's magazines such as *Ladies' Home Journal, Redbook,* and *Good Housekeeping,* told *New York Magazine* that she went to a Lang concert not long after the singer came out and "was amazed. Here was a superstar who no longer had to go off and marry a man and pay him off to pretend she was straight. That's a huge break. I didn't think I'd see it in my lifetime, and I'm only 32."

Keepsake Pages

Were you a *Buffy the Vampire Slayer* fan? If not, try to remember the first time you saw another action heroine and how you reacted.

_____

_____

_____

_____

_____

_____

_____

_____

If you were around for the women's movement, did you feel the next generation of women appreciated all the changes that happened—or, to put it another way, understood what it was like in the bad old days? (If there's a younger woman involved in this conversation, this would be a great time to note how she views the story of the women's movement.)

_____

_____

_____

_____

_____

_____

_____

_____

Okay—the word "feminist." Yes or no? If younger women don't like to call themselves "feminists," do you think that makes a difference? Or is a word just a word?

_____

_____

_____

_____

_____

_____

Have you ever been sexually harassed at work? How did you react? Do you remember the Anita Hill controversy? Do you think it made a difference?

_____

_____

_____

_____

_____

_____

When was the first time you paid when you were on a date?

_____

_____

_____

_____

_____

_____

More Thoughts and Memories

More Thoughts and Memories

14. The New Millennium

Betty Friedan died in 2006 at age 85. She had moved to Washington in her early 70s, happy to be "at the epicenter of politics and public policy," and published a memoir, *Life So Far,* in which she continued settling scores. ("I am the innocent victim of a drive-by shooting by a reckless driver savagely aiming at the whole male gender," said her ex-husband.) Looking back, she said she regretted "that I didn't have a real career" and claimed she "would have loved to have been the editor of the women's page of the *New York Times*"—a feature that had vanished years before, thanks to the movement she led. But Friedan had no second thoughts about what her generation had accomplished. "There's a lot of silly talk that the women's movement is dead. Well it's not dead; it's alive in society!" she wrote. "The way women look at themselves, the way other people look at women, is completely different, *completely different* than it was thirty years ago... Our daughters grow up with the same possibilities as our sons."

She was right on many counts. By the beginning of the new century, women were claiming almost half of the seats in the nation's medical and law schools. They dominated some fields that used to be almost exclusively male, such as pharmacy and veterinary medicine. Forty percent of the new dental school graduates were women, although as late as 1970 the dean of the University of Texas dental school had insisted on admitting no more than two women in every class of a hundred because "girls aren't strong enough to pull teeth."

There were very few fields in which women had not made major inroads. The number of women in science had risen to about 20 percent, up from 3 percent in the early 1960s. (More important, 40 percent of the undergraduate college students majoring in science were women, and girls were taking math and science courses in high school as frequently as boys.) Even in the small, exclusive world of symphony music, where they had traditionally been a rarity, women occupied more than a third of the chairs in top orchestras, thanks in part to a policy of blind auditions that kept judges in the dark about the sex of the competitors for new openings.

"BECAUSE YOUNG MEN ARE RARER, THEY'RE MORE VALUED."

Girls were doing better academically than boys by almost every measure. More than 56 percent of undergraduate college students were female, and their rates of graduation were better. But few schools wanted a student body in which girls vastly outnumbered boys, and colleges were prepared to forgive inferior male grades and achievements in order to keep the sexes balanced. "The reality is that because young men are rarer, they're more valued applicants," wrote Jennifer Delahunty Britz, the dean of admissions at Kenyon, in the *New York Times* essay "To All the Girls I've Rejected." She wondered what messages the nation was "sending young women that they must, nearly twenty-five years after the defeat of the Equal Rights Amendment, be even more accomplished than men to gain admission to the nation's top colleges," then apologized "for the demographic realities."

It was a much-discussed issue for young women and their parents. "The girls are so stressed," said Alison Foster, who talked to students of both sexes at the private Manhattan high school where she worked. "Here we've taught girls to do well in school and be as good as boys, which they've done. Now the girls are better than the boys, and they can't get into college the way boys can. So we've screwed them again."

Instead of celebrating girls' achievements, the nation started to worry. *Newsweek,* in a cover story on "The Boy Crisis," reported with alarm that there were only "44 percent of male undergraduates on college campuses: thirty years ago the number was 58 percent." In Milton, Massachusetts, where there were twice as many girls as boys on the high school honor roll, 17-year-old Doug Anglin filed a civil rights complaint in 2006, claiming the school discriminated against male students.

If society were a person, it would complain that it just couldn't win. There were only two sexes; one was going to have to be in the minority when it came to academic achievement. But while women's failure to realize their potential had been regarded as a regretful shortcoming, the failure of boys seemed to be seen as a threat to civilization itself. Margaret Spellings, George W. Bush's secretary of education, said the dominance of young women in higher education had "profound implications for the economy, society, families, and democracy." Experts worried that all those tests they had imposed on schoolchildren in an effort to chart achievement had somehow encouraged the teachers to run their classes in a less boy-friendly way. "Take Our Daughters to Work Day," which the Ms. Foundation initiated to give girls a sense of possibility, evolved into "Take Our Daughters and Sons to Work Day."

Yet anyone fearing that women were taking over the world needn't have fretted. Their overrepresentation at the top ended with the classroom. Only 17 percent of the partners in major law firms were women in 2005—a figure that wasn't much better than the 13 percent of a decade before. While women held nearly half of lower-level managerial jobs in American businesses, they represented only a handful of CEOs in Fortune 500 companies. More than three-quarters of the American workers making $100,000 to $200,000 a year were male. By the time CBS made Katie Couric the evening news anchor in 2006, most of the people working in TV news were women, including 58 percent of the reporters, 66 percent of the news producers, and 56 percent of the news writers. However, almost 80 percent of the news directors and 68 percent of the assistant news directors were men.

"I THINK IT'S THE MONEY."

At the beginning of the twenty-first century, the overall average hourly pay for female workers had risen above eighty cents for every dollar a man made. But the divide between male and female college graduates was, if anything, getting wider. Part of the difference was due to the fact that professional women tended to work in areas where the pay was lower. For instance, the vast majority of the nation's teachers were still women, including nearly 80 percent of those in elementary and middle schools. The number of male teachers was actually at a forty-year low, at 25 percent. Everyone agreed that the reason was the pay. "If you started paying $100,000 a year, you'd see a lot more men jumping into the field," said Bryan Nelson, the founder of MenTeach, an organization dedicated to encouraging men to go into education.

In an ideal world, the revolution in the national attitude toward a woman's place would have led to a revolution in the pay and prestige accorded to the careers that had traditionally been regarded as women's work, and teachers would have been paid as much as stockbrokers. But that—obviously—had not happened.

It was not as if Americans didn't appreciate how critical good teachers were to the nation's prosperity. Young college graduates in particular saw teaching as a way to "give back" and signed up in droves for Teach for America, a kind of peace corps for urban schoolteachers. In 2007 more than 8 percent of the seniors at Princeton and Wellesley applied to join, along with 11 percent of the graduates at Amherst and Spelman.

Teach for America had been conceived by Wendy Kopp while she was a student at Princeton. She made it the subject of her senior thesis in 1989, and when her professor called the idea "deranged," Kopp begged to disagree. She raised $2.5 million and founded the program the next year. "Teach for America is very hot now," said Serena Savarirayan, a 2001 graduate of Northwestern who originally taught fifth grade in the struggling city of Paterson, New Jersey. But the young recruits did not generally intend to make education their careers. Most saw it as a detour—two years of making a contribution before they returned to their path of upward mobility.

Savarirayan herself thought she would apply to law school, but she fell in love with teaching—with the work, with the kids, and with the intellectual challenge that came with trying to figure out how to help poor and minority students succeed. She moved on to North Star Academy in Newark, a charter school that emphasized rigorous programs, with an eleven-month school year and longer-than-usual school days. She looked ahead to her limitless future and saw it was going to be in education. Her friends and family initially responded with the same stunned puzzlement that might have greeted a young woman in 1960 who announced that instead of majoring in education, she wanted to pursue corporate finance. Savarirayan was undaunted and unsurprised by the lack of enthusiasm for her career choice. "I think it's the money," she said.

"I COULD NOT LET IT SLIDE."

Many economists believed that another part of the wage gap was due to continued discrimination. Certainly some of the women thought so. A new round of class-action lawsuits had begun making their way through the courts, one from women at Wal-Mart, where almost 75 percent of the store department heads were women but only 20 percent of the store managers. In 2007 the Supreme Court was asked to consider the case of Lilly Ledbetter, an Alabama woman who was getting ready to retire as a supervisor in a Goodyear Tire assembly plant when she discovered that she was making a lot less money than the men who held down the same job. Like Lorena Weeks, Ledbetter was a Southerner who had no illusions about what the world would demand of her. "My husband and I grew up in rural Alabama," she said. "If you lived in the country in those years, you worked."

When she went to Goodyear in 1979, Ledbetter was not the first woman the company had hired to work in management on the tire-production floor. But she was the only one who stuck it out. "I realized going in that these people had never adjusted to being around a woman, so I tolerated a lot of discriminatory things," she said. One plant manager told her that Goodyear "did not need women, that [women] didn't help it." Ledbetter worked the night shift, which involved a great deal of overtime, and she was often at the plant twelve hours or more. Her husband would drive her to work and back to reduce the stress.

As in most places, Goodyear's salaried employees were not encouraged to share information about what they were making. So Ledbetter didn't know that as time went on, her salary dropped farther and farther behind those of her male coworkers. Then, as she was approaching retirement, she received an anonymous letter detailing who got what. Ledbetter was being paid 71 percent of what other men with her seniority were getting, and only 87 percent of what the least senior man on the job received. "I was just emotionally let down when I saw the difference in pay and knowing the effect it had on my retirement," she said. "I could not let it slide. I went to the EEOC my next day off."

Goodyear, Ledbetter recalled, "offered me ten thousand dollars" to settle the charges. In response, she calculated the difference between what she had made over the course of her career and what she would have gotten if she'd made as much as the lowest-paid man. She asked for that sum: $60,000. Goodyear returned with a final offer of $15,000, and Ledbetter went to court. The jury awarded her back pay and more than $3 million in damages, which the judge reduced to $360,000 because federal law limited the amount a worker could get for pay discrimination. Lilly, who had been wounded by Goodyear's argument that her low pay was due to bad performance, felt vindicated. But the company appealed, arguing that federal law required her to file a complaint within 180 days of the time the discrimination occurred.

That was the case that went to the Supreme Court, with the EEOC arguing that few employees would know within six months that their salary was different from their peers'. The clock on the 180-day rule should restart each time a discriminatory paycheck is issued, the commission argued. But the Supreme Court sided with Goodyear, 5 to 4. Justice Samuel Alito, who had just taken Sandra Day O'Connor's seat, acknowledged that 180 days was a very short time for workers to figure out they were being discriminated against and file a suit. But that deadline, he theorized, might encourage employees and employer to work out their differences "through voluntary conciliation and cooperation." Ledbetter lost her entire financial award, and she said later that Goodyear sent her a bill for some of the court costs.

Justice Ruth Bader Ginsburg was so angry about the decision that she took the unusual step of reading her dissent from the bench. "In our view, the Court does not comprehend, or is indifferent to, the insidious way in which women can be victims of pay discrimination," she said. Ginsburg was a quiet, low-key justice, not normally given to dramatic gestures. But she had spent much of her professional life fighting for women's rights, and she clearly felt that the new majority created since the departure of her good friend Justice O'Connor intended to undo many of the things that had been accomplished. One of Ginsburg's former law clerks suggested that in talking about Lilly Ledbetter, Ginsburg was also talking about herself. "It's as if after sixteen years on the Court, she's finally voicing some complaints of her own," said Professor Goodwin Liu of the University of California.

When Patricia Lorance had run into a similar problem about time deadlines in her fight to keep her seniority, Congress had amended the Civil Rights Act in response. Ginsburg very pointedly invited lawmakers to do that again, and in 2009, Congress complied with legislation that restarted the 180-day clock every time a discriminatory paycheck was issued. The Lilly Ledbetter Fair Pay Act became the first bill signed into law by President Barack Obama. "I'm so excited I can hardly stand it," Lilly said.

In the decade since she had left her job, the battle had become a new career for her, as well as a distraction from worries about her husband, a loyal cheerleader for her cause who died shortly before her big legislative victory. At 70, she looked much younger, with plenty of fight still in her. "I tell you, working hard will keep you young," she said. As she toured the country giving talks, Ledbetter was approached by women who wanted to share their own stories about pay discrimination. "I had no idea this was such a national problem," she said. "This is not only a person like myself, this is professional people as well. I've heard it from physicians, teachers, nurses, every job you can imagine."

"MY WAY OF SIMPLIFYING MY LIFE."

Even if discrimination and choice of profession were both factors, the biggest reason women's wages were lower was almost certainly their tendency to drop out of the workforce or to scale back to part-time employment when they had children. Young, childless women averaged salaries that were very close to those of young men. A study by Andrew Beveridge, a demographer at Queens College, found that young women in big cities—who tended to stay single and defer having children longer than rural or suburban women—made more than their male counterparts. But once babies arrived, the mothers often fell behind. Banks, law firms, and other demanding employers who expected round-the-clock dedication from their professional employees reported that women were dropping out in droves once they began to have families.

Since World War II, the nation had organized itself economically around the idea that women would be in the workplace. By the new millennium, 47 percent of the nation's workforce was female, and the United States depended more on their contribution to the labor market than did most developed countries. In 2009, as the recession stripped away jobs in male-dominated industries like construction, the *New York Times* reported that "women are poised to surpass men on the nation's payrolls, taking the majority for the first time in American history." But the country had never institutionalized any solution to the child-care quandary. The much-predicted boom in company-run day-care centers never materialized. (Google, the cutting-edge firm that won *Fortune*'s "Best Company to Work For" award two years running, provided in-house day care for its employees. But in 2008 it charged them $1,425 a month for infant care and by 2008 was taking surveys to determine whether the price could be raised to nearly $2,500.) Congress never returned to the idea of making early education the same kind of entitlement that kindergarten and elementary school were. Even child care for the poorest women, which the government was supposed to be supporting, never approached the level of demand. And it was pretty clear that a country that had not yet come to grips with a national health-care plan was not going to create a massive new federal program for working mothers.

→→ ←←

AFTER ALISON FOSTER'S MARRIAGE BROKE UP, she returned to the United States and went to Columbia University for graduate work in counseling psychology, "partly to figure out my own life—why I didn't see this coming." She got a job at a prestigious private school in the city, where her sons could go tuition-free. In the summers, she taught ceramics at a good summer camp, and the boys went there, too. "I figured I could pay for these luxuries I don't have money for," she said. And besides, "having my children in the same school with me was my way of simplifying my life." In a sense, she had re-created those early months in which she brought her baby to work at the wallpaper studio.

"ANY WAY YOU MEASURE IT..."

In 2008 Lisa Belkin, a columnist for the *New York Times* on work issues, wrote a magazine article about husbands and wives who shared housework equally. The most interesting thing about them, she wrote, "is that they are so very interesting." Couples who really split chores were rare, even in homes where both adults worked full-time.

Social scientists had begun studying who did the housework, and "any way you measure it, they say, women do about twice as much around the house as men," Belkin wrote. Perhaps that optimistic study from the 1980s that found husbands had hit the 30 percent point had been true. But if so, that had been just about the end of the progress. "Working class, middle class, upper class, it stays at two to one," said Sampson Lee Blair, who had been studying the issue at the University at Buffalo. When child care was added to the mix, things became even more lopsided. In families where both parents worked, she said, women spent an average of eleven hours a week on child care, and men three.

Belkin introduced her readers to a few couples who were seriously trying to divide household chores evenly, and it seemed like a tortuous process—full of lists and negotiations and struggles on the part of the woman to jettison her higher standards for cleanliness, social niceties such as thank-you notes, and the way the children looked when they were dressed for school. The only households that seemed to arrive at equitable divisions of labor more naturally, Belkin wrote, were lesbian couples.

(Gay men with children had not yet been studied enough to provide a comparison.)

The problem, it seemed, was buried deep in the issue of gender. Husbands who did more around the house than their fathers had done felt they were contributing a great deal, even if it amounted to less than half the time their wives were putting in. Couples struggling to change seemed to do best if they lived in neighborhoods where sharing the housework was more common. As one expert explained, the most important factor in predicting how much a husband would do was how equal a couple's friends' relationships were.

→→ ←←

VICKI COHN POLLARD'S DAUGHTER, Tanya, was horrified when she read the essay her mother wrote about the days of communal life in Baltimore and her theory that "the more responsibility any one person bears for raising a child, the more anger that person will have for the child." And Vicki, who had moved to Maine and become an accomplished acupuncturist, had reservations, too. "If I were to do it over again, I would be more present for her. I think she feels like it hurt her. I think it, too. But who knows? She's a pretty amazing little being."

Tanya got her PhD from Yale and became a college professor, specializing in Shakespeare and Renaissance drama. When she married and had children, she certainly had no plans for communal child rearing. "It's not just that I'm domestic. I'm also private, I guess. I like my own space," she said. But she hardly returned to the stay-at-home pattern of the '50s. When her first daughter, Isabella, was a baby, Tanya and her husband, Will, who is also an academic, shared the responsibilities. "I'd teach two days a week and he'd teach two days a week," she said. "There were a couple of times when Will had to be at Columbia when I was at meetings, and sometimes I'd miss the meeting and sometimes he would. A couple of times I brought Isabella to campus and had a student of mine wheel her around."

Their neighborhood, in Park Slope, Brooklyn, is an epicenter of the evolved American couple. All of Tanya's female friends share the parenting and housekeeping duties with their husbands. They talk in scandalized whispers about the employer who tried to make a man come in to work on a weekend when his baby was a newborn. "Everybody takes it for granted it's the husband's job as much as the wife's to be around," said Tanya. When Tanya and Will had a second daughter in 2007, instead of presents her friends took turns cooking for them, "which basically means that we got a hot meal brought to us once a week." While Tanya's friends don't often take care of her children, she feels secure in the knowledge that "there are a lot of people who I feel I can call on for things like that, which is really, really nice." In some ways, Tanya mused, it wasn't far from that old Baltimore neighborhood after all. "It's funny—my mother regarded it as radical, but I think it's old-fashioned."

"WE MEN MAY NOT BE PREPARED TO BECOME OZZIES."

Belkin, who had a gift for picking subjects that would fascinate and infuriate her female readers, once wrote an article that began with a book club in Atlanta, made up of women who had gone to an Ivy League college and then to top law schools such as Harvard and Columbia: "A roomful of Princeton women each trained as well as any man. Of the ten members, half are not working at all; one is in business with her husband; one works part-time; two freelance; and the only one with a full-time job has no children." They were emblematic, Belkin said, of many high-achieving young American women who had claimed their share of the seats in good schools and professional training. "They start strong out of the gate. And then, suddenly, they stop."

Before most of these accomplished, ambitious women got to the top of the ladder—or even near it—they were leaving work to care for their children, Belkin wrote. A survey of women from the Harvard Business School classes of 1981, 1985, and

1991, she reported, "found that only 38 percent were working full-time." While the older generation felt like failures if they missed having "it all," the younger women were guilt-free. "I've had people tell me that it's women like me that are ruining the workplace because it makes employers suspicious. I don't want to take on the mantle of all womanhood and fight a fight for some sister who really isn't my sister because I don't know her," said Vicky McElhaney Benedict, who graduated from Princeton in 1991, got a law degree, and was, within a few years, a full-time mother with two children.

In some ways, it was the mommy-track fight all over again. The response to Belkin's piece was "a tsunami," she said. "Everybody knew women were leaving. I just wrote about it in the *New York Times.*" For a while, she was getting one or two hundred e-mails an hour. "I got up to go to the bathroom, and when I came back there were sixty more messages."

Was it possible that the women who were educated to be the leaders of their generation were going to opt out? In the early '90s, Claudia Goldin, a Harvard economist, had taken a look at statistics on the work and childbearing history of college women who graduated between 1966 and 1979, and found that only 13 to 18 percent had both children and a career by age 40, even when "career" was defined only as having been working, mostly full-time, for the last three years. A surprisingly large group—28 percent—had not yet had any children, even though the oldest were reaching the end of their potential fertility. The rest had, in the main, focused on children and perhaps intermittent work. Goldin resisted the idea that she had unearthed bad news. A follow-up study, she said, showed that women who graduated in the 1980s had somewhat more success. And another study of graduates of Harvard/Radcliffe found that the amount of time those women took off from work had declined over the years. "There's no indication of 'opting out,' " she said.

Nevertheless, some young, well-educated women in the latest generation made it clear that opting out was already in their plan. In September 2005, the *Times* ran a front-page article, "Many Women at Elite Colleges Set Career Path to Motherhood," that roiled the waters all over again. Louise Story, a young reporter who had done extensive research among the freshmen and senior women in two of Yale's residential colleges, led off with Cynthia Liu, a brilliant, high-achieving sophomore who planned to go to law school—and then become a stay-at-home mom by the time she was 30. Interviews with 138 Yale women, Story said, "found that 85 of the students, or roughly 60 percent, said that when they had children, they planned to cut back on work or stop working entirely."

There was so much outcry that Story felt constrained to publish a special note explaining her research methods. Even *suggesting* that high-achieving college graduates might be choosing not to work seemed to be surrender. How would women achieve equal power in the public world if that world saw their best and brightest as potential dropouts? What if less-privileged younger women took these upper-income stay-at-home moms as a new model and failed to prepare for a career? What if the academic hierarchy began to wonder if educating women was a waste of resources? "It really does raise this question for all of us and for the country: when we work so hard to open academics and other opportunities for women, what kind of return do we expect to get for that?" Marlyn McGrath Lewis, the director of undergraduate admissions for Harvard, told Story.

Nicholas Kulish, a 30-year-old editorial writer for the *Times*, responded with alarm on behalf of the men of his generation. "Well, some of you may want to be Harriets again, but we men may not be prepared to become Ozzies," he wrote. "Returning to the 1950s just doesn't look appealing. For one thing, the way you have us dressing these days, we would get beaten up. More important, though, we may not be able to afford it." These days, Kulish concluded, the heroes of the old situation comedies such as *Ozzie and Harriet* and *Leave It to Beaver* could never support their upper-middle-class families on one paycheck. "Ward Cleaver wouldn't be able to afford a house in the suburbs or Beaver's tuition—unless June went to work, too."

"THE COST OF WOMEN LEAVING . . ."

The whole "opting out" controversy was, in truth, rather irrelevant to the future of American womanhood. If a small sliver of mothers did not have the economic need to work, they had every right to take advantage of the chance to spend extra time with their children, volunteer at the local schools, work for a favored political candidate, or get serious about painting or cooking or yoga or whatever other avocation tugged at their hearts. Many men would choose that sort of life for themselves if they had the chance. In fact, some stay-at-home husbands were doing just that.

But any idea that large numbers of women were going to retire permanently to their homes when they began to have families was buried in the economic meltdown of 2008. Women were going to work throughout their lives. The question was no longer whether they would have jobs but whether they would be able to stick with them consistently enough to make real progress when it came to paychecks and work satisfaction.

Unlike people in many other developed countries, Americans were not, in general, responding to work stress by opting not to have children. In 2006 the United States reached a 2.1 fertility rate—or just over two children per woman—for the first time in thirty-five years. That's almost precisely what demographers regard as replacement level, and it was far higher than in nations such as Italy and Spain. A study at the University of Turin theorized that Italian women's reluctance to have children had to do with the traditional nature of Italian men. Dutch women, whose husbands were much more likely to help with child care and housework, had outside jobs more often than Italian women but still had, on average, more children. French and Scandinavian women, who had access to federally funded child care, also appeared more eager to have families.

But none of those countries matched America's fertility rate. Part of the reason was the increasing number of Hispanic Americans, who tended to have larger families. But even non-Hispanic whites were having babies at rates higher than most of their European peers. Russell Shorto, who examined the issue for the *New York Times,* suggested that the critical factor might actually be employer flexibility—not in offering child care but in being more open to women leaving and reentering the workforce, or agreeing to flexible schedules for those who want to continue working while taking care of small children.

The feminists had worried that if women who were educated in the top colleges dropped out to take care of their kids, the top colleges would stop admitting women, and the top law firms would be reluctant to hire them. But it was conceivable that it might work the other way around. If half of the lawyers and accountants and MBAs were potential mothers, employers might feel compelled to make concessions in order to keep them on the job. "The cost of women leaving and the cost of turnover—and the fact that the majority of accounting graduates were women—were strong drivers of our initiatives," said Wendy C. Schmidt, a principal in the giant accounting firm of Deloitte & Touche in New York, which was a leader in offering flexible schedules and generous sabbatical programs while raising the number of women partners. Lisa Belkin, writing about law firms' growing willingness to reexamine their policies, noted that one "hard-driving white-shoe firm" had successfully petitioned a New York judge to reschedule a hearing set for December 2007 because "these dates are smack in the middle of our children's winter breaks."

"THE CHIEF SOURCE OF IDENTITY AND MEANING."

There were other changes in the way women structured their lives that were both more sweeping and more clearly permanent than any opting-out trend among the most privileged. While the vast majority of Americans still got married, they were spending a larger and larger part of their lives single. At any given point in time, slightly over half of adult American women were either divorced, widowed, or never married. The percentage of women ages 20 to 24 who had never been married jumped to 69 percent in the 2000 census. For ages 30 to 34, the never-married proportion tripled to 22 percent. On all parts of the economic scale, matrimony was being seen less as the start of life and more as a culmination of the achievements of young adulthood. On the upper-economic end, women expected to finish their education, begin careers, and amass either some wealth or money-making capacity before they committed themselves to a husband and children. Poorer women very often saw their path as one that would begin with having children, perhaps move on to a job and savings, and then finish with marriage as the capstone.

While in 1950 only one in twenty American children were born to single women, by 2007 the proportion reached 40 percent. Some of them were the well-planned progenies of lesbian couples or single career women who had concluded that a husband was not going to come along before the biological alarm clock went off. (Of the fifty thousand children who were adopted in the United States in 2001, a third went to single women.) "I can't count how many young women have told me if they don't meet the right man by their early to middle thirties, they'll either adopt or make a trip to the sperm bank and pursue motherhood on their own," wrote Laura Sessions Stepp. But for the most part, the unwed mothers were poor—only 3 percent of children born to college-educated women were out of wedlock, compared to 40 percent of those whose mothers were high school dropouts. While most of those women would get married eventually, fewer than one in six would marry the father of their baby.

In the late 1990s, a team of sociologists led by Kathryn Edin and Maria Kefalas began trying to figure out what caused poor women to choose

motherhood before marriage. They moved into low-income neighborhoods in the Philadelphia area that had a mix of white, Hispanic, and black families. After living with the people they were studying for some time, they concluded that poor American women "saw marriage as a luxury, something they aspired to but feared they might never achieve." Children, on the other hand, were seen as "a necessity, an absolutely essential part of a young woman's life, the chief source of identity and meaning." The world Edin and Kefalas described was one in which poor women believed they could rely on only themselves to build a good life. Men would not necessarily stick around, and those who did would not necessarily treat them properly.

These women thought of having a baby as something that happened early, well before the search for a reliable mate was likely to be completed. During her research, Kefalas got pregnant at age 30 and found that the poor women she was living with "couldn't believe that any woman would postpone childbearing into her 30s by choice." Having babies early, out of wedlock, was a strategy that made perfect sense for the mothers, who generally were not educated for the kinds of careers that needed to be cultivated and built up before the distraction of motherhood arrived. But it was not all that great for the children, who were far more likely than the offspring of two-adult families to be born poor, to be raised poor, and to grow up to be poor adults.

"IT WAS NO BIG DEAL."

Laura Sessions Stepp, who thought she was compromising her career in order to spend more time with her family, created a beat for herself covering adolescent issues for the *Washington Post* and wrote a book on guiding children through their early teens. Rather than downsizing, she had refashioned her work to suit her talents and interests. She was hardly alone. American men and women of all economic groups had to continually retool themselves to keep pace with an economy that no longer had the interest or ability to offer its workers long-term predictable careers. Women, who had been forced to take that kind of approach to their lives anyway, were in some ways better prepared for that economic world than their husbands and brothers.

In the spring of 1998, Stepp found her next big subject when she heard that twenty-five parents in her son's school had been called to a special meeting and told that their children had been involved in a sex ring. About a dozen 13- and 14-year-old girls had been regularly performing oral sex on two or three male students for the better part of the school year.

"It was no big deal," one of the girls told Stepp later.

Stepp's project expanded into an examination of sex among high-achieving high school and college women, *Unhooked: How Young Women Pursue Sex, Delay Love, and Lose at Both*. The girls she talked to strove for straight As and excelled in extracurricular activities such as sports, music, or the school newspaper. But they set their sights much lower when it came to romance. Those who weren't permanently attached went to parties with their girlfriends and then "hooked up" with a boy for a sexual encounter that could mean anything from kissing to oral sex to intercourse, depending on the age, sophistication, and level of attraction of the newly merged parties. Then the partners unhooked and went their separate ways.

"Jamie would flash her fake ID, have a couple of drinks, and dance, either with her girlfriends or, as the night passed, with a guy," Stepp wrote of one of her subjects. "Occasionally, they would kiss while dancing, which the guy took as a signal that she was willing to go back to his room. It seemed awkward to turn him down, she recalled, given the fact that her friends had usually paired off already. Rather than be stranded, she'd go with the guy to his room and fool around in her underwear because it was easier to hook up than come up with a reason not to."

Stepp saw the practice as an avoidance of commitment, a dangerous trend that left young women, especially well-educated young women, with little experience in how to build relationships with men. Not everyone agreed with her dismay. Some felt hooking up was just a new term for sexual behavior that had been going on for decades. "Dating does exist," said Jessica Valenti, the author of *The Purity Myth* and editor of a Web site for young feminists. "The hook-up culture—I'm pretty sure kids always did that. My friends date. Some people hook up without dating, but they do have serious relationships." And, she said, in all the hand-wringing over hooking up, "the idea that it's supposed to be pleasurable is kind of lost. There is such a thing as orgasm."

But Valenti, 29, had her own problems with a culture where preteens wore shirts that said I'M TIGHT LIKE SPANDEX and women had plastic surgery to make their labia smaller. ("In Africa they call it female genital mutilation. Here we call it designer vaginas.") And she worried that young men were so overexposed to pornography that they had trouble getting aroused by regular women—or at least regular women over 25. She saw young women as caught between a conservative culture that obsessed about virginity and a porn culture in which they were urged by jaded cameramen to take off their clothes and writhe for the next edition of *Girls Gone Wild*. "The message is still the same—that women's sexuality doesn't belong to them."

In the new millennia, girls grew up in a world awash in sexuality, thanks to the Internet and cable TV. They connected sex and power very early, shaking their booty at middle-school talent shows and calling up boys to talk dirty in ways they didn't entirely understand but knew would leave the males on the other end of the line flummoxed. A 16-year-old boy told a reporter that girls in his school "overpower guys more. I mean, it's scary." The successors to Madonna sang about men as "prey" who were expected to service them and then go away. The Bratz dolls, sexy competitors to Barbie, wore miniskirts, midriff-baring tops, fishnet stockings, and feather boas, and adults were unnerved to see their owners dressing the same way. Meanwhile their older sisters, who were supposed to be preparing to take over the world, sometimes looked more as if they were planning on a career in the sex-services industry. They had spent their formative years watching *Sex and the City*, whose messages were: (1) Only girlfriends last forever, and (2) Anything worth doing is worth doing in a tutu and stiletto heels.

Valerie Steele, the fashion historian, found it to be just business as usual. "If you're young, you're trying to attract sexual attention. Nothing new whatsoever," she said, recalling the see-through blouses and tight jeans of the '70s. "Short of bringing in an ayatollah, they're not going to get teenagers to dress modestly." Gloria Steinem, who remembered "walking around in a miniskirt and a button that said 'Cunt Power,'" was philosophical. "Are they doing it because they are enjoying it or are they doing it because they feel forced into it? That's the basic question, but body pride and sexuality and adventure is positive." Once, at a lunch, Steinem was seated next to Reese Witherspoon, who had played the Chihuahua-bearing, couture-clad sorority girl who turns out to have a mind like a steel trap in *Legally Blonde*. Steinem recalled that Witherspoon told her she had decided to take the part because of her: "I heard you say we should be able to wear anything we damn well please and still be considered human beings."

There is never going to be a straight narrative when it comes to what women choose to wear and how they want to look. In the early twenty-first century, women were going bare-legged and tossing away the panty hose that had felt like such liberation to an older generation that was used to being encased in girdles. "I stopped wearing panty hose a long time ago because it was painful and they'd always rip," said Michelle Obama. But at the same time, many were embracing Spanx, übergir-

dles made of nylon and spandex, some of which contain the entire body up to the bra line.

"YOU CAN'T SAY A WOMAN'S LIFE IS MORE VALUABLE THAN A MAN'S LIFE."

The women's movement had not created the kind of open and caring society its more optimistic leaders had envisioned. It had merely opened doors, and for all the struggles and silliness, women were still racing through them, making use of the opportunities that came in reach. Somehow, many of those shocking little girls who wanted to let their lace training bras show were growing up to be college students who befuddled the nation by ending the boys' domination of higher education.

They were also demonstrating their willingness to give their lives for their country. After the invasion of Iraq, the Army created a small museum in Fort Lee, Virginia, to honor the women who had fallen during the second Gulf War and its aftermath. By early 2009 the memorial contained 115 names. The female soldiers who gave their lives were truck drivers and helicopter pilots, kitchen workers and medics, and almost everything in between. The majority were under 25. A number were mothers. And although their sacrifice had been honored, it had hardly traumatized the nation in the way opponents of women in the military had once predicted. "I think people have come to the sensible conclusion that you can't say a woman's life is more valuable than a man's life," said Wilma Vaught, a retired Air Force brigadier general who was president of the Women in Military Service for America Memorial Foundation.

At the time of the Iraq invasion, 350,000 women were serving in the American military—about 15 percent of the active-duty personnel. Their performance during the invasion of Iraq and the conflict that followed would make it clear how much the military had come to depend on them. The Iraq experience also underscored Dena Ivey's concern about what would happen when the sexes were mixed in the field. Women returned with post-traumatic stress disorder at much higher rates than men, and experts began to wonder if that was because, along with the inevitable stress of being in danger in a strange, hostile place, women also lived in fear of sexual assault from their fellow soldiers. Studies of female veterans seeking help from the Veterans Administration indicated that high proportions of them had suffered sexual trauma. Representative Jane Harman of California visited a VA hospital in the Los Angeles area and told a congressional panel, "My jaw dropped when the doctors told me that forty-one percent of the female veterans seen there say they were victims of sexual assault while serving in the military." Twenty-nine percent of those women reported having been raped, she added. "Women serving in the U.S. military today are more likely to be raped by a fellow soldier than killed by enemy fire in Iraq."

And while women were still barred from high-risk jobs such as tank operator, Iraq demonstrated how little difference that made. "Frankly one of the most dangerous things you can do in Iraq is drive a truck," an expert in post-traumatic stress disorder told the *New York Times*. There were plenty of women driving trucks. And the impossibility of making a clear distinction between combat and noncombat posts was highlighted early in the war when the U.S. Army 507th Maintenance Company—a unit full of cooks, clerks, and maintenance workers—was separated from a convoy crossing the desert and wound up lost in the hostile city of Nasiriyah. Nine Americans were killed, and the world saw the dazed faces of others who had been taken prisoner, one of them an African-American woman simply saying she was "Shauna" from Texas. It was Shoshana Johnson, a single mother who joined the Army intending to follow her father's career as a cook and who was shot in both ankles before she was taken captive and held for twenty-two days.

Another prisoner, Jessica Lynch, became famous when word went around the nation that Lynch, a tiny blond woman from West Virginia who had joined the military at 18 in hopes of getting enough money to go to college, had valiantly held off hostile forces who surrounded the lost caravan until her gun ran out of bullets. Later, after she was retrieved from an Iraqi hospital, Lynch would make it clear that her rifle had jammed and she had never fired a shot. "Lori was the real hero," she said.

Lynch's best friend in the Army, 23-year-old private Lori Piestewa, was lying beside her in the Iraqi hospital, but the doctors had neither the equipment nor the supplies to treat her severe head injuries, and she died before help arrived. Piestewa, the daughter of a Hopi father and a Hispanic mother, was raised on a reservation in Arizona. She was the first American woman to die in the war.

Piestewa had hoped to become the first person in her family to go to college, but she became pregnant at 17 and got married instead. Two children later, she and her husband divorced, and Piestewa was living with her parents in a trailer on the reservation, where the astronomical unemployment rate left her with very few options. Looking for a way out, she left her children with her parents and enlisted, promising that when she returned, she would build the whole family a real house. She was so determined to make good that when she broke her foot in basic training, she concealed it from her officers. "She didn't want to get held back," said her father. Later, when her unit was deployed to the Middle East, Piestewa had the option of remaining behind for treatment of a badly injured shoulder. But once again, she covered up her physical problems in order to stay with the rest of the company.

The 507th left Kuwait as part of a convoy headed across the desert to Baghdad, but it fell behind because of the weight of its vehicles. The big water truck Lynch was driving broke down, leaving her stranded in the sands until a Humvee raced over and Piestewa, behind the wheel, called out, "Get in, roommate." The lost company eventually found a road; then its leaders made a wrong turn and led the line of trucks into enemy territory in Nasiriyah.

Piestewa's Humvee was in the rear when the men in the front discovered their mistake and tried to turn the line of trucks around. At one point she was offered a chance to switch to a safer car, but Piestewa felt it was her responsibility to stay with Sergeant Robert Dowdy, the senior noncommissioned officer she was driving. Her manner was so serene, another driver said, that she calmed the people around her. "If it wasn't for her, I probably would have freaked out."

As the company attempted to get back out of the city, it came under heavy mortar fire. Piestewa — carrying Dowdy, Lynch, and two other soldiers she had picked up along the way — skillfully and calmly steered her Humvee around the roadblocks until the truck immediately ahead of her jackknifed, and her front wheel was hit by a rocket-propelled grenade as she tried to weave around. The damaged Humvee, out of control and going about forty-five miles per hour, smashed into the truck. Lori Piestewa was fatally injured.

She left behind her parents, a 5-year-old son, and a 3-year-old daughter. Jessica Lynch, who returned home to a huge reception in West Virginia, thanked everyone who had helped her, then concluded, "Most of all, I miss Lori."

Keepsake Pages

Are young women's attitudes toward sex a lot different than when you were growing up? In what ways? Which parts do you think are good, and which worry you?

_____

_____

_____

_____

_____

_____

_____

_____

When did you become aware that women were playing a growing role in the military? Do you think it's a good thing that they're now allowed to have combat duties?

_____

_____

_____

_____

_____

_____

_____

More Thoughts and Memories

More Thoughts and Memories

15. Hillary and Sarah . . . and Tahita

"I'M NOT GOING TO TELL MY
DAUGHTER — OH, I QUIT."

Hillary Clinton's life had been unlike that of any other woman in American history, yet she was also very typical of that whole generation of postwar feminists who had intended to both change everything and have it all. In the '60s, she was a superachiever at an all-female college, where she worried endlessly about the meaning of life and chose boyfriends who were prepared to worry with her. As class-graduation speaker at Wellesley, she shared the stage with Edward Brooke, the first African-American elected to the U.S. Senate since Reconstruction, who Hillary bravely and impolitely dismissed as a typical politician, caring only about what was possible, not what was *right*. In the '70s, she went to law school and cohabited with her boyfriend, who loved the fact that she was so smart. (On the campaign trail in 2008, Bill Clinton would say that when they were at Yale together, he had told Hillary that he knew all the best people of their generation, "and you have the finest mind." While it seemed a little over the top for a law school student to feel he already knew every baby boomer in the nation worth knowing, the audiences liked the show of husbandly pride.)

Hillary intended to take the world by storm but wound up putting her ambitions behind those of her husband. For all that she achieved, for nearly twenty years after her marriage, she was known mainly as Bill's wife. (George McGovern remembers that when he was running for president in 1972, an aide told him that a very bright young lawyer from Arkansas was going to be the campaign's organizer in Texas and that he wanted to "bring his girlfriend," too.) Arkansas was not exactly where the action was for ambitious young legal crusaders, but Hillary moved there because her husband-to-be intended to run for office in his home state. She

waited until she was in her thirties to get pregnant, and there were fertility issues, followed by work-family issues. Later, in her campaigns, she would talk about the time when she had to be in court, and Chelsea was sick and the babysitter called in sick, too. "And it was just that gut-wrenching feeling, and I was lucky enough to have a friend who could come over and watch Chelsea while I ran to court, then ran back home." But that was one bad day. Child care was actually less a problem than the fact that she was responsible for making money while Bill ran for office and served as governor of a state that barely paid its highest elected official minimum wage. She had never envisioned herself as a corporate lawyer, but there she was.

During Bill's presidency, she became the most active first lady since Eleanor Roosevelt, and like her famous predecessor, she created a wide network of supporters dedicated to social issues such as child welfare and women's rights. She visited more than eighty countries and addressed a United Nations conference on women in Beijing, "speaking more forcefully on human rights than any American dignitary has done on Chinese soil," the *New York Times* reported. But she also failed spectacularly in her attempt to reform the nation's health-care system. And, of course, there was the humiliation of her husband's infidelity in what was probably the most public case of adultery since Henry VIII. Ironically, voters seemed to like her better as the betrayed wife than they did when she demonstrated what a marriage of equals might look like in the White House.

Then it was her turn. Before her first lady stint was even over, Clinton started running for the U.S. Senate in New York, a state where she had never lived until she established residency for her campaign. Nevertheless, she won handily and became a very good senator, tending the nuts-and-bolts needs of her constituents while pursuing the big-picture programs like the policy wonk she had always been. She was surprisingly eager to work with Republicans; unsurprisingly interested in the arcane details of complicated legislation.

Women were always her special constituents. Sometimes they saw something of themselves in her. Many of those who had grown up in her era had struggled to balance jobs and family, and wound up putting family first—with no regrets but still with a feeling that their dual burdens had made them miss the chance to do something really big, really wonderful, in the outside world. When Clinton became a senator, they thought about second chances; that even if you were 40 or 50—maybe even 60?—it was still not too late to go for it. And elderly women would always come up to her, saying that they wanted to see a woman in the White House before they died. Some had been born before women could vote, and she could remember all their faces and their stories.

No one knows exactly when she first thought about running for president, but it must have been very early in the game. (Male politicians, after all, tend to start fantasizing with their first election to the board of aldermen or the state legislature.) When Hillary finally announced she was a candidate, the old NOW veterans were thrilled. "I put everything away just to work with Hillary. It was my most devoted time," said Himilce Novas, a Cuban-American writer and college professor. Having a woman elected president would carry a huge symbolic value. "That was a question people would always ask me—when would there be a woman in the White House?" said Muriel Fox. The women's rights leaders had always believed they would live to see the day. But as the years went on, there had perhaps begun to be a little doubt.

In 2007 they were certain again. Clinton seemed like the inevitable Democratic presidential nominee, even to the people who hated her. She had all the money, all the support, and in the early Democratic debates, she cleaned the floor with her opposition, letting the country see that she had the stature, the gravitas, for the job. Then, suddenly, Barack Obama caught fire. No one expected it. He was only 46 and less than three years out of the Illinois state senate. He was supposed to be the presidential candidate *later*, after the Hillary Clinton administration had run its course.

Obama had been born in 1961, to a woman who was a rebel in ways Hillary Rodham would not have dared to try. Ann Dunham, too, was the daughter of an adoring but difficult father—hers had wanted a boy so much he'd named her Stanley, after himself. (She never used the name.) Ann's Kansas working-class parents had a tendency to keep moving west, and she wound up in college in Hawaii, where she married a Kenyan exchange student and had a son when she was still 18. Her husband went off to Harvard, then back to Africa, and the marriage was over. She struggled—as Obama would remind audiences who worried that he seemed "elitist"—as a single mother, sometimes on food stamps. She married an Indonesian businessman and returned with him to Asia, became an anthropologist, and later specialized in microfinancing businesses for women in the developing world. She divorced her second husband but retained her love for his country and its culture. She died of ovarian cancer at 54.

Her early death taught her son to seize the moment. Obama told the public that he had no time to waste becoming more "seasoned" in the Washington ways of doing business; those old ways were the problem, a culture of corruption that was wearing the country down. And it was Hillary—who had always seen herself most of all as an agent of change—who he identified as the emblem of the old. Now he was the one who wanted to do more than just pursue the possible, and his candidacy was as much a history-making event as hers.

Her supporters were outraged, sure Clinton was the victim of a male political establishment that had never really wanted a woman to begin with. Robin Morgan rewrote her famous diatribe "Goodbye to

All That": "Goodbye to the toxic viciousness . . . Goodbye to the HRC nutcracker with metal spikes between splayed thighs . . . Goodbye to the most intimately violent T-shirts in election history, including one with the murderous slogan 'If only Hillary had married O.J. instead!' *Shame.* Goodbye to Comedy Central's *South Park* featuring a story line in which terrorists secrete a bomb in HRC's vagina. . . ." Gloria Steinem asked, in the *New York Times*, whether a black woman with Obama's qualifications would be taken seriously as a candidate, and answered in the negative: "Gender is probably the most restricting force in American life, whether the question is who must be in the kitchen or who could be in the White House," she wrote. But some other women — even women politicians — were uncomfortable with the complaints about sexism. In March 2008, at a Women in Leadership Conference, Alaska governor Sarah Palin told *Newsweek,* "Fair or unfair, I think she does herself a disservice to even mention it, really."

Clinton's staying power was remarkable. Every time she appeared to be hopelessly down, she popped back up. In New Hampshire, when a sympathetic voter asked how she was holding up, Clinton's eyes got moist; many women flashed back to high school and saw the smart girl being bullied by the more popular guys. (She would get misty a few more times during the campaign, always when people were unexpectedly nice to her.) She stunned everyone by taking New Hampshire — the first woman ever to win a primary for the presidential nomination. Then she lost, then she won. But she was not good at organizing in the caucus states, where intensity of devotion mattered more than general popularity, and there were a lot of caucus states. By spring, the party leaders were beginning to mumble — and the TV talking heads beginning to shout — that it was time for her to throw in the towel.

He wants to force me into a corner where I will say, Okay, fine, I give up, I'm the girl, I give up. I'm the nice person, I don't want to have a fight. I'll go home.

Well, I'm not going to do it, she'd tell her aides. In private, she slammed her fist on the table and fumed. *I'm sick of being pushed around in this campaign. I'm not going to give up. I'm not going to tell my daughter — Oh, I quit, because I'm the girl and they're all being mean to me. I'm not going to do it.* Then she went out and did yet another rally, yet another question-and-answer session, yet another interview for local TV in Puerto Rico or Indiana or Montana. Her campaign was far from perfect, but as a candidate, she got better and better as she rolled along, seeming to grow more comfortable in her role at every stop. She began winning the white male vote in working-class states such as Pennsylvania and Ohio, a shift many observers attributed to racism against Obama. Susan Faludi suggested that it might be something more positive: a rethinking by men about the way they viewed women candidates. For most of American political history, she wrote, men had regarded female politicians as versions of "the prissy hall monitor." But there was not any of that in the late-season Hillary, who strode into a bar and traded shots with Pennsylvania workmen, danced the night away in her last-ditch Puerto Rico primary campaign, and joked with reporters in the back of her press plane at the end of the day while nursing a cocktail.

Thanks to the enthusiasm of Democratic voters, who turned out in record numbers, Clinton won eighteen million votes — more votes than any candidate for a presidential nomination had won before 2008. But it was not enough. Obama played by the rules, outorganized the Clinton machine, and won the most delegates. Hillary Clinton was not going to be the Democratic nominee, and 2008 was not going to be the year that the United States of America elected a woman president. But for the first time, a woman had come close, and throughout the rancorous, emotion-laden, endless primary fight, the one question that no one ever felt the need to pose was whether she was strong enough, tough enough, to be commander in chief. By the time the final primaries rolled around, the nation had gotten used to the idea of a woman as a presidential candidate—of a woman as president. And if that was not the White House, it was still a lot.

"WOMEN IN AMERICA AREN'T FINISHED YET."

Clinton's defeat left many of her supporters feeling both sad and, in some cases, angry enough to ignore her pleas to rally around Obama. "I thought I would vote for McCain," said Himilce Novas. "I wanted to show a lesson to the Democratic Party for not having chosen Hillary. This was her time."

Until 2008 men had always been the stars of presidential elections, and it seemed as if women were going to fall back into their familiar roles as undecided voters—the soccer moms and Wal-Mart moms and waitress moms who figured so prominently in the projections of political consultants. Then, on the day after the Democratic convention ended, John McCain suddenly announced that his vice presidential pick was Sarah Palin, the 44-year-old Alaska governor.

"It turns out that women in America aren't finished yet!" Palin told the cheering crowd at her acceptance speech.

Very few people had ever heard of Palin. She had been in office for less than two years, and Alaska—with a population of only 670,000—was a remote territory to most Americans in the Lower 48. Even McCain had met her only once, briefly, before he invited her to his home in Arizona to discuss being on the ticket. The initial reaction among the pundits, politicians, and journalists who make up the nation's chattering class was a kind of stunned silence, followed by predictions of disaster. McCain surrogates such as Senator Lindsey Graham raced around the Republican convention in Minneapolis, assuring everyone that voters would love Sarah because they would feel she was just like them.

All the carping stopped when Palin gave her acceptance speech. The script might have been the work of a veteran Republican speechwriter, but she delivered it with an energy, humor, and passion that stood out from the boilerplate rhetoric that dominated the convention oratory. She became an overnight star. People loved her spirit and the pride she showed in her baby, Trig, who was born with Down syndrome. She was a heady package—vice presidential candidate as action figure. The public learned that she had decorated her office in the capital with the skin of a grizzly her father had killed, and fired the gubernatorial cook, declaring the kids would be fine with mac and cheese. Her handsome husband was part Yup'ik Eskimo, a union member, and a snowmobile champion. "Women like her most of all because she is a woman who is unafraid to push men around, and punch even before being provoked," enthused *Newsweek*. And Palin was also young and attractive—the Web site Wonkette had called her "the hottest governor."

Although Palin's political convictions seemed a little vague, she was very definitely conservative, most particularly when it came to matters such as abortion. The social conservatives who formed the Republican Party's most important base, and who had never felt much attachment to McCain, suddenly discovered a new heroine. Surprisingly, a lot of Hillary's most disappointed fans were intrigued, too. Women voters had never shown much inclination to support female candidates unless they shared their political persuasion, and since Clinton and Palin came from opposite ends of the spectrum, that should have made the Republican vice presidential nominee a hard sell for the Hillaryites. But after her smashing debut at the convention, *Newsweek* reported that thanks to "the Palin Effect," one in three white women said she was more likely to vote for McCain than before the nomination was announced.

As Palin traveled around the country from rally to rally, her crowds were often far larger and more enthusiastic than McCain's. When they were together, she would wow the audience, introduce her running mate—and then people would start to drift away when the man at the top of the ticket launched into his stump speech. Voters loved her or hated her. At first, she was credited with giving her ticket a desperately needed boost. Later, she was blamed for undermining public confidence in McCain's ability to choose good people for his team. But in a country where vice presidential candidates were generally regarded as an afterthought, people couldn't stop talking about Sarah Palin.

"Sarah Barracuda."

Sarah Heath grew up in Wasilla, a small, unlovely exurb forty miles from Fairbanks, where people sometimes called themselves "Valley Trash" to make it clear that they knew the city dwellers looked down on them and that they didn't care. Palin remembered growing up in "a large busy family, where gender was never really an issue... My dad expected us to be back there chopping wood and snowmachining with the rest of them, hunting and fishing and doing all those things that were quite Alaskan." (When asked during her gubernatorial campaign to name her favorite meal, Palin said, "Moose stew after a day of snowmachining.") She was a feisty high school basketball player who got the nickname "Sarah Barracuda" as she led her team to the state championship. She once called that victory the "turning point of my life," and later, when she would try to place herself in the context of the women's movement, she would almost always frame her remarks around Title IX and giving girls equal opportunity to play sports.

Sarah grew up in the world the women's movement had created, and she seems never to have felt constrained by her gender. But like most people in Wasilla, male and female, she did not nourish any grand career plans. Her sister said the only goal they talked about was having children. Sarah roamed through four colleges in five years, never leaving much of an impression. After graduation, she came home to Wasilla, had a brief career in sports reporting, then eloped with her high school

boyfriend, Todd Palin. The newlyweds quickly had two children. Sarah helped with Todd's fishing business, joined the PTA, went to exercise classes, and hunted. ("The protein her family eats comes from fish she has pulled out of the ocean with her own hands and caribou she has shot," *Vogue* would later enthuse.)

In 1992, when Palin was 28, the mayor of Wasilla and a group of his supporters recruited her to run for city council as part of a plan to bring in new blood that would, they hoped, back a sales tax to pay for a local police department. (The smallness of Wasilla politics is written in that first triumph; she won the council election, 530 to 310.) Looking back on her political ascension, Palin would describe herself as a reformer—or, during the 2008 campaign, inevitably, "a maverick"—who waged war against "the old boys' club." But the Wasilla version of the old boys originally thought of themselves as mentors, grooming a nice young mother who could be a conduit to the younger generation of Wasilla voters. John Stein, the mayor, was stunned when he discovered that she intended to run against him in 1996. The entire power structure was stunned when she won and swiftly began firing town officials and replacing them with her own people. "None of that 'Sarah Barracuda' stuff came out until she ran for mayor. But then, boy, did it," Stein said.

It was a pattern that she repeated in her quick rise to the top of Alaska politics. And all the while she was raising a growing family. The Palins' third child, Willow, was born in 1995. While she was mayor, Sarah had another daughter, Piper, and, in a legendary feat of frontier grit, was back at work a day after the delivery. While she was in her second year as governor and lobbying behind the scenes for that vice presidential slot, she had a fifth baby, Trig, after a pregnancy she kept secret even from most of her family until the seventh month. Once again she was back at work within a couple of days.

Palin was a pattern-breaker when it came to the politics-family divide. Traditionally, men started running for office early, while most women waited until their children were grown, and that often left women at the back of the line when it came to getting the best nominations for the highest posts. (While the 2008 election would bring another record number of women into the U.S. House and Senate, their proportion was still under 20 percent in both chambers.) But Palin's large, still-young family did not seem to stand in her way at all. Many young Republican women saw an image of the way they wanted to be — a hard-charging professional who could balance an active family and an outside-the-box, challenging job. "I mean, how cool to have a young woman on the ticket who's doing exactly what I want to do when I grow up," said Jennifer Huddleston, a Wellesley senior who was campaigning for the McCain team in New Hampshire.

"I NEVER THOUGHT I'D HAVE TO RAISE A FAMILY ALONE."

When Hillary Clinton ran for president, no one asked how she was going to balance work and family. Her daughter was grown, and it was pretty clear that Bill could take care of himself. But with Palin, voters were reminded constantly of the issue — this was, after all, the first vice presidential candidate in history to take a breast pump on the campaign trail. After her nomination, the nation flung itself into a debate over whether she could possibly have time for all her responsibilities. In a roundup of national reaction, the *New York Times* found a mother of two in Alabama who was initially impressed but then lost confidence in Palin's judgment after reading that she returned to work three days after Trig was born. There was an evangelical Christian from Ohio who liked the whole package ("The whole family is pro-life, and they put that into practice even when it's not easy"), and another evangelical from Maine who didn't ("A mother with a 4-month-old infant with Down syndrome taking up full-time campaigning? Not my value set"). Phyllis Schlafly, who had been at the Republican convention watch-

ing Palin accept the nomination (and making sure a stern anti-abortion plank was hammered into the party platform), couldn't see what the fuss was about. "People who don't have children or who have only one or two are kind of overwhelmed at the notion of five children. I think a hardworking, well-organized CEO type can handle it well," she said.

Palin responded to the questions by pointing out that this was something no one would ever ask a man. When people wondered how she could be governor with so many kids, she had always said, "How in the world did any other governor do it with four kids or six kids or however many kids they had?" Rather quickly, the country seemed to agree, and the debate subsided. It was, after all, a consensus that many people thought the nation had reached in the '60s and '70s.

Barack Obama had two young daughters, so both tickets featured a candidate with small children. The presidential campaign should have been the ideal platform for a national discussion about the difficulties in balancing work and family responsibilities. But somehow that never percolated to the top, even though Michelle Obama made work-family stress her signature issue. Palin constantly referred to herself as a mother, suggesting that the experience of raising children gave her a special insight into the feelings and needs of average Americans. (Obama, who sent out a clear signal that his campaign was to stick to attacking McCain and leave Palin alone, seemed to agree, sort of, as he damned her with faint praise. "I mean, mother, governor, moose-shooter. I mean, I think that's cool, that's cool stuff," he told a crowd who started to boo at the mention of her name.) But although Palin talked about her family in every public appearance, she never really said much about the challenge American women faced in trying to do it all. Theoretical thinking about large social problems was not generally her strong suit, and she avoided discussions that focused on the difficulties of modern women's lives. When asked about how she could hold down a demanding job and raise a family at the same time, she simply said, "I'm part of that generation where the question is kind of irrelevant because it's accepted."

Michelle Obama had a more conflicted view. When she married and had children, Michelle seemed destined to become a nonfictional version of that other African-American lawyer-mom, Clair Huxtable. She had degrees from Princeton and Harvard Law, a series of great jobs, two adorable daughters, a three-story Georgian Revival house in a diverse, upscale neighborhood near her work, and a husband who outstripped even Bill Cosby's ideal dad. But she discovered it wasn't possible to have it all. "That was a shock to me," she said. "Nobody prepared me for this. We have to be realistic and honest with young women and families about what they will confront, because to say, 'You can do it all and should do it all,' and not to get the support, to me is frustrating."

When Michelle gave birth to her second daughter and Barack's political career went into high gear, she reduced her hours at the University of Chicago, where she was an administrator, but found her part-time job "had a funny way of expanding." Her husband wrote about the strain on their marriage when Michelle found herself saddled with all the household responsibilities: "My failure to clean up the kitchen suddenly became less endearing. Leaning down to kiss Michelle good-bye in the morning, all I would get was a peck on the cheek. By the time Sasha was born—just as beautiful and almost as calm as her sister—my wife's anger toward me seemed barely contained. 'You only think about yourself,' she would tell me. 'I never thought I'd have to raise a family alone.'"

As Michelle saw it, young women shouldn't have to give up on either career or children, "but it becomes a choice you have to make if child care isn't available and salaries aren't high enough to pay off your debt that it took to get the degree, to get the job you're in." During the presidential campaign, she traveled around the country holding roundtable discussions with working mothers. They talked about their inability to find affordable day care, the difficulty of getting time off to tend to sick children or sick parents, and the crushing debt that burdened women who tried to lift themselves up by getting college degrees. (College debt was a favorite issue for the Obamas, who had been saddled with six figures' worth until Barack's famous speech at the 2004 Democratic convention translated into a big book contract that allowed them to pay off the loans.) Michelle was haunted by her meeting with a single mother in her 40s who had gone back to school to get an MBA and was struggling to pay off $100,000 in student loans while supporting an ailing mother and two children in college. And Barack's own sister, Michelle said, was trying to figure out whether she and her husband could afford to have a second child, even though they both had PhDs: "They don't know how they would pay for the cost of child care for a second child—it would wipe out one of their incomes."

Michelle Obama and Sarah Palin were almost exactly the same age, and in their private lives, they both found the answer to work-family tensions in willing relatives. As Hillary Clinton might have said, they had their own villages (or maybe even the equivalent of a commune). Palin's parents and sisters lived nearby and formed an extended family that assumed much of the responsibility for looking after her children, and Todd, whose employers seemed to take a benevolent attitude toward his schedule, was available much of the time. Michelle, who had grown up in Chicago, relied on a network of friends and her widowed mother, Marian Robinson, who moved with them to Washington after the election.

But there were differences. Palin lived in the equivalent of the last Western frontier, a culture where the scarcity of women had always made men more willing to allow them some space. Alaska had never had a female governor before Palin, but once the state got one, people seemed to take an easygoing attitude toward the way she juggled her responsibilities. "There's a greater tolerance here for the integration of family and work," said Gerald McBeath, the chair of the political science department at the University of Alaska. "My students will bring their babies to class, and as long as they're quiet I don't object. It happens quite often." Palin nursed Trig during state budget meetings and took her daughters with her when she traveled to governors' conferences. Her staff apparently didn't object to her habit of bringing the children to the office, and no one questioned what Trig and the girls were doing on the plane when she traveled to out-of-town events. During the vice presidential campaign, reporters discovered that Palin had gotten Alaska to pay for the kids' plane tickets and hotel rooms, claiming that they, too, were engaged in state business.

Palin had been able to mix her two roles, unlike most working mothers, whose employers preferred not to be reminded that there were competing demands on their time. One of the most infamous cases of how complicated and stressful things could get in the Lower 48 involved Jane Swift, a Massachusetts Republican who was elected lieutenant governor in 1999 when she was pregnant with her first child. Swift got into trouble when capitol staff complained they were being dragooned into babysitting, and she made things much worse by claiming that nobody could possibly object to taking care of a baby as adorable as her Elizabeth. When the governor resigned and Swift became acting chief executive, she was pregnant again, with twins, and the hostility toward her was so intense that her opponents tried to keep her from doing state business over the phone when she was confined to bed rest. There was another controversy when she commandeered a state helicopter to fly her home when her daughter was sick. In the end Swift decided to drop her plans to run for governor and retired to private life. "The feeling that I let down my staff, my family, and the public by my actions . . . continues to nag at me," she wrote years later.

"SHE IS PHYLLIS SCHLAFLY, ONLY YOUNGER."

Palin, on the other hand, presented a picture of an almost effortless mix of work and family. (A reporter who followed her around after she was elected governor watched her juggle "two BlackBerrys and a cell phone with one always buzzing" yet appear to be unfazed, "indeed to be having fun," even when she locked her keys in her car and had to borrow her son's jalopy to drive off with her children to the next engagement.) It charmed some women and irritated others. Veterans of the women's movement looked at her and remembered another superachieving Republican wife and mother who had used her extraordinary skills to undermine their feminist agenda. "She is Phyllis Schlafly, only younger," wrote Gloria Steinem in the *Los Angeles Times*. Palin was, by Steinem's lights, wrong on all the issues that mattered most to women, from the right to abortion, to funding for education, to the Lilly Ledbetter Fair Pay Act, which the Republican ticket opposed. If she'd thought even for a millisecond that Palin was the end product of all the battles of the 1970s, Steinem told a friend, "I'd shoot myself."

Hillary Clinton declined to say much about Palin except vague congratulations on her nomination, but the sudden ascent of another very different female politician must have been a torture piled on the already enormous disappointment of losing the Democratic nomination. *Saturday Night Live* aired a hilarious sketch that depicted Clinton and Palin issuing a joint statement against sexism in the campaign. "You know, Hillary and I don't agree on everything," began Tina Fey, playing Palin.

"Anything," interjected Amy Poehler, playing Clinton.

The skit ended with Palin sweetly stating that, whatever their politics, everyone agreed "it's time for a woman to make it to the White House," and Hillary shouting, "I didn't want a *woman* to be president! *I* wanted to be president!"

"These guys are jerks."

As the campaign moved into its final stretch and voters became frightened by the collapsing economy, Palin's appeal dwindled. Her interview with CBS's Katie Couric may have marked the beginning of the end for the Republican ticket—as well as the resurrection of Couric's reputation as a great television interviewer. People began to notice that the Republican vice presidential candidate had a penchant for run-on sentences that trailed off into incomprehensibility. And the sentences, when deconstructed, suggested a minimal grounding in major issues. On the famous question of why she felt Alaska's proximity to Russia counted as foreign-policy experience, Palin told Couric, "As Putin rears his head and comes into the airspace of the United States of America, where do they go? It's just right over the border, it is from Alaska that we send those out to make sure that an eye is being kept on this very powerful nation, Russia, because they are right there. They are right next to our state." The McCain campaign's insistence that Palin's strength lay in her connection to average voters began to look patronizing. When she was unable to name any Supreme Court decision she had ever disagreed with except for *Roe v. Wade,* a McCain adviser told *Newsweek,* "The Court is very important, but Palin is on the ticket because she connects with everyday Americans."

In the end, women voters stuck to their old pattern of voting the candidate, not the gender. There was no Palin Effect: Obama won with a 7 percent gender gap, as women favored the Democratic ticket 56 to 43, while men gave McCain a narrow edge. Some of the McCain staffers angrily leaked stories intended to blame the defeat on Palin: She had spent $150,000 of the party's money on clothes for herself and her family. She had refused to prepare for the Couric interview. She was so uninformed she thought Africa was a country, not a continent. Palin, back in Alaska, said the leaks were

"cruel and it's mean-spirited, it's immature, it's unprofessional, and these guys are jerks."

The clothes issue was always a tender point for female politicians. (Reporters on Hillary Clinton's plane had posted a chart tracking the color of her pantsuits, which some claimed became almost as reliable as a calendar.) But the treatment Palin got for the wardrobe story wasn't much worse than the scorn heaped on John Edwards, a liberal Democrat, for his expensive haircuts. On the other hand, it was hard to imagine a campaign trashing any male vice presidential candidate the way Palin was vilified, with complaints about "diva" behavior, "wacko" comments, and the anecdote about her letting male aides into her hotel room wearing nothing but a bath towel.

"Maybe it's time we let a woman lead us."

Palin wound up the only one of the four national candidates of whom the majority of voters said they had an unfavorable view. But the failure of her candidacy was not a failure for women. At the very minimum, it was a triumph that voters did not seem to regard her floundering as a commentary on anything but Palin herself. On a more positive note, she won over many voters who had tended in the past to be hostile to the whole concept of a woman in the White House. She had a special affinity with younger working-class men. They liked the way she talked about hunting and hockey, and introduced her husband as first dude. They saw her as one of their own, rather than as an outsider parachuting in to tell them how to behave. Younger men with no college education were the people who had always been most threatened by women in the workplace and often the ones most resistant to any idea of being bossed by a woman anywhere. In a somewhat roundabout way, Palin made many of them converts to a new way of thinking. "They bear us children, they risk their lives to give us birth, so maybe it's time we let a woman lead us," a former truck driver told a reporter during a Palin rally in North Carolina.

People spent nearly two years talking about Hillary Clinton and Sarah Palin, and while both women lost, their races had transformed the political conversation. By the time the campaign was over, the idea that women could hold any governmental post, no matter how powerful, was so ingrained that people hardly bothered to take note of the fact that in 2009 the Speaker of the House of Representatives, second in line of succession after the vice president, was a woman, Nancy Pelosi. And the secretary of state, fourth in succession, would turn out to be Clinton herself. Forty years after the Nixon administration had been so deeply unenthusiastic about the idea of trying to put a woman in the cabinet, the country had seen women running virtually every segment of the federal government. When Barack Obama began selecting his administration, there was no speculation about whether it would include any women in the most powerful posts because it was inconceivable that it would not.

"You wear slacks everywhere now."

Meanwhile, Tahita Jenkins, 33, was fired from her job as a New York City bus driver because she refused to wear slacks. "I said, I'm not going to change my religious beliefs just to be a bus driver," she told the media. Jenkins, a single mother, was a member of a Pentecostal church that prohibited women from wearing men's clothing. She brought in a note from her pastor, but transit officials insisted that wearing pants was a safety matter. There was, they said, a danger that a skirt "could get caught on something."

It seems only fair to finish where we started. It had been half a century since American women were publicly humiliated for offenses such as trying to pay a traffic ticket while wearing slacks, and Jenkins is a good reminder that there's no one story to show what that journey meant. So is Edna Kleimeyer, the Cincinnati housewife who had never managed to break her twelve-minute record for ironing a shirt. Kleimeyer was moving on to a retirement home in 2007 when she went through her pile of clothing and realized she owned only one skirt. "You wear slacks everywhere now," she mused. *"Everywhere."* If the changes in women's lives over the last century had gone no farther than the right to wear pants, it would still have made a practical day-to-day difference. And some people would still have felt things had gone too far.

So there you are. American women had shattered the ancient traditions that deprived them of independence and power and the right to have adventures of their own, and done it so thoroughly that few women under 30 had any real concept that things had ever been different. The feminist movement of the late twentieth century created a new United States in which women ran for president, fought for their country, argued before the Supreme Court, performed heart surgery, directed movies, and flew into space. But it did not resolve the tensions of trying to raise children and hold down a job at the same time. Women demolished the sexual double standard and reared new generations of men who appreciated the concept of equal rights for both sexes, even if they did not always act on it. But women did not figure out how to keep marriage from crumbling into divorce, and they were not particularly successful in making their lovers grow into dependable husbands. They had not remade the world the way the revolutionaries had hoped. But they had created a world their female ancestors did not even have the opportunity to imagine. And they still wore silly, impractical shoes.

Keepsake Pages

How do you feel about Hillary Clinton? Has your opinion always been the same—from the time her husband was first running for president—or has it changed?

_____

_____

_____

_____

_____

_____

_____

_____

_____

How about Sarah Palin, when she ran for vice president? Any thoughts?

_____

_____

_____

_____

_____

_____

_____

_____

Do you think there will be a woman in the White House in your lifetime?

_____

_____

_____

_____

_____

_____

_____

_____

_____

_____

_____

_____

_____

_____

_____

_____

_____

_____

_____

_____

_____

More Thoughts and Memories

More Thoughts and Memories

EPILOGUE

Supreme Court Justice Sandra Day O'Connor moved into the new century at the peak of her power and influence. At 75, she was healthy and energetic, and in love with her work, which she pursued with a vigor that continued to exhaust her youthful clerks. When the nation's highest court took up a critical constitutional issue, the outcome depended, more often than not, on her opinion. But her husband, John, was failing. A victim of Alzheimer's disease, he had been stable for a number of years, continuing to accompany his wife on their nightly rounds of the Washington social scene and spending his days in her office, chatting with the staff and visitors. Then in 2005 he began to decline. Determined not to turn his care over to outsiders, Justice O'Connor resigned at the end of the court term in June, going overnight from the most influential woman in the nation to a retiree, alone with a husband who was slipping away. "In those first days after her announcement she didn't answer the phone too often," reported Jeffrey Toobin. "She sat in her office and cried."

Her sacrifice could not save John from the curtain that was falling on his mind. In 2007 she was no longer able to care for him. He was moved into an assisted-living center, where he was miserable and talked of suicide—until he met another Alzheimer's patient and fell in love. It was not unusual, doctors said, for people whose memories of their former life had vanished to suddenly find romance with someone new, and it was often a terrible trauma for the loved ones they had forgotten. But O'Connor regarded it as a blessing. Her son told a Phoenix television station that his mother was "thrilled"

that his father was happy, and would visit with John while he sat on the porch swing, holding hands with his new love, blissfully unaware that the stranger he was chatting with was his wife of fifty-five years, and the woman who had given up a Supreme Court seat for him.

No social movement, no matter how liberating, can bring permanent happiness to the people it touches. We grow old; we lose loved ones. We fall short of our greatest goals and fail to live up to our most optimistic visions of our own character. When history opened up to American women in the late twentieth century, it did not offer them perfect bliss. It gave them the opportunity to face the dark moments on their own terms and to exalt in the spaces between. Here is an update on what it brought to some of the women in this story.

When the women's liberation movement was beginning to erupt in New York and Los Angeles, Louise Meyer Warpness was living in a different world, pursuing a Wyoming farm life that was closer to the patterns of the eighteenth or nineteenth century. But in America, change always arrives eventually. Louise's daughters worked outside the home, and the youngest lived with her future husband before they married. One of her granddaughters is married to an African-American, and another passed through a period of problems with drugs and men before she settled down to marry the father of her baby.

Warpness still lives in the valley where she raised her family. "As I've watched her grow older, I just appreciate her more," says her daughter Jo. "She does her craft work, her needlework. She is such an artist with that. And still such a wise, wise woman. I still admire my mom to the utmost...I can call her, and if I'm down, she'll say, 'What's the matter, honey?' after I've said hello. She just knows us inside. She'll do anything for anybody. And still so intelligent. She has a brain."

In 2002 Sujay Cook became the first woman elected president of the Hampton Ministers' Conference, the largest gathering of black ministers in the world and the place where she had been once snubbed by the powerful minister who refused to shake her hand. (He, in fact, was the one who nominated her.) Coretta Scott King came to the installation. So did Dorothy Height, the revered leader of black women's groups who had tried so hard, and so unsuccessfully, to get representation for women at the great March on Washington. So did Carol Moseley Braun, the first black woman ever to be elected to the U.S. Senate. "I wouldn't miss this," Braun said.

When Reverend Suzan Johnson Cook was called onstage, King, Height, and Braun came on with her. "The place erupted!" she remembered. "They're standing there holding hands with me and I'm like, *Oh my God*."

Despite all those viewings of *Sleeping with the Enemy,* Barbara Arnold's daughter, Alex, fell in love in college and decided she wanted to get married right after she graduated. Her mother didn't fight the idea. "She told me that I'm a lot more independent and sure of myself, which is why she said she was okay with my getting married so young," said Alex, who wryly noted that she had been exactly as old as Barbara had been when she wed. "I always see her as being really confident and capa-

ble, but I guess that was hard-won in her life—that's coming from her report, not mine."

Alex and her husband, David, moved to Washington, where she became the director of communications at the Democratic Legislative Campaign Committee. They had a son in 2007. Soon Alex, who had never been sure how she would decide to handle the work/family divide, returned to her job part-time. "Our generation has backslid in some ways; our mothers really took it forward...," she said. "I hope the next generation finds a better balance. Maybe we're on the verge of that."

In 2000 Lynnette Arthur, the daughter of Dana Arthur-Monteleone and the granddaughter of Gloria Vaz who began her liberation by buying a maroon Malibu, went back to college. To her family's surprise, she "did amazing. I got on the dean's list and graduated with honors." Her grandmother proudly framed her diploma and hung it in the living room. She was the first woman in her family to get a college degree. "They were so proud... Any of my aunts, they probably could have done it, too, but I guess maybe it was a different time in the '70s and '80s," said Lynnette. Now a single mother herself, she is a teacher at a private school in Manhattan, and she is studying for a master's degree.

Lorena Weeks, who made legal history with her fight against the restrictions on the kinds of jobs women could do, lives in the house she and Billy built with the money from her Southern Bell settlement. "On *Barbara Walters* they called it the House That Bell Built," Lorena said. "I wish they hadn't done that, because it hurt my husband." Billy Weeks died in 2000. "If you write anything, don't put in that my husband was all against the suit," Lorena added. "He wasn't. Billy just loved people and he didn't want to hurt people. He loved his friends and he was too good for his own good, bless his heart." She has three granddaughters and eight great-grandchildren. "And isn't it wonderful—five of them are right here within hollering distance." Her son has his own business in back-to-work rehabilitation. One daughter is a bank officer, and the other is county tax commissioner.

Sylvia Roberts, Lorena's attorney, is practicing family law in Baton Rouge. One particular passion, she said, "is preventing teenage dating violence because, boy, once a person gets involved in that, their life is over." Another is displaced housewives: "Just trying to find a way to make use of women, wherever they are."

While Sylvia Acevedo was working as an industrial engineer for IBM, she got word that her unhappy father had snapped completely, killed her mother, and then killed himself. "Now that I've done a lot of therapy and worked on it, I can see it went back generations...I feel much more at peace about it, but for a long time I couldn't talk about it. I was ashamed," she said. IBM, she added, provided her with the equivalent of "a sheltered workshop" while she tried to heal. She eventually moved on to jobs in other software firms and started several businesses. Her current company, CommuniCard, creates tools to help employers communicate with Spanish-speaking workers and consults with large organizations on communications issues.

Not too long ago, Acevedo was helping a client make a pitch to potential investors—"venture capitalists from Northern California. They look at me and they can't even pronounce my name." Remembering the old IBM mentor who told her that businessmen would not listen to her until they were assured she was "like them," Acevedo stopped her presentation and said, "I went to school down the street. You may have heard of it—Stanford? And I was a rocket scientist. So numbers don't faze me." After that, she recalled, "They were like, *Okay.*"

Unable to find work in Montgomery after the bus boycott, Rosa Parks moved to Detroit, where she supported her mother and disabled husband by sewing and working in a clothing factory until Representative John Conyers discovered her plight and hired her as a receptionist. When she died in 2005, her body lay in state in Washington in the Capitol Rotunda—the first woman so honored.

Linda LeClair, the star of the Barnard cohabitation scandals of the late 1960s, changed her name to Grace LeClair a few years later. "It was like—my name got worn out," she says. She worked as a community organizer, an anti–nuclear power activist, a founder of a social investment fund, and an advocate for food issues and housing availability. She is now the executive director of the National Abortion Rights Action League in New Hampshire. She and Peter Behr, her partner in that famous *New York Times* story on cohabitation, are still friends. As to her parents, she said, "We've always been close. They were not happy about that period at all, but we were never out of a relationship." A while ago, LeClair was given a copy of a documentary on the sexual revolution that had a whole section on the Barnard protests. She showed it to her two daughters. "It was really exciting for them to see it," she said. "They've heard the story before, in folklore. But it's like when there were horseless carriages."

Alice Paul died in 1977, without ever knowing that the Equal Rights Amendment was doomed. Her birthplace in Mount Laurel, New Jersey, is now designated a National Historic Landmark.

Sherri (Finkbine) Chessen's real estate career put her six children through college; now her oldest daughter is a lawyer, the senior counsel for the appellate court in San Diego. Her oldest son has followed his mother into real estate. "My next son is a doctor," she said, ticking them off. "The next daughter is a teacher. The next does sports on the radio and does a TV show in Idaho. My baby daughter is a documentary filmmaker. She's making a trilogy of abortion movies. I told her I was passing the torch to her because I was sick of it." Sherri has embarked on another career as an author of children's books.

"If anything, the thalidomide experience brought us closer," she said of her family. "People said I was going to be doomed. I wasn't. I've been blessed."

Pat Lorance never again had a job as good as the tester position she lost in the 1970s. One employer told her when she applied for work that she was qualified but undesirable because she had filed suit against her former company. "I started crying," she admitted. Lorance ended up working in shipping and receiving. "Actually, I've enjoyed everything I've done," she said cheerfully.

But her body gave out. Crippling back problems left her on disability. She lost her home and wound up in public housing, so immobilized by back pain that she was unable to make the bed: "I slept without sheets for four weeks, but I had a place to sleep, honey." Eventually she was able to move into a better apartment that was more accessible to the handicapped. "God's been good to me. He really has," she insisted. "It's been a long haul, but everything's working out good now."

In 1991 Congress responded to *Lorance v. AT&T Technologies* by passing an amendment to the Civil Rights Act that made it clear an employee who was hurt by a discriminatory seniority system could file a court challenge when she was injured by the system, as well as when it first went into effect. Pat Lorance still remembers being told, "I would never

come off the law books. That I'd made a place in history. And I thought, 'Ooooh.'"

After nearly fifty years as little girls' favorite playmate (and endless naked encounters with Ken under the washcloth), Barbie had a midlife crisis in 1999 when she was challenged by the Bratz dolls, with those racy clothes that drove older Americans crazy when they saw them on their granddaughters. In the panic that ensued, Barbie dumped Ken and took up with an Australian surfer named Blaine, who still failed to bring back her popularity. Ken returned to reclaim her in 2006, with cooler clothes, better hair, and a different nose.

Anne Tolstoi Wallach had been too happy about having a job in advertising to think about discrimination when she started her career in the 1950s and '60s. But she hardly failed to notice the changing times. In fact, she wrote advertisements for NOW in the early 1970s. ("Womanpower, it's much too good to waste.") She also kept moving up, to creative director and vice president at Grey Advertising. And as the 1970s ebbed away, she took stock in the most profitable way conceivable. Wallach wrote a novel, *Women's Work,* about a snobby, sexist advertising firm whose authority figures sounded a lot like some of the people she had dealt with earlier in her career. The book brought in a stunning advance of $850,000 in 1980—the equivalent of more than $2 million now. She eventually left advertising to concentrate on her writing and published two other novels and a book of nonfiction. She is working on another novel.

Alison Foster, Anne's daughter, remarried while she was getting her training in counseling psychology. She and her husband work at the same private school in Manhattan that her youngest son still attends and where Alison is dean of students. Occasionally, she says, they fantasize about starting a school of their own, or working together at a boarding school. It's the closest thing she can think of to the communal life she liked so much when she was young.

→＞ ＜←

Maria K. says she tried to raise her sons to understand "a girl's point of view so that they would respect women and know what it felt like to be on the other end. They saw how cruel it could be when a guy hits and runs." Now she has a teenage granddaughter, and she's trying to give different lessons: "When I went to school, you got to be a teacher, a nurse, a secretary, a homemaker. Those were your choices of what you wanted to be. There was nothing else. And now, whether it was the sexual revolution, whether it was the women's rights, whether it was just the passage of time, there are all kinds of things that are available to her that I didn't even know about—being a food scientist, being a journalist, there's just a myriad of things that she can do with her life."

→＞ ＜←

Dena Ivey left the Air Force in 1995 and returned to college in Fairbanks, where she decided that she wanted to become a lawyer. She graduated from the University of Colorado at Boulder Law School, and after a stint working for the Alaska State Commission for Human Rights, she became an assistant district attorney for the state. "I see myself defending victims against a LOT of domestic violence. And I see myself as a defender of traditional Yup'ik values—which do not include smacking people around."

→＞ ＜←

June LaValleur and her partner Jill were together for ten years before they broke up, amicably, sharing custody of a dog that they are very careful not to quarrel in front of. "I'm looking for a partner now," she said. "Gender is not as important as not being a Republican."

(Later, in an update, June reported that she was engaged to a retired engineering professor. He's a Democrat.)

→＞ ＜←

Madeleine Kunin served three terms as governor of Vermont, during which she made a visit to the *New York Times* editorial board, cruising into the building where she had been offered a job in the cafeteria in lieu of an editing slot. (Her delight at the turnaround was not dimmed when a security guard approached the plainclothes policeman who was accompanying her and said, "Welcome to the *Times*, Governor.") She announced in 1990 that she would not run for reelection, wrote her autobiography, and became ambassador to Switzerland, the country where she had been born, becoming what was surely the first U.S. ambassador in memory who was actually able to speak the local languages. Now a college professor, she finds her female students "kind of a puzzle." The young women, she mused, seem to lack "bravado, or confidence. Of course there are lots of exceptions and it's improving, but it's creeping up so much more slowly than I'd have thought when I was elected governor."

→＞ ＜←

Georgia Panter Nielsen got married in 1968, after the airlines' rules against married flight attendants were finally wiped off the books. When she ended her career in 2002, after forty-two years of flying, she was one of about only sixteen hundred flight attendants who had stayed on long enough to reach retirement age, out of the hundreds of thousands who started careers in the sky. Her generation had won their fight to make their jobs real careers rather than a brief interval between college and marriage for attractive young ladies. But what the women's rights movement and union activism achieved, the decline of the airline industry helped take away. Mergers and bankruptcies, crammed planes and rapid turnovers, made it hard to envision enjoying the job for decades on end. "The hourly pay is back to 1990s pay, and staffing is down," said Nielsen. "The work's become so onerous and difficult, they're saying this is again not viewed as a career opportunity so much as a short-term job." When United went into bankruptcy, Nielsen helped organize the retired flight attendants to protect their health care and pensions. "We lobby, we picket, we go to Washington," she reported.

→→ ←←

Wilma Mankiller was awarded the Presidential Medal of Freedom in 1998. She and her husband live in a house in Mankiller Flats, Oklahoma, the traditional home of her family, "surrounded by my books, my art, my grandchildren, and the natural world." In her autobiography, she recalled a meeting she had attended in the Midwest where a man approached her to say he had an important message. "He told me he was an Oneida, and one of the prophecies he had heard was that this time period is the time of the women—a time for women to take on a more important role in society. He described this as 'the time of the butterfly.'"

→→ ←←

In 2000, when she was 66, Gloria Steinem stunned many of her friends by getting married. She wed David Bale, a 61-year-old businessman and social activist from South Africa, in a ceremony at Wilma Mankiller's home in Oklahoma. "The bride wore jeans and a white shirt; the groom, black clothes and an Indian belt," reported the *New York Times*.

"We had both spent our lives doing essentially what we weren't supposed to do, and . . . we ended up in the same place," said Steinem. "I thought to myself, we've spent thirty years equalizing the marriage laws, so why not? And besides, Wilma Mankiller offered us a Cherokee ceremony, so who

can resist that?" It was not quite the same as the time when Angelina Grimké had thrilled all the women's rights advocates in the early nineteenth century by proving that a feminist could find a husband. No one had ever doubted, after all, that Gloria Steinem had the option. But it was quite a moment when she decided to exercise it. She and Bale told each other it wasn't such a big deal; that at their age "till death do you part" wasn't really all that long.

It was, in fact, hardly any time at all. Bale soon developed fatal brain lymphoma and died in 2003 after a terrible decline into confusion and paranoia. "I hope my body goes before my brain and not the other way around. It was hard on him, hard on everyone around him," said Steinem. She returned to a solitary life, to the degree that someone who was constantly traveling or entertaining visiting feminists at home could be alone. Steinem still writes and works full tilt for women's causes, particularly in the developing world. She has given up high heels for boots but even now finds herself continually identified as the attractive feminist. "The part that's hurtful is that having worked hard and continuing to work hard at 73, I still find accomplishments attributed to my appearance. I would have thought I could outgrow that by now."

→→ ←←

Martha Griffiths retired from Congress in 1974, spent several years becoming the first woman to serve on the boards of various corporations, and then accepted the offer to run for lieutenant governor of Michigan with James Blanchard, the Democratic gubernatorial candidate. They were elected as a team in 1982 and 1986, but in 1990, when Griffiths was 78, Blanchard dumped her, citing her age and health. Griffiths, who had lost absolutely none of her feistiness, said that it was women and old people who had given Blanchard his victories and that he ignored them at his peril. Sure enough, he was defeated in a close election. "I don't know if I feel vindicated, but I think it clearly shows that I won it for him the first two times," Griffiths said. She died at 91 in 2003.

＊＞ ＜＊

Nora Ephron, who was told by *Newsweek* that women couldn't be writers, went on to write some of her era's bestselling books and most popular movies, and become far more successful as a director, columnist, and blogger than the men who had once tried to stand in her way. A few years before her death in 2012, she mused about the arc of history. "When the women's movement began to fade, I used to do about ten speeches a year, in part about how not enough had happened," she recalled. But looking back, Ephron concluded that she was completely wrong. "It's a gigantic change. It's unbelievable what happened. It's shocking. It's amazing. And I just look back and think—you must not have been seeing something. Because look at this THING."

ACKNOWLEDGMENTS

→ ←

This book aims to tell the story of what happened to American women since 1960 by combining the public drama of the era with the memories of regular women who lived through it all. To get the second part, my team of interviewers and I sat down with more than one hundred women from around the country, ranging in age from late 80s to their early 20s, who generously agreed to talk about their lives. It breaks my heart that only a few of their stories could be told in any detail. Others are mentioned fleetingly or not at all. But all of them educated me, and the things they told us are, I hope, reflected in the book.

My thanks to interviewees Sylvia Acevedo, Lillian Andrews, Pam Andrews, Michele Araujo, Barbara Arnold, Lynnette Arthur, Dana Arthur-Monteleone, Judy Baker, Josie Bass, Myrna Ten Bensel, Verna Bode, Valerie Bradley, Roberta Brooks, Barbara Jo Brothers, Beverly Burton, Ruth Chesnovar, April Che Chisholm, Valerie Chisholm, Suzan Johnson Cook, Tish Johnson Cook, Rita Coury, Madene Cox, Mary Bell Darcus, Josephine Elsberg, Adelaide Farrell, Yana Shani Fleming, Alison Foster, Lillian Garland, Diane Gilbert, Ellen Goodman, Noella Goupil, Sheri Zoe McWilliams Griffin, Jeannie Gross, Shirley Hammond, Della Taylor Hardman, Joanie Hawkinson, Anna Hay, Alyce P. Hill, Kathy Hinderhofer, Tawana Hinton, Tiffany Hinton, Camara Dia Holloway, Dena Ivey, Dorothea Janczak, Jaime Jenett, Djassi Camara DaCosta Johnson, Emma Jordan, Maria K., Donna Poggi Keck, Edna Kleimeyer, Annemarie Kropf, Joyce Ladner, Sylvia Larsen, June LaValleur, Gayle Lawhorn, Florence Lee, Barbara Lewis, Jo Meyer Maasberg, Linda Mason, Linda McDaniel, Virginia McWilliams, Connie Meadows, Annie Miller, Ellen S. Miller, Marie Monsky, Lucy Murray, Georgia Panter Nielsen, Angela Nolfi, Jennifer O'Connell, Elizabeth Patterson, Susan Meyer Pennock, Sylvia Peterson, Judy Pinnick, Tanya Pollard, Vicki Cohn Pollard, Gloria Pratt, Joanne Rife, Judy Riff, Georgia Riggs, Flori Roberts, Carol Rumsey, Frances Russell, Serena Savarirayan, Frances Sego, Mae Ann Semnack, Margaret Siegel, Jennifer Maasberg Smith, Alexandria Dery Snider, Laura Sessions Stepp, Katherine Stewart, Alice Stockwell, Lenora Taitt-Magubane, Althea Tice, Kimberly Tignor, Barbara Tyler, Gloria Vaz, Anne Tolstoi Wallach, Louise Meyer Warpness, Jane Washington, Mary Helen Washington, Marylyn Weller, Betty Riley Williams, Virginia Williams, Arlene Dent Winfield, Charlotte Wong, and Wendy Woythaler.

The team that interviewed them included Sarah Cox, Amy Jeffries, C. J. Lehr, Christina Lem, Kelly Pike, Daniel Reilly, Susan Rife, Tracy Rzepka, Leigh Shelton, Amy Smith, and Justin Weller. Bronwyn Prohaska provided much of the research for the early sections of the book, and Nick Bunkley helped me track down sources in Michigan.

Special thanks to Marcia Hensley, who brought me many wonderful stories from women in Wyoming, including those of Louise Meyer Warpness, her daughters, Susan and Jo, and her granddaughter, Jennifer Maasberg Smith. Sarah Belanger produced many great interviews, including those of Barbara Arnold and her daughter, Alex, as well as Laura Sessions Stepp's. Carol Lee interviewed, among others, Gloria Vaz, her daughter Dana Arthur-Monteleone, and her granddaughter Lynnette Arthur; Judith Borger's Minnesota interviewees included Dr. June LaValleur. Michelle Jamrisko interviewed Lillian Garland, and Johanna Jainchill interviewed Virginia Williams. Courtney Barnes found many interesting subjects, including one of the early readers' favorites, Maria K., who contacted us as the book was being finished and asked to have her identity disguised to avoid embarrassing her family. Sala Patterson set the interviewing record, bringing me the stories of nineteen women, including those of Tawana and Tiffany Hinton and Sala's mother, Elizabeth Patterson.

For me, one of the greatest pleasures in this project was talking with so many of the people who were involved in the public events described in this story. Thanks to Lisa Belkin, Pat Benke, John Brademas, Pat Buchanan, Jacqui Ceballos, Sherri Finkbine Chessen, Constance Cumbey, Jack Duncan, Mary Eastwood, Jean Enersen, Nora Ephron, Muriel Fox, Jo Freeman, Claudia Goldin, Madeleine Kunin, Grace (Linda) LeClair, Lilly Ledbetter, Pat Lorance, Wilma Mankiller, Gerald McBeath, George McGovern, Faith Middleton, Walter Mondale, Robin Morgan, Cynthia Pearson, Martha Phillips, Lynn Povich, Sylvia Roberts, Marlene Sanders, Pat Schroeder, Valerie Steele, Gloria Steinem, Janet Tegley, Jessica Valenti, Betsy Wade, Diane Watson, Lorena Weeks, and Randi Weingarten for helping me understand what went on. While the people involved in the 2008 presidential campaign talked to me for my *New York Times* column, the interviews they gave me served double duty, particularly those with Hillary Clinton and Michelle Obama.

Amanda Millner-Fairbanks provided me with several boxes full of research and, even better, her company through the last stages of this project.

Thanks to the friends who read this manuscript and shared their thoughts and critiques with me: in particular Trish Hall; my sister, Mary Ann Vinck; my sister-in-law, Kathleen Collins; Nancy Devlin; Eleanor Randolph; Anne Dranginis; and Ann Reardon. My amazing agent, Alice Martell, read it twice, which I definitely regard as service above and beyond the call of duty. Pat Strachan, my editor at Little, Brown, read it first and last and was a constant supportive presence in between. Thanks to all the people at Little, Brown for underwriting this project and being so helpful as we went along, especially Karen Landry, my copyeditor.

Fans of endnotes will notice that I relied on reporting in the *New York Times* along every stage of this narrative. There are a lot of wonderful papers in this country, but even if I weren't biased, I think I'd be in awe of the way the *Times* has devoted its resources to doing serious reporting on American social issues.

Finally, one of the great boons of this kind of enterprise is the chance to thank the people who put up with me while it was being written. So many thanks to Arthur Sulzberger, the publisher of the *Times,* and Andy Rosenthal, the editorial page editor, for giving me a book leave and living with me when I returned in the middle of chapter ten. Thanks to my mother, Rita Gleason, who told me many stories and introduced me to friends who told me theirs. Thanks to my nieces, Becca Gleason and Anna McManus, and my nephew, Hugh McManus, for tutoring me on what the world looks like from the other side of 20. And finally, thanks to my husband, Dan Collins, for life in general.

NOTES

➤➤ ◄◄

Some of the people interviewed for this book, such as Wilma Mankiller, Gloria Steinem, Jo Freeman, and Robin Morgan, have written books of their own that I've also used as resources. Information taken from their books is sourced in the notes. Other quotes are from the interviews, which are listed at the top of each chapter.

INTRODUCTION

Interview: Maria K.

3 On a steamy morning: Jack Roth, "Judge Scolds Woman in Slacks," *New York Times*, August 10, 1960.

3 One early settler wrote: Collins, *America's Women*, 26.

3 One New England Quaker: Chace and Lovell, *Two Quaker Sisters*, 4.

4 "Our men are sufficiently money-making": Douglas, *The Feminization of American Culture*, 57.

4 "She reigns in the heart": Wertz and Wertz, *Lying-In*, 58.

4 *Ladies' Magazine*, a popular periodical: Douglas, *The Feminization of American Culture*, 46.

4 After the Civil War: Jones, *Labor of Love*, 58–60.

4 A 1960 story in the *New York Times*: Marilyn Berger, "Feminine Fashion Has a Place in the Mine," *New York Times*, October 28, 1960.

5 When Betty Lou Raskin: Betty Lou Raskin, "Woman's Place Is in the Lab," *New York Times Magazine*, April 19, 1959.

5 Supreme Court Chief Justice Earl Warren: Kerber, *No Constitutional Right to Be Ladies*, 141.

5 The National Office Managers Association: Charles Ginder, "Factor of Sex in Office Employment," *Office Executive*, February 1961, 10–13.

5 a spokesman for NASA would say: Levine and Lyons, *The Decade of Women*, 35.

I. REPUDIATING ROSIE

Interviews: Beverly Burton, Linda McDaniel, Georgia Panter Nielsen, Angela Nolfi, Sylvia Roberts, Marlene Sanders.

11 "Some of you *do*": "Mlle's Next Word," *Mademoiselle*, January 1960, 33.

11 "I think that when women": Spock, *Decent and Indecent*, 61.

11 *Newsweek*, decrying a newly noticed: "Young Wives," *Newsweek*, March 7, 1960, 57–60.

11 Jo Freeman, who went to Berkeley: Jo Freeman, "On the Origins of the Women's Movement from a Strictly Personal Perspective," in *The Feminist Memoir Project*, 171–72.

11 And once *Mademoiselle* had finished: "The Professional Touch," *Mademoiselle*, June 1960, 82–83.

11 An official for the men-only: Anderson, *The Movement and the Sixties*, 316.

11 When *Mademoiselle* selected seven: "Quo Vadis?" *Mademoiselle*, January 1960.

11 In 1950 only about 9 percent: Stark, *Glued to the Set*, 33.

12 "But all the slapstick": Davis, *Say Kids! What Time Is It?*, 5.

12 "The harshness and crudeness": Ibid., 109.

12 On *Father Knows Best*, younger daughter: Douglas, *Where the Girls Are*, 37–38.

12 When Betty Friedan asked why: Friedan, *It Changed My Life*, 67.

12 Later in the decade: *Star Trek*, "Turnabout Intruder," episode 79.

13 A rather typical episode began: *Bonanza*, "Justice," episode 252.

13 More than 30 percent of American: Nye and Hoffman, *The Employed Mother in America*, 8.

13 The average salary of a female teacher: Bess Furman, "Teacher Pay Half of Seventeen Professions," *New York Times*, May 29, 1960.

13 when the government was reporting: "Mitchell Reports Jobs Plentiful for the 1960 College Graduate," *New York Times*, January 13, 1961.

14 "It is a tradition in the Guggenheimer": Rhoda Aderer, "A Tradition Is Continued by Mrs. Guggenheimer," *New York Times*, January 6, 1960, 94.

14 Esther Peterson, the top-ranking: Peterson, *Restless*, 99.

14 The sociologist David Riesman: David Riesman, "Two Generations," in *The Woman in America*, 91–92.

14 "Tug, there's a whole world": Kerr, *Julie with Wings*, 17–18.

15 The Grace Downs Air Career School: *Mademoiselle*, January 1960, 107.

15 If a stewardess was still on: Lindsy Van Gelder, "Coffee, Tea, or Me," *Ms.*, January 1973, 89.

16 "Hell yes, we have": Walsh, *Doctors Wanted*, 243–44.

16 Although more than half a million: Harrison, *On Account of Sex*, 145, and Peterson, *Restless*, 109.

16 A would-be journalist: Kunin, *Living a Political Life*, 162.

16 When Ruth Bader Ginsburg: Kerber, *No Constitutional Right to Be Ladies*, 202.

16 A report on women in management: Epstein, *Woman's Place*, 6.

16 A federally funded study: David Beardslee and Donald O'Dowd, "Students and the Occupational World," in *The American College*.

17 Marjorie Wintjen, a 25-year-old: Marylin Bender, "Women Equality Groups Fighting Credit Barriers," *New York Times*, March 25, 1973.

17 The *New York Times* was still reporting: Georgia Dullea, "Women Demanding Equal Treatment in Mortgage Loans," *New York Times*, October 29, 1972.

17 Looking back on her life: O'Reilly, *The Girl I Left Behind*, 36.

18 Heinemann's Restaurant: Anderson, *The Movement and the Sixties*, 316.

18 Early in the 1960s: Friedan, *Life So Far*, 113.

2. THE WAY WE LIVED

Interviews: Lillian Andrews, Pam Andrews, Barbara Arnold, Verna Bode, Beverly Burton, Valerie Chisholm, Nora Ephron, Yana Shani Fleming, Alison Foster, Muriel Fox, Shirley Hammond, Tawana Hinton, Maria K., June LaValleur, Gayle Lawhorn, Lorna Jo Meyer, Susan Meyer, Georgia Panter Nielsen, Sylvia Peterson, Judy Riff, Carol Rumsey,

Margaret Siegel, Laura Sessions Stepp, Gloria Vaz, Anne Tolstoi Wallach, Louise Meyer Warpness, Mary Helen Washington, Virginia Williams.

25 In a survey for the *Saturday Evening Post:* George Gallup and Evan Hill, "The American Woman," *Saturday Evening Post,* December 22, 1962, 32.

26 Susan B. Anthony had to be rescued: Fischer, *Pantaloons and Power,* 101–2.

26 But even during World War II: Keil, *Those Wonderful Women in Their Flying Machines,* 259.

27 Wilma Rudolph, the Olympic track star: Rudolph, *Wilma,* 123.

28 One book on dressing: Steele, *The Corset,* 161.

28 *Mademoiselle* advised that when it came: "Questions of Form," *Mademoiselle,* June 1960, 92.

28 When her 12-year-old: Bradford, *America's Queen,* 30.

29 In the fall of 1960: Friedan, *The Feminine Mystique,* 16.

29 As the essayist Jane O'Reilly: O'Reilly, *The Girl I Left Behind,* 40.

29 Only 26 percent: Coontz, *Marriage,* 237.

29 A woman who had reached: Bird, *Born Female,* 50.

29 Writing in the late 1970s: O'Reilly, *The Girl I Left Behind,* 40.

30 *Harper's* bemoaned the fact: Cole, "American Youth Goes Monogamous," 32.

30 In one much-quoted: Gallup and Hill, "The American Woman," 16–32.

30 "Almost all young women": "Shaping the '60s...Foreshadowing the '70s," 30.

31 Joan Bernstein graduated: Couric, *Women Lawyers,* 37–38.

31 In Chicago, which had very: Coontz, *Marriage,* 252.

31 The idea that someone had to be: Monrad Paulsen, "For a Reform of the Divorce Laws," *New York Times Magazine,* May 13, 1962, 22.

32 *Harper's* claimed, "A girl": Cole, "American Youth Goes Monogamous," 32.

32 A science teacher told: Marya Mannes, "Female Intelligence: Who Wants It?" *New York Times Magazine,* January 3, 1960, 44.

32 *Newsweek* reported in 1960: Edwin Diamond, "Young Wives," *Newsweek,* March 7, 1960, 60.

32 At a soon-to-become-famous: Friedan, *The Feminine Mystique,* 153.

32 "Success and a Well-Dressed Wife": "Success and a Well-Dressed Wife Go Together for Young Executives": *New York Times,* April 2, 1960, 27.

33 She indignantly compared: Nan Robertson, "Mrs. Kennedy Defends Clothes," *New York Times,* September 15, 1960, 1.

33 "The food is marvelous": Bradford, *America's Queen,* 189.

34 During the Cuban: Ibid., 240.

3. HOUSEWORK

Interviews: Lillian Andrews, Myrna Ten Bensel, Mary Bell Darcus, Josephine Elsberg, Edna Kleimeyer, Joyce Ladner, Jo Meyer Maasberg, Wilma Mankiller, Virginia McWilliams, Angela Nolfi, Joanne Rife, Louise Meyer Warpness, Marylyn Weller, Betty Riley Williams.

40 "We now expect quite an immigration": Collins, *America's Women,* 235.

41 Sixty percent of families: Chafe, *The Unfinished Journey,* 111–12.

41 A quarter of all families: Rosen, *The World Split Open,* 9.

41 In the famous Levittown: Jackson, *Crabgrass Frontier,* 235.

42 *Ebony* celebrated with an article: "Goodbye Mammy, Hello Mom," *Ebony,* March 1947, 36.

42 A doctoral student: Shapiro, *Something from the Oven,* 73–74.

43 A methodical study: Joann Vanek, "Time Spent in Housework," *Scientific American,* November 1974, 116–120.

43 In the 1950s the average: "New Washer Will Handle Bigger Load," *New York Times,* November 2, 1960.

44 One *New York Times* columnist: Dorothy Barclay, "Family Palship—With an Escape Clause," *New York Times Magazine,* November 18, 1956, 48.

44 "I know that small children": Kerr, *The Snake Has All the Lines,* 61.

44 "Approximately half of *Playboy's*": Ehrenreich, *The Hearts of Men,* 43.

44 "You can hardly pick up": Margaret Taylor Klose, "A Pox on Your Husband's Ego," *McCall's,* April 1960.

45 "The life of many": Giddings, *When and Where I Enter,* 253.

45 A typical woman married: Nye and Hoffman, *The Employed Mother in America,* 5.

45 "Whether one finds it": "The American Female," *Harper's,* October 1962, 115.

45 George Gallup, conjuring up: George Gallup and Evan Hill, "The American Woman," *Saturday Evening Post,* December 22, 1962, 17.

45 Even *Newsweek,* in its: Edwin Diamond, "Young Wives," *Newsweek,* March 7, 1960, 57–60.

46 In 1960 *Redbook:* Friedan, *The Feminine Mystique,* 66.

46 "She is dissatisfied": Diamond, "Young Wives," 57.

46 The (male) president: Harvey, *The Fifties,* 46–47.

47 "of inappropriate and unnecessary": Friedan, *It Changed My Life,* 18.

47 One young mother of four: Friedan, *The Feminine Mystique,* 21.

47 "You'd be surprised": Ibid., 235.

47 "The feminine mystique has succeeded": Ibid., 336–37.

4. THE ICE CRACKS

Interviews: Constance Cumbey, Mary Eastwood, Muriel Fox, Sylvia Roberts, Lorena Weeks.

57 "Women now hold": "Women Likely to Outvote Men," *New York Times,* January 5, 1960.

57 At the end of the decade: Bird, *Born Female,* 162.

57 "The meal begins": Nan Robertson, "GOP Women Facing a Calorie-Packed Week," *New York Times,* July 23, 1960.

57 Meanwhile, nearly two-thirds: George Gallup and Evan Hill, "The American Woman," *Saturday Evening Post,* December 22, 1962, 32.

57 Edna Simpson of Illinois: Chamberlin, *A Minority of Members,* 279.

58 In her unpublished autobiography: Martha Griffiths, *My Letter to Tomorrow,* unpublished manuscript. Thanks to Griffiths's friend Constance Cumbey for sharing this.

58 But in 1946 it was Martha: Lamson, *Few Are Chosen,* 89–90.

58 Griffiths and her husband: Interview, Constance Cumbey.

58 Nevertheless, she felt obliged: Chamberlin, *A Minority of Members,* 263.

58 In her memoirs, the publisher: Graham, *Personal History,* 291.

59 Margaret Price, an official: Harrison, *On Account of Sex,* 74.

59 After the election, 2.4: Ibid., 78.

59 "There is no Alice": Lunardini, *From Equal Suffrage to Equal Rights,* 9.

59 Esther Peterson called them: Peterson, *Restless,* 105.

59 As a good Mormon: Ibid., 13.

60 "Even the youngest": Ibid., 33.

60 "Give her to Kennedy": Ibid., 64.

60 "It is not the policy": Hole and Levine, *Rebirth of Feminism,* 52.

60 She resented the "elite": Peterson, *Restless,* 103.

61 During the 1960 presidential campaign: Ibid., 118.

61 "When I wanted help": Ware, *Beyond Suffrage,* 10.

61 Kennedy's relationship with the great: Paterson, *Be Somebody,* 124.

61 Hyman Bookbinder, who served: Harrison, *On Account of Sex,* 139.

61 But they were about to enter into what Pauli: Rosen, *The World Split Open,* 69.

62 Marguerite Rawalt, a government tax: Unless otherwise noted, this section is based on Judith Paterson's biography of Marguerite Rawalt, *Be Somebody*.

62 One of Rawalt's chief allies: Unless otherwise noted, this section is based on Pauli Murray's book *Pauli Murray: The Autobiography of a Black Activist, Feminist, Lawyer, Priest, and Poet*.

63 "Well, maybe I would": Brauer, "Women Activists," 44.

63 Smith, 80, was: Dan Oberdorfter, "Judge Smith Moves with Deliberate Drag," *New York Times Magazine*, November 12, 1964.

63 "Congressman Smith would": Ibid.

63 In case anyone might: Davis, *Moving the Mountain*, 41.

64 Emanuel Celler of New York: Ibid., 42.

64 Amid the hoots: Fern Ingersoll, "Former Congresswomen Look Back," in *Women in Washington*, 197.

64 "I presume that if there had been": Ibid.

64 "In my judgment": Ibid., 196.

64 Green remembered a male: Ibid., 202.

64 At one point, when she went: Ibid., 203.

64 "For every discrimination": Davis, *Moving the Mountain*, 43.

65 Ida Wells-Barnett, who had: Terborg-Penn, *African American Women in the Struggle for the Vote*, 121–23.

65 A half century later: Fry, "Conversations with Alice Paul," 336–37.

65 While all the black: Ingersoll, "Former Congresswomen Look Back," 197.

65 "We made it!": Ibid., 197.

65 Smith was another widow: The section on Margaret Chase Smith is based on Peggy Lamson's *Few Are Chosen*, 3–29, and Janann Sherman's biography *No Place for a Woman*.

66 "You know, our amendment": Davis, *Moving the Mountain*, 45.

Representative Smith gave conflicting explanations for introducing the amendment. Alice Paul, who believed Smith was sincere, told historian Amelia Fry that Smith warned her his motives would be misconstrued and urged her to find someone else to lead the fight. The evidence seems to me to fall strongly on the side of ridicule and his desire to do mischief to the civil rights bill. Among those who disagree, Jo Freeman makes a thorough argument in her essay "How 'Sex' Got into Title VII."

66 The *Wall Street Journal* invited: Harrison, *On Account of Sex*, 189.

66 "Bunny problems indeed!": "De-Sexing the Job Market," *New York Times*, August 21, 1965, 20.

66 *The New Republic*, a bastion: Harrison, *On Account of Sex*, 188.

67 Aileen Hernández, the only woman: Ibid., 187.

67 "We walked in": Roads, "Interview with Barbara 'Dusty' Roads."

67 Representative James Scheuer of New York: Davis, *Moving the Mountain*, 21.

67 "What are you running": Ingersoll, "Former Congresswomen Look Back," 199.

67 "underground network of women": Friedan, *It Changed My Life*, 96.

67 They "maneuvered me": Friedan, *Life So Far*, 165.

68 The meeting, in Friedan's: Cohen, *The Sisterhood*, 133–35.

68 Friedan remembered that "those five-dollar": Friedan, *Life So Far*, 175.

68 Members joked: Davis, *Moving the Mountain*, 56–58.

68 "What do you call it": Friedan, *It Changed My Life*, 119.

68 As soon as Jo: Jo Freeman, "On the Origins of the Women's Liberation Movement from a Strictly Personal Perspective," in *Gender and Family Issues in the Workplace*, 178.

69 Just finding NOW: Echols, *Daring to Be Bad*, 74.

69 Martha Griffiths, who had naturally: Tinker, *Women in Washington*, 198.

69 "With no money": Friedan, *It Changed My Life*, 121.

69 "You have not heard": Paterson, *Be Somebody*, 152.

69 "I must have relief": Ibid., 176.

69 In Orlando, Ida: Bird, *Born Female*, 165.

69 Lorena Weeks was 9: Unless otherwise noted, the story of Lorena Weeks's suit is based on interviews with Weeks and her attorney, Sylvia Roberts.

70 The head of her union: Herr, *Women, Power, and AT&T*, 81.

5. WHAT HAPPENED?

Interview: Nora Ephron.

78 And, as one nineteenth-century: Kaestle, *Pillars of the Republic*, 123.

78 "Experience in business": Davies, *Woman's Place Is at the Typewriter*, 84.

78 "She's making": "Rosie the Riveter," song by Redd Evans and John Jacob Loeb.

78 The Office of War Information: Colman, *Rosie the Riveter*, 51.

78 two-thirds of those new: Chafe, *The American Woman*, 253.

78 "A Good Man": "A Good Man Is Hard to Find—So They Hire Women," *Time*, November 4, 1966.

78 That year, President Johnson: Bird, *Born Female*, 134–35.

79 "Darling—you are": Litoff and Smith, *Since You Went Away*, 147.

79 "Second, we must": Bird, *Born Female*, 135.

79 During the war, the nation's: Columbus Washboard Company in Logan, Ohio, company history.

79 Half of American homes had: Cherlin, *Marriage*, 35.

79 Even in the best times: Chafe, *The Unfinished Journey*.

79 Family income, adjusted: Cherlin, *Marriage*, 35.

80 Over the '70s and '80s: Coontz, *The Way We Really Are*, 126–27.

80 In the 1970s wives who: Weiss, *To Have and to Hold*, 69.

80 "There is, perhaps, one": "The Liberator," *The Economist*, December 23, 1999.

80 Young unmarried women: Goldin and Katz, "The Power of the Pill," 730–70.

81 It was, as the sociologist: Alice Rossi, "Equality Between the Sexes," in *The Woman in America*, 101.

82 "We have given great offense": Lerner, *The Grimké Sisters from South Carolina*, 139.

6. CIVIL RIGHTS

Interviews: Josie Bass, Valerie Bradley, Suzan Johnson Cook, Emma Jordan, Joyce Ladner, Lucy Murray, Lenora Taitt-Magubane, Mary Helen Washington, Betty Riley Williams, Virginia Williams.

87 Anderson had been blessed: Unless otherwise noted, this section is based on Allan Keiler's *Marian Anderson: A Singer's Journey*, and Anderson's autobiography, *My Lord, What a Morning*.

87 "I don't care if": Freedman, *The Voice That Challenged a Nation*, 57.

87 Sol Hurok, called: William Honan, "Fresh Perspectives on the DAR's Rebuff of Marian Anderson," *New York Times*, May 18, 1993.

88 "I felt like a dog": Olson, *Freedom's Daughters*, 90.

88 Parks, an old schoolmate: Mary Fair Burks, "Trailblazers: Women in the Montgomery Bus Boycott," in *Women in the Civil Rights Movement*, 71.

88 Later, when her husband: Giddings, *When and Where I Enter*, 265.

88 "They've messed with the wrong": Parks, *Rosa Parks*, 133.

88 "My God, look": Ibid., 125.

89 The Women's Political Council: Robinson, *The Montgomery Bus Boycott and the Women Who Started It*.

89 "True, we succeeded": Burks, "Trailblazers," 82.

89 The following morning, Rosa: Rosa Parks, "Tired of Giving In," in *Sisters in the Struggle*, 65.

89 While the ministers pressed: Olson, *Freedom's Daughters*, 122–23.

89 E. D. Nixon of the NAACP: Raines, *My Soul Is Rested,* 49.

89 Later, when Parks's lawyer: Olson, *Freedom's Daughters,* 123, and Robinson, *The Montgomery Bus Boycott and the Women Who Started It,* 136–37.

89 "You have said enough": Collier-Thomas and Franklin, *Sisters in the Struggle,* 70.

89 When Marian Anderson was interviewed: Marian Anderson, interviewed by Emily Kimbrough, *Ladies' Home Journal,* September 1960.

90 Looking for their perfect: Arsenault, *Freedom Riders,* 11–19.

90 Gwendolyn Robinson, a scholarship student: Lefever, *Undaunted by the Fight,* 183–86.

90 A young Marian Wright: Edelman, *Lanterns,* 24.

90 Students had a nine o'clock: Lefever, *Undaunted by the Fight,* 16–17.

90 Alice Walker lasted two years: Ibid., 168.

91 When Diane Nash was nominated: Halberstam, *The Children,* 144.

91 The *Richmond News Leader,* an outspoken: Zinn, *SNCC,* 27.

92 "If anyone gets whupped": Branch, *At Canaan's Edge,* 72.

92 When the Nashville students: Halberstam, *The Children,* 141.

92 In February 1961 Lana Taylor: Zinn, *SNCC,* 39.

92 Smith was another Spelman student: Unless otherwise noted, this section is based on *Soon We Will Not Cry* by Cynthia Griggs Fleming.

92 Ella Baker was well into middle age: Unless otherwise noted, this section is based on *Ella Baker and the Black Freedom Movement* by Barbara Ransby.

93 Septima Clark, a venerable: Brown, *Ready from Within,* 77–78.

93 Septima Clark once referred: Payne, *I've Got the Light of Freedom,* 76.

94 Septima Clark felt the established: Olson, *Freedom's Daughters,* 222.

94 Andrew Young, who was one: Ibid., 142.

94 "Remember, we are not": Zinn, *SNCC,* 106.

94 "People have to be made": Payne, *I've Got the Light of Freedom,* 93.

94 "To our mind lunch-counter": Ibid., 96.

94 Baker wanted the students: Ransby, *Ella Baker and the Black Freedom Movement.*

94 "Where we lived": Cantarow, *Moving the Mountain,* 60.

94 "There was terror": Penny Patch, "Sweet Tea at Shoney's," in *Deep in Our Hearts,* 140.

94 Unita Blackwell, a former: Blackwell, *Barefootin',* 84.

95 "How did I make a living?": Cantarow, *Moving the Mountain,* 73.

95 One former SNCC member: Payne, *I've Got the Light of Freedom,* 97.

95 Elizabeth Jennings, a Manhattan: John Hewitt, "The Search for Elizabeth Jennings," *New York History* 71, 387–415.

95 Pauli Murray was once barred: Murray, *Pauli Murray,* 109.

96 "Oh my God": Arsenault, *Freedom Riders,* 144–45.

96 Warned that any new Riders: Ibid., 181.

96 Susan Wilbur, 18: Ibid., 213–14.

96 Years later, she would tell: Halberstam, *The Children,* 329.

97 When a local resident: Arsenault, *Freedom Riders,* 335.

97 Seeing Lenora enter a church: Lefever, *Undaunted by the Fight,* 134.

97 At the time the demonstrations: Olson, *Freedom's Daughters,* 195.

97 But in Washington, a dying: Ibid., 194.

97 "Diane was a devoted": Ibid., 160.

98 "If the Negro woman": Franklin, *Ensuring Inequality,* 167.

98 Ella Baker was particularly: Ransby, *Ella Baker and the Black Freedom Movement,* 311.

98 In Mississippi, one male: Payne, *I've Got the Light of Freedom,* 271.

98 Anna Arnold Hedgeman—the only woman: Hedgeman, *The Trumpet Sounds,* 178–180.

98 "Nowadays, women wouldn't": Parks, *Rosa Parks,* 166.

98 No woman was invited: Pauli Murray, as quoted in Dorothy Height's "We Wanted the Voice of a Woman to Be Heard," in *Sisters in the Struggle,* 90.

98 "Nothing that women said": Height, "We Wanted the Voice of a Woman to Be Heard," 86–87.

99 Hedgeman proposed that at least: Hedgeman, *The Trumpet Sounds,* 179.

99 "That's them!" This segment is based on information in Unita Blackwell's autobiography, *Barefootin'.*

99 "Violence is a fearful": Olson, *Freedom's Daughters,* 204.

100 But Charles Payne, a Duke: Payne, *I've Got the Light of Freedom,* 265–83.

100 Laura McGhee, a widow: Ibid., 208–18.

100 Fannie Lou Hamer, who was: Unless otherwise noted, this section is based on *This Little Light of Mine,* by Kay Mills.

101 "At first Mrs. Hamer": Blackwell, *Barefootin',* 113.

101 "The spotlight was on": Ibid., 116.

101 "I don't think that anybody": Raines, *My Soul Is Rested,* 107.

102 Marian Wright Edelman said: Edelman, *Lanterns,* 79.

102 Back in Atlanta, Ruby: Fleming, *Soon We Will Not Cry,* 114.

102 Unita Blackwell was disturbed: Blackwell, *Barefootin',* 80–81.

102 At Spelman, Gwen: Fleming, *Soon We Will Not Cry,* 174–75.

103 "The best of all": Ibid., 119.

103 "The first thing you have": Lewis, *Walking with the Wind,* 83–84.

103 "She absolutely did not": Fleming, *Soon We Will Not Cry,* 95.

103 What seemed clear was: Ibid., 104.

103 Two weeks later, Ruby: Ibid., 106–7.

103 "Well, I've found out": Carson, *Silent Voices,* 253. (Carson, who changed the names of the women she interviewed, called Ruby Doris "Sarah.")

104 "He's crazy but he's": Olson, *Freedom's Daughters,* 211.

104 "Since my child": Zinn, *SNCC,* 106.

104 Bevel's compulsive infidelity: Halberstam, *The Children,* 682.

104 By September, there had been eighty: Lewis, *Walking with the Wind,* 274.

104 But the enormous influx: The demographics come from Doug McAdam's *Freedom Summer.*

104 When Penny Patch, a longtime: Penny Patch, "Sweet Tea at Shoney's," 155.

105 "Our skills and abilities": Olson, *Freedom's Daughters,* 310.

105 Things weren't helped: Fleming, *Soon We Will Not Cry,* 137.

105 Dr. Alvin Poussaint, who studied: Ibid., 128.

105 Chuck McDew, a black: Ibid., 132–33.

105 How could the veteran: McAdam, *Freedom Summer,* 103.

105 The white volunteers themselves: Ibid., 150.

105 Although most of the women: Ibid., 110.

105 One of the few young white: Jo Freeman, "On the Origins of the Women's Liberation Movement," in *The Feminist Memoir Project,* 174.

105 Many of the new arrivals: Curry, *Deep in Our Hearts,* 269.

106 Susan Brownmiller, a white: Brownmiller, *In Our Time,* 12.

106 "It had the appearances of a necking party": Unless otherwise noted, this section is based on *From Selma to Sorrow* by Mary Stanton.

106 Leroy Moton, a black volunteer: Branch, *At Canaan's Edge,* 174.

107 Unita Blackwell was also: Blackwell, *Barefootin',* 96.

107 FBI chief J. Edgar: Branch, *At Canaan's Edge,* 177.

108 A poll by *Ladies' Home Journal:* Lyn Tornabene, "Murder in Alabama," *Ladies' Home Journal,* July 1965.

108 Sandra "Casey" Hayden, a longtime: Olson, *Freedom's Daughters,* 334.

108 In an interview in 1995: Ransby, *Ella Baker and the Black Freedom Movement,* 310.

109 "I am not fighting": Mills, *This Little Light of Mine,* 248.

109 Shortly before her death: Olson, *Freedom's Daughters*, 369–70.

7. THE DECLINE OF THE DOUBLE STANDARD

Interviews: Pam Andrews, Barbara Arnold, Josie Bass, Nora Ephron, Alison Foster, Kathy Hinderhofer, Tawana Hinton, Maria K., June LaValleur, Grace (Linda) LeClair, Ellen Miller, Marie Monsky, Georgia Panter Nielsen, Cynthia Pearson, Judy Riff, Carol Rumsey, Laura Sessions Stepp, Louise Meyer Warpness, Wendy Woythaler.

115 In 1968 the *New York Times:* Judy Klemesrud, "An Arrangement: Living Together for Convenience, Security, Sex," *New York Times*, March 4, 1968.

115 The *Times*, which had been: Deirdre Carmody, "Barnard President Delays Action on Defiant Girl," *New York Times*, May 9, 1968; Kathleen Teltsch, "Grades Are Key in LeClair Case," *New York Times*, May 17, 1968.

116 On her arrival, LeClair: Deirdre Carmody, "Coed Disciplined by College Becomes a Dropout at Barnard," *New York Times*, September 4, 1968.

117 "Now don't turn": "J," *The Sensuous Woman*, 116.

117 "A man will go": "Shaping the '60s... Foreshadowing the '70s," 30.

117 In 1961 *Ladies' Home Journal:* Betsy Marvin McKinney, "Is the Double Standard Out of Date?" *Ladies' Home Journal*, May 1961, 10, 12.

118 "far from being a creature": Brown, *Sex and the Single Girl*, 3.

118 "Her world is a far more colorful": Ibid., 4.

118 "You do need a man": Ibid., 2.

118 "brainy, charming, and sexy": Ibid., 1.

118 "And when he finally walked": Ibid.

119 American Medical Association accused him: Allyn, *Make Love, Not War*, 17.

119 a minister visiting: Treckel, *To Comfort the Heart*, 109.

119 In 1972 a survey: Chafe, *Women and Equality*, 122.

120 "I probably wouldn't have": Klemesrud, "An Arrangement."

120 "It is a ridiculous": "Connecticut Retains Ban on Contraceptives," *New York Times*, May 29, 1953.

120 "Her martinis were always": Roraback, "Women and the Connecticut Bar."

121 "If they do that": Asbell, *The Pill*, 239.

121 Griswold and Buxton were given: "Dr. C. L. Buxton, Who Won Fight on Birth Control Ban, Is Dead," *New York Times*, July 8, 1969.

122 But only 4 percent: Watkins, *On the Pill*, 41.

123 "Remember, all of us": Ibid., 109.

123 a Gallup survey found that: Ibid., 115.

123 Gradually, the amount of estrogen: Asbell, *The Pill*, 309.

123 Surgeons removed reproductive organs: Barker-Benfield, *The Horrors of the Half-Known Life*, 120–32.

123 Susan Ford, whose mother: Greene, *Betty Ford*, 50.

124 When 23-year-old: Barbara Winslow, "Primary and Secondary Contradictions in Seattle," in *The Feminist Memoir Project*, 166.

124 Nora Ephron wrote that: Ephron, *Crazy Salad*, 56.

124 By 1975 nearly two thousand: Mann, "Women's Health Research Blossoms."

124 The experts did not: Ehrenreich, *Re-Making Love*, 51.

124 In a 1957 article: Cancian and Gordon, "Changing Emotion Norms in Marriage," 321.

125 Even Helen Gurley Brown, so eager: Brown, *Sex and the Single Girl*, 64.

125 And less than half of married: George Gallup and Evan Hill, "The American Woman," *Saturday Evening Post*, December 22, 1962, 17.

125 Jane Alpert, a high school: Alpert, *Growing Up Underground*, 42.

125 It was no wonder: Ehrenreich, *The Hearts of Men*, 45.

125 In 1970 "Myth of the Vaginal Orgasm": Baxandall and Gordon, *Dear Sisters*, 158.

125 Nora Ephron, reporting on: Ephron, *Crazy Salad*, 55.

126 There was, recalled Anselma: Anselma Dell'Olio, "Home Before Sundown," in *The Feminist Memoir Project*, 166.

126 A letter writer to the *Times:* "TV Mailbag—Dear Jane: Shave," *New York Times*, April 29, 1973.

127 "The whole idea of homosexuality": Friedan, *Life So Far*, 221.

127 When Martha Peterson, the Barnard: Dennis Hevesi, "Martha Peterson, 90, Barnard President in Vietnam Era, Dies," *New York Times*, July 20, 2006.

127 When *Ms.* began: Farrell, *Yours in Sisterhood*, 34.

127 *Time*, which had put: "Women's Lib: A Second Look," *Time*, December 14, 1970.

128 By 1970 the editors: Gene Damon, "The Least of These: The Minority Whose Screams Haven't Yet Been Heard," in *Sisterhood Is Powerful*, 298.

128 "Run, reader, run right": Ibid., 297–98.

129 "Every Sunday when my": Rimmer, *The Harrad Experiment*, 303.

129 "Certainly it was": Priscilla Long, "We Called Ourselves Sisters," in *The Feminist Memoir Project*.

129 "I considered their": Alpert, *Growing Up Underground*, 34–35.

129 At the time, one: Allyn, *Make Love, Not War*, 103.

129 "The invention of the Pill": Morgan, *Sisterhood Is Powerful*, xxxi.

129 Gloria Steinem wrote: Allyn, *Make Love, Not War*, 104.

8. WOMEN'S LIBERATION

Interviews: Nora Ephron, Muriel Fox, Jo Freeman, Maria K., Robin Morgan, Georgia Panter Nielsen, Sylvia Peterson, Vicki Cohn Pollard, Margaret Siegel, Gloria Steinem, Laura Sessions Stepp, Amy Swerdlow, Wendy Woythaler.

135 who promised to refer it: Marjorie Hunter, "5,000 Women Rally in Capital Against War," *New York Times*, January 16, 1968.

135 Grumbling about lawmakers: Ibid.

135 Beating on drums: Firestone, "The Jeannette Rankin Brigade."

136 It was, Swerdlow thought: Swerdlow, *Women Strike for Peace*, 139.

136 "This is not a bedroom": Carroll, *It Seemed Like Nothing Happened*, 34.

137 "By today's standards": Jo Freeman, "On the Origins of the Women's Liberation Movement," in *The Feminist Memoir Project*, 179–80.

137 After that meeting: Brownmiller, *In Our Time*, 18.

137 In a famous remark: Evans, *Personal Politics*, 160.

138 Seattle women were: Barbara Winslow, "Primary and Secondary Contradictions in Seattle," in *The Feminist Memoir Project*, 244.

138 "What I have seen": Vivian Estellachild, "Hippie Communes," in *Dear Sisters*, 225.

138 A few reached out: Brownmiller, *In Our Time*, 18.

138 At the Washington rally: Echols, *Daring to Be Bad*, 114–20.

138 "Was it my brother": Robin Morgan, "Goodbye to All That," in *Dear Sisters*, 53–55.

139 At least one in: Rosalyn Baxandall, "Catching the Fire," in *The Feminist Memoir Project*, 214.

140 the writer Jane: O'Reilly, *The Girl I Left Behind*, 23.

140 Catherine Roraback was 49: Roraback, "Women and the Connecticut Bar."

140 "The history we learned": Morgan, *Sisterhood Is Powerful*, xv.

140 "Women are an oppressed": Baxandall and Gordon, *Dear Sisters*, 90–91.

141 "We take the woman's": Ibid., 34.

141 "No one article": Morgan, *Sisterhood Is Powerful*, xviii.

141 In March 1968: Martha Weinman Lear, "The Second Feminist Wave," *New York Times Magazine*, March 10, 1968.

141 *Washington Post* put its membership: Elizabeth Shelton, "Women's Group Split Over Meaning of Feminism," *Washington Post*, October 24, 1968.

141 When Solanas was arraigned: Marylin Bender, "Valeria Solanas a Heroine to Feminists," *New York Times*, June 14, 1968.

141 Jacqui Ceballos, another NOW: Jacqui Ceballos, president of the Veteran Feminists of America, e-mail, April 6, 2008.

142 The whole episode: Paterson, *Be Somebody*, 183, 190.

142 "We protest," read: "No More Miss America," in *Dear Sisters*, 184.

142 Female passersby, Morgan: Morgan, *Saturday's Child*, 261.

142 A few demonstrators: Brownmiller, *In Our Time*, 40.

143 However, a sympathetic: Ibid., 37.

143 Morgan herself called: Morgan, *Saturday's Child*, 259.

143 "Heartfelt and handwritten": Brownmiller, *In Our Time*, 137.

143 Rosalyn Baxandall, looking: Baxandall, "Catching the Fire," 212.

143 Barbara Epstein, a graduate: Barbara Epstein, "Ambivalence About Feminism," in *The Feminist Memoir Project*, 125.

143 By the end of 1969: Cohen, *The Sisterhood*, 168.

143 "We were considered": Noun, *More Strong-Minded Women*, 88.

143 In a more fanciful: Ibid., 22.

144 "Any time a group": Thom, *Inside Ms.*, 4.

144 its first issue sold: Ibid., 24.

144 Madeleine Kunin, the would-be: Kunin, *Living a Political Life*, 92–93.

144 who demanded to know: Cohen, *The Sisterhood*, 191.

144 The protesters unveiled: Brownmiller, *In Our Time*, 89–91.

144 Susan Brownmiller reported: Ibid.

145 the magazine said 34 percent: Rosen, *The World Split Open*, 301.

145 When field officers: Heilbrun, *The Education of a Woman*, 281.

145 One FBI report: Levine and Lyons, *The Decade of Women*, 29.

146 Betty Friedan once claimed: Friedan, *Life So Far*, 224.

146 She was quoted: Paul Wilkes, "Mother Superior to Women's Lib," *New York Times*, November 29, 1970.

146 "New York's Newest": Heilbrun, *The Education of a Woman*, 121.

146 "The miniskirted pinup girl": Ibid., 144.

146 childbearing, which Ti-Grace Atkinson called: Atkinson, *Amazon Odyssey*, 5.

146 Steinem would say: Cohen, *The Sisterhood*, 322.

146 "I knew that if": Evans, *Personal Politics*, 227–28.

146 She spent an eighth-grade: Steinem, *Outrageous Acts and Everyday Rebellions*, 149.

147 "What Gloria needs": Heilbrun, *The Education of a Woman*, 193.

147 In 1927 a *Harper's* essay: Dorothy Dunbar Bromley, "Feminist—New Style," *Harper's*, October 1927.

147 "I did not agree with the message": Friedan, *Life So Far*, 190.

147 She urged her followers: Carroll, *It Seemed Like Nothing Happened*, 36.

147 Roxanne Dunbar, a radical: Roxanne Dunbar, "Outlaw Woman," in *The Feminist Memoir Project*, 105.

147 Trapped in an interview: Heilbrun, *The Education of a Woman*, 213.

148 "Every so often, someone": Ephron, *Crazy Salad*, 45.

148 Ti-Grace Atkinson's breakaway: Elizabeth Shelton, "Women's Group Split Over Meaning of Feminism," *Washington Post*, October 24, 1968.

148 "I'm not hung up on": Bernice Johnson Reagon, "Women as Culture Carriers in the Civil Rights Movement: Fannie Lou Hamer," in *Women in the Civil Rights Movement*, 213.

148 "Blacks are oppressed": Giddings, *When and Where I Enter*, 308.

148 *Essence* magazine in 1970: Olson, *Freedom's Daughters*, 377.

148 "As a black person": Hicks, *The Honorable Shirley Chisholm*, 84.

148 Chisholm, who became: Freeman, *Women*, 352.

149 On Strike Day itself: Friedan, *Life So Far*, 238–39.

149 Later, at the postmarch: Friedan, *It Changed My Life*, 195.

149 A West Virginia senator: Douglas, *Where the Girls Are*, 163.

149 "It's the funniest thing": Paterson, *Be Somebody*, 198.

150 "We put sex discrimination": Evans, *Tidal Wave*, 67.

150 Roxanne Conlin, who was assistant: Noun, *More Strong-Minded Women*, 125–26.

150 Amelia Fry, a historian: Fry, "Conversations with Alice Paul," xvi–xvii.

150 "Keep the law": Hole and Levine, *Rebirth of Feminism*, 69.

150 At the same time: Paterson, *Be Somebody*, 210.

9 · BACKLASH

Interviews: Sherri Finkbine Chessen, Jo Freeman, Kathy Hinderhofer, Pat Lorance, Robin Morgan, Gloria Steinem, Janet Tegley, Anne Tolstoi Wallach, Louise Meyer Warpness.

159 "She's 92": Dee Wedemeyer, "A Salute to Originator of ERA in 1923," *New York Times*, January 10, 1977.

159 But when a delegation: Janet Tegley, unpublished data.

159 In a birthday interview: Wedemeyer, "A Salute to Originator of ERA in 1923."

160 Married women with a college: Coontz, *Marriage*, 253.

160 "Mothers are the immediate": Dworkin, *Right-Wing Women*, 15.

160 ERA opponents reprinted: Critchlow, *Phyllis Schlafly and Grassroots Conservatism*, 229.

160 By 1974 a consumer's: Carroll, *It Seemed Like Nothing Happened*, 132.

161 Anselma Dell'Olio, who spent: Anselma Dell'Olio, "Home Before Sundown," in *The Feminist Memoir Project*, 166.

161 By the end of the decade: "Changes in Men's and Women's Labor Force Participation," Bureau of Labor Statistics, January 10, 2007.

161 The median income: Coontz, *Marriage*, 258.

161 Patricia Lorance worked at a plant: Pat Lorance's story is based on material in Susan Faludi's *Backlash*, 393–99, and an interview with Lorance.

162 Men told surveyors: Mansbridge, *Why We Lost the ERA*, 23.

162 A National Opinion Research Center: Ibid., 21.

163 A tireless speaker: Critchlow, *Phyllis Schlafly and Grassroots Conservatism*, 141.

163 "I'd drive out": Ginia Bellafante, "At Home with—Phyllis Schlafly; A Feminine Mystique All Her Own," *New York Times*, March 30, 2006.

163 "I think what Phyllis": Elizabeth Kolbert, "Firebrand," *The New Yorker*, November 7, 2005.

164 Many years later, Schlafly: Bellafante, "At Home with—Phyllis Schlafly."

164 "The conservative movement": Michael Murphy, "Conservative Pioneer Became an Outcast," *Arizona Republic*, May 31, 1998.

164 through the "Christian tradition of chivalry," Critchlow, *Phyllis Schlafly and Grassroots Conservatism*, 218.

164 Dr. Benjamin Spock eliminated: Schlafly, *The Power of the Positive Woman*, 27.

165 "I was invited": Felsenthal, *Phyllis Schlafly*, 56.

165 "Household duties": Schlafly, *The Power of the Positive Woman*, 31.

166 "I'd like to burn": Kolbert, "Firebrand."

166 "These people pull at you": Mansbridge, *Why We Lost the ERA*, 146.

167 Some polls showed: Gorney, *Articles of Faith*, 51.

168 "For my first abortion": Brownmiller, *In Our Time*, 104.

168 "I had had an abortion": Steinem, *Outrageous Acts and Everyday Rebellions*, 20.

168 New York, however, was: This section is based on three articles by Bill Kovach in the *New York Times:* "Abortion Reform Approved, 31–26, by State Senate," March 19, 1970; "Abortion Reform Is Voted By the Assembly, 76–73," April 10, 1970; and "Two Key Backers of Abortion Reform in the Legislature Are Defeated Upstate," June 24, 1970.

169 In the first year: Gorney, *Articles of Faith*, 97.

169 "a pregnant street person": McCorvey, *I Am Roe*, 117.

169 "I discovered that if": Ibid., 126.

169 Their combined ages: Gorney, *Articles of Faith*, 154.

170 By the end of the 1970s: "The Fanatical Abortion Fight," *Time*, July 9, 1979.

170 Mary Crisp, the cochair: Douglas Martin, "Mary D. Crisp, 83, Feminist GOP Leader, Dies," *New York Times*, April 17, 2007.

170 Betty Boyer of Ohio: Paterson, *Be Somebody*, 186.

170 "Abortion was about": Noun, *More Strong-Minded Women*, 83.

170 The debate, Representative Barbara Jordan said: Rogers, *Barbara Jordan*, 259–60.

170 "As someone who has loved": Critchlow, *Phyllis Schlafly and Grassroots Conservatism*, 246.

171 "I thought we had it made": Noun, *More Strong-Minded Women*, 172.

171 Miami-Dade County had been: Richard Steele, "A 'No' to the Gays," *Newsweek*, June 20, 1977.

171 "Since homosexuals cannot reproduce": "Maybe There's Something in the Juice," *Time*, February 28, 1994.

171 *Newsweek* reported that a lesbian: Steele, "A 'No' to the Gays."

171 A few years later: Cathleen McGuigan, "Newsmakers," *Newsweek*, November 24, 1980.

171 "It became much more difficult": Barbara Epstein, "Ambivalence About Feminism," in *The Feminist Memoir Project*, 147.

172 "Life felt good": Vivian Gornick, "What Feminism Means to Me," in *The Feminist Memoir Project*, 373–75.

172 "There was such anxiety": Linda Greenhouse, "Defeat of Equal Rights Bill Traced to Women's Votes," *New York Times*, November 6, 1975.

172 One widely distributed: Linda Greenhouse, "What Happens to ERA Now?" *New York Times*, November 9, 1975.

172 "I can't predict": Carroll, *It Seemed Like Nothing Happened*, 271.

10. "YOU'RE GONNA MAKE IT AFTER ALL"

Interviews: Sylvia Acevedo, Suzan Johnson Cook, Barbara Crossette, Maria K., Wilma Mankiller, Sylvia Peterson, Lynn Povich, Pat Schroeder, Gloria Steinem, Gloria Vaz, Betsy Wade, Diane Watson.

177 "You walk into a meeting": Levine and Lyons, *The Decade of Women*, 226.

177 "Helen, are you": Ibid., 206.

178 when Ruth Bader Ginsburg applied: Anderson, *The Movement and the Sixties*, 339.

178 The arbiters of fashion: Brownmiller, *In Our Time*, 4.

178 Jane O'Reilly, recalling: O'Reilly, *The Girl I Left Behind*, 112–13.

178 A "Stamp Out": Baxandall and Gordon, *Dear Sisters*, 40.

178 A fashion report: Marylin Bender, "As Hemlines Go Up, Up, Up, Heels Go Down, Down, Down," *New York Times*, January 27, 1966.

178 And by the end: Nina Hyde, "Grown-Up Glamour," *Washington Post*, May 1, 1978.

178 Wilma Rudolph, a poor: See Rudolph, *Wilma*.

179 "There was no doubt": "The Fastest Female," *Time*, September 19, 1960.

179 the first time "in Clarksville's": Rudolph, *Wilma*, 143.

179 Altha Cleary, who attended: "Sports News," United Press International, December 14, 1980.

179 In 1966 Roberta: John Powers, "Going Route in '66," *Boston Globe*, April 13, 2007.

179 The next year, Kathrine: John Powers, "In '67, Switzer Was 'Magellan' in Sweats," *Boston Globe*, April 13, 2007; Tony Chamberlain, "Feet First," *Boston Globe*, April 16, 2006.

179 "Little girl, you can't": Unless otherwise noted, the section on Billie Jean King is based on *A Necessary Spectacle* by Selena Roberts.

180 "I want her": Selena Roberts, "Tennis's Other Battle of the Sexes," *New York Times*, August 21, 2005.

180 "She won't admit it": "How Bobby Riggs Runs and Talks, Talks, Talks," *Time*, September 10, 1973.

180 ABC paid: Ibid.

181 "I thought it would": Larry Schwartz, "Billie Jean Won for All Women," ESPN.com.

181 "Because of Billie Jean alone": Curry Kirkpatrick, "There She Is, Ms. America," *Sports Illustrated*, October 1, 1973.

181 In Cedar Rapids: Noun, *More Strong-Minded Women*, 77.

181 The women at the University of Kansas: Cindy Luis, "Title IX," *Honolulu Star-Bulletin*, June 2, 2002.

181 Jane L., a ninth-grade: Levine and Lyons, *The Decade of Women*, 71.

181 the sum total of women's: This information was provided by the Women's Sports Foundation.

181 Senator Daniel Patrick Moynihan wrote: Blumenthal, *Let Me Play*, 100.

181 Since an average Big Ten: Cahn, *Coming on Strong*, 250.

182 When Congresswoman Pat: Schroeder, *24 Years of House Work*, 37.

182 Thanks to Title IX: Solomon, *In the Company of Educated Women*, 204.

182 The number of girls playing: Bailey and Farber, *America in the '70s*, 108.

182 The Cedar Rapids Women's Caucus: Noun, *More Strong-Minded Women*, 78.

182 "Second-class citizenship": Cahn, *Coming on Strong*, 251.

182 In 1974 Kathryn: Levine and Lyons, *The Decade of Women*, 14.

182 Billie Jean King was the winner: Roberts, *A Necessary Spectacle*, 66.

183 And, of course, there was: Levine and Thom, *Bella Abzug*.

183 When Chisholm was appointed: Rick Hampson, "Shirley Chisholm Hoping to Be Remembered as Having 'Guts,'" Associated Press, February 12, 1982.

184 Millicent Fenwick, the inimitable: For background, see Amy Schapiro's *Millicent Fenwick: Her Way*.

184 She managed to have: Couric, *Women Lawyers*, 193.

184 Molly Ivins, the great: Ivins, *Molly Ivins Can't Say That*, 18.

185 "The whole world adopted": This section is based on Pat Schroeder's *24 Years of House Work...And the Place Is Still a Mess*.

185 In 1971 there were only: Cox, *Women State and Territorial Legislators*, 328.

186 One afternoon in 1972: Kunin, *Living a Political Life*, 38.

186 When some of them were invited: Ibid., 117.

186 In 1974 Kunin went: Ibid., 182.

187 "To our ear, it still": William Safire, "On Language: Good-bye Sex, Hello Gender," *New York Times Magazine*, August 5, 1984.

187 In the same year: Georgia Dullea, "Birthday Celebration: Gloria Steinem at 50," *New York Times*, May 24, 1984.

187 In 1986 Paula Kassell: Betsy Wade, "Paula Kassell Always Took Women in New Directions," *Women's eNews*, December 6, 2002.

188 After a childhood on Cherokee: This is based on Wilma Mankiller's autobiography, *Mankiller*.

188 "I was so excited": Roraback, "Women and the Connecticut Bar."

188 "In my criminal law": Feigen, *Not One of the Boys*, 5–6.

188 "I liked it right away": The section on women in the skilled-trade unions is based on Jane LaTour's *Sisters in the Brotherhoods*.

190 Their battles began with Eulalie: Barry, *Femininity in Flight*, 162–63.

191 In another case in Miami: Ibid., 167.

191 In 1971 National Airlines: Ibid., 176–84.

191 "In professional terms": Robertson, *The Girls in the Balcony*, 101.

192 At the *New York Times*, the last: Ibid., 133.

193 The women at *Reader's:* Ibid., 209.

11. WORK AND CHILDREN

Interviews: Barbara Arnold, Dana Arthur-Monteleone, Myrna Ten Bensel, John Brademas, Pat Buchanan, Jack Duncan, Alison Foster, Maria K., Faith Middleton, Walter Mondale, Martha Phillips, Vicki Cohn Pollard, Virginia Williams.

199 "They sure do": Felicity Barringer deconstructed this episode, "The Pancake Mix," in the *New York Times*, October 9, 1994.

199 In 1960, 62 percent: Coontz, *The Way We Really Are*, 37.

199 By the middle of the '80s: U.S. Census, Married Couples by Labor Force Status of Spouses, 1986 to the Present.

199 The competition of: Coontz, *Marriage*, 259.

199 In 1977 *BusinessWeek*: Strasser, *Never Done*, 301.

199 While in 1970: Beth Bailey, "She 'Can Bring Home the Bacon,'" in *America in the '70s*, 109.

199 the government would note: Monthly Vital Statistics Report, National Center for Health Statistics, June 27, 1983.

200 by 1976 the number of divorces: Ted Gest, "Divorce: How the Game Is Played Now," *U.S. News and World Report*, November 21, 1983, 39.

200 "It's healthy for the": Ibid.

200 "At that time we were": Friedan, *It Changed My Life*, 415.

200 In California, the average: Lenore Weitzman, "No-Fault Divorce," *U.S. News and World Report*, November 4, 1985, 63.

200 One study found that: Susan Faludi, *Backlash*, 24.

201 Minnette Doderer, who was: Noun, *More Strong-Minded Women*, 166.

201 Lenore Weitzman, a sociologist: Weitzman, "No-Fault Divorce," 63.

201 "My rage centers": Leslie Bennetts, "Displaced Homemakers," *New York Times*, June 15, 1979.

201 The census-takers counted: Lynne M. Casper et al., "How Does POSSLQ Measure Up?" U.S. Bureau of the Census, May 1999.

202 They were right: Faludi, *Backlash*, 16.

202 At Harvard Medical: Klass, *A Not Entirely Benign Procedure*, 33.

202 In 1976, for the first: Lawrence Feinberg, "Half of Black Children Born to Unmarried Women," *Washington Post*, May 4, 1978.

202 it was not until 1968 that the Supreme Court: *Levy v. Louisiana*.

204 "My friends are": O'Reilly, *The Girl I Left Behind*, 9.

204 "I knew that I wanted": Vicki Cohn Pollard, "The Five of Us," in *Dear Sisters*, 222–24.

204 Robin Morgan, living: Morgan, *Saturday's Child*, 232.

204 The estimates of the number: Miller, *The Hippies and American Values*, 88.

205 the thirty-member New World: Noun, *More Strong-Minded Women*, 71.

205 It had been discussed: For more information on this subject, see *The Grand Domestic Revolution* by Dolores Hayden.

205 "The meal is as expensive": Bellamy, *Looking Backward*, 101.

205 "What would shoes be like": Ceplair, *Charlotte Perkins Gilman*, 129–30.

206 Madeleine Kunin, whose political: Kunin, *Living a Political Life*, 113.

207 Actually, the child-care: Cohen, "A Brief History of Federal Financing."

208 One reporter noted, in wonder: Chamberlin, *A Minority of Members*, 317.

208 "Seldom does a bill": Robert Signer, "Child Services Bills Stir Storm," *Chicago Daily News*, March 27, 1976.

208 One letter writer: Judith Miller, "Someone Out There Hates Day Care," *Harper's Weekly*, March 22, 1976, 83.

209 they created such a stir: Richard Fly, "How 'Rights' Letter Came to Houston," *Houston Chronicle*, November 9, 1975.

12. THE 1980S — HAVING IT ALL

Interviews: Sylvia Acevedo, Lynnette Arthur, Sherri Finkbine Chessen, April Chisholm, Suzan Johnson Cook, Jean Enersen, Yana Shani Fleming, Alison Foster, Lillian Garland, Tawana Hinton, Tiffany Hinton, Camara Dia Holloway, June LaValleur, Jo Meyer Maasberg, Wilma Mankiller, Linda Mason, Annie Miller, Ellen Miller, Elizabeth Patterson, Jennifer Maasberg Smith, Laura Sessions Stepp, Randi Weingarten.

216 *Mademoiselle*, which had: Annie Gottlieb, "Do Men Love Women Who Love Work?" *Mademoiselle*, February 1981.

216 A study prepared for: "Poll Finds New View of Women," *Washington Star*, January 6, 1981.

216 A third of the law students: "Law Colleges Add Women as Students," *New York Times*, January 6, 1981.

216 The stubborn gap: Blau, "Trends in the Well-Being of American Women," 129.

216 *Cosmopolitan*, in a welcome: Ruth Franklin, "The '80s Woman — Her Man, Her Job, Her Life," *Cosmopolitan*, November 1980.

216 Ellen Baer, an associate: Ellen Baer, "The Feminist Disdain for Nursing," *New York Times*, February 23, 1991.

216 A Gallup poll showed 88: "In a Poll, Many Women Say Life Is Good," *New York Times*, August 25, 1988.

216 "It really blew": Whittier, *Feminist Generations*, 144.

216 John Molloy, a "wardrobe": Susan Faludi tells the suit story in *Backlash*.

217 A report on the 1985: Jane Mingay, "The High-Style Shoulder," *Maclean's*, May 6, 1985.

217 "We're trying to be": Jennet Conant, "Hold On to Those Hems," *Newsweek*, April 27, 1987.

217 "Shoes have become": Angela Taylor, "Far from the Classic Pump," *New York Times*, August 30, 1983.

217 "When blue jeans": Brownmiller, *Femininity*, 80.

218 Fonda had taken: Kagan and Morse, "The Body Electronic," 164–80.

218 "If you want to trace": Jane Leavy, "Jane Fonda, Good as Old," *Washington Post*, January 26, 1985.

218 The American Society of Plastic: Faludi, *Backlash*, 217.

218 In 1982 the country heard about: "Four Pounds Imperiling Job of a Drum Major," Associated Press, September 26, 1982; "Twirler Fails by 1½ Pounds," Associated Press, September 30, 1982.

218 The average American woman: Faludi, *Backlash*, 171.

218 By the late '80s, there were estimates: Brumberg, *Fasting Girls*, 12.

220 In 1943 the sociologist: Komarovsky, *Women in College*, 91.

220 Striving for "it all": Joe Hagan, "They Fired the Most Powerful Woman on Wall Street," *New York Magazine*, May 5, 2008, 36.

220 While pay for women: Blau, "Trends in the Well-Being of American Women," 130.

220 For the first time, more than half: "Mothers with Babies — And Jobs," *New York Times*, June 19, 1988.

221 But that extra effort: Blau, "Trends in the Well-Being of American Women," 152.

221 In her book *The Second Shift*: Hochschild, *The Second Shift*, 4.

221 In one of the most: Claudia Wallis, "Onward, Women!" *Time*, December 4, 1989.

221 In 1983 the *New York Times*: Georgia Dullea, "When Parents Work on Different Shifts," *New York Times*, October 31, 1983.

221 Harriet Presser, a professor: "Child Care Hassles Cause Birth Decline," *Los Angeles Times*, August 5, 1987.

222 But by 1987 the Bureau: Pamela Mendels, "The Stigma Facing Mommies," *Newsday*, March 27, 1989.

222 The columnist Ellen: Rosen, *The World Split Open*, 327.

222 When she won: Kunin, *Living a Political Life*, 244.

222 Kunin's husband, a doctor: Ibid., 199.

223 Perri Klass, who'd had: Klass, *A Not Entirely Benign Procedure*, 132–33.

223 In 1980 half of American: Komarovsky, *Women in College*, 4.

223 the place where, the *New York Times*: Chafe, *The American Woman*, 243.

224 The number of people: Coontz, *Marriage*, 258.

224 In 1981, in *The Second*: Friedan, *The Second Stage*, quoted in Faludi, *Backlash*, 324.

224 A headline for *New York Magazine*: Patricia Morrisroe, "Born Too Late? Expect Too Much? Then You May Be…FOREVER SINGLE," *New York Magazine*, August 20, 1984.

224 In 1986 a Yale: Faludi, *Backlash*, 9–14.

224 *Newsweek*'s cover showed: Eloise Salholz, "The Marriage Crunch," *Newsweek*, June 2, 1986.

224 As time went on: Felicity Barringer, "Marriage Study That Caused Furor Is Revised," *New York Times*, November 11, 1989.

224 In fact, the career-driven: Faludi, *Backlash*, 15.

224 It was as if the world: Ibid.

224 At one point, Johnson: Cook, *A New Dating Attitude*, 22–23.

225 The national fertility rate: Faludi, *Backlash*, 34.

225 The fertility rate for: Robert Pear, "Sharp Rise in Childbearing Found Among U.S. Women in Early Thirties," *New York Times*, June 10, 1983.

225 Among women who graduated: Goldin and Katz, "Transitions."

225 When Perri Klass got pregnant: Klass, *A Not Entirely Benign Procedure*, 44.

226 In 1982 *Time*: J. D. Reed, "The New Baby Bloom," *Time*, February 22, 1982.

226 Georgia Dullea of the *New York Times*: Georgia Dullea, "Women Reconsider Childbearing over 30," *New York Times*, February 25, 1982.

226 A government study reported: "Infertility Increases in Young Women," United Press International in the *New York Times*, February 10, 1983.

226 There were 2: Kathleen Doheny, "A Boom for In Vitro Fertilization," *Los Angeles Times*, August 7, 1990.

226 When word came that Whitehead: Barbara Kantrowitz, "Who Keeps Baby M?" *Newsweek*, January 19, 1987.

226 Whitehead's lawyer said the baby: Richard Lacayo, "Is the Womb a Rentable Space?" *Time*, September 22, 1986.

226 The Sterns' lawyer played: Mary Shaughnessy, "All for Love of a Baby," *People*, March 23, 1987.

226 "I will never feel": Katha Pollitt, "Contracts and Apple Pie," *The Nation*, May 23, 1987.

226 "Bill and I": "The Life and Custody of Baby M," *Maclean's*, April 13, 1987.

226 who legally adopted: "Now It's Melissa's Time," *New Jersey Monthly*, March 2007.

227 "It was only later": Tamar Lewin, "Partnership in Firm Awarded to Victim of Sex Bias," *New York Times*, May 16, 1990.

228 In 1982 Christine: Unless otherwise noted, this section is based on information in *An Anchorwoman's Story* by Christine Craft.

228 The station claimed the focus group: "Is She a Mutt?" *New York Times*, August 11, 1983.

228 "I have the strong": "New Face of TV News First Seen in the '70s," *Washington Post*, July 23, 2006.

228 "Harry Reasoner didn't want": Virginia Heffernan, "Barbara Walters: The Exit Interview," *New York Times*, September 5, 2004.

228 By the early 1980s: "Television: Keep Young and Beautiful," *The Economist*, August 13, 1983.

229 "The Revolution Is Over": John Leo, "The Revolution Is Over," *Time*, April 19, 1984, 74–78.

229 By the mid-1980s: Faludi, *Backlash*, 30–31.

230 It was, *Time* said: Claudia Wallis, "The New Scarlet Letter," *Time*, August 2, 1982.

230 Near panic ensued: Susan Duerksen, "Millions Must Revise Sex Habits," *San Diego Union-Tribune*, November 7, 1986.

230 In 1981 *Newsweek* announced: Harry Waters, "Television's Hottest Show," *Newsweek*, September 28, 1981.

230 Laura (played by): Readers who want to experience this particular moment of TV history can find it on YouTube.

230 "Rape me": Eric Gelman, "A Perfect Couple," *Newsweek*, September 28, 1981.

230 There had been a great: Brownmiller, *Against Our Will*, 15.

231 Susan Estrich, a Harvard: Estrich, *Real Rape*.

231 On the other side: Katie Roiphe, "Date Rape's Other Victim," *New York Times*, June 24, 1993.

232 In that poll for: "Poll Finds New View of Women," *Washington Star*, January 6, 1981.

232 Ferraro, who was: William Safire, "On Language: Good-bye Sex, Hello Gender," *New York Times Magazine*, August 5, 1984.

232 "Fathers brought their": Kunin, *Living a Political Life*, 306.

232 "Because our tribe": Mankiller, *Mankiller*, 240.

233 "It must be a secretarial": Unless otherwise noted, this section is based on information from *Sandra Day O'Connor* by Joan Biskupic.

234 She took exercise classes: Toobin, *The Nine*, 39.

234 made Sandra Day O'Connor into a jurist: Ibid., 87.

13. THE 1990S — SETTLING FOR LESS?

Interviews: Sylvia Acevedo, Lynnette Arthur, Dana Arthur-Monteleone, Alison Foster, Kathy Hinderhofer, Camara Dia Holloway, Dena Ivey, June LaValleur, Jo Meyer Maasberg, Linda Mason, Jennifer Maasberg Smith, Alex Dery Snider, Laura Sessions Stepp.

241 "I must have been": AnnJanette Rosga, "Notes from the Aftermath," in *The Feminist Memoir Project*, 472–73.

241 "The things I fought": Claudia Wallis, "Onward Women!" *Time*, December 4, 1989.

241 "We don't feel": Farrell, *Yours in Sisterhood*, 105.

242 The cost of college: Coontz, *The Way We Really Are*, 57.

242 Married women who worked: Ibid., 57.

242 In 1989 Felice Schwartz: Felice Schwartz, "Management Women and the New Facts of Life," *Harvard Business Review*, January 1, 1989.

242 "My points touched": Mary Sit, "Derailed by 'Mommy Track,'" *Boston Globe*, October 25, 1989.

242 By 1990, 60 percent: Cotter, "Moms and Jobs."

242 *New York Times* had not dubbed: Tamar Lewin, "'Mommy Career Track' Sets Off a Furor," *New York Times*, March 8, 1989.

242 A coalition of forty-four: Brian Couturier, "Coalition Warns Against Supporting Idea with Legislation," *Los Angeles Times*, March 23, 1989.

244 Reagan never used: Cannon, *Ronald Reagan*, 457.

244 The real Taylor: "Chicago 'Relief' Queen Guilty," Associated Press, March 19, 1977.

244 "When we started the current": "Excerpts from Debate in the Senate on the Welfare Measure," New York Times, August 2, 1996.

244 "When the original welfare": Maureen Dowd, "Washington Talk — Q&A: Daniel Patrick Moynihan," New York Times, February 19, 1987.

244 After the Civil War: Jones, Labor of Love, 58–60.

245 Jason DeParle, who had: DeParle, American Dream, 304.

245 "On welfare Angie": Ibid., 321.

245 In 1995 Norma: McCorvey, Won by Love, 242.

245 "They could have been nice": Douglas Wood, "Who Is 'Jane Roe'?" CNN, June 18, 2003.

246 Even many of the: E. J. Dionne Jr., "Struggle for Work and Family Fueling Women's Movement," New York Times, August 22, 1989.

246 The abortion rate peaked: "Facts on Induced Abortion in the United States," Guttmacher Institute, New York, January 2008.

246 Americans were most likely: Ibid.

246 In South Dakota, an antichoice: Monica Davey, "South Dakota to Revisit Restrictions on Abortions," New York Times, April 26, 2008.

246 More than a century: Collins, America's Women, 245.

246 A native of Oklahoma: Mayer and Abramson, Strange Justice, 84.

247 Time reported that although complaints: Nancy Gibbs, "The War Against Feminism," Time, March 9, 1992.

247 Changing planes in Houston: Mayer and Abramson, Strange Justice, 28.

247 A poll found that 55: Priscilla Painton, "Woman Power," Time, October 28, 1991.

247 A Pentagon report: Eric Schmitt, "Senior Navy Officers Suppressed Sex Investigation," New York Times, September 25, 1992.

247 The "commonsense guideline": Gloria Steinem, "Feminists and the Clinton Question," New York Times, March 22, 1998.

248 Senator Barbara Mikulski, for one: "Year of the Woman," senate.gov.

248 "Maybe you could find": Solaro, Women in the Line of Fire, 197.

248 In the most famous: Cornum, She Went to War.

249 It was not until 1991: Allison Askins for Knight Ridder, "Interracial Marriages on the Rise but Hurdles Remain," Times-Picayune, October 19, 1997.

249 If the country needed: Jane Gross, "In Prom Dispute, a Town's Race Divisions Emerge," New York Times, August 15, 1994.

250 Nora Ephron once joked: Ephron, Heartburn, 81.

250 In 2005 Maureen: Maureen Dowd, "What's a Modern Girl to Do?" New York Times Magazine, October 30, 2005.

251 "What most lesbians remember": Van Gelder and Brandt, The Girls Next Door, 31.

251 In the Washington Post, Kara: Kara Swisher, "We Love Lesbians. Or Do We?" Washington Post, July 18, 1993.

251 New York Magazine put K. D. Lang: Jeanie Russell Kasindorf, "Lesbian Chic," New York Magazine, May 10, 1993.

251 In a reverse case: Yvonne Abraham, "At 80 Schlafly Is Still a Conservative Force," Boston Globe, September 2, 2004.

252 Diane Salvatore, a gay: Kasindorf, "Lesbian Chic."

14. THE NEW MILLENNIUM

Interviews: Lisa Belkin, Alison Foster, Claudia Goldin, Lilly Ledbetter, Tanya Pollard, Vicki Cohn Pollard, Serena Savarirayan, Valerie Steele, Gloria Steinem, Laura Sessions Stepp, Jessica Valenti.

257 "I am the innocent": Margalit Fox, "Betty Friedan, Who Ignited Cause in Feminine Mystique, Dies at 85," New York Times, February 5, 2006.

257 Looking back, she said: Friedan, Life So Far, 375.

257 By the beginning: Jonathan Glater, "Women Are Close to Being Majority of Law Students," New York Times, March 26, 2001; Yilu Zhao, "Beyond Sweetie," New York Times, November 7, 2004.

257 They dominated some fields: Yilu Zhao, "Women Soon to Be Majority of Veterinarians," New York Times, June 9, 2002; Hacker, Mismatch, 2.

257 Forty percent of the new: Hacker, Mismatch, 2; Anderson, The Movement and the Sixties, 20.

257 More important, 40 percent: "Gender Issues: Women's Participation in the Sciences Has Increased," United States Government Accountability Office, July 2004, 3.

257 Even in the small: Goldin and Rouse, "Orchestrating Impartiality."

257 "The reality is that": Jennifer Delahunty Britz, "To All the Girls I've Rejected," New York Times, March 23, 2006.

258 Newsweek, in a cover: Peg Tyre, "The Trouble with Boys," Newsweek, January 20, 2007.

258 In Milton, Massachusetts: Elizabeth Weil, "Teaching Boys and Girls Separately," New York Times Magazine, January 20, 2008.

258 Margaret Spellings, George W. Bush's: Tyre, "The Trouble with Boys."

258 Only 17 percent: Timothy O'Brien, "Why Do So Few Women Reach the Top of Big Law Firms?" New York Times, March 19, 2006.

258 While women held nearly half: "Fortune 500 Women CEOs," Fortune, April 16, 2008.

258 More than three-quarters: David Cay Johnston, "As Salary Grows, So Does Gender Gap," New York Times, May 12, 2002.

258 By the time CBS: Paul Fahri, "Men Signing Off," Washington Post, July 23, 2006.

258 But the divide: David Leonhardt, "Scant Progress on Closing Gap in Women's Pay," New York Times, December 24, 2006.

258 The number of male: Cindy Kranz, "Higher Pay Could Attract Men to Teach, Some Say," Cincinnati Enquirer, December 23, 2008.

260 One of Ginsburg's: Linda Greenhouse, "Supreme Court Memo," New York Times, May 31, 2007.

260 A study by Andrew: Sam Roberts, "For Young Earners in Big City, a Gap in Women's Favor," New York Times, August 3, 2007.

261 By the new millennium: "We the People: Women and Men in the United States," U.S. Census Bureau, January 2005.

261 In 2009, as the recession: Catherine Rampell, "As Layoffs Surge, Women May Pass Men in Job Force," New York Times, February 6, 2009.

261 Google, the cutting-edge: Joe Nocera, "On Day Care, Google Makes a Rare Fumble," New York Times, July 5, 2008.

261 In 2008 Lisa Belkin: "When Mom and Dad Share It All," New York Times Magazine, June 15, 2008.

262 Belkin, who had a gift: Lisa Belkin, "The Opt-Out Revolution," New York Times Magazine, October 26, 2003.

263 Claudia Goldin, a Harvard: Goldin, "The Long Road to the Fast Track."

263 A follow-up study: Goldin and Katz, "Transitions."

263 And another study of graduates: Ibid.

263 In September 2005: Louise Story, "Many Women at Elite Colleges Set Career Path to Motherhood," New York Times, September 20, 2005.

263 "It really does raise": Ibid.

263 Nicholas Kulish, a 30-year-old: Kulish, "Changing the Rules for the Team Sport of Bread-Winning," New York Times, September 23, 2005.

264 In 2006 the United States: Rob Stein, "U.S. Fertility Rate Hits Thirty-five-

Year High," *Washington Post*, December 21, 2007.

264 A study at the University of Turin: Russell Shorto, "No Babies," *New York Times Magazine*, June 29, 2008.

264 "The cost of women": O'Brien, "Why Do So Few Women Reach the Top of Big Law Firms?"

264 Lisa Belkin, writing about: Belkin, "Who's Cuddly Now?"

265 slightly over half of adult: Kate Zernike, "Why Are There So Many Single Americans?" *New York Times*, January 21, 2007.

265 The percentage of women ages: "We the People," U.S. Census Bureau.

265 Of the fifty thousand: Coontz, *Marriage*, 270.

265 "I can't count": Stepp, *Unhooked*, 249.

265 But for the most part: Edin and Kefalas, *Promises I Can Keep*, 207.

265 In the late 1990s: This section is based on information in *Promises I Can Keep* by Kathryn Edin and Maria Kefalas.

265 But it was not all that great: Coontz, *The Way We Really Are*, 150.

266 In the spring of 1998: Stepp, *Unhooked*.

266 A 16-year-old boy: Alex Kuczynski, "She's Got to Be a Macho Girl," *New York Times*, November 3, 2002.

267 "I stopped wearing panty hose": Michelle Obama, interviewed on *The View*, June 18, 2008.

267 "I think people": Donna St. George, "U.S. Deaths in Iraq Mark Increased Presence," *Washington Post*, December 31, 2006.

268 Studies of female veterans: Sara Corbett, "The Women's War," *New York Times Magazine*, March 18, 2007; "Sexual Assault in Military 'Jaw-Dropping,' Lawmaker Says," CNN.com, July 31, 2008.

268 "Frankly, one of the most dangerous": Ibid.

268 Lynch's best friend in the Army: The story of Lori Piestewa is based on information from "A Wrong Turn in the Desert" by Osha Gray Davidson, *Rolling Stone*, May 27, 2004.

15. HILLARY AND SARAH . . . AND TAHITA

Interviews: Muriel Fox, Edna Kleimeyer, Gerald McBeath, George McGovern, Himilce Novas, Michelle Obama.

Unless otherwise noted, this chapter is based on my reporting as a columnist for the *New York Times*.

273 "speaking more forcefully": Patrick Tyler, "Hillary Clinton, in China, Details Abuse of Women," *New York Times*, September 6, 1995.

275 Gloria Steinem asked, in the *New York Times*: "Women Are Never Front-Runners," *New York Times*, January 8, 2008.

275 In March 2008, at a Women: Karen Breslau, "Work Harder, Prove Yourself," Newsweek.com, August 29, 2008.

275 Susan Faludi suggested: Susan Faludi, "The Fight Stuff," *New York Times*, May 9, 2008.

276 "Women like her most": Julia Baird, "From Seneca Falls to . . . Sarah Palin?" *Newsweek*, September 22, 2008.

276 But after her smashing: Ibid.

277 people sometimes called themselves: Lisa Miller and Amanda Coyne, "A Visit to Palin's Church," *Newsweek*, September 2, 2008.

277 Palin remembered growing up: Breslau, "Work Harder, Prove Yourself."

277 (When asked during her gubernatorial): Rebecca Johnson, "Altered States," *Vogue*, February 1, 2008.

277 She once called that victory: S. J. Komarnitsky, "New Mayor, Sharp Knife," *Anchorage Daily News*, October 3, 1996.

277 Her sister said the only goal: Monica Davey, "Little-Noticed College Student to Star Politician," *New York Times*, October 24, 2008.

277 "The protein her family": Johnson, "Altered States."

277 "None of that 'Sarah Barracuda'": Davey, "Little-Noticed College Student to Star Politician."

277 While she was mayor: Evan Thomas and Karen Breslau, "McCain's Mrs. Right," *Newsweek*, September 8, 2008.

278 "I mean, how cool": Amanda M. Fairbanks, "Young, Republican, and Inspired by Palin," *New York Times*, October 29, 2008.

278 In a roundup of national: Jodi Kantor and Rachel Swarns, "A New Twist in the Debate on Mothers," *New York Times*, September 2, 2008.

278 "People who don't have children": Ibid.

278 When people wondered how: Karen Breslau, "An Apostle of Alaska," *Newsweek*, September 15, 2008.

278 Obama, who sent out: Maria Gavrilovic, "It's Stand-Up Comedy Time for Obama," CBS.com, September 8, 2008.

278 When asked about how: Michael Luo, "Working Mother Questions 'Irrelevant,' Palin Says," *New York Times*, September 13, 2008.

279 Her husband wrote about the strain: Barack Obama, *The Audacity of Hope*, 340.

280 During the vice presidential campaign: James Grimaldi and Karl Vick, "Palin Billed State for Nights Spent at Home," *Washington Post*, September 9, 2008.

280 Swift got into trouble: Gail Collins, "The Mommy Track Derails," *New York Times*, January 11, 2000; "The Year of the Stork," *New York Times*, May 11, 2001.

280 "The feeling that": Jane Swift, "In Her Own Words," *Boston Magazine*, January 2003.

280 (A reporter who followed her around): Thomas and Breslau, "McCain's Mrs. Right."

280 "She is Phyllis": Gloria Steinem, "Palin: Wrong Woman, Wrong Message," *Los Angeles Times*, September 4, 2008.

280 *Saturday Night Live* aired: September 27, 2008.

281 When she was unable: *Saturday Night Live*, Jon Meacham, "The Palin Problem," *Newsweek*, October 13, 2008.

281 Palin, back in Alaska: William Yardley and Michael Cooper, "Palin Calls Criticism by McCain Aides 'Cruel and Mean-Spirited,'" *New York Times*, November 7, 2008.

281 Palin wound up the only: Jon Cohen and Jennifer Agiesta, "Perceptions of Palin Grow Increasingly Negative," *Washington Post*, October 25, 2008.

281 "They bear us children": Mark Leibovich, "Among Rock-Ribbed Fans of Palin, Dudes Rule," *New York Times*, October 19, 2008.

282 Meanwhile, Tahita Jenkins: Jeremy Olshan, "Skirt the Issue," *New York Post*, May 31, 2007.

EPILOGUE

Unless otherwise noted, all the information is taken from interviews.

287 "In those first days": Toobin, *The Nine*, 253.

287 He was moved into an assisted-living: "Son: O'Connor Not Jealous of Husband's New Relationship," Associated Press on CNN.com, November 13, 2007.

290 In the panic that ensued: Michael Barbaro, "A Makeover of a Romance," *New York Times*, February 9, 2006.

291 Her delight at the turnaround: Kunin, *Living a Political Life*, 163.

292 In her autobiography: Mankiller, *Mankiller*, 246.

292 "The bride wore": Neil MacFarquhar, "Public Lives: A Feminist Takes the Vows," *New York Times*, September 6, 2000.

292 "I don't know if": Wolfgang Saxon, "Martha Griffiths, 91, Dies," *New York Times*, April 25, 2003.

BIBLIOGRAPHY

✢ ✢

BOOKS

Allyn, David. *Make Love, Not War — The Sexual Revolution: An Unfettered History.* New York: Routledge, 2001.

Alpert, Jane. *Growing Up Underground.* New York: William Morrow, 1981.

Anderson, Marian. *My Lord, What a Morning.* New York: Avon, 1956.

Anderson, Terry. *The Movement and the Sixties.* New York: Oxford University Press, 1995.

Arsenault, Raymond. *Freedom Riders.* New York: Oxford University Press, 2006.

Asbell, Bernard. *The Pill.* New York: Random House, 1995.

Atkinson, Ti-Grace. *Amazon Odyssey.* New York: Links Books, 1974.

Bailey, Beth, and David Farber, eds. *America in the '70s.* Lawrence: University Press of Kansas, 2004.

Barker-Benfield. *The Horrors of the Half-Known Life.* New York: Routledge, 2000.

Barry, Kathleen. *Femininity in Flight: A History of Flight Attendants.* Durham: Duke University Press, 2007.

Baxandall, Rosalyn, and Linda Gordon, eds. *Dear Sisters: Dispatches from the Women's Liberation Movement.* New York: Basic Books, 2000.

Bayer, Linda. *Ruth Bader Ginsburg.* New York: Chelsea House, 2000.

Bellamy, Edward. *Looking Backward.* New York: Signet Classics, 2000.

Bird, Caroline. *Born Female.* New York: Pocket Books, 1971.

Biskupic, Joan. *Sandra Day O'Connor.* New York: Harper Perennial, 2005.

Blackwell, Unita. *Barefootin'.* New York: Crown, 2006.

Blau, Francine, and Ronald Ehrenberg, eds. *Gender and Family Issues in the Workplace.* New York: Russell Sage Foundation, 1997.

Blood, Robert, and Donald Wolfe. *Husbands and Wives: The Dynamics of Married Living.* New York: Free Press, 1960.

Blumenthal, Karen. *Let Me Play: The Story of Title IX.* New York: Atheneum, 2005.

Boston Women's Health Book Collective. *Our Bodies, Ourselves.* New York: Simon and Schuster, 1973.

Bradford, Sarah. *America's Queen: The Life of Jacqueline Kennedy Onassis.* New York: Penguin Books, 2000.

Branch, Taylor. *At Canaan's Edge.* New York: Simon and Schuster, 2006.

Brown, Cynthia Stokes. *Ready from Within: Septima Clark and the Civil Rights Movement.* Trenton: Africa World Press, 1999.

Brown, Helen Gurley. *Sex and the Single Girl.* New York: Pocket Books, 1964.

Brownmiller, Susan. *Against Our Will.* New York: Ballantine Books, 1993.

———. *Femininity.* New York: Fawcett Columbine, 1984.

———. *In Our Time: Memoir of a Revolution.* New York: Delta, 1999.

Brumberg, Joan Jacobs. *The Body Project.* New York: Vintage Books, 1997.

———. *Fasting Girls.* New York: Penguin Books, 1989.

Byrd, Ayana, and Lori Tharps. *Hair Story.* New York: St. Martin's Press, 2001.

Cahn, Susan. *Coming on Strong.* Cambridge: Harvard University Press, 1994.

Cannon, Lou. *Ronald Reagan: A Life in Politics.* New York: PublicAffairs, 2004.

Cantarow, Ellen. *Moving the Mountain: Women Working for Social Change.* Old Westbury, NY: The Feminist Press, 1980.

Caplow, Theodore et al. *The First Measured Century.* Washington, DC: AEI Press, 2001.

Carroll, Peter. *It Seemed Like Nothing Happened: America in the 1970s.* New Brunswick: Rutgers University Press, 2000.

Carson, Josephine. *Silent Voices.* New York: Delta, 1969.

Cayleff, Susan. *Babe: The Life and Legend of Babe Didrikson Zaharias.* Urbana, IL: University of Illinois Press, 1996.

Ceplair, Larry, ed. *Charlotte Perkins Gilman: A Nonfiction Reader.* New York: Columbia University Press, 1991.

Chace, Elizabeth Buffum, and Lucy Buffum Lovell. *Two Quaker Sisters.* New York: Liveright Publishing, 1977.

Chafe, William. *The American Woman.* New York: Oxford University Press, 1972.

———. *The Unfinished Journey.* New York: Oxford University Press, 1999.

———. *Women and Equality.* New York: Oxford University Press, 1977.

Chamberlin, Hope. *A Minority of Members: Women in the U.S. Congress.* New York: Praeger Publishers, 1973.

Cherlin, Andrew. *Marriage, Divorce, Remarriage.* Cambridge: Harvard University Press, 1992.

Clendinen, Dudley, and Adam Nagourney. *Out for Good.* New York: Simon and Schuster, 1999.

Cohen, Marcia. *The Sisterhood.* New York: Fawcett Columbine, 1988.

Collier-Thomas, Bettye, and V. P. Franklin. *Sisters in the Struggle.* New York: New York University Press, 2001.

Collins, Gail. *America's Women: 400 Years of Dolls, Drudges, Helpmates, and Heroines.* New York: William Morrow, 2003.

Colman, Penny. *Rosie the Riveter: Working Women on the Home Front in World War II.* New York: Crown, 1995.

Cook, Dr. Suzan Johnson. *A New Dating Attitude.* Grand Rapids, MI: Zondervan, 2001.

Coontz, Stephanie. *Marriage, a History.* New York: Viking, 2005.

———. *The Way We Never Were.* New York: Basic Books, 1992.

———. *The Way We Really Are.* New York: Perseus Books, 1997.

Cornum, Rhonda. *She Went to War.* New York: Ballantine Books, 1992.

Couric, Emily, ed. *Women Lawyers: Perspectives on Success.* New York: Law and Business, 1984.

Cowan, Ruth Schwartz. *More Work for Mother.* New York: Basic Books, 1983.

Cox, Elizabeth. *Women State and Territorial Legislators, 1895–1995.* Jefferson, NC: McFarland, 1996.

Craft, Christine. *An Anchorwoman's Story.* Santa Barbara: Capra Press, 1986.

Crawford, Vicki et al., eds. *Women in the Civil Rights Movement.* Bloomington: Indiana University Press, 1993.

Critchlow, Donald. *Phyllis Schlafly and Grassroots Conservatism.* New Jersey: Princeton University Press, 2005.

Curry, Constance et al. *Deep in Our Hearts: Nine White Women in the Freedom Movement.*

Athens, GA: University of Georgia Press, 2000.

Davies, Margery. *Woman's Place Is at the Typewriter*. Philadelphia: Temple University Press, 1982.

Davis, Flora. *Moving the Mountain: The Women's Movement in America Since 1960*. Urbana, IL: University of Illinois Press, 1999.

Davis, Stephen. *Say Kids! What Time Is It?* Boston: Little, Brown, 1987.

DeParle, Jason. *American Dream*. New York: Penguin Books, 2004.

Douglas, Ann. *The Feminization of American Culture*. New York: Noonday Press, 1998.

Douglas, Susan J. *Where the Girls Are*. New York: Times Books, 1995.

DuPlessis, Rachel Blau et al., eds. *The Feminist Memoir Project*. New York: Three Rivers Press, 1998.

Dworkin, Andrea. *Right-Wing Women*. New York: Perigee Books, 1982.

Echols, Alice. *Daring to Be Bad*. Minneapolis: University of Minnesota Press, 1989.

Edelman, Marian Wright. *Lanterns: A Memoir of Mentors*. New York: Harper Perennial, 1999.

Edin, Kathryn, and Maria Kefalas. *Promises I Can Keep: Why Poor Women Put Motherhood Before Marriage*. Berkeley: University of California Press, 2005.

Ehrenreich, Barbara. *The Hearts of Men*. New York: Anchor Books, 1983.

Ehrenreich, Barbara, and Deirdre English. *For Her Own Good*. New York: Anchor Books, 1978.

Ehrenreich, Barbara et al. *Re-Making Love: The Feminization of Sex*. New York: Anchor Books, 1987.

Ephron, Nora. *Crazy Salad*. New York: Modern Library, 2000.

———. *Heartburn*. New York: Vintage Books, 1983.

———. *I Feel Bad About My Neck*. New York: Knopf, 2006.

———. *Wallflower at the Orgy*. New York: Bantam, 1970.

Epstein, Cynthia Fuchs. *Woman's Place*. Los Angeles: University of California Press, 1970.

Estrich, Susan. *Real Rape*. Cambridge: Harvard University Press, 1987.

Evans, Sara. *Personal Politics*. New York: Vintage Books, 1980.

———. *Tidal Wave*. New York: Free Press, 2003.

Faludi, Susan. *Backlash: The Undeclared War Against American Women*. New York: Anchor Books, 1991.

Farrell, Amy Erdman. *Yours in Sisterhood*. Chapel Hill: University of North Carolina Press, 1998.

Farrell-Beck, Jane, and Colleen Gau. *Uplift: The Bra in America*. Philadelphia: University of Pennsylvania Press, 2002.

Feigen, Brenda. *Not One of the Boys*. New York: Knopf, 2000.

Felsenthal, Carol. *Phyllis Schlafly: The Sweetheart of the Silent Majority*. Chicago: Regnery Gateway, 1981.

Fischer, Gayle. *Pantaloons and Power*. Kent, OH: Kent State University Press, 2001.

Fleming, Cynthia Griggs. *Soon We Will Not Cry: The Liberation of Ruby Doris Smith Robinson*. Lanham, MD: Rowman and Littlefield, 1998.

Franklin, Donna. *Ensuring Inequality*. New York: Oxford University Press, 1997.

Freedman, Russell. *The Voice That Challenged a Nation*. New York: Clarion, 2004.

Freeman, Jo. *The Politics of Women's Liberation*. Lincoln, NE: Backinprint.com, 2000.

———. *A Room at a Time: How Women Entered Party Politics*. Lanham, MD: Rowman and Littlefield, 2000.

———. *Women: A Feminist Perspective*. Palo Alto: Mayfield Publishing, 1975.

Friedan, Betty. *The Feminine Mystique*. New York: Norton, 1997.

———. *It Changed My Life*. Cambridge: Harvard University Press, 1998.

———. *Life So Far*. New York: Touchstone, 2001.

Fuchs, Victor. *How We Live*. Cambridge: Harvard University Press, 1983.

Gelb, Joyce, and Marian Lief Palley. *Women and Public Policies*. Princeton: Princeton University Press, 1982.

Giddings, Paula. *When and Where I Enter: The Impact of Black Women on Race and Sex in America*. New York: Perennial, 2001.

Ginsburg, Faye. *Contested Lives*. Berkeley: University of California Press, 1989.

Gorney, Cynthia. *Articles of Faith: A Frontline History of the Abortion Wars*. New York: Touchstone, 1998.

Graham, Katharine. *Personal History*. New York: Vintage Books, 1998.

Grant, Joanne. *Ella Baker: Freedom Bound*. New York: John Wiley and Sons, 1998.

Greene, John Robert. *Betty Ford*. Lawrence: University of Kansas Press, 2004.

Hacker, Andrew. *Mismatch: The Growing Gulf Between Women and Men*. New York: Scribner, 2003.

Halberstam, David. *The Children*. New York: Fawcett Books, 1998.

Haney, Eleanor Humes. *A Feminist Legacy: The Ethics of Wilma Scott Heide and Company*. Buffalo, NY: Margaretdaughters, 1985.

Harrison, Cynthia. *On Account of Sex*. Berkeley: University of California Press, 1988.

Harvey, Brett. *The Fifties: A Women's Oral History*. New York: HarperCollins, 1993.

Hayden, Dolores. *The Grand Domestic Revolution*. Cambridge: MIT Press, 1995.

Hays, Sharon. *Flat Broke with Children*. New York: Oxford University Press, 2003.

Hedgeman, Anna Arnold. *The Trumpet Sounds*. New York: Holt, Rinehart, and Winston, 1964.

Heilbrun, Carolyn. *The Education of a Woman: The Life of Gloria Steinem*. New York: Ballantine Books, 1998.

Herr, Lois Kathryn. *Women, Power, and AT&T*. Boston: Northeastern University Press, 2003.

Hersch, Patricia. *A Tribe Apart*. New York: Ballantine Books, 1998.

Hicks, Nancy. *The Honorable Shirley Chisholm, Congresswoman from Brooklyn*. New York: Lion Books, 1971.

Hochschild, Arlie Russell. *The Second Shift*. New York: Penguin Books, 2003.

Hole, Judith, and Ellen Levine. *Rebirth of Feminism*. New York: Quadrangle Books, 1971.

Humes, Edward. *Over Here*. Orlando: Harcourt, 2006.

Ivins, Molly. *Molly Ivins Can't Say That, Can She?* New York: Vintage Books, 1992.

"J." *The Sensuous Woman*. New York: Dell, 1969.

Jackson, Kenneth T. *Crabgrass Frontier*. New York: Oxford University Press, 1985.

Jones, Jacqueline. *Labor of Love, Labor of Sorrow*. New York: Vintage Books, 1995.

Kaestle, Carl. *Pillars of the Republic*. New York: Hill and Wang, 1983.

Kaiser, Charles. *1968 in America*. New York: Grove Press, 1988.

Kamen, Paula. *Her Way: Young Women Remake the Sexual Revolution*. New York: Broadway Books, 2000.

Keil, Sally Van Wagenen. *Those Wonderful Women in Their Flying Machines*. New York: Four Directions Press, 1990.

Keiler, Allan. *Marian Anderson: A Singer's Journey*. New York: Scribner, 2000.

Kerber, Linda. *No Constitutional Right to Be Ladies*. New York: Hill and Wang, 1998.

Kerr, Jean. *Please Don't Eat the Daisies*. Garden City: Doubleday, 1957.

———. *The Snake Has All the Lines*. Garden City: Doubleday, 1960.

Kerr, Laura. *Julie with Wings*. New York: Funk and Wagnalls, 1960.

Klass, Perri. *A Not Entirely Benign Procedure*. New York: Plume, 1994.

Koedt, Anne et al. *Radical Feminism*. New York: Quadrangle Books, 1973.

Koehler, Lyle. *A Search for Power*. Urbana, IL: University of Illinois Press, 1980.

Komarovsky, Mirra. *Women in College*. New York: Basic Books, 1985.

Kunin, Madeleine. *Living a Political Life*. New York: Vintage Books, 1994.

———. *Pearls, Politics, and Power*. White River Junction, VT: Chelsea Green Publishing, 2008.

Lamson, Peggy. *Few Are Chosen: American Women in Political Life Today*. Boston: Houghton Mifflin, 1968.

LaTour, Jane. *Sisters in the Brotherhoods*. New York: Palgrave, 2008.

Lee, Chana Kai. *For Freedom's Sake*. Urbana, IL: University of Illinois Press, 1999.

Lefever, Harry. *Undaunted by the Fight: Spelman College and the Civil Rights Movement*. Macon, GA: Mercer University Press, 2005.

Lerner, Gerda. *The Grimké Sisters from South Carolina*. New York: Oxford University Press, 1998.

Levine, Suzanne, and Harriet Lyons, eds. *The Decade of Women: A Ms. History of the Seventies in Words and Pictures*. New York: Paragon, 1980.

Levine, Suzanne, and Mary Thom. *Bella Abzug*. New York: Farrar, Straus, and Giroux, 2007.

Levy, Ariel. *Female Chauvinist Pigs: Women and the Rise of Raunch Culture*. New York: Free Press, 2005.

Lewis, John. *Walking with the Wind: A Memoir of the Movement*. New York: Harcourt Brace, 1998.

Lifton, Robert Jay, ed. *The Woman in America*. Boston: Beacon Press, 1964.

Litoff, Judy Barrett, and David Smith. *Since You Went Away: World War II Letters from American Women on the Home Front*. Lawrence: University of Kansas Press, 1991.

Lord, M. G. *Forever Barbie*. New York: Walker and Company, 2004.

Lunardini, Christine. *From Equal Suffrage to Equal Rights*. Lincoln, NE: ToExcel Press, 2000.

Mankiller, Wilma. *Mankiller: A Chief and Her People*. New York: St. Martin's, 1993.

Mansbridge, Jane. *Why We Lost the ERA*. Chicago: University of Chicago Press, 1986.

Marks, Lara. *Sexual Chemistry*. New Haven: Yale University Press, 2001.

Mathews, Donald, and Jane Sherron De Hart. *Sex, Gender, and the Politics of ERA*. New York: Oxford University Press, 1990.

Mayer, Jane, and Jill Abramson. *Strange Justice: The Selling of Clarence Thomas*. New York: Houghton Mifflin, 1994.

McAdam, Doug. *Freedom Summer*. New York: Oxford University Press, 1988.

McCorvey, Norma. *I Am Roe*. New York: Harper Perennial, 1984.

———. *Won by Love*. Nashville: Thomas Nelson, 1997.

McLaughlin, Helen. *Footsteps in the Sky*. Santa Clara: Aviation Book Company, 1994.

Mead, Margaret, and Frances Balgley Kaplan, eds. *American Women: The Report of the President's Commission on the Status of Women*. New York: Charles Scribner's Sons, 1965.

Miller, Timothy. *The Hippies and American Values*. Knoxville: University of Tennessee Press, 1991.

Mills, Kay. *This Little Light of Mine: The Life of Fannie Lou Hamer*. New York: Plume, 1994.

Mintz, Steven, and Susan Kellogg. *Domestic Revolutions: A Social History of American Family Life*. New York: Free Press, 1989.

Molloy, John. *The Woman's Dress for Success Book*. New York: Warner Books, 1977.

Morgan, Robin. *Saturday's Child*. New York: Norton, 2001.

———, ed. *Sisterhood Is Powerful*. New York: Vintage Books, 1970.

Murray, Pauli. *Pauli Murray: The Autobiography of a Black Activist, Feminist, Lawyer, Priest, and Poet*. Knoxville: University of Tennessee Press, 2003.

Nielsen, Georgia Panter. *From Sky Girl to Flight Attendant*. Ithaca, NY: ILR Press, 1982.

Noun, Louise. *More Strong-Minded Women: Iowa Feminists Tell Their Stories*. Ames, IA: Iowa State University Press, 1992.

Nye, F. Ivan, and Lois Wladis Hoffman. *The Employed Mother in America*. Chicago: Rand McNally, 1963.

Obama, Barack. *The Audacity of Hope*. New York: Three Rivers Press, 2007.

Olson, Lynne. *Freedom's Daughters*. New York: Scribner, 2001.

O'Reilly, Jane. *The Girl I Left Behind*. New York: Bantam Books, 1982.

Ovington, Mary White. *Black and White Sat Down Together*. New York: The Feminist Press, 1999.

Parks, Rosa. *Rosa Parks: My Story*. New York: Puffin, 1992.

Paterson, Judith. *Be Somebody: A Biography of Marguerite Rawalt*. Austin: Eakin Press, 1986.

Payne, Charles M. *I've Got the Light of Freedom*. Berkeley: University of California Press, 1995.

Peterson, Esther. *Restless*. New York: Caring Publishing, 1995.

Polakow, Valerie. *Who Cares for Our Children?* New York: Teachers College Press, 2007.

Raines, Howell. *My Soul Is Rested*. New York: Penguin Books, 1983.

Ransby, Barbara. *Ella Baker and the Black Freedom Movement*. Chapel Hill: University of North Carolina Press, 2003.

Rimmer, Robert. *The Harrad Experiment*. New York: Bantam Books, 1966.

Roberts, Selena. *A Necessary Spectacle: Billie Jean King, Bobbie Riggs, and the Tennis Match That Leveled the Game*. New York: Crown, 2005.

Robertson, Nan. *The Girls in the Balcony*. Lincoln, NE: Backinprint.com, 1992.

Robinson, Jo Ann Gibson. *The Montgomery Bus Boycott and the Women Who Started It*. Knoxville: University of Tennessee Press, 1987.

Rogers, Mary Beth. *Barbara Jordan: American Hero*. New York: Bantam Books, 1998.

Rosen, Ruth. *The World Split Open*. New York: Viking, 1999.

Rossner, Judith. *Looking for Mr. Goodbar*. New York: Washington Square Press, 1975.

Rudolph, Wilma. *Wilma*. New York: Signet, 1977.

Sanders, Marlene, and Marcia Rock. *Waiting for Prime Time*. Urbana, IL: University of Illinois Press, 1994.

Sanford, Nevitt, ed. *The American College*. New York: John Wiley and Sons, 1962.

Schapiro, Amy. *Millicent Fenwick: Her Way*. New Brunswick: Rutgers University Press, 2003.

Schlafly, Phyllis. *The Power of the Positive Woman*. New York: Arlington House, 1977.

Schroeder, Pat. *24 Years of House Work... And the Place Is Still a Mess*. Kansas City: Andrews McMeel, 1998.

Shapiro, Laura. *Something from the Oven*. New York: Viking, 2004.

Sharan, Farida. *Flower Child*. Boulder, CO: Wisdome Press, 2000.

Sherman, Janann. *No Place for a Woman*. New Brunswick: Rutgers University Press, 2001.

Siegel, Deborah. *Sisterhood, Interrupted*. New York: Palgrave, 2007.

Simmons, Rachel. *Odd Girl Out: The Hidden Culture of Aggression in Girls*. Orlando: Harvest, 2002.

Smith, Lissa, ed. *Nike Is a Goddess*. New York: Atlantic Monthly Press, 1998.

Solaro, Erin. *Women in the Line of Fire*. Emeryville, CA: Seal Press, 2006.

Solomon, Barbara. *In the Company of Educated Women*. New Haven: Yale University Press, 1986.

Spock, Benjamin. *Decent and Indecent*. New York: McCall Publishing, 1969.

Stanton, Mary. *From Selma to Sorrow: The Life and Death of Viola Liuzzo*. Athens, GA: University of Georgia Press, 1998.

Stark, Steven. *Glued to the Set*. New York: Delta, 1997.

Stavis, Ben. *We Were the Campaign: New Hampshire to Chicago for McCarthy*. Boston: Beacon Press, 1969.

Steele, Valerie. *The Corset: A Cultural History*. New Haven: Yale University Press, 2001.

Steinem, Gloria. *Outrageous Acts and Everyday Rebellions*. New York: Signet, 1986.

Steinmann, Marion. *Women at Work: Demolishing a Myth of the 1950s*. Philadelphia: Xlibris Corporation, 2005.

Stepp, Laura Sessions. *Unhooked*. New York: Riverhead Books, 2007.

Strasser, Susan. *Never Done: A History of American Housework*. New York: Henry Holt, 1982.

Swerdlow, Amy. *Women Strike for Peace*. Chicago: University of Chicago Press, 1993.

Tavris, Carol, and Carole Offir. *The Longest War: Sex Differences in Perspective*. New York: Harcourt Brace, 1977.

Terborg-Penn, Rosalyn. *African American Women in the Struggle for the Vote, 1850–1920*. Bloomington: Indiana University Press, 1998.

Thom, Mary. *Inside Ms*. New York: Henry Holt, 1997.

Tinker, Irene, ed. *Women in Washington*. Beverly Hills: Sage Publications, 1983.

Toobin, Jeffrey. *The Nine*. New York: Doubleday, 2007.

Treckel, Paula. *To Comfort the Heart: Women in Seventeenth-Century America*. New York: Twayne, 1996.

Turow, Scott. *One L*. New York: Warner Books, 1997.

Unger, Irwin, and Debi Unger, eds. *The Times Were a Changin': The Sixties Reader*. New York: Three Rivers Press, 1998.

Van Gelder, Lindsy, and Pamela Brandt. *The Girls Next Door*. New York: Simon and Schuster, 1996.

Walsh, Mary Roth. *Doctors Wanted: No Women Need Apply*. New Haven: Yale University Press, 1977.

Ware, Cellestine. *Woman Power*. New York: Tower Public Affairs Books, 1970.

Ware, Susan. *Beyond Suffrage: Women in the New Deal*. Cambridge: Harvard University Press, 1981.

Watkins, Elizabeth Siegel. *On the Pill*. Baltimore: Johns Hopkins University Press, 1998.

Weddington, Sarah. *A Question of Choice*. New York: Penguin Books, 1993.

Weiss, Jessica. *To Have and to Hold: Marriage, the Baby Boom, and Social Change*. Chicago: University of Chicago Press, 2000.

Weitzman, Lenore. *The Divorce Revolution*. New York: Free Press, 1985.

Wells, Helen. *Silver Wings for Vicki*. New York: Grosset and Dunlap, 1947.

Wertz, Richard, and Dorothy Wertz. *Lying-In: A History of Childbirth in America*. New Haven: Yale University Press, 1989.

Whittier, Nancy. *Feminist Generations*. Philadelphia: Temple University Press, 1995.

Zinn, Howard. *SNCC: The New Abolitionists*. Boston: Beacon Press, 1965.

PERIODICALS

Blau, Francine. "Trends in the Well-Being of American Women, 1970–1995." *Journal of Economic Literature*, March 1998.

Blau, Francine, and Lawrence Kahn. "Gender Differences in Pay." *Journal of Economic Perspectives*, Fall 2000.

Brauer, Carl. "Women Activists, Southern Conservatives, and the Prohibition of Sex Discrimination in Title VII of the 1964 Civil Rights Act." *Journal of Southern History*, February 1983.

Cancian, Francesca, and Steven Gordon. "Changing Emotion Norms in Marriage: Love and Anger in U.S. Women's Magazines Since 1900." *Gender and Society*, September 1988.

Cohen, Abby. "A Brief History of Federal Financing for Child Care in the United States." *The Future of Children*, Summer/Fall 1996.

Cole, Charles. "American Youth Goes Monogamous." *Harper's*, March 1957.

Cowan, Ruth Schwartz. "The 'Industrial Revolution' in the Home." *Technology and Culture Magazine*, January 1976.

Finer, Lawrence. "Trends in Premarital Sex in the United States, 1954–2003." *Public Health Reports*, January 2007.

Goldin, Claudia. "The Role of World War II in the Rise of Women's Employment." *American Economic Review*, September 1991.

Goldin, Claudia et al. "The Homecoming of American College Women: The Reversal of the College Gender Gap." *Journal of Economic Perspectives*, Fall 2006.

Goldin, Claudia, and Lawrence Katz. "On the Pill: Changing the Course of Women's Education." *Milken Institute Review*, 2nd quarter, 2002.

———. "The Power of the Pill: Oral Contraceptives and Women's Career and Marriage Decisions." *Journal of Political Economy*, August 2002.

———. "Transitions: Career and Family Life Cycles of the Educational Elite." *American Economic Review*, papers and proceedings, 2008.

Goldin, Claudia, and Cecilia Rouse. "Orchestrating Impartiality: The Impact of 'Blind' Auditions on Female Musicians." *American Economic Review*, September 2000.

Goldin, Claudia, and Maria Shim. "Making a Name: Women's Surnames at Marriage and Beyond." *Journal of Economic Perspectives*, Spring 2004.

Hill, Russell, and Frank Stafford. "Parental Care of Children: Time Diary Estimates of Quantity, Predictability, and Variety." *Journal of Human Resources*, Spring 1980.

Kagan, Elizabeth, and Margaret Morse. "The Body Electronic: Aerobic Exercise on Video." *TDR*, Winter 1988.

Mann, Charles. "Women's Health Research Blossoms." *Science*, August 11, 1995.

O'Neill, June, and Solomon Polachek. "Why the Gender Gap in Wages Narrowed in the 1980s." *Journal of Labor Economics*, June 1993.

Pokras, Robert, and Vicki Georges Hufnagel. "Hysterectomy in the United States, 1965–84." *American Journal of Public Health*, July 1988.

Shannon, William. "A Radical, Direct, Simple, Utopian Alternative to Day-Care Centers." *New York Times Magazine*, April 30, 1972.

"Shaping the '60s…Foreshadowing the '70s." *Ladies' Home Journal*, January 1962.

Vanek, Joann. "Time Spent in Housework." *Scientific American*, November 1974.

Weiss, Robert, and Nancy Morse Samelson. "Social Roles of American Women." *Marriage and Family Living*, November 1958.

PAPERS, ORAL HISTORIES, WEB POSTINGS

Cotter, David et al. "Moms and Jobs: Trends in Mothers' Employment and Which Mothers Stay Home." Council on Contemporary Families. http://www.contemporaryfamilies.org/subtemplate.php?ext=momsandjobs&t=factSheets.

Firestone, Shulamith. "The Jeannette Rankin Brigade: Woman Power?" CWLU Herstory. http://www.cwluherstory.com/CWLUArchive/rankin1.html.

Fry, Amelia. "Conversations with Alice Paul: Woman Suffrage and the Equal Rights Amendment." Suffragists Oral History Project, University of California. http://content.cdlib.org/xtf/view?docId=kt6f59n89c&doc.view=entire_text.

Goldin, Claudia. "The Long Road to the Fast Track: Career and Family." Working Paper 10331, National Bureau of Economic Research.

———. "The Quiet Revolution That Transformed Women's Employment, Education, and Family." Ely Lecture, American Economic Association Meetings, Boston, 2006.

Roads, Barbara. "Interview with Barbara 'Dusty' Roads." *People's Century*, PBS, June 17, 1999.

Roraback, Catherine. "Women and the Connecticut Bar." Oral History Project of the Connecticut Bar Foundation. Interview by Bruce Stave. Center for Oral History, Thomas J. Dodd Research Center, University of Connecticut, July 29, 1999.

Roth, William. "The Politics of Daycare: The Comprehensive Child Development Act of 1971." An Institute for Research on Poverty discussion paper, University of Wisconsin–Madison, December 1976.

INDEX

→→ ←←

ABC-TV, 149, 177, 180, 228
abolition of slavery, 65, 82
abortion, 122, 124, 137, 164, 166–70, 182, 202, 234, 245–46, 248; in America's history, 167–68; Finkbine's experiences and, 166–67; illegal, trauma of, 168; liberalization of state laws on, 168–69; NOW divided over, 170; *Roe v. Wade* and, 169–70, 245, 281; statistics on, 246
Abzug, Bella, 150, 183
accounting, women in, 227–28, 264
Acevedo, Sylvia, 189, 228–29, 241, 248, 289
Adams, Abigail, 58
Adams, John, 58
adoption, 171, 202, 265; unwanted pregnancies and, 122
adultery, 34, 273; as grounds for divorce, 31
Adventures of Ozzie and Harriet, The (TV series), 199
advertising, 79–80; having it all and, 219–20; sexist, of airlines, 191; suburban women as target of, 44; women working in, 25, 26–27, 243, 290
aerobics, 217
affirmative action, 234
African-Americans, 4, 15, 62–63, 119, 229–30, 273; Barbie dolls and, 27; black power movement and, 108–9, 148; children born out of wedlock to, 202; *The Cosby Show* and, 219; extended families of, 202; hair issues and, 28–29, 92, 102–3, 127; injustice to, 87–88; interracial dating and, 29, 249–50; interracial marriage and, 105, 226–17, 249, 250; respectability and standards of behavior for, 90–91, 95; similarities in treatment of women and, 64–65, 82; and Southern racists' paranoia about race-mixing, 107; standards of beauty and, 93, 102–3, 105; stay-at-home wives, 41, 45; white women's relationships with, 104–6; women in California senate, 186; women in U.S. Congress, 148, 183–86; women's liberation movement and, 148. *See also* civil rights movement

Afros, 102–3, 127
Against Our Will (Brownmiller), 230
age: attitudes toward, in women vs. men, 184; of majority, 121
AIDS, 230
Aid to Families with Dependent Children (AFDC), 244
airlines: flight attendants and, 14–15, 67, 190–91, 291–92; sexist advertising of, 191; women not hired as pilots for, 15
Akulian, Ted, 200
Alaska, 63, 249, 276, 277, 280, 291; abortion legalized in, 169; Palin as governor, 275–76, 277, 279–80; Palin's run for vice president and, 280, 281
Alda, Alan, 165
alimony, 200–201
Alito, Samuel, 260
Allyson, June, 32
Alpert, Jane, 125, 129
American Bandstand (TV show), 30
American Baptist Churches, 190
American Medical Association, 119
American Society of Plastic and Reconstructive Surgeons, 218
Amherst College, 258
anchorwoman issue, 228
Anderson, Marian, 87–88, 89–90, 99
Andrews, Lillian, 30, 41
Andrews, Pam, 30, 32, 119, 129
Angelo, Bonnie, 191
Anglin, Doug, 258
anorexia, 218
Anthony, Susan B., 26, 65, 77
anti-Communism, 66, 121, 163–64
Antioch College, 116
Apartment, The (film), 42
appliances, time-saving, 42, 43, 44
Army, U.S., 267, 268
Arnold, Barbara, 27, 119, 126, 203, 288
Aronson, Shepard, 141
Arthur, Adrian, 202
Arthur, Chester Alan, 95

Arthur, Lynnette, 203, 219, 225, 231–32, 241, 250, 288
Arthur-Monteleone, Dana, 202–3, 231–32, 250, 288
athletics, 11, 143–44, 178–82; bans on mixing of sexes in, 179; different prize money for men and women in, 179–80; menstruation and, 27; Riggs's challenges to women tennis players and, 178, 180–81; Title IX and, 150, 181–82, 183, 277
athletic scholarships, 180, 181, 182
Atkinson, Ti-Grace, 141, 142, 146, 148
AT&T, 161–62
attractiveness: appearance rules for flight attendants and, 15, 67, 191; black men's judgment of women based on, 93; feminists' sensitivity to issue of, 142, 146–48; working women judged on basis of, 227, 228. *See also* beauty ideal

baby boom, 45, 80
Baby M, 226
babysitters, 13, 206; fathers as, 221
Baer, Ellen, 216
Bagehot program, 202
Baker, Elaine DeLott, 105–6
Baker, Ella, 92–95, 98, 108, 109, 148
Baker, Josephine, 98
Bale, David, 292
Ball, Lucille, 12, 219
BankAmerica, 182
Barbara Walters (TV show), 288
Barbie dolls, 27, 28, 225, 290
Barnard College, 32, 224; cohabitation scandal at, 115–16, 289; regulations in girls' dormitories at, 116
Barr, Roseanne, 219
Barry, Marion, 97
bars, refusing to serve women if alone, 18
Baruch, Bernard, 66
Bass, Josie, 105, 108, 127
"bastards," 202
Bates, Daisy, 98
Baxandall, Rosalyn, 139, 143

beauty ideal: black community and, 93, 102–3, 105; Miss America demonstration and, 142–43; in 1960s, 27–29; in 1980s, 217–18. *See also* attractiveness
Behr, Peter, 115, 116, 289
Belafonte, Harry, 249
Belkin, Lisa, 261–63, 264
Bell, Griffin, 72
Bellamy, Carol, 172
Bellamy, Edward, 205
Benedict, Vicky McElhaney, 263
benefits (of women's liberation movement), 150
Bennett, Maxine, 127
Bensel, Myrna Ten, 43, 201
Berne, Eric, 191
Bernstein, Joan, 31
Bernstein, Leonard, 33
Bevel, James, 92, 103–4
Beveridge, Andrew, 260
Bird, Caroline, 29
birth control, 80–81, 119; health risks of, 123; laws restricting access to, 120–22; the Pill, 80–81, 82, 119, 120–22, 123, 129; Supreme Court rulings on, 121
birthrate, 42, 199, 202
Blackmun, Justice Harry, 170
black power movement, 108–9, 148
Blackstone, William, 150
Blackwell, Unita, 94–95, 99, 101, 102, 107
Blair, Sampson Lee, 261
Blanchard, James, 292–93
Bloody Sunday (1965), 106
bloomer dress, 26
blue jeans, 102, 126–27, 178, 217
Bode, Verna, 28
body image, 217–18; consciousness-raising and, 139; eating disorders and, 218; sculpting figure through exercise and, 217–18
Bombeck, Erma, 44
Bonanza (TV series), 13, 139, 219
Bond, Julian, 94
Bonet, Lisa, 219
Bookbinder, Hyman, 61
Boston Marathon, 179
Bottoms, Sharon, 252
bouffant hairdo, 28
Bowen, Revonda, 250
Boxer, Barbara, 247–48
Boylan, Betsy Wade, 192–93
"bra burning," 143, 146, 241
Brademas, John, 206, 207, 208, 209
Bradlee, Ben, 187
Bradley, Valerie, 102
Brandt, Pamela Robin, 251
bras, 27–28, 217; going without, 145–46
Bratz dolls, 266–67, 290

Braun, Carol Moseley, 288
breast cancer, 123, 124
breasts: size of, 218; women's hatred of, 139. *See also* bras
Britz, Jennifer Delahunty, 257
Brooke, Edward, 273
Brothers, Joyce, 165
Browder, Aurelia, 89
Brown, David, 117
Brown, Doris, 182
Brown, Helen Gurley, 30, 117–18, 125, 223
Brownmiller, Susan, 106, 143, 144, 168, 178, 217, 230
Brown v. Board of Education, 88
Bryant, Anita, 171
Buchanan, Pat, 208
bulimia, 218
Bureau of Labor Statistics, 222
Burke, Autumn, 184
Burke, Yvonne Braithwaite, 184
Burton, Beverly, 12, 26
Bush, George H. W., 233
Bush, George W., 246
business, women in, 258, 262–63; dressing for success and, 216–17
businessmen, supportive wives of, 32–33
business trips: considered improper for women, 15; men-only "Executive Flights" and, 15, 150; working mothers and, 222–23
BusinessWeek magazine, 199
BUtterfield 8 (film), 117, 128
Buxton, Charles Lee, 120, 121

Cabbage Patch Kids, 225
cabinet-level posts, women in, 57
Cagney and Lacey (TV series), 218–19
Caiazzo, Edward D., 3
California: abortion liberalization in, 169; divorce laws in, 200; gay rights in, 171; women elected to senate of, 186
California Central Savings and Loan Association, 227
Campbell, Jack, 171
Campbell Cookbook, A, 43
Carmichael, Stokely, 108
Carpenter, Karen, 218
Carson, Josephine, 103
Carter, Jimmy, 209
Carter, John Mack, 144–45
Casals, Pablo, 33
CBS-TV, 220, 258
Ceballos, Jacqui, 141–42
Cedar Rapids, Iowa, girls' sports in, 181, 182
Celler, Emanuel, 64
Census Bureau, 199, 201–2, 225
Centers for Disease Control (CDC), 230

CEOs: wives of, 32–33; women as, 258
Chappell, Johnnie Mae, 106
Charlotte Observer, 242
Cherokee Nation, 232–33
Chessen, Sherri (Sherri Chessen Finkbine), 166–67, 223, 289–90
Chicago, divorce law in, 31
Chicago Daily News, 208
Child and Family Services Bill (1975), 208–9
childbearing, 146; birthrate and, 42, 199, 202; delaying of, 225–26, 265; empty nest and, 45; fertility problems and, 226, 230; fertility rate and, 225, 264; Firestone's utopian vision of, 141; leaving workforce after, 31, 262–64; maternity leave and, 227; mortgages and other loans and, 17; postwar baby boom and, 45, 80; trend toward smaller families and, 77, 80; by unmarried women, 202–3, 265 (*see also* single mothers)
child care, 203–9, 232, 242–44; choice of career path and, 242–43; communal living and, 204–5, 262, 291; day-care programs and, 41, 206–9, 222, 244, 245, 261; employer concessions and, 264; extended families and, 103, 202, 203, 279–80; father's participation in, 221–22, 261–62, 264; Gilman's utopian vision of, 205; government support for, 206–9, 222, 244, 261; help from supportive friends and neighbors with, 203–4, 206, 262; hiring help for, 13, 206; husband and wife with differing expectations and, 221; mother's assumption of responsibility for, 25–26; opting-out trend and, 262–64; Palin's candidacy and, 278–79, 280; post-divorce careers hampered by, 200; taking baby to work and, 223
Children's Hour, The (film), 128
child support, 164–65, 200–201
Chisholm, April, 219
Chisholm, Shirley, 148, 183–84
Chisholm, Valerie, 29
chlamydia, 229–30
Choice Not an Echo, A (Schlafly), 164
Civil Rights Act (1964), 290; amended to include job discrimination against women, 63–65, 66–68, 69, 71–72, 82
Civil Rights Memorial (Montgomery, Alabama), 106
civil rights movement, 77, 81–82, 87–109, 116; black manhood as focus in, 97–98, 109; black women as backbone of, 87–95, 99–101; black women pushed into subordinate roles in, 97–98, 108–9; charismatic leader–free organization as ideal in, 94; clothing and hairstyle issues in, 91, 102–3; early, decorum of protests

in, 91; Freedom Rides in, 91, 92, 96–97; generational conflicts in, 102; Liuzzo killing and, 106–8; lunch-counter sit-ins in, 90–91, 92, 94; March on Washington in, 98–99; Mississippi Freedom Democratic Party and, 98, 101; Montgomery bus boycott in, 88–89, 93; in rural Southern towns, 99–101; sexism ascribed to black men in, 108; SNCC founding and, 94–95; violent opposition to, 91, 96–97, 99–100, 104, 105, 106–8; voter-registration projects in, 89, 99–100, 104–6; white women in, 104–6, 108; work/family divide and, 103–4

Clark, Petula, 249
Clark, Septima, 93
Cleary, Altha, 179
"click of recognition," 140
Clinton, Bill, 227, 233, 244, 247, 273, 278
Clinton, Chelsea, 273, 278
Clinton, Hillary, 126, 204, 273–76, 279, 280–82; presidential campaign of, 273–76, 278, 281
Close, Glenn, 230
clothes washing, 39–40, 42, 43, 44
clothing for women, 267; blue jeans, 102, 126–27, 178, 217; in civil rights movement, 91, 102; cultural revolution and, 126; dressing for success and, 216–17; girdles, 27, 28, 145, 178, 217, 267; hats, 27, 183; hemlines, 27, 178, 217; as impediments to work, 26–27; in 1960s, 3, 26–28, 178; in 1970s, 177–78; in 1980s, 216–17; in 2000s, 267, 281, 282; nylon stockings, 27, 28, 90, 178; pants, 3, 26, 90, 177–78, 217, 282; panty hose, 126, 267; of radical feminists, 147; shoulder pads, 217, 219. See also bras; shoes
CNN-TV, 245
Coffee, Linda, 169–70
cohabitation, 81, 115–16, 120, 199, 201–2, 289
college, 31–32, 150, 177, 204, 288; access to birth control at, 122; cost of, 242; debt burden of, 279; finding husband as women's goal in, 30, 31–32; men outnumbered by women in, 77, 216, 257–58; as preparation for homemaking, 46–47; sexual activity at, 119
college dormitories, 116, 250–51
college graduates: gloomy forecast for marriage prospects of, 223–24; opting-out trend among, 262–64; as unhappy housewives, 45–46
Collins, Addie Mae, 106
Collins, Lucretia, 96
colonial era, 3–4
Columbia University, 202
combat, women barred from, 248, 249

Comedy Central, 275
Commerce Department, 15
communal living, 138, 204–5, 262, 291
Comprehensive Child Development Act (1971), 206–9
Congress, U.S., 60, 247–48, 260, 261, 290; abortion issue and, 184; age of majority and, 121; anti–Vietnam War protests and, 135; child care and, 206–9, 222, 244; Civil Rights Act of 1964 and, 63–65, 66–67; Equal Rights Amendment and, 59, 150, 159, 164, 172; exempted from antidiscrimination laws, 185; sex discrimination legislation and, 63–65, 66–67, 150, 182; Title IX and, 181–82; welfare reform and, 244; women in, 57–58, 64, 65–66, 135, 148, 170, 183–86, 247–48, 278, 282. See also Senate, U.S.
Congress of Racial Equality (CORE), 96
Conlin, Roxanne, 150
Connecticut, restrictions on access to birth control in, 120–22
consciousness-raising groups, 139–41, 143
conservatism, political, 163–64, 216
Constitution, U.S., 184
construction, women in, 188–89, 216, 219
consumer culture, 44, 47, 79–80
Continental Airlines, 191
Conyers, John, 289
Cook, Constance, 168
Cook, Ron, 225
cooking, 42–43, 44
Cooper, Eulalie, 190–91
Cornum, Rhonda, 248–49
Coronet magazine, 124
corporate wives, 32–33
corporations, humanistic vision of, 222
Cosby Show, The (TV series), 219, 220, 279
Coughlin, Paula, 247
Couric, Katie, 258, 281
Court, Margaret, 180
Craft, Christine, 228
Craig, May, 63
Crawford, Cindy, 251
credit, women's access to, 17, 150, 182–83
credit cards, 17, 182
Cremer, Patricia, 221
Cremer, Richard, 221
Crisp, Mary, 170
Crossette, Barbara, 187
Cruz, Zoe, 220
Cuban Missile Crisis, 34
culture wars of 1970s, 208, 216
Curry, Connie, 101
custody rights, 200; lesbianism and, 251–52

Dalkon Shield, 123
Dallas (TV series), 219

Damon, Gene, 128
dancing: in 1960s, 30; in 1980s, 219
Darcus, Mary Bell, 40
date rape, 231
dating: dwindling of concept of, 250; hooking up and, 266; interracial, 29, 249–50; in 1960s, 29, 30, 139
Daughters of Bilitis, 128
Daughters of the American Revolution (DAR), 87
Davis, Stephen, 12
Dawson, William, 65
Day, Doris, 117
day-care programs, 41, 206, 245; company-run, 222, 261; government support for, 206–9, 222, 244, 261
death of husband, 31
DeCrow, Karen, 163
Dee, Sandra, 28
DeGeneres, Ellen, 252
Delaney, James, 184
Dell'Olio, Anselma, 161
Dellums, Ron, 185
Deloitte & Touche, 264
Delta, 190–91
Democratic Party, 183; gender gap and, 233; Mississippi Freedom Democratic Party and, 98, 101; women's issues and, 60–61, 164
dentistry, women in, 257
DeParle, Jason, 245
Depository Institutions Amendments Act (1974), 182
diapers, 39, 42, 43
Dick Van Dyke Show, The (TV series), 177
Didrikson, Babe, 178
Different World, A (TV series), 219
Dirksen, Everett, 65
displaced homemakers, 201, 203
divorce, 31, 47, 199–200, 203, 282; alimony and child support after, 164–65, 200–201; ERA and, 165; grounds for, 31; husband's sudden departure and, 201, 203; increase in, 81, 199–200; legal reforms of 1970s and, 164–65, 200–201, 243; women's access to credit after, 17; women's careers after, 200, 201
doctors: women as, 16, 139, 221; women's frustrations with, 123–24. See also medical schools
Doderer, Minnette, 171, 201
dolls, 27, 28, 225, 266–67, 290
Dominick, Clinton, 168, 169
Donaldson, Ivanhoe, 104
double standard, 116, 117; ditched by middle-class young women, 119; Sex and the Single Girl and, 117–18
Douglas, Michael, 230

Douglass, Frederick, 65
Dowd, Maureen, 250
Dowdy, Robert, 269
draft, 137, 138, 165
draft cards, burning of, 138, 143
Dukakis, Michael, 233
Dullea, Georgia, 226
Dunbar, Roxanne, 147
Duncan, Jack, 207, 209
Dunham, Ann, 274
Durr, Virginia, 107
Dutch treat, 250
Dworkin, Andrea, 160
dyeing hair, 226
Dynasty (TV series), 219

East Side/West Side (TV series), 102
Eastwood, Mary, 61, 62, 63, 67, 68
eating disorders, 218
Ebony magazine, 42, 109
economic change, value of women's skills
    and, 77–78
economic downturn of 1970s, 160–61, 162
economic meltdown of 2008, 264
Economist magazine, 80
Edelman, Marian Wright, 102
Ederle, Gertrude, 178
Edin, Kathryn, 265
Edwards, John, 281
Eisenhower, Dwight D., 57, 59, 60
Eisenhower, Mamie, 33
electricians, women as, 188–89
Elsberg, Harold, 41
Elsberg, Josephine, 41, 43–44
Enersen, Jean, 228
engineers, women as, 16, 189, 228–29
Enjoli Perfume, 220, 221
Ephron, Nora, 25, 77, 116, 124, 125, 140, 145,
    146, 148, 250, 293
Epstein, Barbara, 143, 172
Equal Credit Opportunity Act (1973), 150
Equal Employment Opportunity Act (Title
    VII of Civil Rights Act of 1964), 63–65,
    66–68, 69, 71–72, 82
Equal Employment Opportunity
    Commission (EEOC), 67, 68, 70, 190,
    247, 259, 260
Equal Pay Act (1963), 64
"equal pay for equal work," 137. *See also*
    wage gap
Equal Rights Amendment (ERA), 61–62,
    150, 159, 162–63, 171, 182, 184, 186, 207,
    244–45, 257, 289; abortion and gay rights
    debates and, 166, 170, 171; annual
    introduction ritual for, 59; dire
    consequences ascribed to, 164–65; failure
    to achieve ratification of, 172; fairness
    notion and, 162; housewives' resentments

and, 159–60, 164–65; Kennedy
    administration and, 59, 60–61; language
    of, 159, 164; passed by House and Senate,
    150, 159, 164; practical consequences of
    defeat of, 162; Schlafly's campaign
    against, 163–66, 171; state versions of, 172
Ervin, Sam, 150, 159
Essence magazine, 148
Estellachild, Vivian, 138
Estrich, Susan, 231
Evans, Linda, 219
Evans, Sarah, 106
Evers, Medgar, 97
Evers-Williams, Myrlie, 99
Executive Suite (film), 33
exercise, sculpting figure through, 217–18
expectations, of husbands vs. their wives, 221
extended families, 202, 203, 279–80; civil
    rights workers' reliance on, 103–4;
    communal living and, 204–5; supportive
    friends and neighbors as, 203–4

Faludi, Susan, 224, 275
families: extended, 103–4, 202, 203, 204,
    279–80; nuclear, 136, 141, 199, 202, 203,
    204
Farmer, James, 148
farm life, 3–4, 39–41
Fatal Attraction (film), 230
Father Knows Best (TV series), 12, 139, 181,
    204
FBI, 107, 145
Feigen, Brenda, 188
Felsenthal, Carol, 165
Feminine Mystique, The (Friedan), 47
feminism. *See* women's liberation movement
"feminist," use of word, 241
Fenwick, Millicent, 184
Ferraro, Geraldine, 184, 232
fertility problems, 226, 229–30
fertility rate, 225, 264
Fey, Tina, 280
Finkbine, Bob, 166–67
Finkbine, Sherri. *See* Chessen, Sherri
Firestone, Shulamith, 137, 141, 144
Flashdance (film), 219
Fleming, Yana Shani, 27, 219
flexible work schedules, 222, 243, 264
flight attendants, 14–15, 33, 67, 190–91,
    291–92; appearance rules for, 15, 67, 191;
    marriage ban and, 15, 67, 190–91, 291
Fonda, Jane, 217–18
Food and Drug Administration, 123
Ford, Betty, 123
Ford, Gerald R., 208
Ford, Susan, 123
Forman, James, 105
Fortune magazine, 261

Fortune 500, 258
Foster, Alison, 27, 116, 122, 125, 126, 127,
    128–29, 204, 205, 223, 243, 257, 261, 290–91
Fox, Muriel, 32, 58, 68, 69, 141, 142,
    146, 223, 274
fragility, ascribed to women, 231
France, fertility rate in, 264
Francis, Genie, 230
Frank, Reuben, 228
Frankfurter, Justice Felix, 178
Frazier, E. Franklin, 45
"freedom" names, 141
Freedom Rides, 91, 92, 96–97
Freedom Schools, 105
Freedom Summer (1964), 104–6
Freeman, Jo, 11, 68–69, 105, 137, 150
Freud, Sigmund, 11
Friedan, Betty, 12, 18, 32, 136, 141, 142, 146,
    147, 165, 166, 170–71, 200, 224; *The
    Feminine Mystique* and, 47; lesbianism
    and, 127; *Life So Far* and, 257; NOW
    founding and, 67–68; NOW's legal
    actions and, 68–69; Strike Day and, 149
Friends (TV series), 203
friendships, of boys and girls, 29
frigidity, among women, 125
Fry, Amelia, 150

Gallup, George, 25, 30–31, 45, 57, 97, 117,
    118, 123, 216, 234, 249
Garland, Lillian, 226–27
gay men, 127, 262
gay rights, 164, 166, 170–71
Geary, Anthony, 230
"gender gap," in politics, 233
General Hospital (TV series), 230
genital herpes, 230
Gibb, Roberta, 179
Gidget (film), 139
Gilman, Charlotte Perkins, 205
Ginsburg, Ruth Bader, 16, 172, 178, 260
girdles, 27, 28, 145, 178, 217, 267
"girls," referring to women as, 186
Girls Next Door, The (Van Gelder and
    Brandt), 251
Glamour magazine, 146
going steady, 30
Goldberg, Arthur, 60
Goldin, Claudia, 263
Goldwater, Barry, 164
golf courses, segregated, 17
"Goodbye to All That" (Morgan), 138–39,
    274–75
Goodman, Ellen, 222
goodness, women's supposed impulse
    toward, 4
Goodyear Tire, 259–60
Google, 261

Gornick, Vivian, 172
governors, women as, 183, 185, 279–80, 291
graduate and professional schools, 5, 80, 177, 188; quotas for women in, 16, 257. *See also* law schools; medical schools
Graham, Katharine, 58–59
Graham, Lindsey, 276
Graham, Terry, 250
Gramm, Phil, 244
Grasso, Ella, 183
Green, Edith, 64, 101, 181, 182, 183
Grey Advertising, 290
Griffiths, Hicks, 58, 67
Griffiths, Martha, 58, 64, 65, 66, 67, 69, 150, 183, 292–93
Grimké, Angelina, 82, 147, 292
Griswold, Estelle, 120
Gruppo, Claire, 241
Guggenheimer family, 14
Gulf War (1991), 248–49
Gulf War (2003–), 267–69

Hair (Broadway musical), 118–19
hairstyles, 28–29, 145, 147, 217; of African-Americans, 28–29, 92, 102–33, 127
Halberstam, David, 96
Hale, Sarah Josepha, 4
Hamer, Fannie Lou, 100–101, 109, 148
Hammond, Shirley, 27
Hampton Ministers' Conference, 190, 288
Hansberry, Lorraine, 11
Harding, Warren G., 57
Harman, Jane, 268
Harper, Fowler, 120–21
Harper's magazine, 30, 32, 45, 78, 147
Harrad Experiment, The (Rimmer), 129, 229
Harvard Business Review, 16, 242
Harvard Business School, 262–63
Harvard Divinity School, 190
Harvard Law School, 16, 58, 165
Harvard Medical School, 202
Harvard University, 46, 225, 263
Harvey, Claire Collins, 97
hats, 27, 183
having it all: as ideal, 219–20; reality of, 220–23
Hawaii: abortion in, 169; ERA ratified by, 150; fair-employment laws in, 67
Hayden, Sandra "Casey," 108
Head Start, 208
health culture, 217
Hébert, F. Edward, 185
Heckler, Margaret, 183, 208
Hedgeman, Anna Arnold, 98, 99
Heide, Wilma Scott, 200
Height, Dorothy, 93–94, 98, 288
help-wanted ads: divided by gender, 5, 67, 142; mention of race in, 67

hemlines, 27, 178, 217
Hepburn, Audrey, 128
Hepburn, Katharine, 165–66
Hermann, Susan, 96
Hernández, Aileen, 67
Hernandez, Brunilda, 188–89
herpes, genital, 230
Hershey, Lenore, 144
high heels, 27, 137, 147, 178, 217
Hill, Anita, 246–47, 248
Hinderhofer, Kathy, 124, 160, 243
Hinton, Tawana, 28, 119, 122, 127, 223
Hinton, Tiffany, 223
hippie movement, 128, 138
Hispanic Americans, 119, 264
Hobby, Oveta Culp, 57
Hochschild, Arlie Russell, 221
Holloway, Camara Dia, 219, 220, 250
home ownership, 41; access to mortgages and, 17, 41, 78, 165, 182–83; need for two salaries and, 199; by women, 17, 182–83
homosexuality, 262; gay rights and, 164, 166, 170–71. *See also* lesbians
hooking up, 266
Hoover, J. Edgar, 107, 145, 147
Hopkins, Ann, 227–28
House of Representatives, U.S. *See* Congress, U.S.
housewives, 39–47; anti-ERA sentiment among, 159–60, 164–65; corporate wives and, 32–33; displaced by divorce, 201, 203; dwindling status of, 81; emasculation of husbands ascribed to, 44–45; empty nest and, 45; on farms, 3–4, 39–41; Jackie Kennedy as model for, 33–34; prestige lost by, 160, 164; Schlafly's attitude toward, 165–66; in suburbs, 41–44; times spent on domestic chores by, 43; trophy value of, 41; unhappiness of, 11, 45–46
housework, 4, 39–44, 138, 150, 205, 215; clothes washing, 39–40, 42–43, 44; communal living and, 204–5; cooking, 42–43, 44; dumped on women in counterculture movement, 138; farm life and, 3–4, 39–40; *The Feminine Mystique* and, 47; husband's sharing of, 160, 162, 221–22, 261–62; propaganda about glories of, 14, 44, 47; raising of standards for, 43–44; suburban life and, 41–44; time-saving appliances and, 42, 43, 44; time spent on, 43; utopian writers and, 205; working women and, 25–26, 43–44, 220–22, 261–62. *See also* child care
Houston Chronicle, 209
Howard University, 62
Howdy Doody (TV show), 12
"How to Love Your Husband" (Lees), 124–25

Huddleston, Jennifer, 278
Hudson, Rock, 230
Hughes, Genevieve, 96
Human Sexual Response (Masters and Johnson), 125
Humphrey, Hubert, 101
Hurok, Sol, 87
husbands, 282; death of, 31; domestic responsibilities of, 25–26, 160, 162, 221–22, 261–62, 264; emasculation of, ascribed to stay-at-home wives, 44–45; expecting to be waited on by their wives, 221; families suddenly left by, 201, 203

IBM, 78, 229, 289
illegitimacy, 202
"I Love Lucy" (TV series), 12, 199
Indiana University, 179
industrial economy, 4, 78, 80
infantilization of women, 17
insurance, automobile, 17
Internal Revenue Service (IRS), 62, 121
International Brotherhood of Electrical Workers, 188–89
International Women's Year Conference (1977), 170–71
interracial dating, 29, 249–50
interracial marriage, 105, 226–27, 249, 250
intrauterine devices (IUDs), 123
in vitro fertilization, 226
Iowa, legislative reforms in, 150
Iowa State University, 143–44
Iraq, invasion of (2003), 267–69
Italy, fertility rate in, 264
It Takes a Village (Clinton), 204
Ivey, Dena, 249, 267–68, 291
Ivins, Molly, 184

Jackson, Mrs. Willie Lee, 106
Jeannette Rankin Brigade, 135–36, 137, 139
Jehovah's Witnesses, 203
Jenkins, Tahita, 282
Jennings, Elizabeth, 95
Jennings, Peter, 228
Johnson, Bernice, 97
Johnson, Lyndon B., 62, 64, 68, 78, 101, 107
Johnson, Shoshana, 268
Johnson, Suzan (Sujay), 189–90, 224–25, 288
Johnson, Virginia, 125
Johnston, Kathryn, 179
Jong, Erica, 241
Jordan, Barbara, 170, 184
Jordan, Emma, 101, 102
journalism: descriptive language for women in, 187; sex-discrimination suits and, 191–93; TV news and, 220, 228, 258; women working in, 16, 25, 191–93, 242–43

judges, women as, 57, 62; Supreme Court and, 233–34, 260, 287
jury duty, women barred from, 5
Justice Department, U.S., 96
J. Walter Thompson agency, 25, 27, 223

Kassell, Paula, 187
Keenan, Peggy, 4–5
Kefalas, Maria, 265
Kelber, Laura, 189
Kennedy, Florynce, 141
Kennedy, Jackie, 28, 33–34
Kennedy, John F., 33, 34, 57, 58–59, 60, 61, 98
Kenyon College, 257
Kerr, Jean, 44
King, Billie Jean, 178, 179–81, 182
King, Coretta Scott, 288
King, Larry, 180, 182
King, Martin Luther, Jr., 89, 93, 94, 96, 98
KING 5 TV (Seattle), 228
Kinsey, Alfred, 119
Kirschbaum, Kathryn, 182
Klass, Perri, 202, 223, 225–26
Kleimeyer, Edna, 41, 42, 43, 282
Klose, Margaret Taylor, 44
KMBC-TV (Kansas), 228
Knutson, Coya, 58
Koedt, Anne, 125
Komarovsky, Mirra, 220
Kopp, Wendy, 258–59
Ku Klux Klan, 106, 107
Kulish, Nicholas, 263–64
Kunin, Madeleine May, 16, 47, 144, 186, 206, 222, 223, 232, 291

labial-reduction surgery, 266
Labor Department, U.S., Women's Bureau in, 59, 60
labor movement, 60, 69, 292
Ladder magazine, 128
Ladies' Home Journal, 30, 61, 89, 108, 117, 144–45, 171, 252
Ladies' Magazine, 4
Ladner, Joyce, 42, 90–91, 92, 98, 102, 103, 108–9
Landon, Michael, 13
Lang, K. D., 251, 252
La Rue, Linda, 148
laundry chores, 39–40, 42, 43, 44
LaValleur, June, 26, 40, 121, 215–16, 221, 251, 291
law firms: unsympathetic to idea of families, 222; women as partners in, 227, 258
Lawhorn, Gayle, 29, 30
law schools, 5, 58, 165, 182, 188, 216, 233, 257
lawsuits against employers, 259–60, 288, 290; attractiveness issue and, 228; flight attendants and, 190–91; job protection for

pregnant women and, 227; at major newspapers, 191–93; NOW and, 68–69, 70–72; seniority systems and, 162; Weeks v. Southern Bell, 70–72, 191, 288; women's chance to make partner and, 227–28
lawyers, women as, 16, 31, 61, 62, 139, 165, 188, 219, 222, 233–34, 264; African-American, 62–63; consciousness-raising and, 140
leases, women unable to sign, 17
Leave It to Beaver (TV series), 263–64
LeClair, Linda (later Grace), 115–16, 289
Ledbetter, Lilly, 259–60
Lees, Hannah, 124
Legally Blonde (film), 267
leisure gap, 221
lesbians, 127–28, 251–52, 261, 265; gay rights and, 164, 166, 170–71; in military, 249
Levittown, New York, 41
Lewinsky, Monica, 247
Lewis, John, 97, 103
Lewis, Marlyn McGrath, 263
life expectancy, 45; of men vs. women, 44
Life So Far (Friedan), 257
Lilly Ledbetter Fair Pay Act, 260
liposuction, 218
Little League, 77, 179
Liu, Cynthia, 263
Liu, Goodwin, 260
Liuzzo, Viola, 106–8
loans, women's access to, 17, 182–83
Long, Priscilla, 129
Looking Backward (Bellamy), 205
Looking for Mr. Goodbar (Rossner), 229
Lorance, Patricia, 161–62, 260, 290
Los Angeles Times, 280
Louisiana Unemployment Compensation Board, 191
lunch-counter sit-ins, 90–91, 92, 94
Lynch, Jessica, 268, 269

Maasberg, Jo Meyer, 41, 243
MacLaine, Shirley, 128
Mademoiselle magazine, 11, 28, 137, 216
Madonna, 219, 251
maids, 42, 43–44, 220
makeup, 147, 178
male chauvinism, in New Left, 137–39
Mankiller, Wilma, 40, 188, 232–33, 292
Manpower, 79
March on Washington (1963), 98–99
Maria K. (single mother), 5, 31, 122–23, 145, 200, 201, 206, 291
Mariners' Temple (New York), 190
marital status, terms of address and, 187. See also "Ms." title
marriage, 81, 115, 220, 242; airlines' rules against, for flight attendants, 15, 67,

190–91, 291; delaying of, 77, 177, 199, 223–25, 265; egalitarian, 162, 216; as end to women's work life, 14, 15, 16–17, 30–31, 220; interracial, 105, 226–27, 249, 250; premarital sex and prospects for, 116–17, 118; radical feminists' views on, 141; rush into, in 1960s, 30–31, 117; short-term jobs without advancement potential for women before, 14–16, 78; virginity until, 116–17
Martin Marietta company, 69
Mary Tyler Moore Show, The (TV series), 177, 200, 204
Mason, Linda, 220, 222
Massachusetts, restrictions on access to birth control in, 120, 121
Masters, William, 125
maternity leave, 227
math courses, taken by girls, 139, 257
May, Madeleine. See Kunin, Madeleine May
McBeath, Gerald, 280
McCain, John, 276, 278, 281
McCall's magazine, 44, 47
McCarthyism, 66, 121
McCorvey, Norma, 169–70, 245
McDew, Chuck, 105
McDonald, Susie, 89
McGhee, Laura, 100
McGovern, George, 273
McGraw-Hill publishers, 187
McKinney, Betsy Marvin, 117
McNair, Denise, 106
McWilliams, Ike, 40
McWilliams, Virginia, 40
medical schools, 5, 16, 182, 188, 215, 216, 257
Meet the Press (TV show), 63, 64
Meigs, Charles, 4
menstruation, 11, 27
MenTeach, 258
Metropolitan Opera (New York), 89–90
Meyer, Bob, 39, 40
Meyer, Lorna Jo, 28
Meyer, Louise, 26, 39–40, 41, 79, 120
Meyer, Susan, 28
Miami-Dade County (Florida), gay-rights issue in, 171
Miami Herald, 171
Michaels, George, 168–69
middle class, 4–5, 41–42, 79–80
Middleton, Faith, 200
Mikulski, Barbara, 177, 248
military: draft and, 137, 138, 165; homosexuality and, 249; nurses serving with, 191; sexual harassment and assault of women in, 247, 248–49, 268; women in, 165, 248–49, 267–69
Miller, Annie, 225
Miller, Ellen, 116, 225

Millett, Kate, 127–28
Mills College, 46
Milton, Massachusetts, discrimination claimed by boy in, 258
miniskirts, 146, 147, 191, 217, 267
ministers, women as, 190
Mink, Patsy, 181, 183
Miss America demonstration (1968), 142–43, 146
Mississippi Freedom Democratic Party, 98, 101
Mitchell, Bev, 170, 182
Mitchell, John, 150
Mitford, Jessica, 96
Modern Woman: The Lost Sex, 124
Molloy, John, 216–17
"mommy track" controversy, 242, 263
Mondale, Walter, 184, 199, 206, 207, 208, 209, 232
Moneybean, Phoebe, 58
Monroe, Marilyn, 28, 218
Monsky, Marie, 119
Montana, Claude, 217
Monteleone, Tony, 250
Montgomery, Alabama, bus system, 88–89, 93
Moore, Mary Tyler, 177, 200, 204
morality, women as guardians of, 4
Morgan, Irene, 90
Morgan, Robin, 125, 128, 129, 138–39, 140, 142, 143, 163, 204, 274–75
Morrisroe, Patricia, 224
mortgages, 17, 41, 78, 165, 182–83
Mosbacher, Dee, 251
Moton, Leroy, 106–7
Moynihan, Daniel Patrick, 148, 181, 244
Mr. Novak (TV series), 12
Ms. Foundation, 187, 258
Ms. magazine, 127, 144, 181, 187, 189, 241
"Ms." title, 187, 232, 242
Murphy, Matt, 107
Murray, Lucy, 90, 93
Murray, Patty, 247
Murray, Pauli, 61, 62–63, 67, 95, 98, 141
My Little Margie (TV series), 12
"Myth of the Vaginal Orgasm" (Koedt), 125

NAACP, 69, 88, 89, 90, 93, 97
Nash, Diane, 91, 92, 94, 96–97, 98, 99, 103–4
Nation magazine, 226, 234
National Airlines, 191
National Association of Women Lawyers, 62
National Council of Catholic Women, 61
National Council of Jewish Women, 61
National Council of Negro Women, 61, 94, 98
National Lawyers Guild, 140
National Office Managers Association, 5
National Opinion Research Center, 162

National Press Club (Washington, DC), 98, 191–92
National Right to Life Committee, 170
National Woman's Party, 59
Navy, U.S., 247
NBC-TV, 166, 167, 180, 193, 228
Nelson, Bryan, 258
Nelson, Gaylord, 123
Nelson family (Ozzie, Harriet, David, and Ricky), 199
Netherlands, fertility rate in, 264
New England Journal of Medicine, 226
New Frontier, 58–59
New Jersey, state ERA in, 172
New Left, 129, 163; demeaning attitude toward women in, 137–39
New Politics, 137
New Republic magazine, 66
New Right, 159, 163, 208
Newsweek, 11, 25, 32, 45, 171, 224, 230, 251, 258, 275, 276, 281, 293; sex-discrimination suit against, 192
New World Collective, 205
New York City, integration of mass-transit systems in, 95
New York Magazine, 168, 220, 224, 251, 252
New York Post, 143
New York Radical Women, 135–36, 139, 141, 142, 143
New York State: abortion liberalization in, 168–69; divorce laws in, 31, 200; failure of state ERA in, 172
New York Times, 4–5, 14, 16, 29, 32, 44, 57, 66, 120, 126, 127, 141, 142, 168, 169, 217, 221, 224, 226, 232, 242, 245, 246, 257, 261, 268, 273, 275, 278, 292; college cohabitation reported by, 115, 120, 289; descriptive language for women in, 187; Kunin's experiences with, 16, 291; "opting-out" controversy and, 262–64; sex-discrimination suit against, 192–93
New York Times Magazine, 5
Nineteenth Amendment, 57, 149
Nixon, E. D., 88, 89
Nixon, Julie, 142
Nixon, Pat, 149
Nixon, Richard M., 57, 138, 142, 148, 149, 150, 170, 177–78, 184, 207, 208, 234, 282
Nixon, Trisha, 142
Nolfi, Angela, 11, 43
nonviolence strategy, 90, 102, 104
Northwest Airlines, 191
Novas, Himilce, 274, 276
NOW (National Organization for Women), 67–69, 71–72, 77, 143, 149, 160, 170, 172, 191, 200, 274, 290; founding of, 67–68; organizational shortcomings of, 68–69;

radical feminists and, 141–42, 148; *Weeks v. Southern Bell* and, 70–72
nursing, 81, 191, 216
nylon stockings, 27, 28, 90, 178

Obama, Barack, 260, 274, 275, 276, 278, 279, 281, 282
Obama, Michelle, 267, 278, 279
Ochoa, Ellen, 229
O'Connor, John, 233–34, 287
O'Connor, Sandra Day, 233–34, 260, 287
Office of War Information, 78
Olympic Games, 178, 179
Operation Rescue, 245
opting-out trend, 262–64
oral sex, 117
O'Reilly, Jane, 17, 29, 140, 178, 204
orgasms, 124–25
Osgood, Charles, 202
Our Bodies, Ourselves (Boston Women's Health Collective), 124
Our Miss Brooks (TV series), 12
Ozzie and Harriet (TV series), 263

Pacific Southwest Open, 180
Palin, Piper, 277, 280
Palin, Sarah, 275, 276–79, 280–82
Palin, Todd, 276, 277, 279, 281
Palin, Trig, 276, 277, 278, 280
Palin, Willow, 277, 280
Pan Am, 191
Panter, Georgia, 15, 33, 118, 144, 291–92
pants, for women, 3, 26, 90, 177–78, 217, 282; blue jeans, 102, 126–27, 178, 217
panty hose, 126, 267
Parks, Rosa, 88–89, 93, 98, 227, 289
partner, women's chances to make, 227–28, 258
Patch, Penny, 94, 104
patriarchy, 98, 136, 141
Patterson, Elizabeth, 222–23
Paul, Alice, 59, 63, 65, 138, 150, 159, 162, 289
Paul, Saint, 3
Pauley, Jane, 228
pay inequalities. *See* wage gap
Payne, Charles, 100
Pelosi, Nancy, 282
Penthouse magazine, 139
Percy, Charles, 208
Perkins, Frances, 57, 206
Persons of the Opposite Sex Sharing Living Quarters (POSSLQ), 202
Peterson, Esther, 14, 59–60, 61
Peterson, Martha, 115, 116, 127
Peterson, Oliver, 59–60
Peterson, Sylvia, 27, 33, 146, 182–83
pharmacy, women in, 257
Philip Morris company, 180

Phillips, Howard, 208
Phillips, Ida, 69
Phillips, Martha, 207
Piestewa, Lori, 268–69
Pill (oral contraceptive), 80–81, 82, 119, 120–22, 129; health risks of, 123; laws restricting access to, 120–22
pilots, female, 5, 26, 247, 267; airlines' prohibition of, 15
Pincus, Gregory, 123
Pittsburgh Courier, 63
Planned Parenthood, 119, 120, 121, 122
plastic surgery, 218, 266
platform shoes, 178
Playboy, 44, 81, 118
Playboy Clubs, 44, 66, 119; "Bunnies," 66, 67, 119, 146 (*see also* Steinem, Gloria)
"playing the field," 30
Please Don't Eat the Daisies (Kerr), 44
Pleck, Joseph, 221
Poehler, Amy, 280
policewomen, 218–19
Pollard, Robert, 204, 205, 206
Pollard, Tanya, 204, 206, 262
Pollard, Vicki Cohn, 139, 144, 204, 205, 206, 262
Pollitt, Katha, 226
poorer women: birth control and, 120, 121; child-care problems of, 206; children born out of wedlock to, 202; motherhood put before marriage by, 203, 265; welfare reform and, 244–45; women's liberation movement and, 148
pornography, 118, 266
"postfeminists," 231
post-traumatic stress disorder, 268
Poussaint, Alvin, 105
Povich, Lynn, 192
pregnancy: job protection and, 227; teenage, 202–3; unwanted, 122–23. *See also* abortion; birth control
premarital sex, 116–18, 119, 120; birth control pill and, 120; double standard and, 116, 117–18; *Sex and the Single Girl* and, 30, 117–18
Presidential Commission on the Status of Women, 61–63, 67
presidential election of 1960, 57, 60, 61
presidential election of 1972, 208
presidential election of 1980, 233
presidential election of 1984, 232
presidential election of 2008, 274–82; Clinton's campaign in, 274–76, 278, 281; Palin's candidacy in, 276–79, 280–82; work/family divide and, 278–80
President's Advisory Committee for Women, 216, 232
Presser, Harriet, 221

Price, Margaret, 59
Price, Melvin, 163
Price Waterhouse, 227–28
Princeton University, 258–59
Private Secretary (TV series), 12
professional schools. *See* graduate and professional schools; law schools; medical schools
professors, women as, 11
prostitution, 18, 120
protective laws for women, 59, 60, 69, 70–71
Providence Journal, 16
Purity Myth, The (Valenti), 266

Quindlen, Anna, 47
Quinn, Roseann, 229
quotas, 16, 257

Rabinowitz, Lois, 3
Radcliffe College, 46, 168, 225, 263
Radziwill, Lee, 28
Randolph, A. Philip, 98
Rankin, Jeannette, 135–36
rape, 16, 188, 230–32; celebrity-rape trials and, 231; date, 231; of women in military, 268
Raskin, Betty Lou, 5
Rawalt, Marguerite, 62, 65, 69, 71, 142, 143, 150
Rayburn, Sam, 63
Reader's Digest, 193
Reagan, Ronald, 216, 232, 233, 234, 244
Reasoner, Harry, 228
Redbook magazine, 46, 252
Reddy, Helen, 159
Redstockings, 140–41, 168
Republican Party, 159, 276; child-care issue and, 206–7, 208; gender gap and, 233; women's issues and, 60, 164, 170
Reynolds, Debbie, 28
Reynolds, Nancy Clark, 217
Richardson, Elliot, 207
Richmond News Leader, 91
Riesman, David, 14
Rife, Joanne, 16, 46, 47
Riff, Judy, 30, 32, 122
Riggs, Bobby, 178, 180–81
Ringgold High School (Pennsylvania), 218
Ritz-Carlton Hotel (Boston), 18
Roads, Barbara, 67
Roberts, Sylvia, 16, 71–72, 289
Robertson, Carole, 106
Robinson, Clifford, 103
Robinson, Gwendolyn, 90, 102
Robinson, Jo Ann, 88, 89
Robinson, Marian, 279
Rodgers, Mary, 224

Roe v. Wade, 169–70, 245, 281
Roiphe, Katie, 231
Rollins, Avon, 99–100
Romper Room (TV series), 166, 167
Roosevelt, Anna, 68
Roosevelt, Eleanor, 61, 63, 87, 93, 97, 273
Roosevelt, Franklin D., 57, 63, 87
Roosevelt, Franklin D., Jr., 70
Roraback, Catherine, 120–21, 140, 188
Roseanne (TV series), 219
Rosga, AnnJanette, 241
Rossner, Judith, 229
Ruderman, Evan, 189
Rudolph, Wilma, 27, 178–79
RU-486, 246
Rumsey, Carol, 33, 127
running, long-distance, 11, 179
Rustin, Bayard, 98

Safire, William, 187, 232
Salvatore, Diane, 252
Sanders, Marlene, 13
Sanger, Margaret, 120, 123
sanitary napkins, 27
Saturday Evening Post, 25, 30, 45
Saturday Night Live (TV show), 280
Savarirayan, Serena, 259
Savitch, Jessica, 228
Scandinavia, fertility rate in, 264
Scarlett, Frank, 71
Schakowsky, Jan, 146
Scharnau, Ruth Cotter, 143
Schechter, Marshall, 226
Scheuer, James, 67
Schlafly, Fred, 163, 165
Schlafly, John, 251
Schlafly, Phyllis, 163–66, 170, 171, 251, 278, 280
Schmidt, Wendy C., 264
schools, racial segregation and, 88, 89, 90
Schroeder, Jim, 185
Schroeder, Pat, 182, 185
Schwartz, Felice, 242
science, women in, 257
science courses, taken by girls, 139, 257
SCUM (Society for Cutting Up Men), 141–42
Seaman, Barbara, 123
Second Shift, The (Hochschild), 221
Second Stage, The (Friedan), 224
segregation: racial, 87, 87–97, 103 (*see also* civil rights movement); sexual, 17–18, 191–92
Seigenthaler, John, 96
Selma march (1965), 106–8
Semnack, Mae Ann, 42
Semple, Jock, 179

Senate, U.S., 123, 185; African-Americans in, 273; Civil Rights Act of 1964 and, 65; ERA and, 150, 159; Hillary Clinton's stint in, 273–74; Thomas nomination and, 247–48; women in, 57, 65–66, 183, 247–48, 278

seniority systems, 168, 260, 290

Sensuous Woman, The ("J" Garrity), 117

sex, 229–30; Barbie dolls and, 225; casual, backlash against, 229–30; double standard and, 116, 117–18; high-achieving high school and college women and, 266; unwanted pregnancies and, 122–23 (*see also* abortion); virginity and, 116–17, 119, 129, 266; women's enjoyment of, 124–25; young girls' notion of, 266–67. *See also* birth control; premarital sex; rape

Sex and the City (TV series), 267

Sex and the Single Girl (Brown), 30, 117–18

sex education, 120

sex manuals, 124–25

sexual assault, 230–32; of women in military, 268. *See also* rape

sexual harassment in workplace, 246–48

sexually transmitted diseases (STDs), 119, 120, 229–30

sexual revolution, 115–25, 128–29, 199; access to birth control and, 119, 120–22; backlash against, 229–30; cohabitation and, 115–16, 120; frank talk vs. activity in, 119; pressure to have sex and, 128–29; *Sex and the Single Girl* and, 30, 117–18; spirit of free love and, 119; women's pursuit of serious careers and, 80–81, 117

sexual self-expression, 216; Madonna and, 219

Shank, Clare B. Williams, 57

shaving legs, 126, 216

Shaw University, 92

shoes: comfortable, 178; high heels, 27, 137, 147, 178, 217; of radical feminists, 147

Shorto, Russell, 264

shoulder pads, 217, 219

Siegel, Margaret, 27, 137

silk stockings, 92

Simpson, Edna, 57

single mothers, 81, 122–23, 199, 200, 202–3, 223, 265; African-American, 202; removal of stigma attached to, 202; teenage pregnancy and, 202–3; welfare and, 244–45

single women, 30–31, 220, 223–24; access to birth control for, 120, 121–22; earnings of, compared to male counterparts, 260; as home owners, 182–83; increase in number of, 265; limited marriage prospects reported for, 223–25; living together, 127; living with men (*see* cohabitation); *Sex and the Single Girl* and, 30, 117–18

Sisterhood Is Powerful (ed. Morgan), 128

Sixteenth Street Baptist Church bombing (1963), 106

60 Minutes (TV series), 247

skirt-and-sweater sets, 27

slavery: abolition of, 65, 82; marriage compared to, 141

Sleeping with the Enemy (film), 242, 288

Smith, Howard (congressman), 63–64, 66, 67

Smith, Howard K. (journalist), 149

Smith, Jennifer Maasberg, 221, 243

Smith, Margaret Chase, 65–66, 123, 183

Smith, Ruby Doris, 92, 102, 103, 109

Smith, William French, 233, 234

Smith, William Kennedy, 231

Smith College, 32, 46, 47

smoking, 28

sneakers, white, 28

Snider, Alex Dery, 242, 250, 288

Soap, Charlie Lee, 232

soap operas, 230

Social Security, 26, 58, 72, 233

Solanas, Valerie, 141–42

Southern Bell, 70–72, 191, 288

Southern Christian Leadership Conference (SCLC), 93

South Park (TV series), 275

Southwest Airlines, 191

Spain, fertility rate in, 264

Spanx, 267

Spellings, Margaret, 258

Spelman College, 90–91, 102, 258

Spock, Benjamin, 11, 164

sports. *See* athletics

Sports Illustrated, 180, 181

Stanford Law School, 233

Stanton, Elizabeth Cady, 65, 77

Stanwyck, Barbara, 33

Starr, Kenneth, 233

Star Trek, 12

state commissions on the status of women, 67, 68

state legislators, women as, 185–86

Steele, Valerie, 267

Stein, John, 277

Steinem, Gloria, 119, 129, 138, 140, 144, 146–48, 168, 172, 183, 187, 189, 247, 267, 275, 280, 292

Stella, Anthony, 168

Stembridge, Jane, 92

Stepp, Laura Sessions, 28, 29, 137, 216, 242–43, 265–66

Stern, Elizabeth and William, 226

Stevenson, Adlai, 59

stewardesses. *See* flight attendants

Stewart, Justice Potter, 233

Story, Louise, 263

Strike Day (1970), 149

student movement of 1960s, 126, 137; demeaning attitude toward women in, 137–39

Student Nonviolent Coordinating Committee (SNCC), 94–95, 97, 99, 100–102, 103–5, 108–9. *See also* civil rights movement

Students for a Democratic Society (SDS), 137–38

suburbs, 41–47; domestic chores in, 42–44; empty years faced by women in, 45; marketing to women in, 44; men's lives changed by move to, 44–45; social life in, 41; stay-at-home wife as norm in, 41; unhappiness of housewives in, 45–46

success, dressing for, 216–17

suffrage: for African-Americans, 65; for women, 40, 57, 58, 59, 65, 82, 135, 136, 159

suits, for businesswomen, 216–17

Sullivan, Leonor, 64

Sulzberger, Arthur Ochs, 187

Supreme Court, U.S., 178, 202, 227, 249, 281; access to birth control and, 121; discrimination lawsuits and, 259–60; O'Connor's appointment to, 233–34; O'Connor's resignation from, 260, 287; racial segregation and, 88, 89, 95–96; *Roe v. Wade* and, 169–70, 245, 281; Thomas's nomination to, 246–48

surrogate mothers, 226

Susskind, David, 147

Swerdlow, Amy, 135, 136

Swift, Jane, 280

Swimmer, Ross, 232

Swisher, Kara, 251

Switzer, Kathrine, 179

symphony music, women in, 257

syphilis, 120

Taft, Robert, 164

Tailhook, 247

Taitt-Magubane, Lenora, 91, 92, 93, 95, 97, 100, 101, 104

"Take Our Daughters to Work Day," 258

Talbott, Irene, 144

tampons, 27

tax rates, teachers' salaries and, 13

Taylor, Elizabeth, 28, 117

Taylor, Lana, 92

Taylor, Linda, 244

Teach for America, 258–59

teaching, 243; black women in, 93; dearth of women professors and, 11; dressing up for, 27; feminism's impact on, 216; low pay for, 13, 78, 258, 259; women directed into careers in, 13, 78, 81, 258

Technical Virgins Association (TVA), 117

teenage culture, 29–30; dancing and, 30, 219; dating and, 29–30, 266–67; hooking up and, 266

teenage pregnancy, 202–3

Tegley, Janet, 159

television, 41, 80, 230, 241; news broadcasts, 220, 228, 258; in 1960s, 13, 139, 142, 177, 199; in 1970s, 177, 204, 228; in 1980s, 218–20, 228. *See also specific shows*

tennis, 179–81; King-Riggs match and, 178, 180–81

Texas Instruments, 78

thalidomide, 166–67, 290

That Girl (TV series), 177

thinness, 28, 217–18; eating disorders and, 218; exercise and, 217–18

Thom, Mary, 144

Thomas, Clarence, 246–47, 248

Thomas, Helen, 177–78

Thomas, Marlo, 177

Tillinghast, Muriel, 102

Time, 78, 127–28, 179, 180, 226, 227, 229, 230, 241, 247

Time-Life Publishing, 25

Title IX, 150, 181–82, 183, 277

"To All the Girls I've Rejected" (Britz), 257

Toobin, Jeffrey, 234, 287

topless dancers, 119

topless swimsuits, 119

Toscanini, Arturo, 87

Touchdown Club (Washington, DC), 185

trade unions, women in, 188–89

travel, 126; unusual for women in postwar era, 15. *See also* airlines

True Colors (TV series), 249

Trump, Donald, 219

Tulane Law School, 16

TWA, 191

Twenty-sixth Amendment, 121

20/20 (TV show), 251

Twist (dance), 30, 219

Tyler, Judy, 12

Typewriter Trade Journal, 246

typing skills, 25

Tyson, Cicely, 102

Tyson, Mike, 231

Uncle Tom's Cabin (Stowe), 88

Unhooked (Stepp), 266

Union Theological Seminary, 190

United Airlines, 15, 150, 292

United Nations, 220, 273

University of Kansas, 181

University of Texas dental school, 257

unmarried women. *See* single women

upper-income women, options for, 14

U.S. News and World Report, 200

uterus, presumed useless after childbearing, 123

Valenti, Jessica, 266

Vanek, Joann, 43

Van Gelder, Lindsy, 143, 251

Vanity Fair magazine, 251

Variety magazine, 100

Vaught, Wilma, 267

Vaz, Gloria, 26, 187–88, 202–3, 288

Vermont, first women elected to legislature of, 186

Veterans Administration (VA), 268

veterinary medicine, women in, 257

vice president, first woman to run for, 232

Victorian era, 4, 82, 120, 179

Vietnam War, 121, 129, 162, 183; draft and, 137, 138; student protests against, 126, 137, 138; women's protest against (Jeannette Rankin Brigade), 135–36, 137, 139

Villa, Pancho, 189

Virginia Slims tennis tour, 180

Virginia supreme court, 251–52

virginity, 116–17, 119, 129, 266

volunteering, 160

voter-registration projects, of SNCC, 89, 99–100, 104–6

voting rights. *See* suffrage

Vuich, Rose Ann, 186

Waco, Texas, girls' sports in, 181

Wade, Betsy, 192–93

wage gap, 140, 162, 216, 258, 259–61; company policies and, 5; declines in men's pay and job prospects and, 161, 220, 260; Equal Pay Act of 1963 and, 64; lawsuits and, 259–60; Strike Day and, 149; traditional low-salaried jobs for women and, 13, 216, 258; women's reproductive lives and, 260–61

Walker, Alice, 90

Walker, Wyatt Tee, 93

Wallace, George, 65

Wallach, Anne Tolstoi, 25–26, 27, 116, 126, 168, 222, 290

Wall Street Journal, 66

Wal-Mart, 259

Walters, Barbara, 228

Ward, Peggy, 218

Warhol, Andy, 141

Warpness, Louise Meyer, 160, 287–88

Warren, Earl, 5

Washington, Cynthia, 105

Washington, Mary Helen, 28–29, 102

Washington Post, 16, 141, 146, 187, 218, 243, 251, 265

Watergate scandal, 184

Watson, Diane, 186

Webb, Marilyn, 138

Weddington, Sarah, 169–70

Wedowee, Alabama, burning of high school in, 250

Weeks, Lorena, 69–72, 191, 288–89

Weeks, William "Billy," 70–71, 72, 288–89

Weingarten, Randi, 216

Weisstein, Naomi, 137

Weitzman, Lenore, 201

Weld, Theodore, 147

welfare, 202, 206, 244–45

"welfare queens," 244

Weller, Marylyn, 42

Wellesley College, 32, 116, 258

Wells-Barnett, Ida, 65

Wesley, Cynthia, 106

West, Ben, 91

West Point (U. S. Military Academy), 248

Westrich, Joyce, 17,

"What's Wrong with 'Equal Rights' for Women?" (Schlafly), 164

Whitehead, Mary Beth, 226

Wilbur, Susan, 96

Wilder, Billy, 42

Wilkins, Collie, 107

Williams, Betty Riley, 42, 107

Williams, Duvall, Jr., 247

Williams, Esther, 178

Williams, Virginia, 26, 202, 206

Wilson, John Wayne, 229

Winslow, Barbara, 124

Wintjen, Marjorie, 17

Wisconsin, fair-employment laws in, 67

Wise, Stanley, 103

Witherspoon, Reese, 267

Wolff, Larry, 223

Wolfson, Alice, 123

Woman's Dress for Success Book, The (Molloy), 216–17

Women: A Journal of Liberation, 144

Women and Economics (Gilman), 205

Women's Bureau, 59, 60

women's liberation movement, 77, 135–50; accomplishments of, 149–50, 257, 282; backlash against, 159–60, 164–65, 177; blamed for increase in divorce rate, 200; "bra burning" and, 143, 241; changed during 1970s, 171; consciousness-raising groups and, 139–41, 143; FBI investigation of, 145; going braless and, 145–46; housewives' resentment of, 159–60; *Ladies' Home Journal* takeover and, 144–45; male chauvinism in New Left and, 137–39; minority women and, 148; Miss America demonstration and,

142–43, 146; *Newsweek*'s cover story on, 192; radical wing of, 82, 135–37, 141–42, 147, 148; sources of oppression identified by, 136, 140–41; spread of, 143–44; Steinem as public face of, 146–48; Strike Day and, 149; turmoil of 1960s and, 137; unattractiveness equated with, 145, 146, 147; writings of, 144; younger women's views on, 241–42

women's magazines: new suburban housewife and, 44, 47. *See also specific magazines*

women's movement, first wave of (suffragists), 82, 136

Women's Political Council, 89

Women's Wear Daily, 33

Woman's Work (Wallach), 290

Wonkette (Web site), 276

Woodruff, Judy, 228

work/family divide, 25–26, 222–23, 242–43, 273, 274, 282; business travel and, 222–23; choice of career path and, 242–43; dropping out of workforce once babies arrive, 260–61, 262–64; employer concessions and, 264; keeping family invisible while at work, 222; lifestyle arrangements and, 243, 261–62; presidential election of 2008 and, 278; for women in civil rights movement, 103–4. *See also* child care; housework

working mothers: communal living and, 204–5; contemporary, 288; domestic responsibilities of, 25–26, 200, 203–9, 222–23, 242–43, 261–62, 282 (*see also* child care; housework; work/family divide); economic necessity and, 25–26, 80, 161, 165, 199, 220, 242; flexible work schedules for, 222, 243, 264; increase in number of, 78–79, 199, 242; invisible in 1960s, 13; lack of accommodation of societal structures for, 222; "mommy track" controversy and, 242, 263; "opting-out" trend among, 262–64; postdivorce careers and, 200–201; in postwar period, 13–14, 25–26; protective laws and, 69; serious careers sought by, 215–16; single mothers, 223; striving for "it all" and, 219–20; welfare reform and, 244–45

working women: dress codes for, 26–27, 216–17; economic growth and, 78, 79–80, 82; housewives' prestige lowered by, 160; increased demand for women's skills and, 77–78, 82; increased number of, throughout twentieth century, 77–80, 261; invisible in 1960s, 13; lower pay for (*see* wage gap); marriage delayed by, 223–25; mothers as (*see* working mothers); in postwar period, 13–17, 25–27; protective laws for, 59, 60, 69, 70–71; reliable contraception and, 80–81, 82; sexual revolution and, 80–81, 117; short-term jobs without advancement potential for, 14–16, 78; traditional division of labor and, 25–26; unpredictable career paths of, 266; during World War II, 13, 26, 78, 79, 149, 191. *See also specific professions*

World War I, 135

World War II, 13, 26, 78, 79, 80, 87, 135, 149, 178, 191

Woythaler, Wendy, 122, 126, 145

Wyoming: farm life in, 39–40; woman suffrage in, 40

Yale University, 263

Year of the Woman, 248

Yippees, 138

Young, Andrew, 94

Young, Whitney, 148

Young Presidents Organization, 32

Zaccaro, John, 232

Zellner, Bob, 100

Zinn, Howard, 91

Zwerg, Jim, 96